STUDIES IN HISTORIOGRAPHY

Arnaldo Momigliano

HARPER TORCHBOOKS The Academy Library
Harper & Row, Publishers
New York and Evanston

STUDIES IN HISTORIOGRAPHY

Printed in the United States of America.

This book was originally published in 1966 by Weidenfeld and Nicolson, London, and is here reprinted by arrangement.

First HARPER TORCHBOOK edition published 1966 by
Harper & Row, Publishers, Incorporated,
49 East 33rd Street,
New York, N. Y. 10016

Library of Congress Catalog Card Number: 66-27622

To my friends of
the Department of Classics
of the
Hebrew University of Jerusalem

CONTENTS

PREFACE

THE papers collected in this volume represent a selection from my three books, *Contributo alla storia degli studi classici* (Roma, Edizioni di Storia e Letteratura, 1955); *Secondo Contributo* etc. (*ib.*, 1960); and *Terzo Contributo* (in the press). The last three papers were originally written in Italian and have been translated into English for this volume by Mrs Judith Wardman who also prepared the Index.[1]

I am a student of the ancient world, and my primary aim is to understand and evaluate the Greek and Roman historians and the modern historians of the ancient world. Neither common sense nor intuition can replace a critical knowledge of past historians. Ancient history has its own problems of method which are due to the scarcity of the evidence, to the difficulty in the interpretation of ancient languages, and finally to our peculiar relation to what we call the 'classical world'. I am therefore trying to contribute to a more disciplined interpretation of the history of Jews, Greeks and Romans. But I hope that my researches may prove of some interest also to the general student of Humanism and of historiography.

For a more systematic exposition of certain trends of historical thought I should like to refer to my Sather Classical Lectures (1962) on 'The Classical Foundations of Modern Historiography' which I am now preparing for publication.

A.M.

University College London 1965

[1] The papers are unabridged: only the bibliography of the paper on Cassiodorus (*Secondo Contributo*, pp. 219–229) has not been reprinted.

CHAPTER ONE

ANCIENT HISTORY AND THE ANTIQUARIAN*

Per gli ottant'anni del mio maestro Gaetano De Sanctis

Introduction

In the eighteenth century a new humanism competed with the traditional one. It was organized in learned societies instead of being centred in the universities; it was fostered by gentlemen rather than by schoolmasters. They preferred travel to the emendation of texts and altogether subordinated literary texts to coins, statues, vases and inscriptions. Addison discussed the relevance of coins to literary studies[1], and Gibbon, who had taken leave of Oxford, renewed his education by spending twenty pounds on the twenty volumes of the Memoirs of the Academy of Inscriptions. Italy was still the centre of attraction for both the learned and the curious. But it was a more complex Italy, where Etruscan antiquities counted hardly less than Roman ruins, and where extraordinary discoveries began to be announced, from Herculaneum in 1736 and from Pompeii in 1748. Furthermore the antiquities of Greece were growing in significance both for the lucky few – chiefly Englishmen and Frenchmen – who could visit them, and for the larger, but still restricted number who could afford to buy the splendid books in which they were illustrated: primarily the *Antiquities of Athens* by Stuart and Revett (1762).

What is more important, men slowly became aware that they could find beauty and emotion of a new kind if they simply looked at their parish church or at the neighbouring castle – just as they could find poetry if they listened to the songs and stories of isolated farmers. The Grecian, the Celtic and the Gothic revivals, spreading from England to Europe, sealed the triumph of a leisured class which was indifferent to religious controversy, uninterested in grammatical

* *Journal of the Warburg and Courtauld Institutes*, 13 (1950), 285–315. This is a very provisional map of a field that needs much detailed exploration.

niceties, and craved for strong emotions in art, to counterbalance the peace and security of its own existence[2].

Such, if I am not mistaken, is the conventional view of the Age of the Antiquaries: a view which, though it is incomplete, I see no reason to challenge. But the Age of the Antiquaries meant not only a revolution in taste; it meant a revolution in historical method. Here perhaps a student of historiography can intervene. The Age of the Antiquaries set standards and posed problems of historical method which we can hardly call obsolete today.

The whole modern method of historical research is founded upon the distinction between original and derivative authorities. By original authorities we mean either statements by eye-witnesses, or documents, and other material remains, that are contemporary with the events which they attest. By derivative authorities we mean historians or chroniclers who relate and discuss events which they have not witnessed but which they have heard of or inferred directly or indirectly from original authorities. We praise original authorities – or sources – for being reliable, but we praise non-contemporary historians – or derivative authorities – for displaying sound judgment in the interpretation and evaluation of the original sources. This distinction between original authorities and non-contemporary historians became the common patrimony of historical research only in the late seventeenth century. The distinction is of course to be found before that time, but it was not formulated with any degree of accuracy or generally considered to be a necessary presupposition of historical study. In the formation of the new historical method – and consequently in the creation of modern historical writing on the ancient world – the so-called antiquaries played a conspicuous part and posed essential problems. They showed how to use non-literary evidence, but they also made people reflect on the difference between collecting facts and interpreting facts. It is the purpose of this essay to explain, first, the origins of antiquarian research; secondly, why the antiquaries played such a part in the reform of historical method in the eighteenth century; and finally, why in the nineteenth century it became increasingly evident that there was no longer any justification for making a distinction between antiquarian and historical studies.

The origins of antiquarian research

First of all we must ask ourselves who the antiquaries were. I wish I could simply refer to a History of Antiquarian Studies. But none exists[3]. All I can do here is to enumerate a few elementary facts.

I assume that to many of us the word 'antiquary' suggests the notion of a student of the past who is not quite a historian because: (1) historians write in a chronological order; antiquaries write in a systematic order; (2) historians produce those facts which serve to illustrate or explain a certain situation; antiquaries collect all the items that are connected with a certain subject, whether they help to solve a problem or not. The subject-matter contributes to the distinction between historians and antiquaries only in so far as certain subjects (such as political institutions, religion, private life) have traditionally been considered more suitable for systematic description than for a chronological account. When a man writes in chronological order, but without explaining the facts, we call him a chronicler; when a man collects all the facts available to him but does not order them systematically, we set him aside as muddle-headed.

If that is a correct expression of the prevailing feeling about antiquaries, the opinion that the predecessors of modern antiquaries are to be found in Greece during the second half of the fifth century BC must be somewhat qualified.

From a famous passage in Plato's *Hippias maior* (285 d) we learn that the genealogies of heroes and men, the traditions on the foundations of cities and the lists of eponymous magistrates of a city were part of a science called 'archæology'. The speaker is the sophist Hippias whom we know to have composed a list of the winners in the Olympic games. The word 'archæology', as Norden observed long ago, is one that a sophist could easily have invented[4]. There can be little doubt that Plato is transmitting to us a notion which was genuinely familiar to the sophists of the second half of the fifth century BC: the notion of a science called archæology dealing with subjects which today we would call of antiquarian interest. But the form of the treatment may in certain cases have been that of the chronicle rather than that of the systematic handbook. We cannot claim that the 'archæological' books produced by Hippias and his colleagues are invariably the direct predecessors of our *Lehrbücher der Altertümer*. In so far, however, as some of their researches were presented in the form of systematic treatises, they must be linked with modern antiquarian studies.

This was probably the case of the works περὶ ἐθνῶν, ἐθνῶν ὀνομασίαι, κτίσεις ἐθνῶν καὶ πόλεων, νόμιμα βαρβαρικά by Hellanicus, ἐθνῶν ὀνομασίαι by Hippias, περί γονέων καὶ προγόνων τῶν εἰς Ἴλιον στρατευσαμένων ascribed to Damastes or Polus.

I attribute more significance to the fact that already towards the end of the fifth century BC political history and learned research on the past tended to be kept in two separate compartments[5]. Thucydides wrote a kind of history which was more concerned with events of the very recent past than with traditions of the distant past or of distant nations, was more interested in individual or collective behaviour under certain circumstances than in religious or political institutions, and would serve the politician rather than the scholar. Hippias, Hellanicus, Damastes, Charon collected traditions of the past and took pleasure in erudition as such. This, however imperfectly, was the beginning of a distinction which lasted until the nineteenth century AD and even now has not yet completely disappeared. History was chiefly political history. What remained outside was the province of learned curiosity – which the antiquarians could easily take over and explore systematically. This antiquarian research gained impetus after Alexander.

In Hellenistic Greek the word archæology did not preserve the wide meaning it had in Plato[6]. It came to mean simply either history from the origins or archaic history. Flavius Josephus' Ἰουδαικὴ Ἀρχαιολογία is a history of the Jews from the origins to Josephus' own times; Dionysius of Halicarnassus' Ῥωμαικὴ Ἀρχαιολογία is a history of archaic Rome. There was no collective name which covered all the systematic treatises on the past. But such treatises were of course produced in great number, especially as by-products of local history. Their titles allude to either the place or the institution which was the object of research: Ἀργολικά, περὶ τῶν ἐν Λακεδαίμονι θυσιῶν, περὶ ἀδόξων ὀνομάτων, etc. Religious customs and political institutions were the most usual object of study: philology, geography, chronology were made to contribute. In the peripatetic school philosophy and systematic knowledge of the past joined forces[7].

The Romans followed suit. Rome had already produced scholars interested either in the origin of Italian cities or in the peculiarities of Roman institutions or, what amounts to the same thing, in the interpretation of archaic texts, when Varro attempted a systematic survey of Roman life as seen from the point of view of its foundations in the past. None of the Hellenistic scholars seems to have aimed at describing *all* the aspects of the life of a nation as systematically as Varro did. The *Antiquitates divinae et humanae* were greeted by the contemporary Cicero[8] as a revelation. They set a new standard – and perhaps also gave a new name to the science: 'Antiquitates'. With Varro the systematic character of this type of erudition reached perfection. Though we are not certain that he was the first to introduce the name 'Antiquitates', there is some historical justification for calling him the father of modern antiquarian studies. By antiquities he meant a systematic survey of Roman life according to the evidence provided by language, literature, and custom. He asked himself in the *rerum humanarum libri*: '*qui* (*homines*) *agant, ubi agant, quando agant, quid agant*'; and by '*homines*', as St Augustine justly observed[9], he meant the Romans[10]. His research was, of course, more directly relevant to political life than any Hellenistic treatise on the antiquities of a Greek city. A letter by Ateius Capito on his fellow and rival antiquarian Antistius Labeo gives us a glimpse of the political implications of this research for Augustus' contemporaries: '*Sed agitabat hominem libertas quaedam nimia atque vecors, tamquam eorum, divo Augusto iam principe et rempublicam obtinente, ratum tamen pensumque nihil haberet, nisi quod iussum sanctumque esse in Romanis antiquitatibus legisset*'[11]. Yet, in spite of Varro and his followers, 'antiquitates' never became political history[12].

The Middle Ages did not lose the classical interest in inscriptions and archæological remains. Inscriptions were occasionally collected. Monuments were noticed. What was lost, notwithstanding the reminder contained in St Augustine's *Civitas Dei*, was the Varronian idea of 'antiquitates' – the idea of a civilization recovered by systematic collection of all the relics of the past[13]. The stages of the rediscovery of the Varronian idea from Petrarch to Biondo cannot detain us. Biondo's *Roma Triumphans* has already the fourfold classification which many later handbooks preserve under the headings: *antiquitates publicae, privatae, sacrae, militares*[14]. True enough, the word 'antiquitates' meant in the book-titles of the fifteenth century either simply history (*Antiquitates Vicecomitum* by G. Merula, 1486) or ruins of monuments (*Antiquitates urbis* by Pomponio Leto): the original Varronian meaning of a survey of the whole life of a nation was perhaps first reintroduced as a title of a book by J. Rossfield, called Rosinus, in *Antiquitatum Romanarum Corpus*

Absolutissimum (1583). But the notion of the 'antiquarius' as a lover, collector and student of ancient traditions and remains – though not a historian – is one of the most typical concepts of fifteenth- and sixteenth-century humanism. The excitements of the early explorations of the antiquarians in Biondo's times are recorded by the *Iubilatio* of Mantegna's friend, Felice Feliciano[15]. The sober and fastidious scholarship of the great antiquarians of the sixteenth century (Sigonio, Fulvio Orsini, Augustinus, Justus Lipsius) is reflected in their correspondence. They improved on Varro because they combined literary, archæological and epigraphical evidence, their preference being for literary and epigraphical texts. They slowly pieced together Roman chronology, topography, law and religion: they discovered *Roma sotterranea.* They progressively occupied new provinces by extending their research to Greece, to the local antiquities of France, Germany and England and to the oriental kingdoms. They commented on historians and supplemented historians, but usually did not claim to be historians. They modelled themselves on Biondo's *Roma Triumphans* which was not a history, but a systematic survey. Roman history had been written by Livy, Tacitus, Florus, Suetonius, the *Historia Augusta.* There was no reason why it should be written again, because in the main it could be written only as Livy, Tacitus, Florus and Suetonius had written it. Ancient history was still written as part of universal history (a tradition especially cherished by Protestant universities), but the section on Greece and Rome of a universal history would practically amount to a summary of the ancient sources in the right chronological order – hardly the business of serious students of 'antiquitas'[16].

When ancient history was studied for its own sake, independently of antiquarian research and universal history, it was meant either to provide materials for moral and political reflections or to help the understanding of texts read primarily for stylistic reasons. The truth and completeness of the traditional accounts was hardly questioned. To the best of my knowledge, the idea that one could write a history of Rome which should replace Livy and Tacitus was not yet born in the early seventeenth century. The first Camden Praelector of history in the University of Oxford had the statutory duty of commenting on Florus and other ancient historians (1622). As Camden explained, the teacher 'should read a civil history, and therein make such observations as might be most useful and profitable for the younger students of the University, to direct and instruct them in the knowledge and use of history, antiquity and times past'[17]. The first Cambridge professor of history was sacked because his comments on Tacitus were considered politically dangerous (1627)[18]. Both in Oxford and in Cambridge Ancient History was taught in the form of a commentary on ancient historians. Modern people wrote 'antiquitates', not Roman (or Greek) histories.

On the other hand the majority of the *Artes Historicae* of the sixteenth and seventeenth centuries did not treat the work of the Antiquaries as historical work. Those writers who took it into consideration emphasized that the antiquaries were imperfect historians who helped to salvage relics of the past too fragmentary to be the subject of proper history. Bacon in his *Advancement of Learning* (1605) distinguished Antiquities, Memorials and Perfect Histories and defined Antiquities as 'history defaced or some remnants of history which have casually escaped the shipwreck of time' (II, 2, 1). Johann Gerhard Vossius in his *De Philologia Liber* (1650) echoed him: '*Historia civilis comprehendit antiquitates, memorias et historiam iustam. Antiquitates sunt reliquiae antiqui temporis, tabellis alicuius naufragii non absimiles*'. It is worth noticing that Vossius does not consider the antiquities in the *Ars Historica*: here he is concerned only with *historia iusta*. It would seem that '*historia iusta*' or perfect history, if applied to the classical world, was primarily history written by the ancients. What was left out by ancient historians could be salvaged by modern antiquarians[19].

Clear as it may seem, this distinction applied only to the history of classical Greece and Rome. The authority of the ancient historians was such that nobody was yet seriously thinking of replacing them. The situation was different in the study of the other European national and local histories which, except in their beginnings, would coincide with the study of the Middle Ages. No cult of the Middle Ages had yet developed to compete with the idealization of Antiquity. No medieval chronicle could claim such authority as to prevent the rewriting of medieval history. While there was a canonical history of Greece and Rome, there was no canonical history of Britain, France, Germany or Spain. Even the history of Italy as a whole was in a different position from the history of classical Rome. Indeed, political and religious reasons, especially after the Reformation, impelled the radical rewriting of the various national and local histories outside (and usually later than) Greece and Rome with all the aids to study which research in libraries and archives could provide. Sigonio, who did mere antiquarian work when concerned with classical Roman and Greek History, wrote ordinary medieval history in his *Historiarum de Occidentali Imperio Libri XX* (1577) and *Historiarum de Regno Italiae Libri XX* (1580). In the majority of cases it is doubtful whether the students of the past of Britain, France and the rest who called themselves antiquarians meant anything different from the writing of plain history founded on the original evidence. Leland liked to call himself 'antiquarius', and it has even been stated that he was formally appointed antiquarian by the king; for this, however, there seems to be no evidence. But he said that he intended to use the material collected for a work to be entitled *De Antiquitate Britanniae* or else *Historia civilis*. While the student of Latin and Greek antiquities did not feel entitled to consider himself a historian, the student of the antiquities of Britain, France and the rest was only formally distinguishable from the student of the history of those countries – and therefore was inclined to forget the distinction. In the sixteenth and early seventeenth centuries there were both antiquarians and historians (often indistinguishable from each other) for the non-classical and post-classical world, but only antiquarians for the classical world[20].

The situation changed in the second part of the seventeenth century[21]. The difference between the students of the classical world and the students of the non-classical world tended to disappear. Books on Roman and Greek history began to be written which were not subordinated to a scheme of universal history. They were intended either to present an account of events for which the evidence was mainly to be found in coins, inscriptions and archæological remains, or to select and order what was most reliable in the ancient literary evidence, or to offer a reinterpretation of the ancient evidence from some moral and political point of view. Indeed, it is true to say that on the whole each historical work of the late seventeenth and early eighteenth century primarily aims at satisfying one only of these three purposes. Vaillant wrote the history of the Ptolemies and of the Seleucids with the help of coins (1701, 1681); Tillemont wrote the history of the Roman Empire to give what was most reliable in ancient literary sources (1693–1707); Echard (about 1697) and Vertot (1719) introduced into Roman history the popular notion of history by revolutions. The time-honoured form of the discourse was no longer considered sufficient for the third purpose. Even the minor writers of that age were aware of the novelty inherent in the production of books on Greek and Roman history. L. Echard writes in the preface of his *Roman History from the Building of the City to the Perfect Settlement of the Empire by Augustus* (3rd ed., 1697):

There never was anything of this kind in our language before, nor anything relating to the Roman Affairs, but either what has been intermixed with much more other History or what has contained but a few years of this Part. Of these I find none of any note besides Raleigh, Ross, Howel, the Author of the History of the Two Triumvirates, and Pedro Mexia, Author of the Imperial History, the two last of which are Translations.

The Jesuits Catrou and Rouillé prefaced their *Histoire Romaine* (1725 ff.) with these even more telling words:

Jusqu'à nos tems, la République des Lettres se trouvoit destituée d'un secours si nécessaire qu'on s'obstinoit pourtant à lui refuser. A la vérité les sçavants de profession s'étoient épuisés en recherches sur les Coûtumes, sur les Moeurs, sur la Milice, sur le genre de Gouvernement, sur les Loix, et sur l'habillement des Romains . . . Les noms de Tite-Live, de Denis d'Halicarnasse, de Polybe, de Plutarque, et de tant d'autres, les avoient fait respecter, jusqu'à n'oser les incorporer ensemble.

As the two Jesuits explain, the antiquaries preceded the historians, because for a long time nobody dared to replace Livy and his peers.

The antiquaries, by collecting much of their evidence outside the literary sources, helped to make the need for new histories apparent. But the rise of the new historiography on Greece and Rome was bound in the long run to raise the question whether static descriptions of the ancient world had a right to survive side by side with historical expositions. Both points deserve careful analysis. The new importance attributed to non-literary evidence is understandable only against the background of the great reform of historical method which took place in the second part of the seventeenth century. On the other hand the value of the antiquarian approach to Greece and Rome was questioned both in the eighteenth and nineteenth centuries, for different reasons in each century.

The controversy of the 17th and 18th centuries on the value of historical evidence

THE TERMS OF THE CONTROVERSY

In the seventeenth century religious and political disputations had pervaded history and discredited the historian. Bias was easily scented everywhere, and the natural conclusion was to distrust the whole tribe of historians. At the same time attempts were made to put historical knowledge on a safer basis by analysing the sources thoroughly and drawing, if possible, on other evidence than that provided by past historians. A sceptical attitude prevailed, but this scepticism did not always imply complete pessimism as to the possibility of sound historical knowledge[22].

Critical minds emphasized how little was known. La Mothe Le Vayer formulated what was to become known as historical Pyrrhonism in his essay of 1668: *Du peu de certitude qu'il y a dans l'histoire*. R. Simon and Bentley showed to what lengths thorough criticism could go both on sacred and profane history. In 1682 Bayle began to show his hand in the *Critique générale de l'histoire du calvinisme*, where he declared: '*il est bien mal aisé de parvenir jusqu'à l'évidence*'; and also: '*en un mot, il n'y a point de Filouterie plus grande que celle qui se peut exercer sur les monumens historiques*'. In the next decades intellectual Europe was overpowered by the massive erudition and searching criticism of the *Dictionnaire historique et critique*, a best seller, notwithstanding its dimensions. Ernst Cassirer once took Bayle as the prototype of the modern *érudit* who has no other concern than the increase of knowledge[23]. To contemporaries he was Bayle the sceptic, '*l'illustre Bayle qui apprend si bien à douter*', as Baron Holbach sympathetically noted[24]. His historical Pyrrhonism was most obviously related to his distrust of dogmas and pious beliefs. In another Pyrrhonist, Daniel Huet, the bishop and tutor of the Dauphin, who in 1723 made posthumous scandal by his treatise on the weakness of human understanding, absolute scepticism definitely prevails over scepticism on the subject of historical sources. Two circumstances are relevant here. First Huet had arrived at scepticism by way of his long career of pioneer work in the comparative study of religion, of which the most important product is the *Demonstratio evangelica* of 1672[25]. Secondly, a refutation of his Pyrrhonism, next in importance to the classic one by J. P. de Crousaz

(1733), came from an antiquarian – namely L. A. Muratori, *Delle forze dell'intendimento umano ossia il pirronismo confutato*. Muratori, who incidentally would have liked to believe that Huet's posthumous work was a forgery by some adept of the dangerous sect of La Mothe Le Vayer and Bayle, realized that historical knowledge is no longer safe if it is not admitted that there are '*cose sensibili delle quali si ha e si puŏ avere una chiara e indubitata idea*'.

Historical Pyrrhonism was hitting both at traditional historical teaching and at traditional religious beliefs[26]. It was only natural that members of religious congregations (Bollandists, Maurists) should make some of the best contributions towards distinguishing between reasonable and unreasonable doubts in history. But the quest for safe historical rules was not confined to them. The discussion on Pyrrhonism raged in German Protestant universities which were just then making their first conspicuous contribution to historical method. The controversy passed from the hands of historians and philosophers to those of lawyers, who, being traditionally concerned with the reliability of witnesses, could bring a great deal of experience to bear on this subject. All these people tried to determine the characteristics of what they could call reliable evidence. Books of rhetorical rules on the art of historical writing were of course still produced. The Jesuits wrote a few classic ones of this type (P. Rapin, P. Le Moyne). But a new type of treatise on historical writing developed which broke away from the rhetorical *Ars Historica* of the Renaissance and was practically confined to the method of interpreting and criticizing sources. Some text-books were chiefly concerned with textual criticism (authenticity and emendations of texts): the *Ars Critica* by J. Le Clerc (1697) is the most important of them. Others, like H. Griffet, *Traité des différentes sortes de preuves qui servent à établir la vérité de l'histoire* (1769), were mainly concerned with the historical value of original authorities.

One way of answering the question was to make a distinction between literary evidence and other evidence such as charters, inscriptions, coins, and statues. It was assumed that charters and other public statements, coins, inscriptions, and statues were better evidence than literary sources. As one of the lawyers interested in the questions said:

Sunt vero fundamenta et causae quibus dicta veritas innuitur praecipue monumenta et documenta publica quae in archivis imperantium singulari cura adservantur . . . Enim vero, cum non omnibus archiva publica pateant, aut temporum iniuria sint deperdita, alia eorum loco testimonia rei gestae quaerere opus est. Qualia sunt publica monumenta, columnae et statuae apud veteres hinc et inde erectae[27].

Hence the value of a history would depend to a great extent on the quantity of public documents, inscriptions, and coins examined by the historian. In volume VI of the *Mémoires de Littérature de l'Académie Royale des Inscriptions* (1729) four authors (Anselme, De Pouilly, Sallier, Fréret) discussed the traditions on the origins of Rome in a way which implied general examination of the principles of historical criticism. The theme of the discussion was stated thus by l'Abbé Anselme:

J'ay donc avancé que l'antiquité n'est pas esté si dépourvûë qu'on l'a voulu dire des secours nécessaires à l'histoire, et qu'outre les Mémoires qui en ont esté conservez, ce qu'il y a d'obscur et de confus a esté suppléé par des monuments authentiques, qui en ont fait foy . . .[28].

The arguments of the learned academicians were later developed by L. De Beaufort, *Sur l'incertitude des cinq premiers siècles de l'histoire romaine* (1738).

On the other hand, a historian could depend on mere tradition, that is ultimately on accounts of persons who were alleged or claimed to be eye-witnesses. Thus it became essential to determine the criteria whereby tradition can be shown to be good even if it is not supported by independent evidence such as coins, inscriptions, or charters. The selection of a good tradition would of course imply a series of questions on the *bona fides* of witnesses and the means of assessing it, on the interpretation of evidence, on the intentional or unintentional misrepresentation to which the interpretation of evidence may lead. The school of Christian Thomasius specialized in the discussion of the notion of *fides historica.* It was defined in the following way by M. Lupin (*De fide iuridica*, 1699):

Fides historica est praesumtio veritatis de eo quod hominibus accidisse vel ab iis gestum esse dicitur, orta ex coniecturis circumstantiarum quae non saepe fallere solent, nullis tamen ab hominibus inventis aut praescriptis regulis adstricta, sed liberae cuiusvis ratiocinationi, a praeiudiciis tamen vacuae, relicta [29].

The study of the Holy Scriptures was only an extreme case of analysis of a tradition almost unsupported by independent evidence. The formulation of internal criteria sufficient to establish the *bona fides* of the sources was the only way to answer the sceptic in the absence of independent documentary sources or of any considerable amount of epigraphic and archæological material[30]. The whole discussion on the miracles of Jesus between Charles Blount (1680) and Charles Leslie (1698) and between Th. Woolston (1727) and Bishop Sherlock (1729) turned on the reliability of the writers of the Gospels as witnesses. To Blount who implied that there is no better evidence for the miracles of Jesus than for the miracles of Apollonius of Tyana, Leslie replied by what he called his 'Short and Easy Method' of selecting good witnesses. Whether the method was as short and easy as Leslie thought is another matter. Even when, under the influence of J. D. Michaelis, more attention was given to Hebrew antiquities, the discussion of the *bona fides* of the sources remained the main method of assessing the truth of the Bible.

In Roman History, Perizonius' *Animadversiones Historicae* (1685) were a sound attempt at methodical analysis of literary evidence without much appeal to documentary evidence. When the wave of historical Pyrrhonism was dangerously mounting he defended his position, that of moderate criticism, in his *Oratio de fide historiarum contra Pyrrhonismum Historicum* (1702). His main argument was that in certain cases historians can be trusted because they speak against the interest of the cause they are defending.

Complex philological criticism such as Perizonius was attempting did not come into its own until the beginning of the nineteenth century when a more subtle technique enabled scholars to discover the literary sources (if any) of literary sources. In the eighteenth century nobody had yet any precise notion of the sources of Diodorus or Tacitus. Nor as yet was the personality of the historian himself an object of conspicuous interest, except in a few cases. Also the idea that a tradition is entitled to respect as the mouthpiece of popular beliefs did not command wide attention. As long as these aspects were not carefully considered, it was inevitable that official documents, inscriptions, and coins should appear more reliable than literary evidence merely based on tradition. It was first of all a question of number. Common sense would offer insuperable resistance to the notion that thousands of documents, coins, and inscriptions could be forged as easily as isolated literary texts.

THE EMPHASIS ON NON-LITERARY EVIDENCE

In 1671 Ezechiel Spanheim, the founder of modern numismatics, reminded his readers of Quintilian's *obiter dictum*: '*Alii ab aliis historicis dissentiunt*' (II, 4, 19). He had a remedy:

Non aliunde nobis certius quam in nummis aut marmoribus antiquis praesidium occurrit. Nec certe ratio hic aut eventus fallit. Subsidia quippe reliqua, dubiam semper transcriptorum exemplarium fidem, haec autem sola primigeniam Autographorum dignitatem prae se ferunt.

In another passage the allusion to the contemporary discredit of historians is even more explicit:

Multa iisdem historiarum aut Annalium conditoribus, vel odio vel amore, vel incuria sunt perperam tradita, quae emendari hoc tempore aut revinci, nisi publicis quibusdam tabulis, non possunt.

In 1679 Jacques Spon with the ardour of an apostle of a new method proclaimed the superiority of archaeological evidence in his *Réponse à la critique publiée par M. Guillet.* He challenged his opponent:

Il nous fera voir dans ses premières dissertations comment par un miracle inoui les Auteurs anciens, tout hommes qu'ils estoient, avoient moins de passion que le marbre et que le bronze d'apresent, et comment au contraire le bronze et le marbre d'alors estoient plus susceptibles de passion que les hommes de ce siècle.

In 1697 Francesco Bianchini published *La Istoria Universale provata con monumenti e figurata con simboli degli antichi.* What makes it very remarkable is the underlying conviction that archaeological evidence (or, as Bianchini calls it, '*storia per simboli*') makes a firmer basis for history than literary evidence. According to Bianchini ordinary chronographers do not realize that they are mistaken in quoting only literary evidence. Archaeological evidence is at the same time 'symbol and proof of what happened' ('*le figure dei fatti, ricavate da monumenti d'antichità oggidì conservate, mi sono sembrate simboli insieme e pruove dell'istoria*'). Bianchini knows that the superiority of archaeological evidence is generally admitted by his contemporaries. The study of ancient monuments is '*accommodato al genio della età nostra*'. Others had spoken in the same spirit of the seventeenth century as 'the century of numismatics'. Later Francesco Bianchini applied his method to the ecclesiastical history of the first centuries. He died before finishing his work which was completed and published by his nephew Giuseppe Bianchini in 1752: *Demonstratio Historiae Ecclesiasticae quadripartitae comprobatae monumentis pertinentibus ad fidem temporum et gestorum.* Addison therefore echoed a widespread opinion when he observed: 'It is much safer to quote a medal than an author for in this case you do not appeal to Suetonius or to Lampridius, but to the emperor himself or to the whole body of a Roman Senate.'

Bianchini was an astronomer. Jacques Spon was a doctor. So were his friends Charles Patin, Charles Vaillant and other numismatists and antiquarians. One of them, H. Meibomius, observed in 1684: '*Et nescio quidem an peculiari aliquo fato Medici nos veteris nummariae rei studio teneamur.*' They brought something of the scientific method of direct observation into historical research[31].

The Pyrrhonists did not fail to point out that even charters, inscriptions, coins and monuments are not beyond doubt or suspicion. They may be falsified, they may be differently interpreted. F. W. Bierlingius, the author of the two remarkable dissertations *De iudicio historico*, 1703, and *De pyrrhonismo historico*, 1707, wrote:

Ars inscriptiones interpretandi adeo fallax est, adeo incerta . . . Numismata iisdem dubiis obnoxia sunt . . . Vides ergo, quicumque demum proferantur historiarum fontes, et antiquitatis monumenta, omnia laborare sua incertitudine[32].

Another moderate sceptic, Gilbert Charles Le Gendre, in his *Traité de l'opinion ou Mémoires pour servir à l'histoire de l'esprit humain*, which passed through four editions between 1735 and 1758, insisted on the doubtful value of archaeological evidence: '*le marbre et l'airain mentent quelquefois*'. It is worth noticing that he amplified the section on misleading monuments after the first edition. Evidently the point was becoming increasingly important[33].

To judge from contemporary evidence, the Pyrrhonists, however, failed to impress the majority of scholars. Jacques Spon and other antiquarians were acclaimed in one of the many dissertations directed to establish the value of inscriptions in Law:

Bene sit, praecamur, piis manibus Gruteri, Reinesii, Sponi, Fabretti, ceterorumque qui ad describendas e lapidibus, saxis, marmoribusque inscriptiones antiquas, romanas imprimis, studium suum laudabiliter contulerunt. Neque enim, si recte componantur singula illa monumenta, ad veteris solum Historiae corroborandam fidem et ad pleraque capita mythologiae et omnis generis antiquitatum explicanda egregie conducunt sed etc . . .[34].

In 1746 the systematic comparison of literary with non-literary evidence was accepted as an orthodox criterion against historical Pyrrhonism in Joh. Aug. Ernesti, *De fide historica recte aestimanda*[35].

The same opinion was expressed in 1747 by Chr. A. Crusius, *Weg zur Gewissheit und Zuverlässigkeit der menschlichen Erkenntnis* and is codified in one of the most important treatises on historical method of the century, the *Allgemeine Geschichtswissenschaft* by J. M. Chladenius (1752). In Göttingen the historian's readiness to take over the study of non-literary evidence was officially recognized in 1766 with the foundation of the Historical Institute. It was Gatterer's creation and was chiefly devoted to those auxiliary sciences (diplomatics, numismatics, etc.) which – as Chr. G. Heyne explained in the inaugural speech – '*historicis argumentis fidem faciunt*'[36]. Individuals who had preferred non-literary to literary evidence had not been lacking in former centuries. Ciriaco d'Ancona can easily be credited with this preference[37]. In the late sixteenth century Antonio Agostino (Augustinus) expressed the same belief in an incidental sentence: '*Yo mas fe doi a las medallas y tablas y piedras, que a todo lo que escriven los escritores*'[38]. His contemporary Claude Chifflet observed: '*Veteres historiae controversias nummorum antiquorum cognitio componit*'.[39] Such quotations could probably be multiplied. They do not alter the fact that non-literary evidence became especially authoritative in the late seventeenth and early eighteenth centuries.

The extraordinary story of Père Hardouin can be understood only in this context. He is notoriously a pathological case. Starting from the study of numismatics, he found contradictions between coins and literary texts and slowly reached the conclusion that all the ancient texts (except Cicero, Virgil's *Georgics*, Horace's *Satires* and *Epistles* and his beloved Pliny the Elder) had been forged by a gang of Italians in the late fourteenth century. He even identified the leader of the gang: Severus Archontius, who absentmindedly left his trace in a passage of the *Historia Augusta* (Firmus Sat., 2, 1) as a numismatist. Hardouin carried the contemporary bias for non-literary evidence and the contemporary suspicion of literary evidence well beyond the verge of madness. But his contemporaries did not laugh. They answered at length. La Croze wrote a whole volume against Hardouin (1708). Dom Tassin and Dom Toustain justified their big *Nouveau Traité de Diplomatique* (1750–65) by asserting *inter alia* that it would make it impossible for a new Hardouin to repeat his exploits. The discovery of the falsification of the whole of St. Augustine and of the *Divina Commedia* were, as is well known, among the details of Hardouin's discoveries[40].

When we survey the achievements of the antiquaries in formulating the rules for the proper interpretation of non-literary evidence, we must make a sharp distinction. The success in establishing safe rules for the use of charters, inscription and coins as regards both authenticity and interpretation was complete. The resistance encountered by Mabillon's *De Re Diplomatica* (1681) was no more than one could expect for a work which was admittedly polemical. Such attacks as that by the Jesuit P. Germon, *De veteribus regum francorum diplomatibus et arte secernendi antiqua diplomata vera a falsis Ad R. P. Mabillonium disceptatio* (1703), were primarily symptomatic of the conflict between religious orders. Soon Mabillon's work was generally recognized as authoritative. His palaeographical researches were extended to Greek writing by Montfaucon who gave its present name to the new discipline in his *Palaeographia graeca* (1708)[41]. On the other hand Scipione Maffei perfected the classification of the Western hands and formulated the rules of epigraphical criticism in the *Istoria Diplomatica* (1727) and in the posthumous *Ars Critica Lapidaria* (1765). As for coins, a series of great scholars from Spanheim to Eckhel (1792) left no doubt about the proper way of handling them.

Vases, statues, reliefs and gems spoke a much more difficult language. The imposing literature on Emblemata which had accumulated since Alciato was not likely to improve the clarity of this language. Given a monument with images on it, how can we understand what the artist meant? How can we distinguish between what is only ornamental and what is meant to express a religious or philosophical belief? The history of the attempts to create a scientific iconography from, say, Jacques Spon, *Miscellanea Eruditae Antiquitatis* (1679) to J. Spence, *Polymetis* (1747), passing through *L'Antiquité expliquée* by Montfaucon (1718), is still to be written. Winckelmann's lifelong concern with iconography, culminating in the *Versuch einer Allegorie besonders für die Kunst* (1766), is to be understood in this context. Whatever the importance of the results reached by Winckelmann and his predecessors, the amount of agreement among antiquarians was incomparably less in this field than in the fields of numismatics, epigraphy, and diplomatics[42]. Anyone who has read Franz Cumont's *Le Symbolisme Funéraire des Romains* which appeared in 1942 and Professor A. D. Nock's criticism of this book in the *American Journal of Archaeology* of 1946 may suspect that after two centuries we are still far from a generally accepted interpretation of certain types of imagery.

If it is true that we are still suffering from the failure of the eighteenth-century antiquarians to produce a convincing dictionary of the figurative arts, the immediate developments were not affected. Armed with his treatises, of more or less permanent value, on numismatics, diplomatics, epigraphy, and iconography, the eighteenth-century antiquarian could venture into old and new fields with a confidence that his predecessors lacked. He could turn himself into a historian or could help historians to write histories of a new kind. It will be enough to recall what is perhaps the greatest contribution of the eighteenth-century examination of non-literary evidence to historical knowledge: the discovery of pre-Roman Italy.

AN EXAMPLE OF THE EXTENSIVE USE OF NON-LITERARY EVIDENCE

The quarrelsome giant Thomas Dempster is a picturesque figure of the Scottish Catholic emigration to Italy in the early seventeenth century. He died a professor of Humanities in Bologna in 1625 leaving a reputation of much knowledge and little judgment which does not do full justice to the principal work he published during his life, a new edition of Rosinus' *Antiquitates*. I have not yet been able to ascertain how it happened that his manuscript *De Etruria Regali* remained unpublished until it fell into the hands of Thomas Coke, afterwards Earl of Leicester, about a century later. Coke was right in saying in his Preface: '*Hoc quidem mirum videri potest ita disposuisse Fortunam ut de rebus Etruscorum antiquis scribere et Britanno homini contingeret unice, et quod idem liber in Britanni pariter hominis manus incideret.*' Dempster had collected only the literary and some epigraphical evidence on Etruria. It is significant for the greater emphasis of the eighteenth century on archaeological evidence that the editor felt the impossibility of publishing the manuscript as it stood: he asked the antiquarian with a great family name, Filippo Buonarroti, to add the monumental evidence. The book, a strange composite of the antiquarian learning of two centuries, appeared in Florence in 1723. It made an unusual hit. In the seventeenth century not much had been published on the Etruscans after Inghirami and Reinesius (1637). Now there was a flow of books and dissertations. The Accademia di Cortona with its Lucumoni and its important dissertations was founded by Onofrio Baldelli in 1726; the Società Colombaria of Florence started in 1735. Everyone recognized that Dempster was the source of inspiration for the new interest in Etruria. But this interest was not primarily literary. It was chiefly centred in the study of archaeological evidence. The Etruscan Museums of Volterra, founded by Guarnacci, of Cortona, founded by Baldelli, and of Montepulciano, founded by P. Bucelli, originated in those years. By 1744 the so-called Etruscan vases had already acquired the right to a room of their own in the Vatican. The archaeological revival spread from Tuscany to the other parts of Italy: the Accademia di Antichità Profane in Rome was founded in 1740; the Accademia degli Ercolanesi in 1755. The discovery of Herculaneum and Pompeii was the most conspicuous result. Thomas Dempster made a hit because the Italian scholars were looking for a new focus for their patriotic feelings and cultural interests. Deeply rooted in their regional traditions and suspicious of Rome for various reasons, they found what they wanted in the Etruscans, Pelasgians and other pre-Roman tribes. Local patriotism was gratified by the high antiquity of pre-Roman civilizations. The new trend of interest in non-literary evidence suggested the possibility and provided the technique of exploration. The antiquarian method, combined as it was with the patriotic revival, produced scholars of an excellence unknown in Italy for over a hundred years[43].

The juvenile essay published by Vico in 1710 – *De antiquissima Italorum sapientia* – was concerned with metaphysics and had little relation to ancient times, except in the title. One point is worth bearing in mind about Vico. Very conversant with the linguistic, theological and juridical learning of his age, he was practically untouched by the methods of Spanheim, Mabillon, and Montfaucon. He admired Mabillon, and refers at least once to Montfaucon, but did not assimilate their exact scholarship. He was isolated in his times partly because he was a greater thinker, but partly also because he was a worse scholar than his contemporaries. The antiquarian movement of the eighteenth century passed him by[44].

Many fantastic theories were produced like Guarnacci's *Origini italiche* where Etruscans and Samaritans came dangerously close. Even the shrewd and internationally minded Denina indulged in an idyllic description of Italy before Roman rule with her peaceful society of small cities and states. Indeed even Tiraboschi started his *Storia della Letteratura Italiana* from the Etruscans. The celebration of pre-Roman Italy which is so frequent in the early Risorgimento[45] is not less characteristic of the eighteenth-century Italian historians.

Here are the roots of many of the ideas of Gioberti's *Primato*. Yet serious research went together with mythical thinking. To suspect Etruscans whenever so-called Etruscan vases were found meant putting the problem on an archaeological basis, and that was unusual. The discoveries in Southern Italy soon compelled the admission that many of these vases were of pure Greek workmanship – a notion already familiar to Winckelmann. The idea that the *Tabulae Eugubinae* were Etruscan was definitely exploded[46]. Gori's collection of monuments proved to be of lasting importance and at the end of the century Lanzi's *Saggio di lingua etrusca* gave an excellent sample of methodical research.

When Wilamowitz came to Italy in 1925 he made a speech in Florence in which he recommended the history of pre-Roman Italy as a good subject for future Italian scholars. It was easy for Croce to point out that the idea was at least one century old in Italy. He could have said that it was two centuries old[47].

The Italians went back to Greece via Etruria and Magna Graecia in the eighteenth century. The Sicilian coins which prince Torremuzza collected and Goethe went to see, the Herculanensan papyri, and finally what were at last recognized as Greek vases, spoke Greek. The discussion between those scholars like Passeri who admitted the priority of Greece and those like Guarnacci who supported the claims of Etruria made people realize how close the connections between Etruria and Greece had been. A new feeling of intimacy with the Greek world is noticeable in Italy in the eighteenth century after the long interval of the Counter Reformation. The *Fasti Attici* by O. Corsini (1744) and the *Monumenta Peloponnesia* by P. M. Paciaudi (1761) extended the interest from Magna Graecia to Greece itself. Several elements of the complex which made it possible for Foscolo to be an Italian and for Leopardi to write his poetry can be traced back to museums, necropolises and learned societies[48].

The conflicts between antiquarians and historians in the 18th and 19th centuries

THE CONFLICT IN THE EIGHTEENTH CENTURY

What characterizes the writing of history in the late seventeenth and early eighteenth centuries is the large number of historians whose main concern was to ascertain the truth of each event by the best methods of research. They shared this preoccupation with the contemporary antiquarians whose methods, in fact, they often followed. Thus, though the difference between a book of history and a book of antiquities remained formally clear, the aims of the historians were often identical with those of the antiquaries. Both aimed at factual truth, not at interpretation of causes or examination of consequences. In the words of Mark Pattison's retort to De Quincey, thinking was not their profession[49]. When the 'philosophic' historians began to attack erudition, the prestige of both antiquaries and 'learned' historians was affected. In their quest for reliable evidence the learned historians and antiquaries had been apt to forget that history is a reinterpretation of the past which leads to conclusions about the present. The philosophic historians (Montesquieu, Voltaire) asked questions about the present. Indeed, they asked questions about the general development of mankind of such a sweeping nature that exactness in detail might easily seem to be irrelevant; and to which, incidentally, literary sources might easily seem to provide a more satisfactory answer than the *thesauri* of the antiquaries. Voltaire approved of the doubts of his more learned colleagues on many details of the historical tradition, but he did not feel the need of replacing them by better established details. He brushed them away as irrelevant and asked for a different approach to history. The idea of civilization became the main theme of history, and political history was subordinated to it. Matters such as art, religion, custom and trade, which had so far been left to the province of the antiquary, became typical subjects for the philosophic historian – but hardly in the manner of the antiquaries. Many shared Horace Walpole's distaste for the people who thought everything ancient worth preserving as such. The *Discours Préliminaire de l'Encyclopédie* (1751) could not be more explicit:

> *Le pays de l'érudition et des faits est inépuisable; on croit, pour ainsi dire, voir tous les jours augmenter sa substance par les acquisitions que l'on y fait sans peine. Au contraire le pays de la raison et des découvertes est d'une assez petite étendue et souvent au lieu d'y apprendre ce que l'on ignoroit, on ne parvient à force d'étude qu'à désapprendre ce qu'on croyoit savoir.*

As Gibbon noticed:

> In France . . . the learning and language of Greece and Rome were neglected by a philosophic age. The guardian of those studies, the Academy of Inscriptions, was degraded to the lowest rank among the three royal societies of Paris: the new appellation of Erudits was contemptuously applied to the successors of Lipsius and Casaubon.

Vertot, Middleton, Ferguson and Gillies, in reinterpreting the political history of Greece and Rome, hardly concerned themselves with discussions on sources.

In the field of ancient religion, the long-standing collaboration of the antiquary with the philosopher was disturbed. In the seventeenth century it had become increasingly apparent that Oriental languages and history were necessary to the understanding of Christianity. In 1617 John Selden published his epoch-making *De Diis Syris*. In 1627 D. Heinsius made the point in the *Aristarchus Sacer* that even the language of the Gospels could not be understood without some knowledge of Oriental languages. Islam became better known and later attracted sympathies. Acquaintance with mediaeval Jewish philosophy brought up the problem of the origin of idolatry in terms which had already been formulated centuries before. Johann Gerhard Vossius' treatise *De theologia gentili et physiologia christiana sive de origine et progressu idololatriae* (1641) was accompanied by text and translation of Maimonides' *Mishne Torah*. Contact with pagan peoples in Asia and in America sharpened men's eyes to the characteristic features of paganism. The questions asked by the scholars were: (*a*) how polytheism came to replace primitive monotheism; (*b*) what had been the relation between Mosaic law and the institutions surrounding nations; (*c*) what sort of confirmation, if any, could be found for Hebrew and Christian truth in pagan texts. The method of answering these questions was usually a combination of etymology with the comparison of dogmas and rituals. The sacrifice of Phrixus might be compared with that of Isaac; Sarapis and Joseph, the son of Jacob, might be the same person. The name of Vulcanus was easily found to be identical with that of Tubalcain. Even the destruction of Troy was taken as a prophetic description of the destruction of Jerusalem by Nebuchadnezzar. Hebrew and Phoenician derivations were made fashionable by Estienne Guichart and Samuel Bochart. In 1700 Thomas Hyde made available Parsi texts – not always with happy consequences.

The answer to the question of origins varied from Euhemerism to the intervention of devils and tricks of philosophers and priests. But it was more or less generally recognized that some country – preferably Egypt – had been the centre of diffusion of a philosophic monotheism. The Jesuit A. Kircher satisfied himself that the *Mensa Isiaca* provided evidence for an Egyptian belief in the Trinity (1652). H. Witsius

(1683) could defend the originality of Jewish monotheism against John Marsham and John Spencer only by maintaining that the Egyptians derived their monotheistic beliefs from the Jews. Though there was nothing unusual or unorthodox in the view that some pagans had known the truth independently of Jewish and Christian revelation, the number of the pagans now admitted to the true knowledge of God might have dangerous implications. One understands why English Deists from Herbert to Toland cultivated comparative religion so keenly and why their opponents from Cudworth to Warburton were compelled to do the same. The Deistic controversy was fought with weapons supplied by the *antiquitates sacrae*[50].

Towards the end of the seventeenth century it also became clear that the study of religion would increasingly have to reckon with the non-literary evidence collected by the antiquarians. Spanheim promised a numismatic work on religion which never materialized, but coins were generally admitted to be great conveyors of religious ideas. In 1700 De La Chausse proclaimed that gems were another boon to the student of religion:

Evvi da tanti artefici espresso in picciol spazio tutto ciò e ancor più di quello che l'istoria ci palesa di considerabile, la religione degli antichi, il culto de' lor dei . . . gli arcani più occulti dei gentili; e sotto misteriose immagini e portentose figure scopresi la superstiziosa dottrina di molte nazioni[51].

Collections of images of gods had, of course, been common throughout the Renaissance period. The sixteenth-century repertoires by Du Choul and Cartari were still reprinted. But now iconography was made to serve the new comparative science of religion. The popular writer A. Banier, in *La Mythologie et les Fables expliquées par l'Histoire* (1738), insisted on the necessity of using '*médailles, inscriptions, monumens historiques*' to explain ancient religion. It is characteristic that the first edition of the *Gründliches Mythologisches Lexicon* by B. Hederich which appeared in 1724 referred only to literary sources, but the second edition of 1770 added sections on iconography. The so-called Etruscan vases excited discussions on religious matters. Yet it is impossible to avoid feeling that the further we advance into the eighteenth century the less central these researches become for the study of religion. The more philosophic spirits of the age found it unnecessary to stoop to collect and interpret the literary and non-literary evidence on ancient religion. The factual knowledge of President De Brosses, Ch. Fr. Dupuis, N. A. Boulanger, Baron de Sainte-Croix, J. B. G. de Villoison and even of the enormously diffuse A. Court de Gébelin was narrow. They constantly reflected on principles. They were busy formulating general theories about the origin of religion or more specifically of religious mysteries, and did not take the trouble to get a clear picture of what the antiquaries were doing. The more thoughtful students of religion seemed to have become unaware of the evidence collected and of the problems formulated by the antiquarians. Much of the past work was lost on them. On the other hand too many of the people who knew the evidence were obviously unaware of the difficulties of their subject. The antiquarians themselves forgot the lesson of wisdom provided by Montfaucon's *Antiquité expliquée*, which exploded so many complicated interpretations of religious symbols. Unable to reflect on principles they speculated on details. Stukeley transferred the Trinitarian nonsense of Kircher from Egypt to Stonehenge. D'Hancarville fascinated many of his betters by his misuse of vases. R. Payne Knight endeavoured under the guidance of coins 'to explore the vast and confused labyrinths of political and allegorical fable and to separate as accurately as we can the theology from the mythology of the ancients' – and he proved to be not less wild than D'Hancarville. It was characteristic that a serious worker, P. E. Jablonski, should avoid non-literary evidence as much as possible in his *Pantheon Aegyptiorum* (1750)[52].

THE CONFLICT IN THE NINETEENTH CENTURY

Up to the end of the seventeenth century the antiquaries had been left undisturbed in two activities. They had cared for that type of evidence which the ordinary political historian was apt to leave aside; and they had studied those subjects – customs, institutions, art, religion – which were outside the province of the political historian and could be best examined on non-literary evidence. In the early eighteenth century they lost the control of non-literary evidence. The more the 'learned' historians accepted the antiquarian's method of checking literary by non-literary evidence, the less the antiquarians could claim numismatics, diplomatics, and epigraphy as their own subjects. But they remained the teachers of the four 'antiquitates' – *publicae, privatae, sacrae, militares*. The right of the antiquarians to exist was not challenged in the eighteenth century.

The 'philosophic' historians had no use for their erudition and did not try to direct it into new channels. The question changed its aspect and became a more definite challenge to the antiquarians when, towards the end of the century, it became evident (thanks chiefly to Winckelmann and Gibbon) that erudition and philosophy were not incompatible. The combination of philosophic history with the antiquarians' method of research became the aim which many of the best historians of the nineteenth century proposed to themselves. It is still the aim that many of us propose to ourselves. It means two difficult things: the constant repression of the *a priori* attitude inherent in the generalizing approach of the philosophic historian and, on the other hand, the avoidance of the antiquarian mentality with its fondness for classification and for irrelevant detail. The antiquary was a connoisseur and an enthusiast; his world was static, his ideal was the collection. Whether he was a dilettante or a professor, he lived to classify. In certain cases his habits of mind were reinforced by the methods obtaining in subjects with which he was closely connected. *Antiquitates sacrae* bordered on theological territories; *antiquitates publicae* were hardly distinguishable, if applied to Rome, from Roman Public Law. In both fields systematic and dogmatic teaching was traditional. But history was now beginning to pervade theology and jurisprudence. A new notion, both exacting and comprehensive, of human development left little space for mere descriptions of the past.

The question to ask about the antiquarian studies in the nineteenth century is not why they were discredited, but why they survived so long. The answer is that the antiquarian mentality, naturally enough, was not unsuited to the nature of the institutions with which it was mainly dealing. It is easier to describe law, religion, customs, and military technique than it is to explain them genetically. Often the nature of the evidence is such that one has to combine items belonging to different historical periods in order to obtain the picture of an institution. Where the historian is reluctant to tread lest he may offend against the proper chronological sequence, the antiquarian is ready to introduce himself. Classification can dispense with chronology.

That explains why doubts on the possibility of unifying antiquarian and historical studies lingered long even in well-informed minds and were the object of lively debates. F. A. Wolf in his *Darstellung der*

Altertumswissenschaft (1807) tried to distinguish between history concerned with '*Das Werdende*' and antiquities concerned with '*Das Gewordene*'[53]. F. Ast felt that there was a distinction between '*Altertumswissenschaft*' and the political history of antiquity (1808)[54]. E. Platner distinguished between history which describes a nation '*in seiner Bewegung*' and antiquities which describe it '*in seiner Geschlossenheit und Ruhe*'[55]. F. Ritschl in *Ueber die neueste Entwicklung der Philologie* (1833)[56] was perhaps one of the first to deny entirely the existence of such things as '*Altertümer*' and made many other acute remarks, but Boeckh in the *Enzyklopädie*, though denying '*Altertümer*' in general, maintained the distinction between political history and '*Staatsaltertümer*', the one concerned with events, the other with institutions. Boeckh was obviously influenced by the long tradition of dogmatic teaching of law and political institutions in the juridical faculties[57].

G. G. Gervinus (1837) and J. G. Droysen (1868) did not deal with this problem in their text-books of *Historik* and therefore probably thought it out of date. But this should not blind us to the fact that the teaching and writing of 'antiquitates' as something different from history has lasted until a few decades ago. '*Kunstaltertümer*' were organized by Chr. G. Heyne when Winckelmann had already invented the history of art. '*Kultaltertümer*' were written after K. O. Müller had shown what a history of Greek religion could be. There were '*Kriegsaltertümer*' even after H. Delbrück's *Geschichte der Kriegskunst* (1900), and L. Friedländer did not immediately achieve the transformation of '*Privataltertümer*' into '*Sittengeschichte*'. The '*Staatsaltertümer*' were yet more tenacious, supported as they were by the example of Mommsen's systematic '*Staatsrecht*': not until this century have German scholars been persuaded to turn '*Staatsaltertümer*' into '*Rechtsgeschichte*' or '*Verfassungsgeschichte*'[58]. Nor was the survival of the antiquarian approach to history a mere German idiosyncrasy, though it must be admitted that outside Germany fewer people worried about this problem. France remained traditionally the best home for the antiquaries until not so many years ago.

Occasional relapses into the antiquarian state of mind must be expected even in the future. But the idea of 'antiquitates' is now dead because the corresponding idea of political history founded upon literary evidence is dead. The historians have recognized that the traditional subject of antiquarian research can be transformed into chapters of the history of civilization with all the necessary apparatus of erudition.

The antiquary rescued history from the sceptics, even though he did not write it. His preference for the original documents, his ingenuity in discovering forgeries, his skill in collecting and classifying the evidence and, above all, his unbounded love for learning are the antiquary's contributions to the 'ethics' of the historian. We cherish the memory of Jean Mabillon not only for the *De Re Diplomatica* but for the *Traité des Études Monastiques* where he recommended: '*Avoir le coeur dégagé des passions, et sur tout de celle de critiquer*'[59].

APPENDIX 1 [60]

John Leland, King's Antiquary

The article on John Leland in the *Dictionary of National Biography* states (p. 892): 'In 1533 Leland was made King's antiquary, an office in which he had neither predecessor nor successor.'

The evidence for this statement is not given and, apparently, is not easy to find. The notion that Leland was made King's Antiquary goes back, as far as I can ascertain, to the *Life of Camden* by T. Smith (1691) in which one finds this characteristic passage (p. XXVII):

(Lelandi) industriam perquam laudabilem annua pensione e fisco Regio soluta favore suo fovit Rex Henricus VIII illumque Antiquarii quo merito gloriatus est Lelandus titulo insignivit. Munus istud, quod dolendum est, ab isto tempore omnino desiit: licet unus et alter (vix enim plures numerantur) superbum illud Historiographi Regii, *nescio an satis pro dignitate, nomen sustinuerint.*

T. Smith did not quote any evidence, and A. Hall in the *Vita Auctoris* with which he prefaced his edition of Leland's *Commentarii de scriptoribus britannicis* (1709), gave T. Smith as his evidence for the same statement:

ut illum non modo bibliothecae suae praefecit, verum etiam magnifico Antiquarii titulo liberalissime donavit. Unus est inter Anglicae scholae Proceres, virorum eruditorum semper feracissimae, qui ad tanti nominis fastigium conscenderit
– Habeat secum, servetque sepulchro.

W. Huddesford's Life of Leland (1772), p. 9, is even more precise: 'By a commission under the Broad-Seal, Ann. Dom. 1533, in the 25th of his reign, he was appointed the King's Antiquary; the first and indeed the last, that bore that honourable office.' But he gives as evidence Wood's *Athenae Oxonienses*, and Wood (ed. Bliss), I, p. 198, says something different: '(Leland) had a commission from him under the broad seal, an. reg. 25, Dom. 1533, whereby he was impowered to make a search after England's antiquities, etc.'

Leland, in his 'Newe Yeares Gyfte to King Henry the VIII', called *The Laboriouse Journey and Searche for Englandes Antiquitees* (ed. Huddesford, no page number), stated that in the 35th year of 'your prosperouse reygne' he obtained a 'moste gracyouse commyssion to peruse and dylygentlye to searche all the lybraryes of Monasteryes and collegies of thys your noble realme.' He signed his pamphlet 'Joannes Leylandus Antiquarius'. The signature, in the best humanistic style, does not necessarily imply that he had been appointed King's Antiquary. The question, to which I should like to have an answer from competent students, is whether T. Smith had other evidence besides this signature.[61]

APPENDIX II [62]

A Select List of Studies on Pre-Roman Italy
(*about* 1740–1840)

Amaduzzi, G. C., *Delle origini italiche di Monsig. Mario Guarnacci, Esame critico con una apologetica risposta, etc.* (Venice 1773).

Amati, G., *Sui vasi etruschi o italogreci recentemente scoperti* (Rome 1830).

Balbo, C., Delle origini degli antichi popoli italiani, *Antologia Ital.* (1846), pp. 213–33; 247–62.

Bardetti, S., *De' primi abitatori dell'Italia*, opera postuma (Modena 1769); *Della lingua dei primi abitatori dell'Italia*, opera postuma (Modena 1772).

Bianchi Giovini, A., *Sulle origini italiche di A. Mazzoldi, Osservazioni* (Milan 1841); *Ultime osservazioni sopra le opinioni del Signor A. Mazzoldi intorno alle origini italiche* (Milan 1842).

Bini, G. C., see Lami, G., *Lettere gualfondiane.*

Bonaparte, L., *Catalogo di scelte Antichità Etrusche trovate negli scavi del Principe di Canino* (Viterbo 1829).

Bourguet, Louis, *Spiegazione di alcuni monumenti degli Antichi Pelasgi trasportata dal Francese con alcune osservazioni sovra i medesimi* (Pesaro 1735).

Campanari, Sec., Dei primi abitatori d'Italia, *Giornale Arcadico, LXXXIV* (1840), pp. 241–72.

Carli Rubbi, G. R., *Delle antichità italiche* (Milan 1788–91).

Cattaneo, Carlo, *Notizie naturali e civili su la Lombardia.* Introduzione, I (Milan 1844).

Del Bava, G. M. Riccobaldi, *Dissertazione istorico-etrusca sopra l'origine, l'antico stato, lingua e caratteri della Etrusca nazione* (Florence 1758).

Delfico, M., *Discorso preliminare su le origini italiche*, in *Dell'antica numismatica della città d'Atri nel Piceno* (Teramo 1824).

Denina, C. G. M., *Delle Rivoluzioni d'Italia* (Turin 1769–70).

Durandi, Jacopo, *Saggio sulla storia degli antichi popoli d'Italia* (Turin 1769); *Dell'antico stato d'Italia. Ragionamento in cui si esamina l'opera del p. S. Bardetti sui primi abitatori d'Italia* (Turin 1772).

Fabroni, G., *Degli antichi abitatori d'Italia* (Florence 1803).

Ferrari, Guido, *Dissertationes pertinentes ad Insubriae antiquitates* (Milan 1765).

Fourmont, E., *Réflexions sur l'origine, l'histoire et la succession des anciens peuples*, 2nd ed. (Paris 1747).

Fréret, N., *Recherches sur l'origine et l'histoire ancienne des différents peuples de l'Italie*, in *Histoire de l'Académie des Inscriptions* (1753), XVIII, pp. 72–114.

Gori, A. F., *Museum Etruscum*, Florence, 3 vols. (1737–43); *Difesa dell'Alfabeto degli antichi Toscani pubblicato nel 1737 dall'autore del Museo Etrusco, disapprovato dall'illustrissimo Marchese S. Maffei* (Florence 1742); *Storia Antiquaria Etrusca del principio e de' progressi fatti finora nello studio sopra l'antichità etrusche* (Florence 1749).

Guarnacci, Mario, *Origini italiche o siano memorie istorico-Etrusche sopra l'antichissimo regno d'Italia e sopra i di lei primi abitatori*, 3 vols. (Lucca 1767–72) (2nd ed., Rome, 1785–87).

Inghirami, F., *Monumenti Etruschi o di Etrusco nome disegnati*, 6 vols. (Fiesole 1821–6); *Lettere d'Etrusca Erudizione* (Fiesole 1828); *Etrusco Museo Chiusino . . . con aggiunta di alcuni ragionamenti del Prof. D. Valeriani*, etc. (Florence 1832–4); *Storia della Toscana*, 16 vols. (Fiesole 1841–3); *Pitture di Vasi Etruschi*, 2nd ed., 4 vols. (Florence 1852–6).

Lami, G., *Lettere Gualfondiane sopra qualche parte dell'antichità etrusca* (Florence 1744); *Lezioni di antichità toscane* (Florence 1766).

Lanzi, L. A., *Saggio di Lingua Etrusca* (Rome 1789); *De' vasi antichi dipinti volgarmente chiamati etruschi* (Florence 1806).

Maffei, Sc., *Ragionamento sopra gli Itali primitivi in cui si scuopre l'origine degli Etruschi e dei Latini*, in *Istoria Diplomatica* (Mantua 1727), pp. 201–60; *Trattato della nazione etrusca e degli Itali primitivi*, in *Osservazioni Letterarie*, vols. IV–VI (Verona 1739–40). *Cf.* also *Osservazioni Letterarie*, III (1738), p. 233 (a review of T. Dempster, *De Etruria Regali*).

Mazzocchi, A. S., *Sopra l'origine dei Tirreni*, in *Saggi di dissertazioni . . . lette nella nobile Accademia Etrusca di Cortona*, III (1741), pp. 1–67.

Mazzoldi, A., *Delle origini italiche e della diffusione dell'incivilimento italiano all'Egitto, alla Fenicia, alla Grecia e a tutte le nazioni asiatiche* (Milan 1840) (2nd ed. Milan 1846); *Risposta alle osservazioni di A. Bianchi Giovini* (Milan 1842).

Micali, G., *L'Italia avanti il dominio dei Romani*, 4 vols. (Florence 1810) (2nd ed., Florence 1821); *Storia degli antichi popoli italiani* (Florence 1832); *Monumenti inediti a illustrazione della storia degli antichi popoli Italiani* (Florence 1844).

Passeri, G. B., *Lettere roncagliesi* in A. Calogierà, *Raccolta di Opuscoli*, XXII–XXIII (Venice 1740–2); *Dell'Etruria omerica* in A. Calogierà, *Nuova Raccolta di Opuscoli*, XVIII (1768); *In Thomae Dempsteri libros de Etruria regali Paralipomena* (Lucca 1767); *Picturae Etruscorum in vasculis*, 3 vols. (Rome 1767–75).

Quadrio, F. S., *Dissertazioni critico-storiche intorno alla Rezia* (Milan 1755).

Romagnosi, D., *Esame della storia degli antichi popoli italiani di G. Micali in relazione ai primordii dell'italico incivilimento*, in *Biblioteca Italiana*, LXIX–LXX (1833).

Rosa, G., *Genti stabilite tra l'Adda e il Mincio prima dell'Impero Romano*, (Milan 1844).

Tonso, A., *Dell'origine dei Liguri* (Pavia 1784).

Valeriani, D., see Inghirami, F., *Etrusco Museo Chiusino*.

[ADDITIONAL NOTE (1954). – A reprint now in my possession of the anonymous article *Storia degli Studi sulle Origini italiche* quoted below p. 37 n. 43 shows that it was written by Antonio Casati.]

[1] J. Addison, Dialogues upon the usefulness of Ancient Medals, *Miscellaneous Works*, III (1830) pp. 59–199.

[2] See, for instance, C. Justi, *Winckelmann und seine Zeitgenossen* (3rd ed. 1923, 1st ed. 1866); L. Hautecoeur, *Rome et la Renaissance de l'Antiquité à la fin du XVIII siècle*, 1912 (*Bibl. Écoles Athènes et Rome*, 105); L. Cust and S. Colvin, *History of the Society of Dilettanti*, second issue 1914 (1898), pp. I-XLI; E. D. Snyder, *The Celtic Revival in English Literature* (Cambridge, Mass. 1923); P. Yvon, *Le Gothique et la Renaissance Gothique en Angleterre* (Caen 1931); K. Clark, *The Gothic Revival, An Essay in the History of Taste* (2nd ed. London 1950); H. R. Steeves, *Learned Societies and English Scholarship* (New York 1913).

Essential documents: Comte de Caylus, *Recueil d'Antiquités*, 1752–67; G. B. Piranesi, *Antichità romane*, 1756; R. Wood, *Ruins of Palmyra*, 1753; Idem, *Ruins of Baalbec*, 1757; R. Chandler, *Marmora Oxoniensia*, 1763; A. Gori, *Symbolae litterariae*, Florence and Rome, 1748–51. Baudelot de Dairval, *De l'utilité des voyages et de l'avantage que la recherche des antiquitez procure aux sçavans*, I (1686) pp. 1–70 is an invaluable document for the 'ethics' of the antiquarians.

[3] The best is in C. B. Stark, *Systematik und Geschichte der Archäologie der Kunst* (Leipzig 1880). Much information also in J. W. Thompson and B. J. Holm, *A History of Historical Writing*, II (1942) and of course in J. Sandys, *A History of Classical Scholarship* (Cambridge I–III, 1906–8); Ch.-V. Langlois, *Manuel de Bibliographie Historique* (Paris 1901).

For England *cf.* H. B. Walters, *The English Antiquaries of the Sixteenth, Seventeenth, and Eighteenth Centuries* (London 1934). For France, S. Reinach, Esquisse d'une histoire de l'archéologie gauloise, *Revue Celtique*, XIX (1898) pp. 101–17, 292–307 (see also below p. 33 n. 20).

[4] E. Norden, *Agnostos Theos*, 1913, p. 367. *Cf.* also Themist., 26, 316 [H. Kesters, *Antisthène et la dialectique* (Louvain 1935) p. 164]. A. Körte, Die Entstehung der Olympionikenliste, *Hermes*, XXXIX (1904) p. 221.

[5] F. Jacoby, Charon von Lampsakos, *Studi Italiani Fil. Class.*, XV, 1938, p. 218, is here essential. The distinction between Hippias' 'archaeology' and Thucydides' notion of history is evident. Less evident, though I should think very perceptible, is the distinction between Hippias' 'archaeology' and Herodotus' ἱστορία. Hippias collected and made available information which (1) was not easily accessible, (2) often came from a distant past, (3) lent itself to the form of a catalogue. Herodotus' history consists of one main action, is chiefly concerned with the recent past and (at least in principle) gives the more trustworthy tradition without suppressing the less trustworthy (Jacoby, Pauly-Wissowa, *Real-Encyclopädie*, Suppl. II, s.v. Herodotus, col. 467 ff.). Compare what Dionysius of Halicarnassus says in *De Thucyd.* 5.

[6] *Cf.* Dionys. Hal. I, 4, 1; Strabo XI, 14, 12, p. 530; Diod. Sic. ii, 46, 6; Flavius

Josephus, *Ant. Iud.*, I, 1, 5; I, 3, 94 (on Hieronymus Aegyptius *cf.* Jacoby, P. W. VIII, col. 1560).

We do not know what the Archaeology registered among the works by the philosopher Cleanthes was. The name of Archaeology was given retrospectively to a work by Semonides on Samos (seventh century BC); see Suidas, s.v. Σιμμίας, and P. Maas, P.W. IIIA, 185. It was also given to the Atthis by Phanodemos (fourth century BC). Cfr. also Philostr. *Vita Apoll. Tyan.* ii, 9 and Proclus, *Comm. ad Timaeum*, p. 31 C–E (I, pp. 101–2 Diehl.). The 'Ρωμαική ἱστορία (Steph. Byz. s.v. 'Αβοριγῖνες) and the 'Ρωμαική ἀρχαιολογία (Steph. Byz. s.v. Νομαντία) by King Juba must be the same work (F. Jacoby, P.W., IX, col. 2392).

[7] F. Jacoby, *Klio*, IX (1909) p. 121; *cf. Atthis* (1949) p. 117 (on Philochoros as a historian who separated history from antiquities). *Cf.* also A. Tresp. *Die Fragmente der griechischen Kultschriftsteller* (1914) (*Religionsg. Versuche und Vorarbeiten*, XV, I) and his article in P.W. Suppl. IV, col. 1119.

[8] *Ac. Post.*, I, 8.

[9] *De civ. dei*, VI, 4.

[10] Varro's place in the history of antiquarian research needs study. Bibliography in H. Dahlmann, P.W. Suppl. VI, s.v. Terentius Varro and F. Della Corte, *Enciclopedisti latini* (Genoa, Di Stefano 1946) pp. 33–42 (also *La filologia latina dalle origini a Varrone* (Turin 1937) p. 149). The fragments of the *Antiquitates* are to be found in R. Merkel, ed. of Ovid's *Fasti* (1841) CVI, and P. Mirsch, *De M. Terenti Varronis Antiquitatum Rerum Humanarum libris XXV*, in *Leipziger Studien*, V (1885) p. 1.

On the difference between Roman and Greek antiquarians see the acute remarks by F. Jacoby, *Fr. Gr. Hist.*, IIIa, Kommentar zu 273, p. 248 ff.

[11] Aul. Gell., XIII, 12, 2.

[12] *Cf.* the mentions of antiquarians in Plinius *N.H.*, Praef. 24; Tac. *Dial.* 37. The whole history of Roman antiquarian studies from Fenestella to Johannes Lydus is still to be written. On Plutarch see bibliography in K. Ziegler, in Pauly-Wissowa, s.v. Plutarchos, col. 222 of the off-print.

[13] Recent information on medieval antiquarian studies is contained in J. Adhémar, *Influences Antiques dans l'Art du Moyen Age Français* (London, The Warburg Institute, 1939) pp. 43–131; F. Peabody Magoun, The Rome of two Northern Pilgrims, *Harv. Theol. Rev.*, XXXIII (1940) pp. 267–90; R. Valentini and G. Zucchetti, *Codice Topografico della Città di Roma*, III (1946) (*Fonti Storia d'Italia*) with the important review by A. Degrassi, *Epigraphica*, VIII (1946) pp. 91–93; and in the numerous studies by A. Silvagni on epigraphical collections in the Middle Ages (*Diss. Pont. Accad. Archeol.*, XV (1921) p. 151; *Rivista Archeologia Cristiana*, XV (1938) pp. 107 and 249; *ibid.*, XX (1943) p. 49; *Scritti in onore di B. Nogara* (1937) p. 445 etc.). *Cf.* also B. Lasch, *Das Erwachen und die Entwickelung der historischen Kritik im Mittelalter* (Breslau 1887) and M. Schulz, *Die Lehre von der historischen Methode bei den Geschichtschreibern des Mittelalters* (Berlin 1909).

[14] Biondo's method in its relation to ancient antiquarian research has not yet been studied. *Cf.* C. S. Gutkind, *Deutsche Vierteljahrs. f. Literaturwissenschaft*, X (1932) p. 548, for a recent account of Poggio. *Cf.* also P. Joachimsen, *Geschichtsauffassung und Geschichtschreibung in Deutschland unter dem Einfluss des Humanismus*, 1910, I, pp. 15 ff.

A point of great importance is the relation between philological and antiquarian research, at least since Poliziano's *Liber Miscellaneorum* (the significance of which is rightly appreciated by G. Funaioli, Lineamenti di una storia della filologia attraverso i secoli, *Studi di Letteratura Latina*, I (1946) p. 284) and Coelius Rhodiginus (Ludovico Ricchieri), *Antiquae Lectiones* (1516). This, too, needs detailed research. For the beginnings of Egyptology there is the classical work by K. Giehlow, Die Hieroglyphenkunde des Humanismus, *Jahrb. d. Kunsthist. Sammlungen des allerhöchsten Kaiserhauses*, XXXII (1915) pp. 1–222. *Cf.* also E. H. Gombrich, Icones symbolicae, *Journ. Warburg Institute*, XI (1948) pp. 163–92.

[15] The evidence on the word 'antiquarius', 'antiquario', 'antiquary', etc. in the European literatures has not yet been collected. The *Vocabolario della Crusca* gives A. Caro, *Lettere Familiari* (ed. Milan 1807) III, p. 190, 'e poiché io mi avveggo al vostro scrivere che siete in ciò piuttosto istorico che antiquario', and S. Speroni, *Dialogo della Istoria* in *Opere* (Venice 1740) II, p. 300, 'Antiquari . . . cioè amatori ed ammiratori di cose antiche'. But notice S. degli Arienti, *Le Porretane*, Novella III, written in 1487: '(Feliciano da Verona) cognominato Antiquario per aver lui quasi consumato gli anni soi in cercare le generose antiquità de Roma, de Ravena et de tutta l'Italia'. *Cf.* also the letter by Antonio Leonardi to Felice Feliciano on Ciriaco d'Ancona in G. Colucci, *Antichità Picene*, XV (1792) p. CLIV. On the reference of the *OED* s.v. Antiquary to Leland as the recipient of the title Antiquary from Henry VIII, see Appendix, p. 27–28. W. Camden called himself an 'antiquarius': see the *Epistula* in *Britannia* (1586). For the meaning of 'antiquitates' before Rosinus notice also A. Fulvio, *Antiquitates urbis Romae* (1527); Pirro Ligorio, *Antichità di Roma* (1553); O. Panvinio, *Antiquitates Veronenses* (1648) (posthumous). A work apparently called *Antiquarium* by G. Bologni (1454–1517) is partly published in *Supplemento II al Giornale dei Letterati d'Italia* (Venice 1722) p. 115. See on this G. Mazzucchelli, *Gli scrittori d'Italia*, II, 3, p. 1490. A poem by A. Fulvio is called *Antiquaria urbis*, (Rome 1513). The *Commentaria super opera diversorum auctorum de antiquitatibus loquentium* by Annius of Viterbo, 1498, are, as is well known, a collection of forged ancient historians: *cf.* O. A. Danielsson, Annius von Viterbo über die Gründungsgeschichte Roms, *Corolla Archaeologica Principi Gustavo Adolpho dedicata*, 1932, p. 1.

For the seventeenth century *cf.* also F. Baldinucci, *Notizie de' Professori del Disegno* (opera postuma, Florence 1728) VI, p. 76: [Il granduca Cosimo III] lo costituì sopraintendente di esse [avanzi della dotta e venerabile antichità] e come oggi si dice suo antiquario'. The reference is to Bastiano Bilivert.

The text of the *Iubilatio* in P. Kristeller, *Mantegna* (1902) pp. 523–4. An important text for the antiquarians of the end of the fifteenth century is offered by the introductory pages of B. Rucellai, *De urbe Roma*, in *Rerum Italicarum Scriptores ab anno aerae christ. millesimo ad millesimum sexcentesimum*, II (Florence 1770) pp. 783–4, on which see F. Gilbert, *Journ. Warburg Inst.*, XII (1949) p. 122. The name of Iacopo Antiquari (on whom see G. B. Vermiglioli, *Memorie di I.A.*, Perugia 1813) lent itself to puns which are instructive. Marsilio Ficino in a letter to him (*Epistolae* (Venice 1495) CXXXIX): 'Ceteri te Iacobe tantum cognominant antiquarium; academia vero et antiquarium pariter et novarium tamquam antiquitatis innovatorem atque cultorem. Quid autem esse aliud opinamur renovare antiqua quam aurea illa saecula revocare regnante quondam Saturno felicia.' *Cf.* also Ioh. Baptista Mantuanus, *Opera* (Antwerp 1576) III, pp. 316–17:

> Tanta humanarum facta est mutatio rerum
> Ut videar mundo vivere nunc alio.
> At quoniam noster manet Antiquarius aevi
> Maxima pars, mundus qui fuit ante manet.
> Optima pars et res et rerum nomina servat.
> Este alacres, mundus qui fuit ante manet.

[16] The chief works of the antiquaries of the sixteenth–seventeenth centuries are collected in the *Thesauri* by J. G. Graevius (Roman antiquities, 1694–9) and

J. Gronovius (Greek antiquities, 1697–1702) with the Supplement by J. Polenus (Venice 1737). Their results are summarized in S. Pitiscus, *Lexicon Antiquitatum Romanarum* (*Sacrae et Profanae, Publicae et Privatae, Civiles et Militares*) (Venice 1719). The *Bibliotheca Antiquaria* by J. A. Fabricius, 1713 (3rd ed. 1760) remains the invaluable guide to that literature, but *cf.* also D. G. Morhofius, *Polyhistor* (Lübeck 1708) Lib. V, cap. ii, De scriptoribus antiquariis. Ducange's two *Glossarii* (1678, 1688) are, of course, to a certain extent, to be reckoned among the products of antiquarian research. For an early seventeenth-century definition of antiquarian studies *cf.* G. Naudé, *De Studio liberali* in *Variorum Auctorum Consilia et Studiorum Methodi* collected by Th. Crenius (Rotterdam 1692) pp. 602–3. The history of the studies on Christian Rome is to be found in G. B. De Rossi, *La Roma Sotterranea Cristiana*, I (1864) pp. 1–82. The chief work, A. Bosio, *Roma sotterranea*, was published in 1632. A study of the antiquarian research in the seventeenth century should include an examination of the catalogues of the cabinets. For a classification of antiquarian studies in the seventeenth century see M. Schmeizel, *Versuch zu einer Historie der Gelehrheit* (Jena 1728) p. 758. But notice the definition by J. A. Fabricius, *op. cit.*, p. 228: 'quicquid enim agunt homines, quoscumque ritus et mores observant, vel publice susceptos obeunt, vel privatim et domi'. For the evolution from mere numismatics to historical studies see J. Tristan, *Commentaires historiques contenans l'histoire generale des Empereurs, imperatrices, Caesars et tyrans de l'empire romain illustrée, enrichie et augmentée par les inscriptions et enigmes de treize à quatorze cens Medailles* (Paris 1635). This is clearly a step towards a history of the Roman Empire.

[17] See H. Stuart Jones, *Oxoniensia*, VIII–IX (1943–4) p. 175. Part of the evidence had already been published by W. H. Allison, *Amer. Hist. Rev.*, XXVII (1922) p. 733. The method of the first Camden Praelector, D. Whear, is clearly expounded in his *Relectiones Hyemales, De Ratione et Methodo legendi utrasque Historias civiles et ecclesiasticas* (Oxford 1637). The purpose of his teaching can be easily gathered from the Introductory Oration which in the English translation of 1685 reads: 'History is the Register and Explication of particular affairs, undertaken to the end that the memory of them may be preserved, and so Universals may be the more evidently confirmed, by which we may be instructed how to live well and happily'. The Ciceronian inspiration is, of course, indicated by Whear. The second edition of the English translation (1694) contains also Dodwell's *Invitation to Gentlemen to acquaint themselves with Ancient History* which is written in the same spirit and tries (not very successfully) to overcome the classical objection to any utilitarian defence of Ancient History: 'Why may not our modern Histories suffice for accomplishing Gentlemen, which are generally written in Tongues more intelligible by Gentlemen?' (VIII). Invaluable evidence for the teaching in Oxford is also provided by the lectures delivered by D. Whear and preserved in ms. (Auct. F. 5. 10–11) in Bodley's Library. I hope to publish a specimen of them.

[18] J. B. Mullinger, *The University of Cambridge* (1911) III, pp. 87–9.

[19] For instance P. Beni, *De Historia* (Venice 1622) I, pp. 26–7, recognizes the value as historical sources of coins, inscriptions, etc., but 'verae et germanae historiae laus litterarum monumentis ac narrationi sit reservanda'.

[20] *Cf.* for instance R. Flower, Laurence Nowell and the discovery of England in Tudor times, *Proceed. Brit. Acad.*, XXI (1935) pp. 47–73; D. Douglas, *English Scholars* (London 1939); M. McKisack, Samuel Daniel as Historian, *Review of English Studies*, XXIII (1947) pp. 226–43. Also E. N. Adams, *Old English Scholarship in England from 1556 to 1800* (Yale 1917).

[21] *Cf.* in general E. C. Scherer, *Geschichte und Kirchengeschichte an den*

Deutschen Universitäten (Freiburg i. Br. 1927); M. Scheele, *Wissen und Glaube in der Geschichtswissenschaft. Studien zum historischen Pyrrhonismus in Frankreich und Deutschland* (Heidelberg 1930); G. Gentile, Contributo alla storia del metodo storico, in *Studi sul Rinascimento* (2nd ed. 1936) pp. 277–302; H. Müller, *J. M. Chladenius, 1710–59. Ein Beitrag zur Geschichte der Geisteswissenschaften, besonders der historischen Methodik* (Berlin 1917); R. Unger, Zur Entwicklung des Problems der historischen Objektivität, *Aufsätze zur Principienlehre der Literaturgeschichte*, I (1929) p. 87.

[22] Besides the well-known works by P. Hazard and B. Willey, *The Seventeenth Century Background* (1934) *cf.* for instance: R. Pintard, *Le libertinage érudit dans la première moitié du XVII siècle* (1943) I, p. 45; M. Rossi, *Alle fonti del deismo e del materialismo moderno* (Florence 1942); J. V. Rice, *Gabriel Naudé* (Johns Hopkins Studies in Romance Literatures, XXXV) (1939); F. L. Wickelgren, *La Mothe Le Vayer, thèse* (Paris 1934); H. Robinson, *Bayle the Sceptic* (New York 1931).

[23] *Die Philosophie der Aufklärung* (1932) p. 269.

[24] B. de Holbach, *Système de la Nature*, II, ch. 12 (ed. 1821, p. 354, n. 1), already quoted by P. Hazard, *La pensée européenne au XVIIIe siècle*, III, p. 33.

[25] A. Dupront, *P. D. Huet et l'exégèse comparatiste au XVIIe siècle* (Paris1930). I cannot enter into the more theological discussions on the relations between historical truth and religious beliefs, but see at least Jean Le Clerc, *La vérité de la religion chrétienne*, in *De l'incredulité* (Amsterdam 1696) for the references to historical method (p. 327).

[26] L. Traube, *Vorlesungen und Abhandlungen* (1909) I, p. 13 ff. is still fundamental. Very valuable information is provided by L. Wachler, *Geschichte der historischen Wissenschaften*, II (Göttingen 1820) and by S. von Dunin Borkowski, *Spinoza* III (1936) pp. 136–308, 529–550. *Cf.* also N. Edelman, *Attitudes of Seventeenth-Century France toward the Middle Ages* (New York 1946).

[27] C. O. Rechenberg, *De autoritate* (sic) *historiae in probandis quaestionibus iuris et facti* (Leipzig 1709) p. 8 .*Cf.* for instance M. Schmeizelius, *Praecognita historiae ecclesiasticae* (Jena 1721) p. 85: 'Historici authentici praeferendi sunt non authenticis: illi sunt qui ex Archivis, Actis et instrumentis publicis scripserunt, isti qui ex libris vulgaribus sua hauserunt'; Io. Iac. Griesbachius, *Dissertatio de fide historica ex ipsa rerum quae narrantur natura iudicanda* (1768) in *Opuscula Academica*, ed. Io. Ph. Gabler (Jena 1824) I, p. 206: 'Quid enim contra genuina documenta publica auctoritate firmata . . . ulla cum specie dici potest?' See also J. F. Eisenhart, *De auctoritate et usu inscriptionum in iure* (Helmstedt 1750); Chr. A. Crusius, *Weg zur Gewissheit und Zuverlässigkeit der menschlichen Erkenntnis* (Leipzig 1747) pp. 1041 ff. Von der historischen Wahrscheinlichkeit.

[28] M. De Pouilly, *Nouveaux essais de critique sur la fidélité de l'histoire*, pp. 71–114, and Sallier's answer, pp. 115–46, are especially worth noticing in this volume. Another treatise on historical method which has never been analysed properly is provided by the Prefaces and Propylaea of the *Acta Sanctorum* (1643 ff., especially 1675 ff.). *Cf.* also R. P. Honoré de Sainte Marie, *Réflexions sur les règles et sur l'usage de la critique* (1713–20) which I know in the Latin translation, *Animadversiones in regulas et usum critices* (Venice 1751).

[29] In the same sense C. A. Hübener, *Historicus Falso Suspectus*, diss. (Halle 1706). The dissertation which can be said to have started all the discussion in Germany is J. Eisenhart, *De fide historica commentarius, accessit Oratio de coniungendis iurisprudentiae et historiarum studiis* (Helmstedt 1679). Eisenhart discusses the meaning of *fides, auctoritas, notorium facti* and *notorium iuris* and gives rules for establishing the reliability of evidence. His influence is particularly evident on the two dissertations *De iudicio historico* (1703) and *De pyrrhonismo*

historico (1707) by F. W. Bierlingius, which are reprinted with changes in the same author's *Commentatio de pyrrhonismo historico* (Leipzig 1726). On pp. 225 ff. see the discussion De fide monumentorum ex quibus historia depromitur. What he says on p. 96 can be taken as typical of the new critical attitude: 'Historicum genus scripturae tantum abest ut a citationibus abhorreat, ut potius lector suo quodam iure illas postulare queat. Prima statim quaestio, quae historias legenti in mentem venit, haec est: unde auctor haec sua desumsit? Num testibus usus est idoneis atque fide dignis?'

[80] J. D. Michaelis, *Compendium antiquitatum Hebraeorum*, 1753; *Mosaisches Recht* (1770) are the pioneer works in Hebrew antiquities. It is remarkable that Montfaucon had been reluctant to collect evidence on Hebrew archaeology. On Michaelis' predecessors see S. von Dunin Borkowski, *Spinoza*, III, pp. 149–52.

[81] H. Meibomius, *Nummorum Veterum in illustranda imperatorum romanorum historia Usus* (Helmstedt 1684); *cf. Epistola de rei medicae simul ac nummariae scriptoribus praecipuis* by Christophorus Arnoldus in P. Parisius, *Rariora Magnae Graeciae Numismata*, altera editione renovata accurante Joh. Georgio Volckamero, Med. D. (1683). Chr. Arnoldus mentions, among others, the doctors W. Lazius, F. Licetus, A. Occo, C. Patin, L. Savotius (the author of *Discours sur les médailles antiques*, Paris 1627), J. Spon, J. Vaillant.

On the reputation of numismatics in the late seventeenth century *cf.* Ph. J. Reichartus, *De Re Monetali Veterum Romanorum* (Altdorf 1691) where (pp. 84–89) there is a hymn to numismatics ('nullum libero homine dignius, nullum iucundius, nullum ad res victoris terrarum orbis populi probe cognoscendas est utilius' etc.); G. Cuperus, *Utilitas quam ex numismatis principes capere possunt* in *Apotheosis vel consecratio Homeri sive Lapis Antiquissimus* (Amsterdam 1693); I. M. Suaresius, *De numismatis et nummis antiquis* (Rome 1668). The best bibliography is in A. Banduri, *Bibliotheca Numismatica* in *Numismata Imperatorum Romanorum a Traiano Decio*, I (1718). There is a list of numismatic works of the seventeenth century in M. P. Tilger, *Dissertatio historico-politica de nummis* (Ulm 1710) pp. 40–5; on p. 41 Tilger calls the seventeenth century 'numismaticum'. *Cf.* also B. G. Struvius, *Bibliotheca Numismatum antiquiorum* (Jena 1693).

Above all, compare *Introduction à la Connoissance des Médailles* by Ch. Patin, 3rd ed. (Padua 1691) p. 8: 'Et mesme l'on peut dire que sans les Medailles l'Histoire dénuée de preuves passeroit dans beaucoup d'esprits, ou pour l'effet de la passion des Historiens, qui auroyent escrit ce qui seroit arrivé de leur temps, ou pour une pure description de memoires, qui pouvoyent estre ou faux ou passionez.' *Cf.* an interesting reaction to all this enthusiasm in Abbé Geinoz, Observations sur les médailles antiques, *Histoire de l'Acad. Royale des Inscriptions* (1740) XII, pp. 263ff.; on p. 280: 'Avec les livres sans les médailles on peut sçavoir beaucoup et sçavoir bien, et avec les médailles sans les livres on sçaura peu et l'on sçaura mal.' But see on the other hand H. E. Froelich, *Utilitas rei numariae veteris* (Vienna 1733) and the letter by P. M. Paciaudi 'a Sua Eccellenza il Sig. Bali d'Alsazia d'Hennin' published as an appendix to F. A. Zaccaria, *Istituzione antiquario-numismatica* (Venice 1793) pp. 354–64, where he attacks Bayle's *obiter dictum* on coins ('monumens que les modernes emploient impunément pour satisfaire leurs caprices sans se fonder sur un fait réel') in *Dictionn.* (ed. 1730) IV, p. 584, s.v. *Sur les libelles diffamatoires.*

Declarations of great methodical importance are also contained in J. Spon's preface to his *Recherche des antiquités et curiosités de la Ville de Lyon* (1673) (the book incidentally contains a list 'des principaux antiquaires et curieux de l'Europe'). An adequate study of J. Spon is wanted; *cf.* A. Mollière, *Une famille médicale Lyonnaise au XVIIe siècle – Charles et Jacob Spon* (Lyons 1905) (very sketchy). On Bianchini as a historian, B. Croce, *Conversazioni critiche* (1924) II, pp. 101–9. Further bibliography in the article by F. Nicolini in *Enciclopedia Italiana*. On Bianchini and Montfaucon, E. De Broglie, *Bernard de Montfaucon* (Paris 1891) I, p. 336.

For Bianchini's method compare what he says in *Demonstratio*, p. XIV: 'Sunt igitur claustra quaedam et sepimenta, imo et vestigia veritatis historicae, saxa, laminae, tabellae, corpora denique omnia signata literis, aut insculpta symbolis, sive etiam ornata figuris et imaginibus pertinentibus ad notas chronologicas, nomina, ritus, consuetudines illorum temporum, quibus ab Historia assignantur . . . Neque enim Scriptorum suorum tanta cuique fiducia seu potius arrogantia insedit ut auctoritate antiquorum marmorum et signorum emendari detrectet.'

[32] *De pyrrhonismo historico*, p. 50. See above.

[33] Among moderate sceptics compare Jo. Burchardus Menckenius, *Quod iustum est circa testimonia historicorum* (Halle 1701); *Id.*, *De Historicorum in rebus narrandis inter se dissidiis horumque causis*, in *Dissert. Literariae* (Leipzig 1734); Fr. Gladov and G. Fürbringer, *De erroribus historicorum vulgaribus* (Halle 1714); A. H. Lackmannus, *De testimoniis historicorum non probantibus* (Hamburg 1735). An anonymous dissertation, *De incertitudine historica*, is contained in *Additamentum ad Observationum Selectarum Halensium ad rem litterariam spectantium tomos decem*, pp. 148 ff., no date (but 1705?). The best dissertation of this kind is possibly P. F. Arpe, *Pyrrho, sive de dubia et incerta historiae et historicorum veterum fide argumentum* (Kiel 1716) (available in the Bibliothèque Nationale): twelve chapters systematically collect all the possible sources of deviation from truth.

[34] I. Wunderlich, *De usu inscriptionum romanarum veterum maxime sepulchralium in iure* (Quedlinburg 1750); *cf.* M. A. Greve, περὶ ἅπαξ εἰρημένων *sive de auctoritate unius testis* (Wittenberg 1722).

[35] Jo. Aug. Ernesti, *Opuscula Philologica*, 2nd ed. (Leyden 1776) p. 68. *Cf.* also J. Priestley, *Lectures on History and General Policy* (1788) and N. Fréret, *Observations générales sur l'histoire ancienne*, in *Oeuvres complètes*, I (1796) pp. 55–156.

[36] Chr. G. Heyne, *Opuscula Academica* (1785) I, p. 280. B. Hederich, *Anleitung zu den führnemsten historischen Wissenschaften*, 3rd ed. (Wittenberg 1717) is taken to be the first handbook of the auxiliary sciences of history. As it seems to have had little circulation outside Germany (I have been able to see it only in the Bibliothèque Nationale), it is perhaps permissible to warn the reader that it is an elementary summary of universal history, Roman antiquities, mythology, geography, chronology, genealogy, etc.

[37] 'Maiorem longe quam ipsi libri fidem et notitiam praebere videbantur' – Franciscus Scalamontius, *Vita Kyriaci Anconitani* in G. Colucci, *Delle Antichità Picene* (1792) XV, p. LXXII. On Ciriaco, see E. Ziebarth, *Neue Jahrbücher f. das class. Altert.*, IX (1902) p. 214; XI (1903) p. 480; also G. Voigt, *Die Wiederbelebung des class. Alterthums* (1880) 2nd ed., I, pp. 271 ff.

[38] *Dialogos de medallas, inscriciones y otras antiguedades* (Tarragona 1587) p. 377. *Cf.* the Italian translation, *Dialoghi di Don Antonio Agostini tradotti in italiano* (Rome 1592) p. 261: 'io dò più fede alle medaglie, alle tavole e alle pietre che a tutto quello che dicono gli scrittori'. On this great scholar who exercised a deep influence on the antiquarians of the late seventeenth century (Spanheim is the best instance) a monograph is wanted. The most recent researches I know are by P. S. Leicht, Rapporti dell'umanista e giurista Antonio Agostino con l'Italia, *Rend. Accad. Italia*, VII, 2 (1941) p. 375; J. Toldrá Rodón, El gran renacentista español D.A.A., *Boletín Arqueológico*, XLV (1945) p. 3; C. M. del Rivero, D.A.A. principe de los numismaticos españoles, *Arch. Español de Arqueología*, XVIII (1945) p. 97; F. de Zulueta, D.A.A., *Boletín Arqueológico* XLVI (1946) p. 47 (the translation of an English paper which had already appeared as the David Murray Lecture, Glasgow, 1939). I owe Augustinus' passage to C.

Mitchell of the Warburg Institute. A more moderate opinion in the same sense was expressed by S. Erizzo, *Discorso sopra le medaglie antiche* (Venice 1559) p. 2.

[39] *De numismate antiquo liber posthumus* (Louvain 1628) p. 12 (on the author see J. Ruysschaert, *Juste Lipse et les Annales de Tacite* (Louvain 1949) p. 48).

[40] The theory of the forgery is formulated first in *Chronologiae ex nummis antiquis restitutae prolusio de nummis Herodiadum* (Paris 1693) p. 60. For a typical statement by Hardouin see *Ad Censuram scriptorum veterum prolegomena* (London 1766) p. 15: 'Nos mense Augusto anni 1690 coepimus in Augustino et aequalibus fraudem subodorari, in omnibus mense Novembri suspicati sumus: totam deteximus mense maio anni 1692.' On his method, p. 172: 'De his quae leguntur in historia scripta nihil omnino nummi veteres habent; sed prorsus contrarium exhibent: et quod maius esse in historiis fabulositatis indicium potest? Nihil fere eorum quae sunt in nummis sculpta historia scripta repraesentat; et non est istud alterum certum νοθείας argumentum? Et quid mirum mentitos esse in historia profana qui sacram perverterunt aut adulterarunt?' See also his *Observationes in Aeneidem* in *Opera Varia* (Amsterdam 1723) pp. 280 ff. It begins with 'Virgilio numquam venit in mentem Aeneidem scribere.' As an example of his criticism see his comment on *Aen.* VIII, 505: 'Corona non fuit aevo Augusti. In nummis antiquis non vidi ante saeculum XII iam senescens.' The paper on Dante was republished in Paris in 1847 with the title *Doutes proposés sur l'âge de Dante par P.H.J.* (It appeared in the *Journal de Trévoux*, 1727.)

The best essay on Hardouin is by G. Martini, Le stravaganze critiche di padre J. H., *Scritti di paleografia e diplomatica in onore di V. Federici* (Florence 1944) pp. 351–64. *Cf.* M. Veyssière de la Croze, *Vindiciae veterum scriptorum contra J. H.* (1708). On Severus Archontius, see also *De J. Harduini . . . Prolegomenis . . . epistola quam . . . scripserat* Caesar Missiacus, vulgo C. de-Missy (London 1766) p. 15.

[41] *Cf.* Anonymous (P. Jacq.-Phil. Lallemant?), *Histoire des contestations sur la Diplomatique* (Paris 1708); V. Thuillier, *Histoire de la contestation sur les études monastiques*, in *Ouvrages posthumes* de D. Jean Mabillon et D. Thierri Ruinart (1724) I, p. 365. *Cf.* E. Marthène, *Histoire de la congrégation de Saint-Maur*, especially Vol. IV ff. (1930 ff.); P. Gall Heer, *Johannes Mabillon und die Schweizer Benediktiner* (St Gallen 1938). The *Correspondance inédite de Mabillon et de Montfaucon avec l'Italie* (1846) is invaluable.

[42] On Winckelmann the best study to date is C. Antoni, *La lotta contro la ragione* (1942) p. 37.

[43] E. Fiesel, *Etruskisch* in *Geschichte der indogermanischen Sprachwissenschaft* (Berlin 1931); G. Gasperoni, Primato, onore e amore d'Italia negli storici ed eruditi del Settecento, *Convivium*, XI (1939) 264; F. Mascioli, Anti-Roman and Pro-Italic Feeling in Italian Historiography, *Romanic Review*, XXXIII (1942) pp. 366–84. But the anonymous Storia degli studi sulle origini italiche, *Rivista Europea*, I (1846) pp. 721–42; II (1847) pp. 102–38 is still invaluable. On N. Fréret, M. Renard, *Latomus*, III (1939) pp. 84–94; on Herculaneum *cf.* for instance M. Ruggiero, *Storia degli scavi di Ercolano* (Naples 1885); G. Castellano, Mons. Ottavio Antonio Bayardi e l'illustrazione delle antichità d'Ercolano, *Samnium*, XVI–XVIII (1943–5) pp. 65–86, 184–94. On M. Guarnacci, L. Gasperetti, Le Origini Italiche di Mario Guarnacci e l utopia della Sapientia Antiquissima, *La Rassegna*, XXXIV (1926) pp. 81–91. An interesting contemporary survey of the antiquarian studies is provided by A. F. Gori in Admiranda Antiquitatum Herculanensium Descripta et Illustrata, *Symbolae Litterariae* (Florence 1748) I, pp. 31–38. Several works by G. Gasperoni (on which C. Calcaterra, *Giorn. Stor. Lett. Ital.*, CXXVI (1949) p. 383) study the Italian erudi-

tion of the eighteenth century. See for instance, *La Storia e le lettere nella seconda metà del sec. XVIII* (Jesi 1904); *La scuola storico-critica nel sec. XVIII* (Jesi 1907).

M. Maylender, *Storia delle Accademie d'Italia* (Bologna 1926 ff.) provides information on academies.

[44] G. B. Vico, *La scienza nuova seconda*, ed. F. Nicolini (1942) I, p. 206; II, p. 225. The recent *Bibliografia Vichiana* by B. Croce and F. Nicolini (Naples 1947) is an invaluable mine of information on the philological studies of the eighteenth century. *Cf.* also F. Nicolini, *Commento storico alla Seconda Scienza Nuova* (Rome 1949).

[45] B. Croce, *Storia della storiografia italiana nel secolo decimonono*, 3rd ed. (1947) I, p. 52.

[46] The history of the problem is related in the introduction by G. Devoto to his edition of the *Tabulae Iguvinae*, 2nd ed. (1940).

[47] B. Croce, *Conversazioni critiche*, IV (1932) pp. 150–2.

[48] C. Sigonio was the last great Italian antiquarian of the Renaissance to study a Greek subject. The next important work is perhaps F. E. Noris, *Annus et Epochae Syromacedonum in vetustis urbium Syriae nummis* (Florence 1691). All the other important studies of Greek antiquities of the seventeenth century are not Italian (J. Selden, *Marmora Arundelliana* (1628); F. Rous, *Archaeologia Attica* (1637); E. Feith, *Antiquitates Homericae* (1677); J. Spon, *Miscellanea Eruditae Antiquitatis* (1679); J. Potter, *Archaeologia Graeca* (1702), and above all the various monographs by J. Meursius collected by G. Lami (Florence 1741–1763).

Cf. A. Curione, *Sullo studio del greco in Italia nei secoli XVII–XVIII* (Rome, Tosi 1941). The whole problem of the study of Greek in Italy must be examined again.

[49] M. Pattison, *I. Casaubon*, 2nd ed. (1892) p. 449. The whole page is relevant. *Cf.* B. Croce, *La letteratura italiana del Settecento* (1949) p. 241.

[50] On the studies of the seventeenth century, see O. Gruppe, *Geschichte der klassischen Mythologie und Religionsgeschichte* (1921) p. 45; L. Capéran, *Le problème du salut des infidèles* (Toulouse 1934) p. 257; M. M. Rossi, *La vita, le opere e i tempi di Edoardo Herbert di Cherbury* (1947) (especially vol. III); Idem, *Alle fonti del deismo e del materialismo moderno* (Florence 1942). *Cf.* also G. Mensching, *Geschichte der Religionswissenschaft* (Bonn 1948) p. 39. A few characteristic works: A. Kircher, *Oedipus Aegyptiacus* (Rome 1752); E. Dickinson, *Delphi Phoenicizantes* (Oxford 1655); Z. Bogan, *Homerus* Ἑβραΐζων (Oxford 1658); J. Hugo, *Vera historia romana* (Rome 1655); S. Bochart, *Geographia Sacra* (*Phaleg et Canaan*) (Caen 1646); H. Witsius, *Aegyptiaca et* δεκάφυλον (Amsterdam 1683); J. Spencer, *De Legibus Hebraeorum Ritualibus* (Cambridge 1685); T. Hyde, *Historia religionum Veterum Persarum eorumque Magorum* (Oxford 1700) (he was attacked without explicit mention by Montfaucon, *L'Antiquité expliquée*, II, Part 2, p. 395). On the history of the *Mensa Isiaca* which played such a part after L. Pignorio's edition (Venice 1605), see E. Scamuzzi, *La Mensa Isiaca del Regio Museo di Antichità di Torino* (Rome 1939). There is an interesting allusion to the *Mensa Isiaca* in R. Cudworth, *The True Intellectual System of the Universe*, in *Works*, II (Oxford 1829) p. 119.

M. M. Rossi, *Alle fonti del deismo*, seems to me to have explained (pp. 26 ff.) why the comparative study of religion became a weapon in the hands of Deistic thinkers, though their opponents never denied a natural revelation to pagans.

[51] M. De La Chausse, *Le Gemme antiche figurate* (Rome 1700), Proemio.

[52] The best catalogue of works is in O. Gruppe, *Geschichte der klassischen Mythologie*, quoted pp. 58 ff. Among recent works notice A. W. Evans, *Warburton and the Warburtonians* (Oxford 1932); F. Venturi, *L'Antichità Svelata e l'idea del*

progresso in N. A. Boulanger (Bari 1947); S. Piggott, *W. Stukeley* (Oxford 1950). The titles of the books mentioned in the text are: Ch. de Brosses, *Du culte des dieux fétiches* (1760); A. Court de Gébelin, *Monde primitif analysé* (1773 ff.); Ch. Fr. Dupuis, *Origine de tous les Cultes* (1794); N. A. Boulanger, *Antiquité dévoilée* (1766); Baron de Sainte-Croix, *Mémoires pour servir à l'histoire de la religion secrète des anciens peuples*, with an appendix by J-B. d'Ansse de Villoison (1784) (*cf.* also the edition of 1817 under the title *Recherches historiques et critiques sur les mystères du paganisme*); P. F. Hugues d'Hancarville (alias Ancarville), *Recherches sur l'origine, l'esprit et les progrès des arts de la Grèce* (London 1785); R. Payne Knight, *The Symbolical Language of Ancient Art and Mythology* (1818) (reprint New York, 1876); [T. Blackwell] *Letters Concerning Mythology* (London 1748); N. S. Bergier, *L'origine des dieux du paganisme* (1767), and J. Bryant, *A New System or an Analysis of Ancient Mythology* (1774), are equally typical. A good introduction to all this literature is provided by the anonymous *Essai sur la religion des anciens grecs* (Geneva 1787), II, pp. 183–223 (the author is said to be N. Leclerc de Sept Chênes).

[53] This definition was still repeated by E. Meyer, the last great historian, to my knowledge, who accepted the distinction between history and antiquities as legitimate: Zur Theorie und Methodik der Geschichte, *Kleine Schriften*, 2nd ed. (1924) I, p. 66.

[54] F. Ast, *Grundriss der Philologie* (Landshut 1808) p. 12.

[55] E. Platner, *Ueber wissenschaftliche Begründung und Behandlung der Antiquitäten* (Marburg 1812) p. 14.

[56] F. Ritschl, *Opuscula Philologica*, V (1879) p. 1. Ritschl made the point 'Warum also nicht lieber den unbehaglichen Schlendrian ganz aufgeben und den Stoff der sogenannten Antiquitäten in angedeuteter Weise in natürliche aus den Unterschieden menschlicher Geistesthätigkeit selbst abgezogene Bereiche vertheilen?' The line from Ritschl to Droysen is clear.

[57] See also L. von Ulrichs, *Handbuch der klassisschen Altertumswissenschaft* (1886) I, p. 22 for another definition (and defence) of Antiquity. On all this literature about Enzyklopädie und Methodologie der Altertumswissenschaft, which I do not propose to examine in detail, see A. Bernardini and G. Righi, *Il Concetto di Filologia e di Cultura Classica nel Pensiero Moderno* (Bari 1947).

[58] For the discussion on 'Staatsrecht' and 'Staatsaltertümer' see provisionally my note in *Journ. Roman Studies*, XXXIX (1949) p. 155. I hope to write later on the influence of antiquarian studies on the rise of sociology.

[59] A first draft of this paper was read at the Warburg Institute in January 1949. I am grateful for helpful discussion to the members of the Institute, to Professor C. Dionisotti, Dr F. Jacoby, Dr N. Rubinstein, Mrs M. I. Henderson, Dr R. Pfeiffer, Dr B. Smalley, and to the Principal of Brasenose, Mr Hugh Last.

[60] I am grateful to Miss M. McKisack for having discussed with me the subject of this Appendix.

[61] E. N. Adams, *Old English Scholarship* (1917) p. 17, who repeats the common opinion, seems to refer to the Preface by John Bale to the 1549 ed. of the *Laboriouse Journey*. The reference would be misleading, as Bale calls Leland only 'a moste dylygent sercher of the Antiquytees of thys oure Englyshe or Brytthyshe nacyon'. I notice with pleasure that T. D. Kendrick, *British Antiquity* (1950) p. 47, note 1 reaches the same conclusion. Mr Kendrick does not discuss the texts mentioned above.

[62] This list does not aim at being complete. See also G. F. Gamurrini, *Bibliografia dell'Italia Antica*, I (Arezzo 1905). For Sicily, see B. Pace, *Arte e civiltà della Sicilia antica* (Rome 1935).

CHAPTER TWO

GIBBON'S CONTRIBUTION TO HISTORICAL METHOD*

It is seldom that the antiquarian and the philosopher are so happily blended.

GIBBON, Ch. IX

WE shall not ask of Gibbon new methods in the criticism of sources. In the *Decline and Fall* we find no trace of the new type of patient analysis of sources which his German contemporaries were just beginning to develop. The reviewer in the *Göttingische gelehrte Anzeiger* of 1788, though full of admiration for Gibbon, immediately emphasized the superiority of German source-criticism. Gibbon, taken as a whole, never went beyond a superficial impression of the comparative value of his sources. He did not even ask himself regularly what lay behind his immediate sources. He had no safe criterion for deciding that Herodian is more reliable than the *Historia Augusta* or that Dio Cassius is more or less reliable according to the opportunity he or his sources had to witness the events he relates. This is not to suggest that in certain cases Gibbon cannot characterize a source with great shrewdness. For instance he saw that the life of Severus Alexander in the *Historia Augusta* is, as he says, the 'mere idea of a perfect prince, an awkward imitation of the Cyropaedia'. Yet he did not make the observation a starting point for any of those researches which were to occupy later students. The question 'why is the life of Severus Alexander a panegyric?' never seems to have occurred to him. Nor did he try to ascertain the role of this biography within the series of biographies which compose the *Historia Augusta*.

Gibbon was not a pioneer in the study of sources, but he knew them extraordinarily well. He still had that familiarity with the classical and Byzantine writers which characterizes the great *érudits* of the seventeenth and early eighteenth centuries, and he added a know-

* *Historia* 2, 1954, 450–63.

ledge of medieval chroniclers. He also knew the best commentaries on every source available at his time and had digested the results of innumerable dissertations on major and minor points of scholarship. The famous twenty volumes of the *Mémoires de l'Académie des Inscriptions* which started his new education at the price of twenty pounds were only a beginning. He became gradually acquainted with an enormous mass of learned dissertations and treatises. Few or none of the great names of the erudition of the seventeenth and eighteenth centuries are missing from his notes. He went through the quartos and folios of the Benedictine publications, laying aside those religious prejudices which might have biased him against their authors and editors. He got hold of the most important geographical descriptions of the scenes of his history. It was no easy task if we reflect that he spread his net so as to take in both China and Spain. He did not know Oriental languages, but gives the impression of having read in translation many of the Oriental chronicles and poems that were available in his time. Needless to say, he was acquainted with numismatics and with epigraphy and read both the Fathers of the Church and ecclesiastical history as well as ordinary political history. Of Roman Law he had more than a little knowledge, and was conversant with at least some of the medieval juridical texts which had been brought to light in his time. The catalogue of his library which has been prepared by Mr Geoffrey Keynes (as far as the evidence is still available) confirms the range of his reading. He paid £3,000 for books from January 1785 to June 1788, three years and a half, and in 1788 he counted between six and seven thousand volumes on his shelves.

We must, however, remind ourselves that if the facts about Gibbon's erudition are well known, the story of his intellectual formation is not yet clear. We know the writers who were consulted by him in his maturity much better than the writers who contributed to form his mind. Pioneer work in this field has been done by Mr Christopher Dawson in his admirable paper on Gibbon read to the British Academy in 1934. I owe much to this paper and would strongly recommend the study of it. But I propose to make my own way in a slightly different direction. My former studies on the historiography of the eighteenth century have persuaded me that, in order to understand Gibbon, we must start from the great conflict of his time between antiquarians or *érudits* and philosophic historians[1].

Gibbon is the heir of a great tradition of learned studies, but in a new fashion. For, to begin with, there is courage and purpose in his display of learning. Here we must go back to that page of his autobiography in which he regrets that the intellectual air of Paris was hostile to the *érudits* and that his beloved Academy of Inscriptions had sunk below the dignity of the sister academies: 'The learning and language of Greece and Rome were neglected by a philosophic age.' This will bring home to us that there is no direct continuity, strictly speaking, between Gibbon and the *érudits*. On the contrary, there is a caesura which is represented by the intellectual movement of the French Encyclopedists.

The erudition of Bayle, Le Clerc, Leibniz is not surprising in its context. They naturally belonged to the age of great erudition; they breathed the atmosphere of Montfaucon, Mabillon, Spanheim. The same still applies to Muratori. But Gibbon was no simple survivor of a former age, nor indeed was he a provincial exponent of a somewhat old-fashioned tradition of studies. He was entirely at home in the new Paris of the encyclopedists and he shared many of their convictions. French was a language he felt his own and in which he started his career as a writer. D'Alembert and Voltaire were not less familiar to him than were Bayle, Spanheim and Muratori. We shall soon see that the scheme of his history was inspired by Montesquieu and Voltaire. Yet these were the very people who discouraged and even despised the erudition of which he was so fond.

The eighteenth-century conflict between the old-fashioned historical method of the *érudits* or antiquarians and the newfangled approach of the philosophic historians can perhaps be best illustrated by a reference to the now almost forgotten book *Monumenta Peloponnesia* by the Italian P. M. Paciaudi which appeared in 1761. Paciaudi explains that the philosophers could see no purpose in all those quotations which were the delight of the *érudits* and especially in all those conjectures which more or less inevitably accompany scholarship. He, Paciaudi, and the other antiquarians looked with horror at the invasion of the holy precincts of history by a fanatic gang of philosophers who travelled very light. He himself, however, had to admit that too many antiquarians were wasting their time in idle conjectures.

Thus, on the one side was what we may call the traditional school of learned historians. They had prevailed in Europe until the middle of the eighteenth century and had given many proofs of patience, critical insight and honesty. They had provided France, Italy,

Germany and England with very important collections of their national historical sources, though, as we may incidentally remember, Gibbon would always regret that England had not yet found her Muratori. These *érudits* were not simple providers of bare facts. They were often attacking or defending political and religious institutions. Many of them were devoted members of religious orders; others were free-thinkers. One of the latter influenced Gibbon so much as to affect even his style. Gibbon learnt from Bayle to blend malice and erudition. Bayle the sceptic, the libertine, the knight-errant whose lady had the voluptuous name of Erudition, was ever present to Gibbon's mind. But he learnt no less from the pious Jansenist Tillemont, so scrupulous and candid in collecting the evidence and in separating ascertained facts from personal opinions.

On the other side a new school of philosophic history had developed which was characterized by an interest in what came to be called civilization. The historians of this school examined the progress of mankind as it was reflected in political institutions, religion, trade, custom. Naturally enough, given their interests, they did not aim at establishing the authenticity of individual facts, but at outlining the development of the human species. Their books were more in the nature of essays than of learned treatises. While the *érudits* took pride in lengthy notes (leaving however the nineteenth century to produce the longest footnote in literature, the 165-page footnote in the *History of Northumberland*)[2], the philosophic historians seldom set out their evidence and aimed at being readable. They selected what they thought the most relevant facts according to a preconceived theory. They discussed rather than narrated. '*Malheur aux détails*', exclaimed Voltaire as early as 1738, '*c'est une vermine qui tue les grands ouvrages.*'[3] D'Alembert's *Discours préliminaire à l'Encyclopédie*, which provoked Gibbon, expanded on this theme.

The revolutionary importance of the philosophic historians must not of course be minimized even for a moment. They realized that an accumulation of facts does not make a history, and that the components of civilization, such as law, religion and trade, are more important than diplomatic treaties or battles. They finally overcame the one-sided view of history which confined it to political and military events. In a way we modern students of history are all disciples of the philosophic historians. Every time we study the history of population, religion, education, commerce, we are treading in the steps of Montesquieu, Voltaire, Hume, Condorcet.

But there was a great danger that philosophic history of this kind would continue to be written in a capricious way, with a haphazard choice of facts. The learned historians had collected and systematized a number of rules for the proper use of evidence. The *Ars Critica* by Le Clerc, the so-called *Propylaea* of the *Acta Sanctorum*, together with the *De re diplomatica* of Mabillon, are some of the best instances of this type of introduction to historical method. All these rules meant very little to the philosophic historian, and one can envisage the possibility that they might have become obsolete. Students of the last three centuries of history were not directly affected by these conflicts. The philosophic historians did not object to detailed research about modern history, and the standards of research about recent periods were far less exacting than those upheld by the antiquarians. But where the ancient and medieval history was concerned, a learned experience accumulated over centuries of scholarship with an extraordinary faculty for discrimination was in danger of being lost. Those who still remained faithful to the old gods of erudition were increasingly divorced from the living forces of the culture of their time besides being open to the attacks and irony of the philosophers. It was no joke to become a target for Voltaire.

At this point Gibbon stepped in. He aimed at blending in himself the philosopher and the antiquarian. His first work, the *Essai sur l'étude de la littérature*, written in 1759 and published in 1761, already shows how seriously he had thought about problems of method and how advanced he was on the way to becoming a philosophic historian with an antiquarian bias. He celebrated Bayle's *Dictionnaire* as '*un monument éternel de la force et de la fécondité de l'érudition combinée avec le génie*'; he discussed historical pyrrhonism '*utile et dangéreux*'; he wanted an '*histoire philosophique de l'homme*', but protested strongly against D'Alembert's contempt for erudition. It is evident that when he finished his *Essai* in 1759 he had already selected the points in which he could not agree with his French masters. In literature his sympathies were for the ancients against the moderns; in philosophy he thought that an invaluable help to the knowledge of human nature would come from the minute study of the ancient world. Though by now an admirer of Voltaire, he was convinced that the good cause would be helped by erudition. Indeed, his concrete historical interests were already running in the direction of his future masterpiece. He discussed the origins of polytheism, he inserted into his Essay an irrelevant digression on the first treaty between Rome and Carthage and even proposed to himself the problem of the causes of the Roman decline. For some years more he still felt that 'the ages of the world and the climates of the globe' were open to his choice. He wandered round in his search of a subject for historical study. There was indeed serious danger that he might occupy his best years in writing a history of the Liberty of the Swiss, though the materials were 'fast locked up in the obscurity of a barbarous old German language' which he did not understand. Eventually, his earlier and more genuine interests in Antiquity and Christianity emerged victorious[4].

The sections of Gibbon's diaries which have so far been published provide other important evidence on his intellectual formation. Gibbon, even when he had other literary projects in mind, mainly read books on Greece and Rome. It is clear that all his education had prepared him to prefer the decline of Rome to any non-classical subject. In 1762 he noted that Voltaire was not 'a man to turn over musty monkish writers to instruct himself'. On the other hand he pointed to Erasmus whose 'learning was all real and founded on the accurate perusal of ancient authors' and whose genius 'could see thro' the vain subtilties of the school, revive the laws of criticism, treat every subject with eloquence and delicacy, sometimes emulate the ancients, often imitate them, and never copy them'. He also criticized l'Abbé de Mably for 'attributing more consequences to the particular characters of men, often ill drawn, than to the general manners, character, and situation of nations'[5].

The later French section of the diaries which has recently been published under the title of *Journal de Lausanne* shows even greater maturity of judgment. In 1762 Gibbon apparently still admired the popular historian Vertot who specialized in revolutions of any country – Rome, Sweden, Portugal. A year later, in 1763, he remarked tartly that Vertot's books were historical novels: '*Ses ouvrages qui se font lire comme des romans ne leur ressemblent que trop.*' He was by now well aware of the recent revolutionary developments in Italian archaeology following the discoveries of Etruscan cemeteries and of Herculaneum. He planned therefore a new description of ancient Italy, but wanted it to be written *en philosophe* in order to discover the influence of geographical conditions on Roman history. The reading of Rutilius Namatianus which he started for its geographical interest re-opened for him the problem of the decline of Rome.

The pages of the *Journal* written on this subject in December 1763 can hardly be overrated. The little poem by Rutilius touched upon all the aspects of Roman life in the early fifth century AD when it was written. Gibbon felt that Rutilius was both a witness and a victim of the decline of Rome. He sympathized with the Pagan who had seen his own religion collapsing under the weight of old age and involving the Empire in its fall[6]. Gibbon never found time to write his projected account of '*l'état de la littérature en France, les gens de lettre, les Académies et le Théâtre*'. But his remarks about the coins of the Cabinet du Roi show how his mind was working in Paris: '*J'eus le plaisir, ou si l'on veut le chagrin, de suivre la décadence des beaux arts depuis le siècle* (sic) *d'Alexandre et d'Auguste où la plus petite monnaye de cuivre est d'une gravure exquise jusqu'aux tems ténébreux du bas-empire dont les médailles laissent entrevoir à peine les traces de la figure humaine*' (February 24th, 1763).

The still unpublished diary of the Italian journey stops (except for a few unimportant notes) at the gates of Rome; and the pages on Turin, Milan, Genoa, Lucca, Florence and other northern cities are inevitably filled with details about things seen and persons met.

Reflections on wide topics are seldom reported. Two of them deserve special mention. The Egyptian antiquities of the Turin collection prompted the remark: '*J'avoue cependant que l'Égypte toute curieuse qu'elle est, est trop éloignée, trop obscure et trop énigmatique pour m'intéresser beaucoup*' (May 6th, 1764).

In Florence he found time to read part of the *Histoire de Dannemarc* by P. H. Mallet, and to reflect on the causes and effects of the spreading of Christianity among the German barbarians[7]. The decline of Rome – the spreading of Christianity: the two subjects were slowly becoming associated in Gibbon's mind.

In 1769 the *History of the Reign of the Emperor Charles V* by William Robertson appeared. Robertson could only confirm Gibbon in his inclination to scholarship. Though Robertson accepted much of Voltaire's view of the Middle Ages, he was unable to approve his cavalier disregard of conventional historical rules. He wrote:

I have not once mentioned M. de Voltaire, who, in his Essay sur l'Histoire générale, has reviewed the same period and has treated of all these subjects. This does not proceed from inattention to the works of that extraordinary man, whose genius, no less enterprising than universal, has attempted almost every different species of literary composition . . . But as he seldom imitates the example of modern historians in citing the authors from whom they derived their information, I could not with propriety appeal to his authority in confirmation of any doubtful or unknown fact[8].

It is clear that Robertson, like Gibbon, was concerned with the problem of maintaining the standards of historical research. I doubt, however, whether Robertson arrived in time to exercise a deep influence on the formation of Gibbon's historical method. Gibbon was by then steadily working on his *Decline and Fall.* Besides, there are some striking differences between Robertson and Gibbon. I am of course only concerned with the first section of the *History of the Reign of the Emperor Charles V* – that is *A View of the Progress of Society in Europe from the Subversion of the Roman Empire to the Beginning of the Sixteenth Century* which can properly be compared with the theme and method of the *Decline and Fall.* Robertson made his researches chiefly on medieval legal and constitutional history and did pioneer work on land tenure. He did not study the rise of Christianity and of Islam, the barbarian invasions, the religious controversies, which are the subject of Gibbon. He did not aim at a full recital of events. The text of his *View* is very brief and sketchy. The 'Proofs and Illustrations' which he appends to it are in the nature of short independent dissertations which (as he says) 'belong more properly to the province of the lawyer or antiquary than to that of the historian.' At least in this section Robertson is very far from achieving the closely knit texture of Gibbon's history. He cannot claim, as Gibbon can, to be the perfect blend of philosopher and antiquarian.

The man who, though in a field very different from Gibbon's, really achieved something comparable in his historical work is Winckelmann. He too assimilated all the work of the antiquarians who had studied the artistic remains of Greece and Rome and interpreted them according to philosophic notions. His *History of Ancient Art*, which appeared in 1764, was not too late for Gibbon's studies in his formative years. Though Gibbon never went beyond the purchase of a German dictionary in his quest for the German language, he could soon read the book in the French translation of 1766. But he never showed (as far as I am aware) a marked interest in the man who was striving like himself to blend the philosopher with the antiquarian. Winckelmann from the very nature of his studies was almost untouched by those ideas which affected Gibbon. He disliked French culture and belonged to the Platonic tradition. Not being a political historian, he remained outside the main preoccupations of his age which were also Gibbon's preoccupations. I doubt whether Gibbon learnt much from him.

Gibbon cannot and certainly would not claim any originality in the realm of philosophic ideas. His faith in human reason, his vague deism, his hatred of superstition, intolerance, cruelty, are clearly reminiscent of Voltaire. He also shared Voltaire's indecision as to whether constitutional government or the enlightened despot were the better regime for a state.

Being an Englishman, he is altogether favourable to parliamentary forms when supported by a strong aristocracy and self-conscious commons. His adopted country, Switzerland, obviously reinforced his approval of self-government of the aristocratic type. But his Antoninus Pius and Marcus Aurelius and Theodoric are modelled on the eighteenth century benevolent despot.

His own problem, the decadence of the Roman Empire, had been discussed by Montesquieu and by Voltaire, and there is hardly any idea of Gibbon on the subject which has not its parallel in the former or in the latter. Montesquieu emphasized the fact that the very transformation of the Roman republic into a monarchy was ultimately bound to destroy Rome. He explained that the end of the republic implied the introduction of a mercenary army which proved to be less capable of defending the Roman State. Gibbon had perhaps been impressed more favourably than Montesquieu by the efficiency of the imperial legions. But he admitted that the 'victorious legions, who in distant wars acquired the vices of strangers and mercenaries, first oppressed the freedom of the republic and afterwards violated the majesty of the purple'.

At the same time Gibbon brought into special prominence, as Voltaire had done, that the Christians joined hands with the Barbarians to destroy the Empire. All his theory about the effects of the spreading of Christianity is an expanded version of what Voltaire wrote in two chapters (XI and XII) of the *Essai sur les moeurs*: '*Le christianisme ouvrait le ciel, mais il perdait l'empire.*'

Christopher Dawson was of course right in observing that Gibbon followed a historical tradition going back to the Italian humanists of the fifteenth century when he embraced the history of the period between 200 AD and the fall of Constantinople under the name of History of the Decline and Fall of the Roman Empire. Dawson was also right in pointing to Vertot as a popularizer of the notion followed by Gibbon that history changes by revolutions rather than by slow evolution. Yet, though Gibbon knew his Italian humanists, such as Flavio Biondo, and his Vertot, it can be doubted whether in either case he was directly influenced by them. Montesquieu extended his reflections on the greatness and decadence of Rome to the fall of Constantinople: this must have been decisive for Gibbon. Again, the idea that revolutions rather than slow changes make history underlies much of Voltaire's writing. Whatever may be the ultimate roots of Gibbon's opinions on the past, the opinions themselves came to him from the great French thinkers of his own century.

What then is new in Gibbon? What is new is evidently the *History of the Decline and Fall of the Roman Empire.* Gibbon's leading political, moral and religious ideas are those of Voltaire. But he was aware that facts are needed in history. Here the facts are collected, sifted, made to live again by a man who had no doubt about what to love and hate, but knew also how to describe, to measure effects, to draw a line between good and bad evidence. The intellectual horizon of the eighteenth century was indeed vast. Europe was too small for it. Curiosity and sympathy went to extra-European nations and religions, Islam included. The study of religion and law received a new meaning. The discovery of the new celestial city of the philosophers, to use the terminology of Professor Carl Becker, gave the criterion by which to judge the terrestrial city of priests, monks, scholastic philosophers and feudal lords. Potentially this new history was ready before Gibbon. But only Gibbon had the knowledge and the imagination to put it together and call it to life. Thus his *Decline and Fall* is both a complex and vivid picture of the Middle Ages from a certain point of view and a unique self-portrait of the eighteenth-century mind.

Gibbon was not entirely sincere when he wrote about the Roman Empire: 'The story of its ruin is simple and obvious; and instead of inquiring *why* the Roman Empire was destroyed, we should rather be surprised that it had subsisted so long.' Gibbon knew that there was something to be explained about the decline of Rome and thought that Christianity offered the main element of the explanation. But he must not be made responsible for the D. Phil. candidate's dream of sleeping beauty: somewhere in the wood the true cause of the decline and fall of the Roman empire lies hidden and only waits to be awakened by him, the lucky D. Phil. candidate. To Gibbon the decline and fall of Rome suggested a picture of new societies, laws, customs, superstitions, something to be described in its various stages rather than to be deduced from certain premises. Even the two controversial chapters on Christianity are not merely a contribution to the explanation of the decline of Rome. Gibbon himself says plainly what the two chapters mean, and we must accept his declaration as both correct and of consequence. Chapter XV was written to describe the spread of Christianity as a natural event. Chapter XVI was meant to show more fully than Voltaire had done that the persecutions of the Christians by the Pagans compared favourably with the persecutions of Christians by Christians[9].

It may seem surprising that with so much explosive material received from the French encyclopedists, Gibbon soon gained universal authority. The many attacks against his chapters on Christianity made little impression on the general readers and were not even taken very seriously in the circles in which they were produced. Three observations may perhaps contribute to explain this state of affairs. First of all, Gibbon's erudite method proved to be effective also from the point of view of success among general readers. They realized that he produced his evidence and left it open to his critics to find fault with him. Secondly, he gave an optimistic answer to the question on the future of civilization. If he accused Christianity of having destroyed ancient civilization, he was also certain that modern civilization was strong enough to resist the attacks of the barbarians. He dismissed all fears in that simple sentence which none of us can read without envying the man who wrote it: 'Europe is secure from any future irruption of barbarians; since, before they can conquer, they must cease to be barbarous.' Finally, his history, notwithstanding its reputation for naughtiness, is almost conventional in its solemnity and decorum. People educated by Plutarch to expect noble deeds and wise words were not disappointed. Unconventional in his religious opinions, and malicious, Gibbon was nevertheless paying full homage to the amiable prejudice that history is a theatre where you must play your part with appropriate words and gestures. This is enough to create a distance between us and Gibbon. All his psychological approach ignores the subtleties and the pitfalls of more modern studies of human behaviour. But what in the *Decline and Fall* has now merely the charm of old-fashioned manners made a direct appeal to eighteenth-century readers. Gibbon's ideas satisfied only the enlightened, but his presentation pleased the educated generally[10].

To sum up, I submit that Gibbon broke new ground not by his ideas on the decline of Rome, but by offering the treasures of erudition to the contemplation of the philosophic historian. By doing so, he unexpectedly reconciled two methods of writing history which so far had seemed to be inevitably opposed. First of all, he presented the theories of the philosophic historians in a much more persuasive way. Secondly he showed that erudition did not necessarily imply lack of elegance and reflection. But perhaps the most important consequence was that something new came out of his combination. Philosophic history ceased to be approximate and arbitrary and was submitted to the traditional rules of historical criticism. Nobody could refute Voltaire or Condorcet or even Montesquieu's *Considérations* by checking their references or by pointing to the flaws in their method of collecting evidence, but it was perfectly possible to apply this type of control to Gibbon. In truth Gibbon has been annotated and corrected perhaps more than any other modern historian. The controversies arising from his history were no longer a matter of subjective impression but could be discussed in terms of documentary evidence. All those critical devices which had been current among the *érudits* were made available to the philosophers. A new type of philosophic history emerged. It combined the learning of one school of thought with the philosophic imagination of the other. The work of reconciliation meant in fact that the tradition of criticism which we associate with the names of the great Bollandist and Maurist scholars and with Muratori was not submerged under the weight of philosophic history. It passed into the historical method of the nineteenth century together with Gibbon's synthesis of the philosopher and of the antiquarian.

By rescuing the details from that *malheur* to which Voltaire had doomed them, Gibbon made it possible both to preserve and to render more trustworthy what was after all the most endearing quality of classical historiography: the art of detailed narrative. Indeed it is Gibbon's speciality that we never can be quite sure whether he displays erudition for the sake of a good story or tells a good story as a contribution to learning. Thanks to his great erudition and to a native capacity for choosing what is picturesque, he is far more amusing than any other historian except Herodotus. If we compare his pages with those of Voltaire, we can see the difference that erudition can make in writing history. Where Voltaire produces an epigram, Gibbon has the fullness of well documented details. One enjoys his reliability, but one feels that there is life behind the evidence. It would be mischievous to call Gibbon a predecessor of the nineteenth century romantic historians who delighted in purveying atmosphere, though he certainly could feel the fascination of evoking the past and claimed to have conceived the plan of his work in the most romantic circumstances. He was too much of a 'rational voluptuary' not to control his emotions, but one can see that the age of Walter Scott, Chateaubriand and Augustin Thiérry would find something to learn – indeed something to enjoy – in the pages of the unromantic Gibbon.

I have stressed the fact that Gibbon's novelty is to be found in the reconciliation of two historical methods rather than in a new interpretation of a historical period. But I have no doubt about the importance of the support Gibbon gave to Voltaire's thesis about the causes of the decline of Rome. This thesis is inevitably disappointing to us. The very attitude of the free-thinkers of the eighteenth century made it difficult for them to see how Christianity had worked on the world. They did not dislike Christianity because they liked Paganism, though they sometimes affected to do so. They saw in history the struggle between a few wise men, the predecessors of themselves, against the violence, the superstition and the stupidity of the majority. From their point of view Christianity did not introduce into history anything which was really new and which therefore would explain something otherwise destined to remain unexplained. Not only did they fail to appreciate the new constructive elements which Christianity introduced into moral life. They failed also to understand the common people of the pagan world. They identified Paganism with a few enlightened philosophers, and not surprisingly found them to their taste. Then they came to dislike the Byzantine Empire, because it was theocratic, and the Western Middle Ages, because their culture was dominated by monks and priests.

However, we owe it to Gibbon that the problem of the relations between Christianity and the political and social developments of Europe has come to stay in European historiography. Gibbon followed Voltaire in boldly sweeping away every barrier between sacred history and profane history. This was something new. Take the three historians whom Gibbon studied and admired, Sarpi, Tillemont, Giannone. Sarpi wrote the History of the Council of Trent purely as a political history without a close analysis of religious feelings and their influence on secular affairs. Tillemont separated the history of the Church from the history of the Roman emperors. Giannone, in what he called the Civil History of the Reign of Naples, dealt not with Christianity as a religion, but with the Church as an organization rival to the State. Giannone's posthumous *Triregno*, first published in the nineteenth century, shows his truly sovereign mind conceiving a far ampler design of philosophy of history, but neither Voltaire nor Gibbon could have been acquainted with it.

What can be disputed is whether the historians of the nineteenth century learnt from Voltaire and Gibbon all that they could about the central problem of the relations between the religious developments and the political developments in Europe. History in the nineteenth century was ruled by German professors who lived and worked in universities where church history was taught in the theological faculties and political history in the philosophical faculties. The momentous consequences of the separation between sacred history and profane history in the German universities of the nineteenth century can hardly be overrated. The German historians of the nineteenth century normally studied either political history or church history without probing deeply into their connections. When the Marxists reacted against this separation, they performed a useful service. But they themselves were confined in their movements by their own peculiar prejudice that religion can be understood only in terms of class conflicts: they themselves were unable to recognize both the spring and the complexities of religious life. Voltaire and Gibbon really found their heirs outside Germany – or rather outside the academic circles in which German methods prevailed. Their problems fructified in the minds of the French, Italian and English Liberal historians, such as Constant, Guizot, B. Malfatti, Lecky, Milman, and Lord Acton – that Lord Acton who was such an admirer of German professors and so utterly unlike any of them. These liberal historians tried to write the History of European Civilization including both politics and religion.

This is not the place to examine why, with the exception of Lecky and Milman, they did not succeed in producing the books they had in mind. Constant, Guizot, Lord Acton, Malfatti left sketches or torsos rather than completed works. Maybe their failure is partly due to the fact that each of them sacrificed his own studies to political duties: they had first to build the Europe that they wanted to describe.

The task of rewriting Gibbon has been left to the twentieth century. We too may well find that we must first build a humane, liberal Europe before we can study its past. Meanwhile a simple example will suffice to show in what terms we might now restate Gibbon's problem of the inter-relations between Christianity and the Roman Empire. Gibbon, as we know, has written one of his most amusing and naughty chapters about the monks: 'The freedom of the mind, the source of every generous and rational sentiment, was destroyed by the habits of credulity and submission; and the monk, contracting the vices of a slave, devoutly followed the faith and passions of his ecclesiastical tyrant.' This applies to all monks – to the anachoret of Egypt and the Benedictine. Gibbon admitted, it is true, that 'the monuments of Greek and Roman literature have been preserved and multiplied by their indefatigable pens'. But this remains a detail on which he puts as little emphasis as possible. The whole work of Cassiodorus at Vivarium is dealt with in a sentence in a note of chapter XXXVII. To us it is evident that St Benedict and Cassiodorus mark the beginnings of a new society in the West: a society forming itself in Italy among the ruins of the Ostrogothic state. St Benedict conceived his monasteries as the nuclei of a new society economically autonomous and religiously sound. Cassiodorus perceived the possibility of making the monasteries the centres of a new learning where the Christian writers, beginning with the Bible, should be emended and elucidated according to the methods of profane scholarship. It remains to be seen how far St Benedict and Cassiodorus were successful in their enterprises. But no account of the Ostrogothic rule and of the following wars can overlook the creative efforts of St Benedict and Cassiodorus. They had the vision of a busy, educated, holy society while Theodoric's kingdom was going to pieces. Gibbon who admires Theodoric has few words for the men who tried to save the relics of civilization and to found new centres of spiritual and economic life while the Ostrogothic building was collapsing.

I should be happy if I could leave Gibbon at that, taking him simply as the historian who by combining philosophy and erudition and by a native touch of artistry, educated on classical models, triumphantly carried the results of eighteenth century thought into the nineteenth century. But there is something in Gibbon both enchanting and deceptive which suggests that no formula of that kind will really exhaust the richness and depth of his personality. Was he not speaking of himself when he said:

A rational voluptuary adheres with invariable respect to the temperate dictates of nature and improves the gratifications of sense by social intercourse, endearing connexions and the soft colouring of taste and the imagination?

Though one may suspect that he was less confident in the destiny of mankind than he would like us to believe, he was at least persuaded with the help of statistics that his own personal destiny had been singularly fortunate[11].

[1] On the antiquarian studies of the eighteenth century my paper Ancient History and the Antiquarian, *Journ. Warburg and Courtauld Inst.*, 13 (1950) p. 285 [reprinted above]. The best general study on Gibbon is perhaps G. Falco, *La Polemica sul Medioevo* (Turin 1933) pp. 191–340. I regret that I have not been able to use the important book by G. Giarrizzo, *E. Gibbon e la cultura europea del Settecento* (Napoli 1954) and P. Fuglum, *E. G. His view of life and conception of history* (Oslo 1953).

[2] I rely on the authority of F. Haverfield, *The Roman Occupation of Britain* (1924) p. 83.

[3] *Oeuvres complètes, Correspondance* III (1880) p. 30 (A M. l'Abbé Dubos).

[4] The references to the *Essai* in the ed. 1761 are to pp. 15, 49, 105.

[5] D. M. Low, *Gibbon's Journal to January 28th 1763* (London 1929) pp. 104, 129, 147–8, 183. *Cf.* p. CX for the composition of the *Essai*.

[6] G. Bonnard, *Le Journal de Gibbon à Lausanne, 17 Août, 1763–19 Avril 1764* (Lausanne 1945) pp. 122, 167, 177. *Cf.* G. Bonnard, L'importance du deuxième séjour de Gibbon à Lausanne dans la formation de l'historien, in *Mélanges Ch. Gilliard* (Lausanne 1944) and the penetrating remarks by L. S. Sutherland, *Engl. Hist. Rev.* LXI (1946) 408. Important for Gibbon's formative years, H. S. Offler, E. G. and the making of his Swiss History, *Durham Univ. Journal*, XLI (1949) 64.

[7] The pages of the *Journal on Paris* are now available in G. R. de Beer, G. A. Bonnard, L. Junod, *Miscellanea Gibboniana* (Lausanne 1952) 93–107. The reflections on Christianity suggested by Mallet are translated into English and reported in *Miscellaneous Works*, III, 2 ed. (1814) 231–8. But the most typical remark is suppressed. The last paragraph reads in the original (July 16th, 1764): 'Un protestant diroit encore que le Christianisme du Xme siècle étoit bien plus difficile à digérer que celui du Vme: il l'est assurément pour un raisonneur, mais je crois que le raisonnement a eu assez peu de part dans ces changémens, et quand on croit déjà aux absurdités de sa propre secte, se rebute-t-on pour quelques mystères de plus?'

[8] *History of the Reign*, etc., 7 ed., I (1792) p. 477.

[9] On this section *cf.* the acute analysis by J. B. Black, *The Art of History* (1926) pp. 165–9, and F. Meinecke, *Historismus*, I, p. 252.

[10] For contemporary opinion *cf.* J. E. Norton, *A Bibliography of the Works of E. Gibbon* (Oxford 1940) and also Sh. T. McCloy, *Gibbon's Antagonism to Christianity* (1933).

[11] This paper owes much to discussion with C. Dionisotti, M. I. Henderson, H. M. Last, J. J. Seznec, B. Smalley.

CHAPTER THREE

GEORGE GROTE AND THE STUDY OF GREEK HISTORY*

To Anna Laura

It was about twenty-five years ago that the name of Gower Street first impressed itself on my mind. I was reading Mrs Grote's biography of her husband. Some of you may remember how Grote is described as returning 'from the meetings of Council quite over-wearied, taking a shilling fare of hackney coach from Gower Street to Highbury Barn, and walking thence across the field-path to his house in Paradise Place'[1].

Thus, in my admittedly rather imperfect map of a mythical London, the Gower Street of George Grote had its place beside the Baker Street of Sherlock Holmes and the George Street of Giuseppe Mazzini, near the Euston Road. The transition from myth to reality is always complicated. Yet for once the reality was not inferior to the myth. Because the first member of University College I ever met personally was Norman Baynes, that great historian who typifies so much of what is best in the tradition of the College.

To teach Ancient History in the College of George Grote and Norman Baynes must have seemed a severe responsibility to my predecessors Professor Cary and Professor Jones. For me the responsibility is even more serious because my predecessors fulfilled their task with distinction, setting high standards both of teaching and research. Yet two considerations give me courage. First of all, like the Stoic emperor, I can thank the gods for having given me good teachers and having made me acquainted with many good men. Secondly, when as a special lecturer in 1946 I was so cordially introduced to the life of University College by the present Master of Birkbeck, I soon came to appreciate the propitious atmosphere of this institution born in liberty for liberty. The earliest days of the College provide the example of the first Italian professor, Antonio Panizzi, who combined to good effect love for the country in which

* An Inaugural Lecture delivered at University College London on 19 February 1952.

he was born with love for the country which had given him sanctuary in his hour of need.

It is the tradition of this College that the Professor of Ancient History takes responsibility for Oriental, Greek, and Roman history. This is certainly a wise provision, even if it is not necessarily compatible with the mortal nature of a mere historian. Today it is Greek history that presents most difficulties both to the teacher and to the researcher. Oriental history is still in that happy stage in which the almost vertiginous increase of evidence lends plausibility to the convention that thinking is a work of supererogation for the historian. As for Roman history, it was put solidly on its feet a hundred years ago by Theodor Mommsen and nobody has yet succeeded in turning it upside down; it is still safe to assume that he who does not know Roman law does not know Roman history. But all students of ancient history know in their heart that Greek history is passing through a crisis; and in order to clarify the nature of this crisis I now ask you to reconsider with me Grote's contribution to the study of Greek history against the background of the work of his predecessors and successors.

May I remind you that it is uncertain whether Greek history was invented in England or in Scotland? The two claimants are the Englishman William Mitford, who published the first volume of his *History of Greece* in 1784 but did not finish his work until 1810, and the Royal Historiographer of Scotland John Gillies who in 1786 published a complete Greek history in two volumes in quarto and by 1778 had already published a discourse 'on the history, manners, and character of the Greeks from the conclusion of the Peloponnesian War to the battle of Chaeronea'.

Between the Scot and the Sassenach I shall of course maintain strict neutrality. We continentals never knew of such a thing as Greek History with capital letters until the end of the eighteenth century or the beginning of the nineteenth century when it became generally known that Greek history was being taken as seriously in *ultima Thule* as Roman history was on the Continent. This was the important point. In the eighteenth century handbooks of Greek history were not uncommon on the Continent, some of the most popular books being in fact vulgarizations translated from English into French, German, and Italian. Diderot translated into French the *Grecian History* of Temple Stanyan in 1743, and the rather low-level compilation by Oliver Goldsmith enjoyed popularity on the Continent as long as it did in England[2]. What was really new was, however, political discussion embodied in a Greek history, such as one could read in Mitford and Gillies.

The priority of Mitford and Gillies in the study of ancient Greek politics seems to be well established. But it has not yet been noticed that Mitford and Gillies themselves were stimulated by a discussion on the decline of Greece in the fourth century BC which started in France and continued in Ireland before passing to England – or Scotland. In the age of enlightened despotism Philip of Macedon would naturally arouse more sympathy than Demosthenes. Philip had been a patron of historians and philosophers exactly as the historians and philosophers of the eighteenth century expected their kings to be. The first to raise Philip to a research subject in the seventeenth century was Pufendorf, the great international lawyer[3], but the first full-scale apologetic biography was written about 1736 by the French gentleman Claude Mathieu Olivier[4]. L'Abbé de Mably, another conspicuous name, followed with his *Observations sur les Grecs* on the same line in 1749. Then the subject was taken up in two stately volumes by Thomas Leland, Fellow of Trinity College, Dublin[5]. The curious poetical preface of this book explicitly says that Leland had Frederick of Prussia in mind while writing on Philip of Macedon. The date of publication, significantly enough, was 1758, the year of the treaty between England and Prussia.

The comparison of Philip of Macedon with Frederick the Great, once made, was unlikely to be forgotten, since it carried conviction. Both kings gave an unexpected turn to history by a singular combination of military abilities, intellectual interests, and ruthless cunning which made them well suited to their role as leaders of nations which were expanding while their more civilized neighbours were declining. John Gillies took up the comparison at great length in his *View of the reign of Frederick II with a Parallel between that Prince and Philip II of Macedon* published in 1789. It must be added that Gillies travelled in Prussia and met Frederick several times. But he had already written in 1778 that discourse on the Greek History of the fourth century BC which considered even wider issues of contemporary life – nothing less than the consequences of the American revolution. In his eyes the Athenian democrats were forerunners of the American rebels:

If that turbulent form of government [namely republics] should be established in a new hemisphere, and if popular assemblies and senates should be there entrusted with the right to exercise power, why might they not abuse it as shamefully as before? Why might not the ancient barbarities be renewed, the manners of men be again tainted with a savage ferocity?[6]

The savage ferocity of which Gillies was afraid was apparently that of the Athens of Demosthenes.

Gillies was not, however, the fool that an isolated quotation can make him look. He had the sweep of imagination of the true historian and was the first to realize that Lysias and Isocrates could be made to contribute to a history of Athens. Uncritical about the early ages to the point of accepting literally the story of Helen of Troy, he introduced new and interesting ideas into the political history of Greece. Later, in 1807, he performed a feat for which nobody has yet given him credit. He was the first to write *in extenso* the history of the Graeco-Macedonian States from the death of Alexander to the reign of Augustus[7]. Here again I suspect, though I am not certain, that he was inspired by contemporary events. His Romans conquering the Greek States are not unlike the French conquering Europe under Napoleon.

However that may be, the simple facts I have stated compel us to revise ideas on the development of historiography in the nineteenth century. It is commonly believed – and I have said so myself – that Niebuhr was chiefly responsible for starting the discussion on Demosthenes and Philip in Germany during the Napoleonic wars and that Droysen discovered the analogy between Macedon and Prussia. Droysen is also credited with the original idea of a history of the period intervening between Alexander and Augustus[8]. It now appears that the discussion of the Fourth Century in terms of modern political principles – and even of Prussia – had started almost a century before Droysen. Though Droysen's penetrating vision of the Hellenistic age as the age of transition between Paganism and Christianity cannot be compared with Gillies' limited political interests, it is undeniable that he had a predecessor in this respect too.

As an anti-democratic historian of Greece, Gillies was soon superseded by Mitford, chiefly because the latter's *History of Greece* was richer and more reliable in scholarly details. Yet, as August Boeckh, a good judge, remarked, Mitford had more information and less political judgment than Gillies. During most of his working life Mitford had before him the experience of both the American and French revolutions. A determined supporter of the rights of kings, he was admired by his political friends of *The Quarterly Review* and respectfully hated by Byron and by the young Macaulay[9]. When the Philosophic Radicals decided to intervene in the study of ancient history, it was inevitable that Mitford's work, already in its fourth edition, should become their chief target.

We associate the philosophic radicals with population and taxation problems, with the pleasures and pains of self-interest, and with the refusal to mention good taste. But when John Arthur Roebuck visited the Utilitarian Society for the first time he found its members in 'a low, half-furnished, desolate sort of room' discussing 'a critique for some review of an edition of a Greek author'[10]. The importance that the Utilitarians attributed to Greek history can be illustrated by a sentence of John Stuart Mill:

> The battle of Marathon, even as an event in English history, is more important than the battle of Hastings. If the issue of that day had been different, the Britons and the Saxons might still have been wandering in the woods[11].

About 1822 it was settled that Grote would make Greece his province. In later years Mrs Grote, who seldom underrated her husband, and never herself, claimed to have inspired the idea of the Greek history in the autumn of 1823. Chronology seems to be against her claim[12]. In October 1823 she herself wrote to G. Warde Norman:

> The Grecian History prospers, and G[rote] is more absorbed in it than ever. He has nearly concluded the account of the Greek colonies. Into this part of the work he has infused some useful doctrines both as to political economy and the principle of population.

In the printed text, Greek colonization occupies chapter 22 and the following in the second part. Even if the first draft was shorter, it is clear that the work had already been progressing for some time.

Roman history was not yet apportioned. Warde Norman and John Stuart Mill, then little more than seventeen years old, were both thinking of writing it. Mill, precise as always, had decided to start it when he reached the age of twenty. Both projects fell through. The only book on Roman history inspired by the radical school, the *Inquiry into the Credibility of the Early Roman History* by Sir George Cornewall Lewis, another lifelong friend of Grote, appeared in 1855.

In 1826 Grote felt sure enough of himself to launch a major attack on his predecessor Mitford. It filled fifty pages of *The Westminster Review* and was ostensibly a discussion of Clinton's *Fasti*

Hellenici[13]. Clinton of course drops out after the first page This article is still the best introduction to the thought of Grote. Already he shows that sympathy for small states which led him later to make a close study of the politics of Switzerland. He exalts the 'unparalleled stimulus to the development of individual talent' provided by Greek society, and finally he interprets Greek democracy as the form of government coinciding not with the interests of the poor, but with the interests of society as a whole.

Whether by accident or design *The Quarterly Review* published a defence of Mitford and an attack on the Greek Courts of Justice at about the same time[14]. The Radicals replied in *The Westminster Review* of 1827, but this time the anonymous article was written by Charles Austin. Mitford and the *Quarterly* were castigated for forty pages[15]. This vigorous start was followed by delays. Grote's banking business and his election to Parliament retarded the progress of the work. There was an interruption of ten years between 1831 and 1841. When Grote picked up the thread of his book he had to decide whether he could compete with his old schoolfellow Connop Thirlwall, whose *Greek History* had begun to appear in 1835[16].

The society of Trinity College Cambridge where Thirlwall developed into an historian was strikingly different from that of Threadneedle Street, where Grote convoked his friends in the early morning before his banking business started. Yet the two groups had much in common. Hurrell Froude's description of those wonderful Cambridge fellows who 'know everything, examine everything, and dogmatize about everything'[17] might as easily apply to Grote's society. Both societies disliked Mitford, read German, and were attacked by *The Quarterly Review*[18]. Both aimed at a liberalization of English political and intellectual habits and wanted them to be founded on firm philosophical principles. These similarities between the 'apostles' of Trinity College and the radicals of Threadneedle Street explain why the stories of Thirlwall and Grote have so many qualities in common and why ultimately Thirlwall's was superseded by Grote's.

This is not to deny the importance of the differences between the two schools. According to Thirlwall and his friend Julius Charles Hare, Niebuhr and Schleiermacher were giving more than what Grote called the inestimable aid of German erudition; they were providing a philosophy of history, a theological system – in a word, a faith. Thirlwall introduced Schleiermacher's theology to the English, and Hare put into his volume *Guesses at Truth* as much German romantic philosophy of history as the English language was capable of taking. The radical philosophers of London were unsympathetic to Schleiermacher's theology, though not to his Platonic studies, and followed Niebuhr only up to a point. This became evident when Sir George Lewis published his *Inquiry into the Credibility of the Early Roman History* which criticized Niebuhr's historical method as too subjective. Grote showed a large measure of agreement with his friend in an article in *The Edinburgh Review* which is his only contribution to Roman studies[19]. Later he wrote privately to him about another of his books: 'I wish I could think that it would be successful in repressing the German license of conjecture.'[20]

Furthermore, the two Trinity men and their associates, including Arnold of Rugby, were fighting within the walls of the old universities for a reform of the prevailing methods of teaching the classics. They wanted the empirical knowledge of the classical languages characteristic of the English school to be replaced by scientific investigation of the classical literatures as pursued in German universities. Grote was less directly interested in this reform and probably less anxious at heart to have it brought about.

There cannot be two opinions on Thirlwall's intellectual qualities. His scholarship was fine, his judgment sure; his straightforward and incisive style was better suited to historical writing than that of Grote. But he could not put his whole heart and mind into a Greek History as Grote could. Neither his theology of German origin nor the gentle worldly wisdom which we can see in his letters was necessarily drawing him to scenes of the Persian wars or to the Athenian market-place. Grote, on the contrary, found all that he wanted in ancient Greece: the origins of democratic government and the principles of freedom of thought and of rational enquiry. His major discovery in the field of Greek thought—the revaluation of the Sophists—was the result of his search into the relations between Greek democracy and intellectual progress. Thirlwall really loved Germany; Grote loved Athens. He loved Athens without any romantic nostalgia as a state which was formed for the sake of the good life. He saw a parallel between the education imparted by the Sophists and Socrates and that imparted in modern universities.

And there is a further point. Nothing was more important to the Philosophic Radical than the careful examination of evidence. His voice became particularly solemn when he spoke of the 'law respecting sufficiency of the evidence'. Bentham, the two Mills, Sir George Lewis, Grote, and John Austin, our great professor of jurisprudence whose lectures were so good that only John Stuart Mill understood them, were all engaged in examining the laws of evidence. When a proper study of the contribution of this group to English historiography is made, it will probably show that the importance of Sir George Lewis and his influence on his friends have not yet been properly appreciated. Lewis is well remembered as the prodigious man who succeeded in being at different stages of his career a student of the Romance languages and of ancient astronomy, an editor of Greek texts, a critic of Comte and Niebuhr, a translator of Boeckh and Karl Otfried Müller, an investigator of English law and administration, the author of *An Essay on the Influence of Authority in Matters of Opinion* and of *A Treatise on the Methods of Observation and Reasoning in Politics* – not to speak of his public offices. What really unifies his activity – as Walter Bagehot came near to seeing – is his passion for rigorous examination of the evidence[21]. This passion Grote shared, and he brought to its support an immense capacity for minute work.

I have often wondered whether John Stuart Mill's famous letter on Grote written to Carlyle in 1833 must be taken seriously. A letter to Carlyle was by definition an embarrassed letter; and a letter by John Stuart Mill to Carlyle was the least likely to be the exception. But let us suppose that Mill was perfectly sincere when he wrote to Carlyle:

> [Grote] is a man of good, but not first-rate intellect, hard and mechanical, not at all quick; with less subtlety than any able and instructed man I ever knew. . . . After all I had said of him you will be surprised to learn that he reads German[22].

The answer to Mill is surely contained in Mr Garrod's remark about Scaliger and Bentley: 'Learning, consummate learning, is a thing a good deal more rare than genius.'[23]

Respect for the law of evidence brought Grote to what was then the revolutionary conclusion that Greek history had to be divided into two neatly separated compartments: legendary Greece, historical Greece. Grote never denied that the legends on early Greece might contain a good deal of history. He simply confessed his inability to separate history from myth without 'collateral evidence and without possibility of verification'[24]. Thus he broke with K. O. Müller and his English admirers. It is easy for us made wise by the discoveries of Mycenae, Crete, Troy, and Boghaz-Keui to react against Grote's scepticism. He could justly reply that Mycenae, Crete, Troy, and Boghaz-Keui have provided the collateral evidence that he lacked.

What gives Grote's *History* its almost unique distinction is this combination of passionate moral and political interests, vast learning, and respect for the evidence.

The natives of Europe used to be civilized in the nineteenth century, and these qualities of Grote were immediately recognized by almost everyone. John Stuart Mill, notwithstanding his grudges against Grote and their temperamental differences, commented with admiration in *The Spectator* and in *The Edinburgh Review* upon the volumes of the *Greek History* which appeared from 1846 onwards. He greeted them as the first attempt at a philosophic history of Greece[25]. Not less admiring was the *Revue des Deux Mondes*, in which the first volumes were discussed by Prosper Mérimée[26]. Even the *Quarterly* was swept off its feet. It forgot to protest against the rehabilitation of Cleon and only made a very mild reservation about the sophists: indeed it celebrated 'the strict attention to the laws of evidence' and 'the high moral tone which breathes through the whole work'[27]. The only notable exception was Richard Shilleto, the distinguished Cambridge don, who wrote a pamphlet entitled *Thucydides or Grote?* He was candid: 'I cannot refrain from saying . . . that I am thankful that [Mr Grote] is not a member of either of the old universities of our land.' Mr Shilleto was answered by another Cambridge man who happened to be George Grote's brother, and nothing more was heard of him in this connection[28].

It would be pleasant to follow in greater detail than is possible here the steps of the *Greek History* towards popularity and authority. There is for instance a letter by Auguste Comte promising to read it in order to find confirmation of his own theories, though in obedience to mental hygiene he was no longer reading books[29].

As I have mentioned, the study of Greek history had been almost unknown to the Continent before the end of the eighteenth century. In the first half of the nineteenth century in so far as research on detail was concerned the situation was reversed by the industry of the German universities. Three or four epoch-making works emerged, such as K. O. Müller's books on the Dorians and on mythology,

Boeckh's *Public Economy of Athens*, and Droysen's *History of Hellenism*. With the exception of Droysen, whose importance was not recognized until much later, these works were immediately influential. But the general histories of Greece (such as those by Graff, Plass, and Roth) remained poor compilations. Only Duncker's *History of Antiquity* which included Greek history to 479 BC had some independent value for its clear presentation of the archaic age and for its interpretation of Themistocles' personality: it was later translated into English. No distinguished Greek history appeared in France either, until 1851. Victor Duruy who published one in that year had to rewrite it ten years later under the impact of Thirlwall and Grote[30].

In fact Grote's history set new standards and gave new impulse to the writing of Greek history. Under Grote's archonship a new era started. His work, either in the original or in its French and German translations, travelled everywhere and impressed every classical student by its approach to the legends, by its revaluation of Greek political life, and above all by its insistence on the close connexion between political and intellectual history. Grote utilized in full the results of German scholarship and assessed their value with independent judgment. His twelve volumes were neatly planned and consistently readable. In England, Freeman was inspired to write the *History of Federal Government* to cover an aspect which Grote had almost overlooked, in part for chronological reasons[31]. In the next generation the restless and fertile mind of Bury wrestled continuously with problems that Grote suggested to him[32]. In France, Grote influenced a long series of researches on social and constitutional history, especially of Athens.

But it was in the German world that Grote created the greatest commotion. The German professors could hardly believe their ears when they heard that he was a banker. But they took his challenge seriously. All the German studies on Greek history of the last fifty years of the nineteenth century are either for or against Grote. The German scholars produced their famous series of Greek histories in answer to Grote: Kortüm (1854), Curtius (1857), Busolt (1885), Holm (1886), Beloch (1893), to which the *History of Antiquity* by E. Meyer (Vol. II, 1893) must be added. Two of the most penetrating researches on special periods of Greek history – the study of Demosthenes and his age by A. Schaefer (1856) and the history of Athenian politics after Pericles by Beloch (1884) – were directly inspired by Thirlwall and Grote. In 1854 the veteran scholar Schömann thought it necessary to devote a whole book to the discussion of Grote's opinions on the Athenian constitution[33]. In 1873 Hermann Müller-Strübing, an extravagant but learned German scholar who lived in London, wrote what amounted to a pamphlet of 735 pages against the German adversaries of Grote[34]. Later Theodor Gomperz took pride in acknowledging how much his *Greek Thinkers* owed to Grote, whom he knew personally[35]. I suspect that Gomperz was in fact Grote's greatest pupil. The reputation of the English historian spread outside the circle of the specialists. Karl Lehrs has left a description of how Heinrich Theodor von Schön, the Prussian Minister, anxiously awaited the appearance of each new volume of the *History*[36]. Johann Jacoby, the democratic leader, made extracts from Grote for political propaganda[37]. In 1890 Pöhlmann wrote one of the first examinations of Greek democracy from a quasi-Marxist point of view to refute Grote[38]. In 1893 Wilamowitz-Moellendorff concluded his survey of the studies of Greek history with Grote; and a very significant page it was. Wilamowitz wanted to replace the unpleasant political discussions on Cleon and Demosthenes inspired by Grote with sober study of Greek constitutional law. We shall soon see the consequences[39].

In Italy, Grote was not unknown. His theories on Greek legends were mentioned a few months after their publication in the *Rivista Europea* of 1847[40]. When Grote died, Pasquale Villari, already famous as a student of Savonarola, wrote to J. S. Mill deploring the loss[41]. But in the first seventy years of the nineteenth century the Italians seem to have accepted too literally Lodovico Antonio Muratori's invitation to leave the Greeks and Romans and devote themselves to medieval history which was at the roots of their present troubles. When I consider how little was apparently written on Greek history in Italy at that time, I sometimes wonder whether by strange chance some such work has not eluded me. Anyway the Italian universities recognized the need of importing teachers of Greek history from Germany. Holm and Beloch wrote their histories of Greece as professors in Italian universities. The results of this infusion of German scholarship were soon evident and almost spectacular. In 1898 Gaetano De Sanctis, a pupil of Beloch, produced at the age of twenty-eight a history of Athens which put Italian studies in the forefront and which is still unsurpassed. Both Beloch and De Sanctis were keen students of Grote; at their schools of Rome and Turin Grote has been discussed by three generations of students who are now teachers in their turn[42].

After 1900 the decline of creative work on Greek history became evident. The age in which practical politicians and moralists were interested in Greek was ushered out by Wilamowitz on the one hand and by John Ruskin on the other. As Ruskin's once-famous words on Grote are no longer well remembered, I may perhaps quote them:

> Grote's History of Greece . . . There is probably no commercial establishment between Charing Cross and the Bank, whose head clerk could not write a better one, if he had the vanity to waste his time on it[43].

While Greek history was taught more and more in old and new universities everywhere, few important books, either on archaic or on classical Greece, were published. In Germany, E. Meyer never finished the Greek section of his *History of Antiquity*, and Wilamowitz gave priority to literary studies in what was perhaps the least clearly directed period of his extraordinary activity. In Italy, De Sanctis devoted himself chiefly for many years to the study of Roman history. The general level of production sank rapidly. It is true that the history of the Hellenistic States was attracting the attention of some of the best men – Tarn in Great Britain, Wilcken in Germany, Holleaux in France, Rostovtzeff in Russia and then in America, Cardinali in Italy. But it would be naïve to suggest that the history of Greece proper is an exhausted field. The opposite is true. Never before have so many fundamental discoveries challenged the historian.

With the discovery of inscriptions and papyri, the written evidence has been increased in the last seventy or eighty years as it had not been since the end of the sixteenth century. The amount of lyric poetry has been almost doubled, filling gaps in the most obscure periods of Greek history. Pindar is no longer alone, Menander can speak for himself, the study of Athenian constitutional history has been transformed by the discovery of the *Atheniensium res publica*, and the history of the Athenian empire has been made possible by inscriptions. Greek elements have been found in Jewish, Indian, Arabic, and perhaps Hittite, sources.

Archaeology has been no less generous with help and problems. It has extended the evidence for Greek history which used to begin with Homer any moment after 1000 BC to about 2000 BC; it has added two new periods, the Minoan and the Mycenaean, and has given us the possibility of seeing the Greek cities and sanctuaries as they were. We are apt to forget that seventy or eighty years ago Cnossus, Mycenae, Delphi, Olympia, Smyrna, Priene, and Olynthus did not exist for historical purposes. Nor were the museums organized to provide direct evidence for the historical evolution of ancient Greece. A few months ago I was walking through the rooms of the Museum of Syracuse – that monument to the genius and patience of Paolo Orsi. It was natural to ask oneself what K. O. Müller or George Grote would have given for such an orderly collection of the evidence showing all the stages through which the Greeks passed in Sicily from the first contacts with the natives to the not inglorious Byzantine end.

Finally, archaeology combined with comparative philology has broken for ever the isolation of Greek history. The Indo-European invasion of Greece, once a wonder in itself, has become a part of a vast chain of events in the eastern Mediterranean. The study of Hellenization has been extended to the Indus, that of Orientalization to the Pillars of Hercules. We know what Greek art and religion became in Etruscan, Celtic, and Scythian hands – indeed in Roman hands.

If evidence in itself were a source of inspiration, what could be more inspiring than all this evidence of which Grote and his generation knew practically nothing?

It is to be admitted that between the two wars the interest in Greek political and cultural history was again on the increase, perhaps more in Germany and in Italy than elsewhere. In the tense atmosphere of the Weimar republic Wilamowitz returned to greatness, producing the unbroken chain of masterpieces of his old age from the book on Pindar to *Der Glaube der Hellenen*. We are proud to have here among us Dr V. Ehrenberg who has contributed so much to revising Greek constitutional history. In Italy official emphasis on Roman imperialism persuaded the honest to return to Greek history. The grand old man of ancient history, as Professor Cary called De Sanctis[44], produced in 1939 what is perhaps the only Greek history of this half century bearing the imprint of a strong personality. Also, much work was done in Italy towards a reinterpretation of the fourth century BC. More recently one has noticed a new interest in Greek constitutional history in the United States, chiefly due to Professor Larsen of Chicago; and Professor Gomme has revived the study of Thucydides in this country. Perhaps, though it is not devoted to political history, one should not omit a book by the Regius Professor of Greek at Oxford – *The Greeks and the Irrational* – which opens such wide perspectives on the achievements and failures of classical Greece. But even if some of these developments had not been disturbed in the way we know they were, they could not represent more than the symptoms of a possible change for the better in a situation which is frankly critical. The most important aspects of this crisis appear to me to be the following four.

First, we are increasingly interested in social and economic history, but the available evidence is as yet insufficient to provide those statistics without which no proper social and economic history of Greece can be written. Furthermore the evidence, such as it is, is almost invariably archaeological, and therefore can be used only after classification by highly specialized methods. The technical difficulties are such and the rewards in results are so problematic that no serious economic and social historian of ancient Greece has yet appeared.

Secondly, the prevailing approaches to history – Marxism, psychoanalysis in its different varieties, sociology in its different varieties, the neo-Spenglerism of the first Toynbee and the neo-Augustinianism of the second – have the merits and demerits which everybody knows or should know. But in any case they are unilateral approaches, ill-suited to be applied without integration and correction, as they usually are, to the eminently many-sided history of Greece. The trouble is that people who do not accept unilateral approaches too often have no approach at all.

Thirdly, Fustel de Coulanges prophesied as long ago as 1872 that historical evidence would be distorted more and more for partisan purposes[45]. But what nobody seems to have expected is that evidence would be distorted for no purpose at all, simply because of lack of common sense. Yet this is what has been happening with alarming frequency in recent years. Perhaps it is not altogether surprising that our generation should find it increasingly difficult to assess the value of evidence, but the consequence is that idle and misleading speculation is a factor with which the Greek historian has constantly to reckon. Much of the recent work on early Greek traditions is pre-Grotean in character.

Fourthly, the study of Greek political ideas has become increasingly divorced from the study of political events and institutions.

Nobody can speak without admiration of Professor Jaeger's *Paideia* – one of the most influential books of our time in the classical field, original in its outlook, subtle in its analysis. Yet, it is necessary to repeat that it is written with insufficient reference to the political and social history of Greece.

I hope I have not put an undue amount of self-righteousness into my last paragraphs. As Benedetto Croce once remarked, intellectual failures are collective phenomena from which no contemporary can presume to escape. We all partake of the cruel dullness of our age. But it seems to me that we shall never be able to talk about Greek history without embarrassment until we return to first principles. The first principles were stated by Grote: Greek history is essential to the formation of the liberal mind, but in its turn the liberal mind is religious in examining the evidence. A hundred years after its appearance, the limits and shortcomings of Grote's *History* are only too obvious. We need not quarrel about Cleon. It will be enough to say that, when Grote committed his most notorious mistake by identifying the Athenian liberty of the fifth century with absolute liberty, he overlooked the warning already given many years before by Benjamin Constant in his classic essay on the differences between ancient and modern ideas of liberty.

If we agree with Grote that so much of our intellectual patrimony has its origins in Greece and that it is our duty to assess it with careful analysis of the evidence, then we can see better what is worth studying in Greek history. We want to explain how the Greeks emerged from the North to get in touch with the great empires of the second millennium BC, how they founded their big states, how they survived the crisis of the beginnings of the Iron Age, how the new centres of civilization developed that Homer and Hesiod knew, and how the Greek mind created the new politics, philosophy, art, and poetry of the sixth and fifth centuries. We want also to know how the Greeks came to attribute universal validity to their conceptions and proceeded to hellenize both the West and the East and what happened in these encounters. Athens must remain the centre of a Greek history. But beyond the borders of classical Greece we expect to perfect our knowledge of Southern Italy, where Greek and Roman civilization cannot be disentangled, of Syria where Christianity was born, and of Egypt where Christianity and Greek philosophy were fused and monasticism was invented. Finally, we must know what

Greece contributed to the creation of the new Rome, Constantinople, and how she impressed her mark on the Moslem civilization from Baghdad to Toledo.

If this is the history of Greece that we would like to know, it is also easy to mention the parts of it we know least. We have no up-to-date history of archaic Ionia, of the Athenian empire, of Magna Graecia in the fifth and fourth centuries BC, of the Seleucid empire, of the province of Achaea under the Roman empire. The studies of Greek private law are deplorably behindhand and those of public law can be improved. There is no history of Greek agriculture, or of Greek coinage; and that of Greek trade is out of date. Finally, a history of Greek political theories after Aristotle and of historiography after Thucydides is still to be written. The continuity in political and historical thought has often been postulated; it has never been described. On these subjects the Roman and the Greek historian become one, and the Byzantine historian is the indispensable collaborator. Felix Jacoby's masterly collection of the fragments of the Greek historians, a unique achievement in the philological field, has made the task possible, if not easy.

These, to my mind, are the fields of research in which we can usefully engage ourselves and our pupils, atomic bombs permitting. I trust that in so doing we shall be acting in the spirit of George Grote. He may or may not be classified as a Whig historian, and the Whig historian may or may not have committed all the sins that Professor Butterfield has visited upon him so thoroughly. When all is said, it remains true that Grote possessed the all-redeeming virtue of the liberal mind. He was determined to understand and respect evidence from whatever part it came; he recognized freedom of speech, tolerance, and compromise as the conditions of civilization; he respected sentiment, but admired reason. One can take some pride in being a teacher or a pupil in the College which for more than forty years provided so many joys and so many tribulations for George Grote[46].

[1] Mrs Grote, *The Personal Life of George Grote* (1873) p. 57.

[2] French translation in 1802; Italian translation, Florence, 1807; Greek translation, Vienna, 1806; German translation, Leipsic, 1792; Spanish translation, Madrid, 1822. Some of these are from the abridgement.

[3] De rebus gestis Philippi Amyntae F., *Dissertationes Academicae Selectiores* (Lund 1675) pp. 109–95: Pufendorf discusses constitutional points.

[4] *Histoire de Philippe* (Paris 1740–60) I, LI: 'C'est l'histoire d'un Prince habile et heureux, qui n'est heureux que parce qu'il est habile.'

[5] *The History of the Life and Reign of Philip, King of Macedon* (1758); the poetical preface is by Samuel Madden.

[6] *The Orations of Lysias and Isocrates translated from the Greek with some account of their lives, and a discourse on the history, manners, and character of the Greeks from the conclusion of the Peloponnesian War to the Battle of Chaeronea* (1778) p. LXIII.

[7] *The History of the World from the Reign of Alexander to that of Augustus* (1807); *cf.* also J. Gast, *The History of Greece from the accession of Alexander till its final subjection to the Roman Power* (1782); A. Boeckh, *Encyklopädie und Methodologie* (1877) p. 346.

[8] *Cf.* Momigliano, *Filippo il Macedone* (Firenze 1934); Genesi storica e funzione attuale del concetto di Ellenismo, *Giorn. Crit. Filos. Ital.*, XVI (1935) and papers there quoted.

[9] Byron, *Don Juan*, Canto XII, 19 and note; Macaulay, *Miscellaneous Essays*, in *Works*, VII (1866) ed. Lady Trevelyan, 683–703 (written in 1824).

[10] *Life and Letters* (London and New York 1897) p. 27; *cf.* for what follows G. L. Nesbitt, *Benthamite Reviewing, The First Twelve Years of The Westminster Review* (New York 1934).

[11] *Early Grecian History and Legend* reprinted in *Dissertations and Discussions*, II (1859) 283. J. S. Mill's early interest in Roman and Greek History is well known: *Autobiography*, ed. H. J. Laski, pp. 10–11.

[12] Mrs Grote, *The Personal Life of George Grote*, p. 49, compared with [Mrs Grote], *The Philosophical Radicals of 1832* (1866) p. 65, and above all G. Grote, *Posthumous Papers* (1874) p. 26.

[13] *The Westminster Review*, V (1826) 269–331.

[14] *The Quarterly Review*, XXXIII (1826) 332–56.

[15] *The Westminster Review*, VII (1827) 227–68.

[16] For an impressive testimonial on Grote, *cf.* Thirlwall's *Letters to a Friend* (1882), ed. A. P. Stanley, p. 323.

[17] *Remains of Hurrell Froude* (1838) I, 310, already quoted by J. Thirlwall, *John Connop Thirlwall, Historian and Theologian* (1936) p. 62.

[18] J. C. Hare, *A Vindication of Niebuhr's History of Rome from the Charges of the Quarterly Review* (Cambridge 1829). The useful account of this period of English historiography by K. Dockhorn, *Der deutsche Historismus in England* (Göttingen 1950) is discussed by me in *Rivista Storica Italiana*, LXIII (1951) 592. *Cf.* now D. Forbes, *The Liberal Anglican Idea of History* (Cambridge 1952).

[19] *Minor Works*, pp. 205–36.

[20] *Life of G. Grote*, p. 264.

[21] *Cf.* W. Bagehot, in *Biographical Studies* (1895) ed. R. H. Hutton, pp. 223, 357; L. Stephen, *The English Utilitarians*, III (1900) 334, and my essay, G. C. Lewis, Niebuhr e la critica delle fonti, *Rivista Storica Italiana* (1952). See also Lewis' *Letters* (1870), which contain much about his friendship with Grote. The *Treatise on the Methods of Observation and Reasoning in Politics* has a section *On the Treatment of Political History*, I, 181–323. A review of Grote's History by Lewis, in *Edinburgh Review*, XCI (1850) 118–52. *Cf.* Mrs Grote's *Life*, p. 195.

[22] *The Letters of J. S. Mill*, I (1910) 58.

[23] H. W. Garrod, *Scholarship, its Meaning and Value* (Cambridge 1946) p. 10.

[24] *Cf.* his essay Grecian Legends and Early History (1843) in *Minor Works*, p. 75.

[25] *Spectator* of 4 April 1846. The most important reviews of Grote's books by

Mill are collected in *Dissertations and Discussions*, II (1859) 283–334, 510–54; III (1867) 275–379; IV (1875) 188–230.

[26] *Revue des Deux Mondes*, XVIII (1847) 52–69; *cf.* also Kortüm's review in *Heidelberger Jahrbücher* (1846) 641–52, for an instructive account of the Greek studies in Germany.

[27] *The Quarterly Review*, LXXVIII (1846) 113–44; LXXXVI (1850) 384–415; LXXXVIII (1850) 41–69; XCIX (1856) 60–105. The last article was written by Dr William Smith, the lexicographer. As Mrs Grote says, 'It was an additional pleasure on the part of the Historian to find, in his unknown critic and eulogist, a pupil of his own cherished institution, University College.' *Life*, p. 231.

[28] J. G[rote], *A few remarks on a pamphlet by Mr Shilleto entitled 'Thucydides or Grote?'* (Cambridge 1851). The respect which soon surrounded Grote's name is shown by the pamphlet by E. M. Cope, *Plato's Theaetetus and Mr Grote's criticisms* (Cambridge 1866).

[29] 'Quoique, par régime cérébral, je ne lise presque rien, il me tarde de m'assurer directement si le jugement que ma grande théorie historique m'a conduit à formuler sur cette civilisation se trouve suffisamment conforme à votre profonde appréciation spéciale,' Grote, *Posthumous Papers*, p. 90.

[30] Compare J. P. Mahaffy's remarks in his introduction to the English translation of V. Duruy (1898) and see also W. Vischer, Ueber die neueren Bearbeitungen der griechischen Geschichte (1861) in *Kleine Schriften*, I (1878) 511–33.

[31] *Cf.* Freeman's reviews of Grote, now in *Historical Essays*, II (1873).

[32] The importance of Bury's History of Greece is perhaps underrated by N. H. Baynes in his classic memoir of Bury (1929); *cf.* also Baynes and H. M. Last in *Dict. Nat. Biogr.*, suppl. 1922–30, s.v. J. B. Bury.

[33] English translation by B. Bosanquet (Oxford 1878).

[34] *Aristophanes und die historische Kritik* (Leipzig 1873).

[35] Th. Gomperz, *Essays und Erinnerungen* (1905) pp. 33, 184–96. *Cf.* his son's biography, H. Gomperz, *Th. G.*, I (Vienna 1936) index s.v. G. Grote.

[36] K. Lehrs, *Populäre Aufsätze aus dem Altertum*, 2nd ed. (1875) p. 478. See also J. von Döllinger, *Akademische Vorträge*, II (1889) 174–6 (written in 1872).

[37] J. Jacoby, *Geist der Griechischen Geschichte, Auszug aus Grote's Geschichte Griechenlands*, nach dessen Tode hrsg. von F. Rühl (Berlin 1884).

[38] Published in *Deutsche Zeitschrift für Geschichtswissenschaft* and republished in *Aus Altertum und Gegenwart* (München 1895) pp. 315–42. Pöhlmann has acute remarks on Ricardo's influence on Grote; *cf.* his speech *Griechische Geschichte im 19. Jahrh.* Festrede der Münchener Akademie (1902) in *Aus Altertum und Gegenwart*, Neue Folge (1911) 277–322. Grote's influence on German historiography is ignored by H. von Srbik, *Geist und Geschichte vom deutschen Humanismus bis zur Gegenwart*, II (1951).

[39] *Aristoteles und Athen*, I (1893) 375–81. But see also J. G. Droysen, *Briefwechsel*, II 442 (written in 1857).

[40] G. Rosa, Dei miti greci e latini, *Rivista Europea* (1847) p. 432: but Rosa calls Grote 'Gregorio' and must know him indirectly through reviews. An Italian translation of Grote, which began to appear in Naples in 1855, was discontinued after three volumes.

[41] J. S. Mill, *The Letters*, II, 332.

[42] See my account in C. Antoni and R. Mattioli, *Cinquant'anni di vita intellettuale italiana. Scritti in onore di B. Croce*, I (1950) 85–106; *cf.* A. Ferrabino, *La dissoluzione della libertà nella Grecia antica*, 2nd ed. (Padua 1937) p. 44.

[43] J. Ruskin, *Arrows of the Chace* (1886) in *Works*, ed. Cook and Wedderburn, XXXIV, 586. In a letter of 1864 Ruskin says 'The only two works of value on Rome

and Greece are by a polished infidel, Gibbon, and a vulgar materialist, Grote,' *Works*, XVIII, p. XXXIV.

[44] *Journ. Hell. Studies*, LIX (1939) 296.

[45] De la manière d'écrire l'histoire en France et en Allemagne depuis cinquante ans, *Revue des Deux Mondes*, CI (1872) 241–51.

[46] I am indebted to H. M. Last, G. Pugliese Carratelli, and P. Sraffa for information.

CHAPTER FOUR

FRIEDRICH CREUZER AND GREEK HISTORIOGRAPHY*

Alla cara memoria di Leone Ginzburg morto nelle carceri di Roma il 5.II.1944.

THE name of Professor Friedrich Creuzer of Heidelberg University is associated with two of the most typical episodes of the Romantic period. His reluctance to throw in his lot with the gifted Caroline von Günderode led to her suicide (1806) – and to the vindictive remarks by Caroline's friend and champion, Bettina Brentano: 'Creuzer came to visit Savigny in Marburg. Repulsive as he was, it was inconceivable that he could interest a woman.'[1] His *Symbolik und Mythologie der alten Völker* (1810–12) was an attempt to give a scientific basis to the Neoplatonic interpretation of Greek mythology[2]. Though soon dismissed by responsible philologists, it was greeted with enthusiasm by philosophers like Schelling[3], lastingly influenced the erratic genius of Bachofen[4], and altogether played a very important part in the development of mythological studies.

We do not propose to offer any contribution to the discussion of these two episodes. There is another aspect of Creuzer which is much less known and deserves attention: his study of Greek historiography. It belongs to the early phase of his life, before Caroline von Günderode and the *Symbolik* appeared on his horizon. Indeed, it belongs to those years around 1800 which mark the beginning of a new era for historical studies in Europe and can still offer much inspiration. What was done in ancient history was then immediately relevant to history in general. The methods of Greek and Roman history were still exemplary. The results thus obtained were of general interest. Ancient history has now become a provincial branch of history. It can recover its lost prestige only if it proves again capable of offering results affecting the whole of our historical outlook. One of the ways

* *Journal of the Warburg and Courtauld Institutes* 9 (1946), 152–63.

is, quite simply, to regain contact with those writers of the past who treated classical subjects of vital importance to history in general. Creuzer produced a book of this kind. In writing his *Historische Kunst der Griechen* he was fully aware that the Greeks invented what we admit to be true historiography and that any understanding of Greek historiography is not possible without a firm grasp of the principles of historiography at large.

Friedrich Creuzer's *Die historische Kunst der Griechen in ihrer Entstehung und Fortbildung* is now read in the second edition of 1845 – twelve years later than H. Ulrici's *Charakteristik der antiken Historiographie* (1833). Inevitably, one forgets that the book had first appeared in 1803. A recent comparison between the two editions confirmed my suspicion that the second edition, though it was increased by almost two hundred pages of *Nachträge* and enriched with bibliographical notes, did not introduce any change into the text. What one reads in the text of pp. 1–252 of the second edition[5] is what Creuzer had already published in 1803[6]. The impression one may get from the notes of the second edition that Creuzer was indebted to some books later than 1803, and especially to the *Entwurf einer Theorie der Geschichte* by W. Wachsmuth[7], published at Halle in 1820, is therefore misleading. Wachsmuth, who dedicated his book to Creuzer, was certainly his friend, and Creuzer liked to mention him in his notes to the second edition, but the text was in no way affected by him or by any of the other writers later than 1803 who are listed in a note on pp. 2–3. Creuzer's book is nothing more nor less than the first modern history of Greek historiography, as the contemporary review in the *Göttingische Gelehrte Anzeigen* immediately recognized[8]: an epoch-making book, though it receives no mention in the *Geschichte der Philologie* by Wilamowitz and is barely referred to in Sandys' *Classical Scholarship*. Creuzer's *Symbolik* has remained famous and is again enjoying a revival of popularity in the train of the fashionable interest in symbols and symbolism[9]. Its refutation by Lobeck's *Aglaophamus* is, indeed, a part of its prestige. But the *Historische Kunst der Griechen*, which was a healthy inspiration, is relegated to the dubious obscurity of books which are assumed to be superseded. Only O. Regenbogen, in writing his remarkable essay on Herodotus[10], was struck by the fact that he had been anticipated by Creuzer and acknowledged it in eloquent words. Yet his characterization of Creuzer's personality – '*rationalistische*

Polyhistorie und romantische Einfühlungsfähigkeit' – is, as I hope to show, neither exhaustive nor correct[11].

Vossius was still, at the end of the eighteenth century, *the* book on Greek historiography[12]. He was far from being a mere antiquarian. Both his *Historici Graeci* and his *Historici Latini*[13] have their complement in his *Ars Historica* (1623), the hero of which is Polybius. But his interest in historiography was to discover principles, not to describe a development. Theory provided criteria by which to judge the ancient practice, and ancient practice gave illustrative material to the *Ars Historica*. That was only a particular case of the general relation between history and philosophy: '*Est enim historia, ut non semel dictum, philosophia exemplis constans. Haec philosophiae et historiae affinitas ac coniunctio facit, ut philosopho praecepta sua liceat historicorum exemplis illustrare, et vicissim historicus possit facta quaedam ad philosophorum praecepta expendere*' (*Ars Hist.*, chap. 18).

It is hardly necessary to add that this approach was everywhere crumbling long before Creuzer's appearance on the scene. In the second part of the eighteenth century one could read scores of dissertations inspired by the principle that historians are the voice of their times and must be examined in relation to what was called the genius of their age. The authority of Herodotus and Thucydides was steadily growing. Indeed Herodotus – naïve, cosmopolitan, '*historien des moeurs*' and an imitator of Homer – was becoming very popular[14]. Thucydides also was better appreciated as a student of politics[15]. It remained true, however, that Vossius' *Historici Graeci* had not been replaced as a whole by a more modern history of Greek historiography. Besides, Creuzer was entitled to ask himself whether the reaction against Vossius had gone far enough. In 1797, when he wrote his first essay on Herodotus and Thucydides[16], he had been a pupil of Schiller in Jena[17], was well acquainted with Herder's work and had just been reading the new little book *Die Griechen und Römer* by F. Schlegel[18]. The Romantic wind was blowing around him. Other inspiration in the same sense, though not pointing so clearly in the new direction, was to be found in some students of the history of philosophy whom he had known well in his undergraduate years, for instance D. Tiedemann[19]. The preface to *Herodotus und Thukydides* declares that the ancient historians had not yet been 'philosophically' studied to such good purpose as the most ancient Greek poets. It also says that a complete understanding of Herodotus will be possible only after the successful completion of the research still in progress on the epic poems: the allusion to F. A. Wolf (and to F. Schlegel?) is obvious. Many other allusions in this essay and in the following dissertation *De Xenophonte historico* (1799) leave no doubt that Creuzer was already thinking of a new and up-to-date history of Greek historiography.

Examined in itself, the pamphlet on Herodotus and Thucydides cannot be said to be more than an acute and pointed restatement of current contemporary opinions. It was Creuzer's aim to prove that Herodotus and Thucydides had different conceptions of history for reasons depending partly on the times in which they lived and partly on the subject they chose. Thucydides had the advantage of a stricter ideal of truth. Herodotus was superior in the depth and variety of human interests. As in many contemporary studies, the difference between Herodotus and Thucydides is no longer examined in the abstract, but in relation to their historical environments. The historical perspective does not lead to complete relativism, but helps to attribute a value of his own to each historian. The special value of Herodotus is found in his wider humanity, according to a famous passage of Herder's *Briefe zur Beförderung der Humanität*[20].

The dissertation *De Xenophonte historico* seems to me to represent a definite step forward. The survival of more traditional patterns of judgment is evident in the Latin form and academic purpose of the booklet. But the sharp differentiation between the pragmatism of Polybius and that of the early Greek historians, the analysis of the differences between Xenophon's and Herodotus' religion, and the conclusion that Xenophon marks the beginning of the decline of Greek historiography because he is more subjective and superstitious, show that Creuzer was getting into shape the idea of a new history of historiography.

What was really only rudimentary in these first essays was the interest in the relation between poetry and history, in so far as it could help to define both the specific quality of Greek historiography, and the nature of historiography in general. On these points Chr. Gottl. Heyne, F. Schlegel – and the intense philosophic discussion of the beginning of the new century which proceeded through the Schlegels to Fichte and Schelling – were decisive. Heyne's *Historiae scribendae inter Graecos primordia* was printed in 1799. F. Schlegel's *Geschichte der Poesie der Griechen und Römer* appeared in 1798. The *Athenaeum* was started in the same year, and Schelling's *System des transcendentalen Idealismus* was published in 1800. As we have said, *Die historische Kunst der Griechen* was first edited in 1803.

It was Creuzer's opinion, when he wrote his *Historische Kunst*, that no one could talk of Greek historiography without having a clear notion of what historiography was. Thus, he inserted a brief theory of historiography for which, as he says, he had '*die Ansicht der Neueren vor Augen gehabt*' (p. 187). This theory was not be considered an external criterion imposed upon Greek historiography, but a hermeneutic hypothesis to be checked on the Greek texts (p. 175). Historiography, according to Creuzer, tries to discover the unity ('*übersinnliche Einheit*') and meaning of empirical facts by the application of critical research and of an artistic process of synthesis. The task of the student of historiography is to find out the critical methods and the artistic proceedings whereby historians establish the facts in their own individuality and formulate the ideas which are behind the facts. So far as Greek historiography is concerned, one has to examine two problems: (a) the origin of Greek historical thought; (b) its development from Herodotus onwards.

The origin of Greek historiography is to be found in epic poetry. The evolution happened in four stages: (1) Homeric poems; (2) epic cycle; (3) 'logographoi'; (4) Herodotus. Each of these stages must be analysed from the point of view of (a) style; (b) method of ascertaining the facts; (c) disposition of the facts, in order to see how the Greeks became increasingly aware of the difference between fine artistic creation and the recounting of facts. Only Homer and Herodotus present their facts, not in a superficial order, but in a real artistic unity. The traditional opinion that Herodotus was an imitator of Homer is given a deeper meaning[21]. The fact that Herodotus, like the poets, read his historical compositions to the Greek public is taken to confirm the theory that history developed from poetry. In the analysis of the unity of Herodotus, Creuzer writes his most impressive pages. They are almost a hymn to the birth of history.

The second part of the book on the development of Greek historiography is simpler and shorter. Creuzer does not go beyond Xenophon. The rest is decay because the artistic element of historiography was suffocated by narrow didactic preoccupations. Herodotus, Thucydides and Xenophon had method in ascertaining facts; they had also art. Herodotus was inspired by a religious-national idea;

Thucydides by a political idea – though, according to Creuzer, more in his description of single events than in the general annalistic plan of his work – whereas Xenophon's inspiration is clearly ethical and is accompanied by a nice sense for harmony. All these forms of historiography are legitimate because their ideas are not personal reflections of the writer like the ideas of Polybius, but objective patterns. Creuzer cannot help regretting that Thucydides had to miss the freshness of Herodotus (*'jener Reiz der jugendlichen Historie'*, p. 224), but realizes that a political historian could not do otherwise. On the other hand pragmatic history with a view to utility, as in Polybius, is little less than the great enemy of sound historical thought. In so far as modern historians are influenced by Polybius rather than by Herodotus or Thucydides – not a little, one understands, being Vossius' personal fault – ancient historiography of the severe style is superior to modern historiography. Modern historiography, admittedly, is often better in one of the elements which contribute to the writing of history, namely critical research, but harmony between facts and ideas is lacking in it. With the modern, what is not pragmatic is aprioristic. In the modern world the alternative to pragmatic historiography is philosophy of history *'nach welcher der Geist, statt sich in religiöser Betrachtung über die Natur zu erheben, aus stolzer Willkür sich eine Natur erschuf'* (p. 201). Only the new history by Johannes Müller may be compared with Herodotus (p. 197) – good German prose, *'gemütlich'*, better than the professorial style or than French frivolity.

It is obvious that the brothers Schlegel were the most profound influence on the author of the *Historische Kunst der Griechen*. Even Herder, Lessing and F. A. Wolf were, at least in part, seen by the young Creuzer through the eyes of the two Schlegels. Many years later, in a review which appeared in the *Heidelberger Jahrbücher*, XVIII, 1825, Creuzer proclaimed the great debt of his generation to them[22]. From F. Schlegel he borrowed the idea of the origin of Greek historiography from the epic cycle[23] and through Schlegel assimilated the Wolfian conception of the Greek world as a spiritual unity. On the other side it is probable that A. Wilhelm Schlegel sharpened his eye for style. Generally, the atmosphere of Creuzer's book is that of the brothers Schlegel: the same deep concern with poetry and language, the same underlying assumption that the study of Greek literature will illuminate the nature of the human mind or, to put it in a way which the brothers Schlegel would not have rejected, that if one wants to understand a thing one must follow up its historical origin.

This influence, however, has clear limits. The more speculative work of the two brothers on methodology of history and philology was not known to Creuzer because it was confined either to unpublished lectures (A. W. Schlegel) or to unpublished drafts (Friedrich). Neither wrote a specific history of historiography, and Friedrich, the nearer to Creuzer, seems to have thought in his early phase that history of historiography could be treated as pure literary history – an idea against which Creuzer felt that he still had to protest twenty years later in the review of the *Heidelberger Jahrbücher* quoted above[24]. In those years Friedrich Schlegel, though so emphatic on the necessity of history for '*Selbstkenntniss*', was much more directly concerned with the problem of the philosophy of philology which would form a fit prelude to the higher synthesis of poetry and philosophy. Even if it were true that his philosophy of philology, if developed, would have been a full philosophy of history, it is at least certain that Creuzer was not aware of it[25]. Creuzer was not specifically interested in the problem of hermeneutic, but in that of historiography. The extension of research to a field which the two brothers had left almost untouched implied a somewhat different attitude towards the problem of history.

In this situation Heyne's memoir on the origin of Greek historiography in the Göttingen *Commentationes* of 1799 (vol. XIV) was providential. What young F. Schlegel had suggested in a few words – the origin of Greek historiography from the epos – was independently demonstrated by the veteran Master at great length and in a sober scholastic Latin. Creuzer, who was after all an academic scholar, could find in it solid ground on which to build his book. F. Schlegel provided the inspiration, Heyne the foundation.

I should not care to commit myself on the relation of the *Historische Kunst* to the great contemporary systems of philosophy. Creuzer, in his old days, when he had entirely lost faith in his juvenile attempt at writing theory and history of historiography together, spoke of it as '*ein Kantisch-Fichtescher Lappen*'[26]. Direct or indirect echoes from Kant and Fichte are easy to catch in his pages. His conception of art as freedom and of historical events as nature can perhaps be described as approximately Kantian. But Kant and Fichte (at least until 1813) both deprecated empirical history (and historiography) as a mere 'rhapsody' of facts and, whatever their special points, were agreed that the only history which made sense was the history *a priori* of human liberty[27]. It seems clear that Creuzer was proceeding in a different direction. In his modest way he was busy, together with many of the very best of his generation, in re-establishing the value of empirical history within the frame of the new idealism. Though I should not be able to say how much Schelling meant to Creuzer in those years, a glance at Schelling, the main motive force of this reaction, can, better than anything else, remind us of what was happening. By Schelling, Herder was vindicated and Schiller's conception of art was 'erected into the principle of knowledge and existence' (to echo Hegel's solemn words).

In his essay on the Philosophy of History (1798)[28] Schelling denied the possibility of history *a priori*, indeed of any philosophy of history, and attributed to the field of history those events which are neither periodical nor otherwise bound by necessary laws. '*Was a priori zu berechnen ist, was nach notwendigen Gesetzen geschieht, ist nicht Objekt der Geschichte.*' The historian was also said to be a poet ('*Dichter*') without much explanation. The *System des transcendentalen Idealismus* (1800) strongly reaffirms that '*die Willkür ist . . . die Göttin der Geschichte*' and that what is necessary cannot be historical. The new analysis of necessity and liberty, however, shows that a line is to be drawn between pragmatic history (historiography) and universal history, the latter aiming at the real object of human life: '*Das allmähliche Entstehen der weltbürgerlichen Verfassung.*' Only such a history, which admits liberty and necessity together, is directly connected with (indeed absorbed into) the supreme sphere of art. The practical conclusion which Schelling himself derived in 1802 in his *Vorlesungen über die Methode des academischen Studiums* (published in 1803 and therefore probably not known to Creuzer before he finished his book) was not far from Creuzer in the general attitude to the historians of the past. Herodotus and Thucydides were opposed to Polybius and Tacitus as the authentic historians to the pragmatic ones. Modern historians were depreciated with the partial exception of Gibbon and the more complete exceptions of Machiavelli and J. Müller. Sound historiography was described as a synthesis of reality and ideality obtained by art[29]. As the *Vorlesungen über die Methode* show a great change in many points of Schelling's thought, it may be emphasized that in the matter of history the continuity is patent.

That the times were ripe for this conception is confirmed by

A. W. Schlegel's expression of analogous ideas in lectures which were not published during his life and therefore probably did not affect Creuzer. In the *Vorlesungen über schöne Litteratur und Kunst* of 1801–2 the conception of an empirical history based on universal ideas is neatly formulated[30]. In the *Vorlesungen über Enzyklopädie* of 1803, which were written under the influence of Schelling's new book *Vorlesungen über die Methode*, the artistic character of historiography was defined in an impressive formula: history was called '*Poesie der Wahrheit*'. It goes without saying that pragmatic historiography was attacked, and Johannes Müller praised as the really great historian of the age[31].

Thus, what makes it legitimate to relate Creuzer to Schelling is the common conception that art is *the* instrument whereby empirical history is possible. Creuzer's formulations are very brief and somewhat superficial, and it would be both unfair and grotesque to press them or to measure them by the standards of compact systems. Creuzer never drew a rigorous distinction between pragmatic and universal history and never tackled the problem of the transcendental unity of necessity and liberty which was basic for Schelling. What, to my mind, makes the interest of Creuzer's pages is that he did not simply theorize as to what historiography ought to be, but showed in a history of historiography what historiography is. Being chiefly interested in history of historiography he came to defend the autonomy of empirical history by writing history of historiography. On the other hand his theory of historiography proved to be a very sensitive instrument for the analysis of Greek historiography. No other student of Greek historiography has ever made better remarks on the artistic unity of Herodotus, Thucydides and Xenophon. A history of modern historiography did not appear, so far as I know, until 1812; it was the *Geschichte der historischen Wissenschaften* by L. Wachler. And Wachler, though of an admirable erudition, cannot be compared with Creuzer in grasp of ideas.

The broader issues can only be hinted at. The conception that historiography is the discovery of ideas by an artistic process combined with a critical method is to be found again in Schleiermacher and W. von Humboldt and may be taken as typical of the first phase of the so-called 'Historismus'[32]; by which first phase we mean the defence of empirical history against the theory of a history *a priori* whether in the dualistic form of Kant and Fichte or in the monistic one of Hegel. The determining influence of Schelling's philosophy in this movement is proved by its relevance to Schleiermacher, Humboldt and Boeckh[33]. Furthermore, because of the dependence of Ranke, Gervinus, Boeckh and Droysen on Humboldt, much of the historical research of the nineteenth century appears to be founded on those presuppositions. All that is claimed here is that the *Historische Kunst der Griechen* is on the same lines and deserves attention for its early date, for the unusual emphasis on the history of historiography and for its solid contribution to the knowledge of Greek historiography.

As was only natural, Creuzer had meantime been made aware by his studies that a collection of the surviving fragments of ancient historians was needed. He planned such a collection and in 1806 published the first part of the *Historicorum Graecorum Antiquissimorum Fragmenta* including Hecataeus, Charon and Xanthus. This collection of fragments, though taken over by others, was never completed[34]. Creuzer, under the influence of Frau von Günderode and Görres, was proceeding towards the *Symbolik* in a direction nearly parallel to that chosen by F. Schlegel and Schelling. Yet he and his pupils prepared much of the material for the other more successful collection we still have on our shelves, Müller's *Fragmenta Historicorum Graecorum* (1841) – a modest confirmation of the truth that even a collection of fragments can arise only out of problems.

The *Historische Kunst der Griechen* had other early recognitions besides the review in the *Göttingische Anzeigen*. F. A. Wolf described it to Goethe as a good book[35], and in the famous report to the French Institute on learning in Germany by Charles Villers, Creuzer obtained a very honourable place[36]. Echoes of the book are to be found everywhere in the following years[37]. The first serious attack on the method of the book appeared in the life of Herodotus published by F. C. Dahlmann in 1823. The very concept of logographoi was denied; the epic style of Herodotus qualified; his religion taken as a negative element: Herodotus was no longer the poet of history, but the brilliant, competent political historian of the type which Dahlmann himself was going to be[38]. It was already significant that a *life* of Herodotus should be presented as an *essay* on Herodotus. From a different angle, the criticism of H. Ulrici in his *Charakteristik der antiken Historiographie* (1833) was not less radical. Intensely religious, Ulrici thought that the task of the historian was to give '*das Bild des göttlichen Gedankens und Willens*'. For lack of true religion no Greek or Roman could do that. They were too much tied to the sensible world to be able to grasp pure ideas. The Christian idea of mankind was inevitably alien to them: a true universal history was impossible for them: their historical art was a substitute for historical science. In so far as Polybius in his universalism and Tacitus in his moralism are nearer to Christianity, they are greater historians than Herodotus and Thucydides. If Thucydides is superior to Herodotus because his irreligion goes deeper into human nature than Herodotus' traditional piety or superstition, Polybius' universalism (if I understand Ulrici right) implies a deeper conception of humanity than that of Thucydides. Without a real knowledge of Providence, ancient historiography was also without a proper knowledge of the development of arts and science. Only modern historiography is scientific – or philosophic.

If Dahlmann brought home the new realistic trends of political historiography after the Romantic orgy, Ulrici showed the evolution of Romantic philosophy itself from its early humanistic phase to the religious one. He spoke of the necessity of taking Christianity into account in a history of historiography. One may add that Ulrici had an admirable mastery of all Greek and Roman historiography and a shrewd capacity for pointed formulations which make his book much better reading than Creuzer's. His pages on the religion of Xenophon, for instance, are still the best on the subject.

Nearer to Creuzer in advocating the perennial value of Greek historiography and the need of artistic intuition in history was W. Roscher in his juvenile book on Thucydides (1842). A pupil both of Humboldt and of Ranke, he found in Thucydides his congenial spirit. Yet, in Roscher again, it is possible to see the growing detachment from Creuzer. Roscher studied Thucydides as a guide to political realities, whereas Creuzer was concerned with the relation between history and art.

Ulrici became a pure philosopher, Roscher turned out a great economist and student of politics, Dahlmann became a politician and modern historian: none of them in his maturity had either time or inclination to carry on research on Greek historiography. Here are some of the forces which led the following generation to neglect the study of Greek historiography. The Greek historians were no longer asked to answer problems of importance. They were left to useful, yet brutal, erudition until towards the end of the century when Eduard Meyer expounded his historical method by an analysis of Thucydides[39]. But E. Meyer remained an exception. Few classical scholars are seriously interested in problems of historical method. This fact, rather than Creuzer's connection with the *Symbolik*, explains why (as far as my knowledge goes) his *Historische Kunst der Griechen* has never been critically re-examined[40].

[1] *Goethes Briefwechsel mit einem Kinde*, 2nd ed. (1837) I, p. 110. From a letter, An Goethes Mutter, pp. 80–126. Later Bettina Brentano devoted a whole novel to the idealization of her friend, *Die Günderode* (1840). *Cf.* also her husband, A. von Arnim's novel *Isabella* (1812). We need not enter into Bettina's peculiar methods of literary composition.

[2] Creuzer did most valuable work as an editor of Neoplatonic texts; Proclus and Olympiodorus (Frankfort 1820–2), Plotinus (Oxford 1835).

[3] Einleitung in die Philosophie der Mythologie, in *Sämmtl. Werke*, II, 1, p. 89.

[4] *Versuch über die Gräbersymbolik der Alten* (1859).

[5] F. Creuzer's *Deutsche Schriften*, neue und verbesserte Auflage, III. Abtheil. (1845). The quotations in the text are from this edition.

[6] I used the copy of the first edition in the possession of Trinity College, Cambridge. The book is in the British Museum.

[7] I hope to write on this work in connection with Gervinus' and Droysen's *Historik*.

[8] In the 33rd issue, 27 February 1804, p. 321, an instalment almost entirely devoted to Creuzer's book. The obscurity of the style was, however, reprimanded: 'Ist es die Terminologie einer neueren Schule, welche diese Dunkelheit verursacht, oder lag sie in den Ideen des Verfassers?' The reviewer was almost certainly Chr. Gottl. Heyne (*cf.* F. Creuzer, Aus dem Leben eines alten Professors, in *Deutsche Schriften*, V, 1 (1848) p. 26).

[9] E. Cassirer, *Philosophie der symbolischen Formen*, II, p. 21; A. Baeumler in J. J. Bachofen, *Der Mythus von Orient und Occident* (1926) p. CIV ff.; E. Howald, *Der Kampf um Creuzers Symbolik. Eine Auswahl von Dokumenten* (1926) etc. For a highly significant recent debate *cf.* F. Cumont, *Recherches sur le symbolisme funéraire des Romains* (1942) (on Creuzer p. 13) and A. D. Nock, Sarcophagi and Symbolism, in *Amer. Journ. Arch.*, L (1946) p. 340.

[10] *Die Antike*, VI (1930) p. 203. *Cf.* also the same author's Thukydides als politischer Denker, in *Das humanistische Gymnasium* (1933) pp. 2 ff. Regenbogen echoes E. Rohde's judgment (see following note).

[11] Creuzer was born in Marburg in 1771. He studied in Marburg and Jena (where he was in 1790), but got his doctorate in Tübingen in 1799. Professor *extraordinarius* in Marburg in 1800, *ordinarius* in 1802, he passed to Heidelberg in 1804 and remained there to the end of his life (1858), except for a brief period of residence in Leyden (1809) after Frau von Günderode's suicide – *cf.* Guigniaut, *Notice historique sur la vie et les travaux de George-Frédéric Creuzer* (Institut Impérial de France, séance publique annuelle du 31 juillet, 1863), 1864; K. B. Stark, *Vorträge und Aufsätze* (1880) pp. 390–408 and 480–507 with some important letters by Creuzer; C. Bursian, *Gesch. d. class. Philologie in Deutschland* (1883) p. 562; W. Rehm, *Griechentum und Goethezeit* (1936) p. 322; and the article

in *Allgem. Deutsche Biographie.* The often uninspiring literature on Frau von Günderode must be consulted: *cf.* especially E. Rohde's well-known essay *F. C. und K. v. G.* (1896); K. Preisendanz, *Die Liebe der Günderode. F. Creuzer's Briefe an C. v. G.* (1912); R. Wilhelm, *Die Günderode, Dichtung und Schicksal* (1938) pp. 114 ff. The best on the subject is still Bettina Brentano.

[12] *De historicis graecis libri tres* (1624) (2nd ed., 1650). They were still useful enough in the nineteenth century to be re-edited 'auctiores et emendatiores' by A. Westermann in 1838. D. Wyttenbach's *Selecta Principum Historicorum* (Amsterdam 1794) is an anthology showing a marked preference for Polybius' pragmatism.

[13] *De historicis latinis* (1627) (2nd ed., 1651).

[14] *Cf.* for instance Abbé Geinoz, Défense d'Hérodote, *Mém. Acad. Inscr.*, XXIII (1756) p. 101; M. de Rochefort, Sur la morale d'Hérodote, *ibid.*, XXXIX (1777) p. 1; Voltaire, *Le Pyrrhonisme de l'Histoire* (1768) in *Oeuvres complètes*, XXXIX (1825) p. 334; C. A. Böttiger, *De Herodoti historia ad carminis epici indolem propius accedente*, I–II (1792–3).

[15] *Cf.* J. D. Heilmann, Krit. Gedanken von dem Charakter und der Schreibart des Thucydides (1758), in *Opuscula* II (1778) pp. 87–208; Abbé de Mably, *De la manière d'écrire l'histoire* (ed. London, 1789, *Oeuvres*, XII), p. 340 and the significant judgment in J. J. Barthélemy's *Voyage du jeune Anacharsis*, 3rd ed. (Paris 1790) V, 413 (1st ed., 1787): 'Hérodote, Thucydide et Xénophon seront sans doute regardés à l'avenir comme les principaux de nos historiens, quoiqu'ils diffèrent essentiellement par le style . . . Hérodote voit partout une divinité jalouse. . . . Thucydide ne découvre dans les revers que les fautes des chefs de l'administration ou de l'armée: Xénophon attribue presque toujours à la faveur ou à la colère des dieux les bons ou les mauvais succès.' It is only fair to add that the most famous apology for Thucydides belongs to the late seventeenth century: Père Rapin, *Les comparaisons des grands hommes: La comparaison de Thucydide et de Tite-Live*, II (Paris 1684) pp. 65–162 (Engl. transl. Oxford 1694), but *cf.* the remarks by A. Dain, Thucydide au XVIIe siècle, in *Congrès de Strasbourg de l'Ass. Budé, 1938* (Paris 1939) pp. 95–6.

[16] Republished in *Deutsche Schriften*, III, 2, pp. 591 ff. Reviewed in *Gött. Gelehrte Anz.* (1798) n. 122, pp. 215–16 (Manche brauchbare Materialien zu einer Geschichte der historischen Kunst unter den Griechen, woran es uns bisher noch fehlt).

[17] Schiller's *Was heisst und zu welchem Ende studiert man Universalgeschichte* had been written a year before (1789) Creuzer's residence in Jena. *Cf.* also *Ueber die aesthetische Erziehung* (1795), 25. Brief; B. Mugdan, *Die theoretischen Grundlagen der Schillerschen Philosophie* (1910) (*Kantstudien*, Erg.-H. 19); F. Meinecke, *Sch. und der Individualitätsgedanke* (1937). I regret that I have been unable to find anywhere a short essay published by the Tübingen poet and professor K. Ph. Conz – known especially for his connections with Schiller and Hölderlin – which has the title *Einige Bemerkungen über die historische Kunst der Alten* and was published in the short-lived *Museum für die Griechische und Römische Litteratur* (1795). Creuzer knew and appreciated it. (*Cf.* G. Cless, *Der schwäbische Dichter K. Ph. Conz 1762–1827* (Tübingen 1913). The article was not reprinted in Conz's three volumes of *Kleine prosaische Schriften*, published in Tübingen, 1821–2 (2 vols.) and Ulm, 1825. For an idea of the teaching of history of historiography in German universities at that time, *cf.* M. Fülleborn, *Encyclopaedia philologica* (1798) (2nd ed. 1800) which, as is well known, summarizes F. A. Wolf's lectures (*cf.* also F. A. Wolf's Darstellung der Altertumswissenschaft, in *Museum d. Altertumsw.*, I (1807) p. 61).

[18] Reprinted in *Prosaische Jugendschriften*, ed. Minor, I (1882) (2nd ed. 1906).

[19] *Cf.* especially D. Tiedemann, *Geist der speculativen Philosophie* (1791). Creuzer wrote the official obituary of Tiedemann in 1803; *Opuscula selecta* (1854) p. 163. Also Reinhold's *Ueber den Begriff der Geschichte der Philosophie* in Fülleborn's *Beyträge zur Geschichte der Philosophie*, I (1791) pp. 5–35, was almost certainly well known to Creuzer. Reinhold was a professor in Jena. The classic formulation of the principles of a history of philosophy was given in 1798 by W. G. Tennemann's *Gesch. d. Philosophie.*

[20] 'Also bleibt der Geschichte einzig und ewig Nichts als der Geist ihres ältesten Schreibers, Herodots: der unangestrengte milde Sinn der Menschheit' (*Brief* 121).

[21] 'Erst aus der inneren Einheit einer grossen Weltbegebenheit, welche der homerische Sinn und der gebildete Geist des Herodotos aufzufassen wussten, konnte die volkommnere Organisation einer Historie aufblühen' (p. 122).

[22] *Deutsche Schriften*, III, 2, pp. 7 ff.

[23] *Geschichte der Poesie der Griechen und Römer*, ed. Minor, I, p. 342.

[24] *Deutsche Schriften*, III, 2, p. 20. The passage by F. Schlegel referred to is in *Die Griechen und Römer*, ed. Minor, I, p. 77.

[25] On F. Schlegel and philology compare especially C. Enders, *F. Schl. Die Quellen seines Wesens und Werdens* (1913) p. 351; J. Körner, *Romantiker und Klassiker* (1924); K. Börries, *Die Romantik und die Geschichte* (1925); F. Imle, *Fr. v. Sch.'s Entwicklung von Kant zum Katholizismus* (1927); J. Körner, F. Schl.'s *Philosophie der Philologie* mit einer Einleitung herausgegeben, *Logos*, XVII (1928) pp. 1–72; *Id.*, Introd. to F. Schlegel's *Philosophische Schriften* (1935); F. Gundolf, *Romantiker* (1930) pp. 9 ff.; V. Santoli, Filologia, Storia e Filosofia nel pensiero di F. Schlegel, *Civiltà moderna*, II (1930) p. 117; *Id.* Introd. to F. Schlegel's *Frammenti critici e scritti di estetica* 1936; A. Emmersleben, *Die Antike in der romantischen Theorie. Die Gebrüder Schlegel und die Antike* (1937). A. Schlagdenhauffen's big work, *F. Schlegel et son groupe. La doctrine de l'Athenaeum, 1798–1800* (1934) must be consulted, but is superficial. On F. Schlegel in general see also V. Grönbech, F. Schlegel i Aarene 1791–1808, *Det Kgl. Danske Vidensk. Selskab* XXII (1935); O. Mann, *Der junge Schlegel* (1936); L. Wirz, *F. Schlegel's philos. Entwicklung* (1939) (*Grenzfragen z. Theol. u. Phil.* 13).

[26] Aus dem Leben eines alten Professors, in *Deutsche Schriften*, V, I (1848) p. 26. *Cf.* also the very important review of Schöll's *Geschichte der griechischen Literatur* in *Wiener Jahrbücher der Literatur*, LXI (1833) pp. 164–210 = *Deutsche Schriften*, III, 2, pp. 28 ff. It may here be noted that the insistence of Lessing on the distinction between dramatic truth and historical truth (for instance *Hamburgische Dramaturgie*, 11 Stück, ed. Reclam, p. 49) was important to Creuzer: *Hist. Kunst*, 2nd ed., pp. 162, 192, etc.

[27] *Cf.* for instance F. Medicus, Kants Philosophie der Geschichte, *Kantstudien*, VII (1902) pp. 1–22, 171–229 (*cf.* also IV (1900) pp. 61–7); E. Lask, *Fichtes Idealismus und die Geschichte* (1902); K. R. Brotherus, *I. Kants Philosophie der Geschichte* (Helsingfors 1905); W. G. Herbst, *J. G. Fichtes Geschichtsphilosophie nach den Prinzipien der Wissenschaftslehre* (1913), and in general X. Léon, *F. et son temps* (1922–7); M. Gueroult, *L'évolution et la structure de la doctrine de la science chez Fichte* (1930). I do not know W. Steinbeck, *Das Bild des Menschen in d. Philosophie J. G.* (1939). See also below n. 32 and De Ruggiero and Collingwood quoted in the following note.

[28] *Sämmtl. Werke*, I, I (1856) p. 461. On Schelling and history *cf.* G. Mehlis, *Schellings Geschichtsphilosophie in den Jahren 1799 bis 1804* (1906); A. Pötzsch, *Studien zur frühromantischen Politik und Geschichtsauffassung* (1907); H. Knittermeyer, *Sch. und die romantische Schule* (1929), and the monographs by L. Noack (1859); E. v. Hartmann (1869); E. Bréhier (1912) and N. Hartmann (*Die Philo-*

sophie des deutschen Idealismus, I (1923). Also G. De Ruggiero, *Storia della Filosofia*, IV, 4, 2nd ed. (1946) p. 337 and R. G. Collingwood, *The Idea of History* (1946) p. 111.

[29] *Vorlesungen*, 2nd ed. (1813) p. 221 (10. Vorlesung) 'Auch die wahre Historie beruht auf einer Synthesis des Gegebenen und Wirklichen mit dem Idealen, aber nicht durch Philosophie, da diese die Wirklichkeit vielmehr aufhebt und ganz ideal ist: Historie aber ganz in jener und doch zugleich ideal sein soll. Dieses ist nirgends als in der Kunst möglich . . .' In K. Chr. F. Krause, *Grundriss der historischen Logik* (1803) 'historisch' means simply 'empirisch': Krause does not discuss historiography.

[30] *Deutsche Literaturdenkmale*, XVII (1884) p. 14.

[31] The *Vorlesungen über Enzyklopädie* are, as far as I know, still unpublished. There is a summary in R. Haym, *Die Romantische Schule*, 5th ed. (1928) pp. 911–912. – On J. Müller *cf.* P. Requadt, *J. v. M. und der Frühhistorismus* (1929). Two typical formulations of Müller's ideas will be found in *Sämmtliche Werke*, VIII (1810) pp. 412–14 (on Tacitus); XI, pp. 330–41 (on historical style).

[32] It is perhaps evident that F. Meinecke, *Entstehung des Historismus* (1936), though of great importance for the historiography of the eighteenth century, does not describe the 'Entstehung des Historismus' which is to be found in philosophers and philologists whom Meinecke does not consider. More relevant is his later book of essays, *Vom geschichtlichen Sinn und vom Sinn der Geschichte* (1939) (*cf.* especially his chapter on Schleiermacher). For discussions on Meinecke *cf.* E. Seeberg, *Hist. Zeitschrift*, CLVII (1938) p. 241; C. Antoni, *Dallo storicismo alla sociologia* (1940) ch. 3; B. Croce, *La storia come pensiero e come azione* (1938) p. 51. C. Antoni has given an invaluable introduction to the problem in *La lotta contro la ragione* (1942). *Cf.* also his *Considerazioni su Hegel e Marx* (1946). A. Korff, *Geist der Goethezeit*, vol. III (1940) (*Frühromantik*), is unfortunately known to me only indirectly; *cf.* De Ruggiero, *Storia della Filosofia*, IV, 4 (1946) pp. 424 ff. For earlier discussions: R. Fester, *Rousseau und die deutsche Geschichtsphilosophie* (1890); I. Goldfriedrich, *Die historische Ideenlehre in Deutschland* (1902); W. Dilthey, *Der Aufbau der geschichtlichen Welt in den Geisteswissenschaften* (1920); E. Troeltsch, *Der Historismus und seine Probleme* (1922). For a discussion of J. Thyssen, *Geschichte der Geschichtsphilosophie* (1936), *cf.* C. Antoni, *Considerazioni su Hegel e Marx*, p. 156.

[33] On Schleiermacher and Schelling, H. Süskind, *Der Einfluss Schellings auf die Entwicklung von Schleiermachers System* (1909); *Id.*, *Christentum und Geschichte bei Schl.* (1911); G. Wehrung, *Schl. in der Zeit seines Werdens* (1927). More generally: R. B. Brandt, *The Philosophy of Schl.* (1941). On Humboldt and Schelling *cf.* E. Spranger, *Hist. Zeitschrift*, C (1907) p. 541. On Boeckh, J. Wach, *Das Verstehen*, I (1926) p. 168. On Droysen, H. Astholz, *Das Problem 'Geschichte' untersucht bei J. G. D.* (1933); E. Rothacker, *Hist. Zeitschrift*, CLXI (1940) p. 84; C. Antoni, *Considerazioni su Hegel e Marx*, pp. 118–25.

[34] Ctesias and Ephorus were edited respectively by another Heidelberg professor, Chr. F. Bähr (Frankfort 1824) and by M. Marx (Karlsruhe 1815), the second with Creuzer's preface. The edition of Philistus and Timaeus by Fr. Göller (Leipzig 1818) was also, perhaps, indirectly inspired by him: see K. B. Stark, *Vorträge und Aufsätze* (1880) p. 483. Hellanicus' fragments had already been collected by F. G. Sturz in 1787: his *Pherecydes* appeared in 1789. Bähr also finished a commentary on Herodotus which Creuzer had started.

[35] *F. A. Wolf. Ein Leben in Briefen* . . . besorgt . . . durch S. Reiter, I (1935) p. 358 (letter of 30-1-1804).

[36] *Cf.* the English translation of the report in *The Classical Journal* IV (1811) p. 143.

[37] For instance in Wachler, mentioned in the text, or in Chr. D. Beck, *Nonnulla de iudicio artis historicae classicorum scriptorum* (1805).

[38] F. C. Dahlmann, Herodot, aus seinem Buche sein Leben, *Forschungen auf dem Gebiete der Geschichte*, II, 1 (1823). Against Creuzer: p. 213 (*cf.* p. 109). Dahlmann, typically, tried to prove that Herodotus never made public recitations of his history.

[39] *Forschungen zur alten Geschichte*, II (1899) pp. 269–436.

[40] I am indebted to Mrs M. I. Henderson, Dr F. Jacoby, Professor H. M. Last, and Dr R. Pfeiffer for discussion. My friends V. Santoli and C. Antoni could not contribute when this paper was written (1944).

CHAPTER FIVE

M. I. ROSTOVTZEFF*

THE *Social and Economic History of the Roman Empire* by M. Rostovtzeff appeared in 1926 when I was an undergraduate. Soon I was given the book to read by my teachers, and I have not yet forgotten the impression it made on me.

All seemed, and indeed was, extraordinary in the book. Even the external appearance was unusual. We were accustomed to books on ancient history where the archaeological evidence, if used at all, was never presented and explained to the reader. Here a lavish series of plates introduced us directly to the archaeological evidence; and the caption of each plate really made us understand what one could learn from apparently insignificant items. The notes were something unusual too. Learning we knew, but here was overwhelming learning on out of the way subjects. And, of course, the main novelty was the text itself. Some other contemporary historians with whom we were well acquainted – De Sanctis, Beloch, Ed. Meyer, Tarn – were great men, not less great than Rostovtzeff. Even as undergraduates we could see that some of our teachers (such as Beloch and De Sanctis) analysed the ancient sources with a surer touch than Rostovtzeff. But Rostovtzeff delighted and surprised us by what seemed to us his uncanny gift of calling things ancient to life. He guided us through the streets of Rome, Pompeii, Nîmes and Trèves and showed how the ancients had lived.

It was little we knew of the man who was giving us such a thrill. But what we heard was in keeping with the impression made by the book. We were told that Rostovtzeff was a Russian liberal who had taught in the University of St Petersburg until 1918 and had become an exile when the Bolsheviks seized power. We also knew that he was a man of great physical strength and exceptional memory, passionate and egotistic, capable of lecturing in six different languages and of quarrelling in as many. De Sanctis, who had been his friend for

* *The Cambridge Journal*, 7 (1954), 334–46.

thirty years, told us with a smile that one night in Athens he had had some difficulty in saving a Greek cabman from the wrath of Rostovtzeff, who had underestimated (or perhaps fully appreciated) the powers of Greek wine. A German archaeologist had another story about Rostovtzeff. On the eve of his departure from Germany Rostovtzeff had been invited to visit the cellars of a famous wine producer of the Rhine valley. The next Rostovtzeff knew was that he was approaching the station of Vienna: the railway ticket had been carefully tied to his buttonhole by his German host.

A few years later, in the early thirties, one had plenty of opportunities of meeting Rostovtzeff in Rome. Short, tough, with strange, forbidding, and yet sad, blue eyes, he lived up to his reputation without any difficulty. These were the years of the excavation of Dura-Europos, and he would lecture in five languages on his work there without needing a note. He was in his sixties, but his energy seemed unspent. He could still pass from an intense season of excavations at Dura to another not less exacting season of research in the wonderful library of the German Archaeological Institute in Rome. He was perhaps less aggressive than in his younger days. Nobody disputed his greatness. The University of Yale surrounded him with unique respect and gave him all the means for his work. Though he was still bitter about Russia, one felt that America had really become his home. Perhaps the quality most noticeable in him was his love for street life. The streets, the gardens, the manifold out-of-door activities of a Mediterranean city appealed to him immediately. One could see that his love for classical history was inspired by his intimate acquaintance with and his great love of modern Southern life – whether in the Mediterranean or in Anatolia. Pompeii had been his favourite city since his youth. Later he fell in love with Ostia and Leptis Magna. The recovery of another city, Dura on the Euphrates, was one of the great achievements of his life.

So much for a first impression. But Rostovtzeff poses very difficult questions to the students of historiography who want to know something more precise about him. He left Russia when he was forty-eight. We shall see that it would be wrong to assume that he had reached intellectual maturity before leaving Russia. Rostovtzeff was one of the very rare men who are capable of developing until old age. The crisis of the exile gave new impetus to his mind. It is safe to assume that the exile made Rostovtzeff the great man he was. However, the first forty-eight years of his life count for something.

We are all doing him a great injustice in speaking about him without a proper knowledge of his Russian background. But this knowledge I found very hard to obtain. As far as I know, Rostovtzeff did not write an autobiography, and none of the studies on Rostovtzeff known to me – not even that by the American critic, Meyer Reinhold, which appeared in *Science and Society* in 1946 – contributed anything of importance to the knowledge of the first part of his life. The obituaries which came to my notice are disappointing in this respect. Strange as it may seem, not even the Russian teachers of Rostovtzeff are mentioned[1].

To explain this situation, two facts should be borne in mind. Russian is a language normally unknown to ancient historians, and Rostovtzeff, even before his exile, had to write much of his work in Italian, French and, above all, German in order to be understood by his colleagues. Furthermore he translated or had translated into English, Italian, French and German much of the work he originally published in Russian. Thus he became widely known among people who neither cared for nor thought of his Russian background. On the other hand, in Russia it has become impossible to speak freely about Rostovtzeff. In the first years after the revolution things were perhaps easier. Anyway in 1925 the Soviet authorities published a manuscript on the ethnography and history of Southern Russia which Rostovtzeff had left behind while escaping. The first to be surprised about the publication was Rostovtzeff himself, who of course was not asked to see the book through the press. But later, as far as I can judge on limited evidence, talk on Rostovtzeff was either discouraged or controlled. The work by B. Buzeskul on *Universal History and its representatives in Russia in the XIX century and at the beginning of the XX century* – which was published posthumously in 1931 – does not consider Rostovtzeff's activity after 1914 and gives little more than a summary of his earlier work[2]. The bibliography on Russian historians published by Madame Švedova in 1941 contains the name of Rostovtzeff in the index of names, but not in the text[3]; the section on Rostovtzeff seems to have been suppressed in manuscript or proofs. The much discussed history of Russian historiography by N. I. Rubinstein, which appeared in Moscow in 1941, devotes a few insignificant lines to Rostovtzeff and does not examine his activity after 1918[4]. More recent books such as that by Maškin on Augustus[5] and that by Ranovič on the eastern provinces of the Roman Empire[6], both published in 1949, discuss Rostovtzeff briefly as a typical representative of un-Russian, bourgeois historiography, though one of them refers to a review by Mr Last in the *Journal of Roman Studies* to prove that Rostovtzeff did not even please his bourgeois colleagues.

So the Russian background is not studied by Western scholars because they know little about Russian historiography, nor by Russian scholars, because the name of Rostovtzeff is unpleasant. One hopes that Rostovtzeff's Russian pupil, Elias Bickerman, now a professor at Columbia University, and a great historian himself, will sometime write about his master. He is the only one who can do it properly, having known Rostovtzeff before 1918.

The fact that until 1914 Rostovtzeff worked in close collaboration with German scholars and was one of the few foreigners they respected is both significant and deceptive. No doubt Rostovtzeff joined the new school of research on Hellenistic and Roman history that developed in Germany towards the end of the last century. This school emphasized the importance of regional administrative and agrarian history, invented the new science of papyrology and rewrote the history of Hellenistic and Roman Egypt. Ulrich Wilcken was the leader of the school, but Max Weber, later to become the greatest German sociologist, was behind the new interest in agrarian history, and two first-class students of Roman law, Mitteis and Partsch, were soon won to the study of Romano-Egyptian law. Old Mommsen and the younger, yet very authoritative, Hirschfeld approved and encouraged the new trend, though it was a reform of their method. Mommsen and Hirschfeld, with their keen legal minds and their perfect command of literary sources and inscriptions, studied the organization of the Roman empire from the centre. Wilcken chose to study that province of the Roman empire, Egypt, that was least typical of the Roman empire as a whole. He proved that the Roman province of Egypt preserved much of the social and administrative structure of the former Hellenistic kingdom. Wilcken and his friends emphasized the Hellenistic influences on the Roman empire and made people aware that Roman law and Roman administration looked quite different if seen at work in a remote province. The discovery of thousands of documents on papyri made it possible to apply the methods of modern sociological research to ancient history. Quantitative analysis was applied to fields where only vague conjectures had been possible. For many years Rostovtzeff studied Hellenistic history and the Roman provinces of the East on the evidence of papyri and legal texts. He wrote a book on tax-farming and another, more important, on the history of the Roman Colonate in its relations to Hellenistic land-tenure. The history of the Roman Colonate was published by Wilcken in a special supplement to his *Archiv für Papyrusforschung* and made Rostovtzeff's reputation. His juvenile studies on the so called Roman *Tesserae* were clearly modelled on the epoch-making study of Wilcken on Ostraca.

Yet the activity of Rostovtzeff was not confined to these researches, nor were these researches as similar to those of Wilcken as might seem at first. While writing books on administration and land tenure, Rostovtzeff made himself a master of Hellenistic and Roman archaeology. He travelled widely, taking notes on monuments having a bearing on social life. He studied Pompeii with special care and produced a monograph on Hellenistic landscape painting which was a contribution to social studies. Though he knew how to use his eyes, he was never an art critic. His interest in style was always less than his interest in subject matter. He saw that landscape painting reflected contemporary life and was important evidence for housing, agriculture, trade, not to speak of religion. Furthermore, he applied his knowledge of Hellenistic art to the study of the archaeology of Southern Russia. Russian prehistory was developing fast under the guidance of men like N. P. Kondakov, B. V. Farmakovskij and V. A. Gorodcov, whose *Prehistoric Archaeology* is said to have made a deep impression when it appeared in 1908. The tombs of Southern Russia yielded treasures which now fill the Museum of the Hermitage and showed that during the Hellenistic period nomadic tribes of Iranian origin played an important part in the composite civilization of the Black Sea region. Rostovtzeff, who already knew the Hellenistic side of this civilization, soon proved to be an authority on Scythians and Sarmatians as well. In following up his Nomads, he reached the borders of China and tackled problems of Chinese art whenever they could throw light on the Iranian elements of Southern Russia. In addition to his many contributions to journals, he produced (in 1914) the standard work on wall-painting in Southern Russia. At the same time, he prepared a work on the Scythians in Southern Russia which, as I have already said, was first published by the Soviet authorities in 1925 and was then re-elaborated in the German translation supervised by Rostovtzeff himself in 1931. A third book on Iranians and Greeks in Southern Russia appeared first in Russian and then in an English version published at Oxford in 1922.

I have no qualification to judge this work on Southern Russia. But it is highly appreciated by the few students of this subject, for instance Sir Ellis Minns. What a classical scholar can say is that it was something more than pioneer research on the fringes of the Classical World. Classical scholars too often forget that Greek and Roman civilizations themselves were precarious, though glorious, achievements at the fringes of a well-developed world of nomadic or semi-nomadic tribes. It was the business of the Hellenistic kingdoms and of the Roman empire to contain the nomads and enlarge the fringe of cities. But ultimately the nomads broke through, and this was the end of the Roman empire. For obvious reasons Celts and Germans have always been kept under observation by students of the Classical world. But their forms of life and sources of strength can be fully understood only if seen against the background of the wider semi-nomadic world to which they belonged. The Southern Russian tribes transmitted to the West impulses which came from as far as China. It was Rostovtzeff who brought home to classical scholars what the nomads had meant. Later Alföldi and Altheim developed the theme and enlarged the scope of research by calling in Huns and Turks, but in doing so they were no more than Rostovtzeff's pupils, whose judgment is perhaps less sound than their teacher's. It is not surprising that a Russian should have been the first to recognize the importance of the nomads for classical history. He himself lived beyond the classical fringe of Mediterranean cities. And here we begin to perceive what Rostovtzeff owed to his Russian origins.

Nor is that all. We noticed Rostovtzeff's interest in agrarian history, in Hellenistic planned economy and in the city life of the middle class. All these three elements play an important part in Russian historiography of the late nineteenth and early twentieth centuries.

Roman agrarian history had of course been made fashionable by Max Weber, but agrarian history in general was a speciality of Russian historians. In a country where agrarian problems were both archaic in form and contemporary in substance, the study of the peasantry could hardly escape attention. Perhaps because the analysis of Russian agrarian problems might easily get one into trouble – Semevskij was banned from teaching for his work on the peasant question in Russia – many distinguished Russian historians studied the agrarian history of other countries. Kareev and Lučickij studied the French peasantry, and P. Vinogradoff wrote his epoch-making book on English Villeinage before being called to the Oxford chair of Jurisprudence. The study of Roman colonate was introduced into Russia as early as 1886 by an enthusiastic admirer of Fustel de Coulanges, I. M. Grevs; and the subject became quite fashionable. It is easy, indeed perhaps too easy, to account in this way also for the Russian interest in the economic organization of Hellenistic Egypt. Living under the Czars, the Russian professors could understand the complicated regulations of the Ptolemies more readily than could their Western colleagues living in the pre-1914 world of free competition. Rostovtzeff's most distinguished predecessor in this field was Michael Chvostov, who also did some work on land ownership in France before the revolution. After having written papers on the agrarian problems of archaic Athens and Sparta, Chvostov published in 1907 his *History of the Eastern Trade of Greco-Roman Egypt*. Later he published a study of the textile industry in Egypt in which he went into its technical aspects. Chvostov, who died in 1920, was two years younger than Rostovtzeff but developed more quickly and influenced him. The Russians had an obvious interest in Hellenistic and Byzantine history. Thus Rostovtzeff also found in Russia many good students of the later Greek world as a whole: it will be enough to mention the two epigraphists, V. V. Latyšev and A. V. Nikitskij, and the historian of Hellenistic Athens, S. A. Žebelev. Rostovtzeff later proved to have learnt from all of them.

Finally, Rostovtzeff found in Russia a keen interest in ancient and medieval city life. In this case contrast rather than similarity provided the motive. Russia is proverbially lacking in cities with a history comparable to those of Italy, Ancient Greece and Germany – the lands of city States *par excellence* –or even of France, Spain and Great Britain. A friend of mine was an attaché to the Italian Embassy in Moscow a few years ago when the Russians celebrated the eight-hundredth anniversary of their capital. A Russian woman asked him rather defiantly: 'Have you got in Italy eight-hundred-year-old cities like Moscow?' My friend had to think a little before he could find an Italian city less than a thousand years old: finally he produced it – Alessandria della Paglia. Czarist Russia had its peasants and was very often inclined to idealize them, but it had very little of the active and prosperous bourgeoisie which built, beautified and ruled the Western cities. Bourgeoisie may seem a vague and misleading term to us, but obviously was not to the Russian liberals who deplored the absence in their country of the merchants of London, Ghent and Florence. Here again it is no chance that one of the most sensitive studies of French and Italian medieval cities was produced by N. Ottokar, then a professor in the University of Perm and now the professor of medieval history in the University of Florence. It was as a Russian liberal, longing for the creative *bourgeois* society of the Western World, that Rostovtzeff travelled to discover the cities of the Mediterranean fringe.

These are simple indications of the complexity of the currents of ideas that fertilized the mind of Rostovtzeff before the tragedy of exile fell upon him. For tragedy it was. And the tragedy was made worse perhaps by an unhappy period spent in Oxford. Rostovtzeff, who had no mean opinion of himself, was made even more aggressive by the upheaval of exile, and probably did not realize that the average Oxford don knew Greek and Latin much better than he did. He antagonized and in some cases offended his hosts, but many of these seem to have failed to perceive his rapid progress towards absolute greatness. The consequence was that Rostovtzeff was lost to Europe. He left England and taught in the American University of Wisconsin for a few years before finding a permanent and happy home at Yale in 1925.

Whoever goes through the gigantic output of Rostovtzeff in the period 1918–26 has some idea of the crisis through which he passed. It was a feverish production, lacking formal perfection, often marred by vulgar mistakes in detail, but exceptional in originality, relevance to contemporary life and variety. The giant had been hit, but was hitting back. Rostovtzeff was trying both to conclude all the work he had been accumulating before his exile and to meet the challenge of exile by tackling new problems. He still had much to say on his old themes of Southern Russia, Hellenistic land tenure, landscape painting, Asiatic animal style. But he was also maturing the twin masterpieces of the economic and social histories of the Roman empire and of the Hellenistic world. A first sketch of the main thesis of the Hellenistic work appeared in the *Journal of Egyptian Archaeology* in 1920: a first formulation of the basic theory of his Roman volume was published in the *Musée Belge* in 1923. Before 1918 Rostovtzeff had been a man of exceptional learning in the archaeological and papyrological field and of conspicuous originality in any theme he treated, but had given no precise sign of becoming a great historian. He had reached the age of forty-eight without finding the great theme – the inspiration – which could unify his knowledge and mature his mind. Exile provided the shock that transformed him. The Russian liberal rapidly became a great liberal historian. He joined the line that from Guizot and Grote to Marc Bloch and the Hammonds has proved to be singularly capable of a comprehensive view of human nature and the only one seriously interested in the social consequences of intellectual liberty. A liberal faith was Rostovtzeff's inspiration, and the ancient bourgeoisie was made the theme of the two works which were to occupy their author for the next twenty years.

As it happened, the *Economic and Social History of the Roman Empire* was finished first and appeared fifteen years before the Hellenistic history. The differences between the two works are conspicuous, but they should not make one forget that the basic inspiration is the same. When Alexander destroyed the Persian empire, he opened the gates of the East to Greek soldiers, traders, farmers, sailors, teachers, doctors, engineers. These people built cities in the Greek way and spread the Greek language and Greek customs. Centuries later the Romans took over the Hellenistic monarchies of the East and established their rule over the tribal communities of Spain, Gaul and Africa. History repeated itself. A new enterprising minority romanized the West and revitalized the declining bourgeoisie of the East by an infusion of new men and ultimately of social security. The Hellenization of the East and the Romanization of the West were not planned, strictly speaking, by any government. They were the result of the work of people who firmly believed in their way of life and attracted to it the upper class of their subjects. The Roman and Greek cities spreading from Gibraltar to the Euphrates and beyond were the results of this activity. They told a story of adventure, work, prosperity which appealed to Rostovtzeff and made him forget the darker sides of the efforts whereby Greeks and Romans built their cities. Born in a country where the bourgeoisie was hard to find, he came to idealize the Hellenistic and Roman bourgeoisie. He loved Rhodes more than any other Hellenistic state because no other was ruled so completely and successfully by its bourgeoisie. He was equally appreciative of the *petit bourgeois* who boasted of his trade on his tombstone and of the wealthy financier who built theatres and gymnasia for his own city. Slaves and peasants attracted Rostovtzeff's attention only in so far as they helped, or interfered with, the activity of the city builders. Agrarian history, to which Rostovtzeff had devoted so much important research when he was in Russia and in the first years of his exile, played only a secondary part in the two great Histories. This is serious enough, and we shall come back to it, as it is essential to the understanding of Rostovtzeff. He is not the historian of Roman and Hellenistic society as a whole. He is primarily the historian of their traders, gentlemen farmers, and professionals. He is never so good as when he can show how they extended the range of their activity and spread prosperity and comfort where they stepped in.

Yet it is evident that the triumph of the Hellenistic and of the Roman bourgeoisie was comparatively short and incomplete. In the second century BC the Hellenistic middle class was already declining. In the third century AD the city life of the empire was vitally affected by inflation, wars and military tyranny. Twice Rostovtzeff was faced by the problem of explaining the decline of city life. In respect of the Hellenistic bourgeoisie he never hesitated. He fastened the responsibility for its fall on both the Hellenistic kings and the Roman invaders. The kings paralysed the middle class by their planning and regulations and wars: the Romans completed the work of destruction since they destroyed cities, increased taxation, disorganized traffic and terrorized individuals before being persuaded by Augustus that it was in their interest to give security to the Eastern middle class.

In the case of the Roman empire, Rostovtzeff was not so certain of himself. Under the impact of the Russian revolution he thought he had discovered the clue to the decline of Rome in the conflict between the bourgeoisie and the peasantry. According to the theory he first made public in the *Musée Belge*, 1923, the peasants remained outside the civilization of the Roman empire. They hated the bourgeoisie and found an opportunity for revenge when they became more numerous in the Roman army. Helped by emperors who sympathized with them, they rebelled against the cities and spread disorder. The Red Army of the third century ruined the Roman State of the Caesars, just as the Red Army of the twentieth century ruined the Russian State of the Czars. This is the famous theory that has provoked so much discussion. Norman Baynes among others found no difficulty in proving that in the third century AD the peasants were not less terrorized by the army than the city dwellers[7]. These criticisms certainly affected Rostovtzeff, but in any case he was bound to see things differently as soon as he became less preoccupied with Russian affairs. Already in the book of 1926 he leaves space for the alternative explanation that the Roman bourgeoisie was weakened by State intervention and barbarian attacks just as the Hellenistic bourgeoisie had been weakened by State intervention and Roman attacks. Later, in the German edition of his book (1929), he deleted all explicit mention of the Red army of peasants. Finally in an article in the *Economic History Review*, 1930, he emphasized State intervention only as the cause of the Roman decline and dropped his theory of the peasant rebellion.

One easily sees that the *Social and Economic History of the Roman Empire* is a book not very clearly and coherently thought out. It was written much more quickly and with much less thorough knowledge of the evidence than the later book on Hellenistic history. It was also emotionally disturbed by his impressions of the Russian revolution. The image of a Red peasant army for which there was really no evidence took hold of Rostovtzeff against his better judgment. He was unable to combine it with the other explanation that State control progressively cut the roots of free initiative and prosperity. But without his painful experience of the Russian revolution Rostovtzeff would probably not have described the bourgeoisie of the Roman empire with such loving care. Though his theory of the alliance between peasants and army proved to be delusive, we know that there were peasant rebellions in the empire and we know also that peasant discontent occasionally allied itself with religious movements. The part played by the peasantry in the history of the third to the fifth centuries AD has still to be assessed fairly.

When Rostovtzeff turned to the completion of the *Social and Economic History of the Hellenistic World* he was peacefully established in America. I was perhaps not the only reader to miss in the Hellenistic history the generous impatience, the emotional intensity of the book on Rome. Something of the old fire had gone out, but the new history was a much more careful piece of research. Rostovtzeff had learned to examine the evidence more prudently and patiently. He had in the meantime returned to field archaeology, and the excavation of Dura-Europos with all the work of interpretation it implied had been a wonderful discipline both for himself and for the American pupils he trained there.

Not much can be said here about the rediscovery of Dura, except in so far as it is relevant to Rostovtzeff's interpretation of Hellenistic and Roman civilization. The story is better read in Rostovtzeff's little book *Dura and its Art* which appeared in 1938. Dura was a mere name until its site was identified by chance after the First World

War and soon attracted the attention of the great Franz Cumont. Cumont excavated there on behalf of a French academy and published his results in 1926. This encouraged the University of Yale and Rostovtzeff to take over the excavations (about 1928) when it became clear that the French did not intend to go on. Dura was first a Macedonian colony on the border of the Euphrates, then it became a Parthian city and included large sections of population of Iranian and Semitic origin. Later it was occupied by the Romans and received a garrison. It was finally destroyed in the third century, and its ruins were slowly buried in the desert. The new Pompeii suited Rostovtzeff well and confirmed his ideas about the composite character of Hellenistic civilization. He analysed admirably the various elements that went to make the history of Dura. Never dogmatic because of his liberal education, he proved also to be much more discriminating, much more patient in interpreting the ruins of Dura, than one would have expected from his earlier work. The volumes of the reports on the excavations, though written to a great extent by his collaborators and pupils, were the results of their common study under his direction and represented his third great life work – which alone would suffice to make the glory of a historian.

In the *Social and Economic History of the Hellenistic World* there is not so evident a hiatus as that between the two interpretations of the decline of the empire which one can discover in the Roman book. But there is a more subtle conflict of points of view. Elsewhere I have tried to explain that the Hellenistic history is the result of the superimposition of two books[8]. One analyses the causes of the decline of Hellenistic social life under the impact of State intervention and Roman invasion. The other is an inventory of the main achievements of Hellenism in the economic and social field. What unifies the two books to a certain extent is the emphasis on the creative work of the Hellenistic bourgeoisie. The bourgeoisie deserves the credit for the achievements of the Hellenistic civilization, and the Hellenistic kings and the Roman generals are responsible for its shortcomings. But Rostovtzeff did not succeed in fusing together the two themes of his book. Something separates the main section on the consequences of State intervention and Roman invasion from the final section on the achievements of Hellenistic civilization, though I should be embarrassed to say what it is.

A critical evaluation of Rostovtzeff should therefore start from the prominent position he assigns to the bourgeoisie in his Hellenistic and Roman histories. In my opinion, Rostovtzeff is essentially correct in assuming that both the Hellenization and the Romanization of the territories of the Roman Empire resulted from the activities of the urban middle class. But four rather obvious remarks come to my mind:

(1) Rostovtzeff did not make a close enough study of the problem of political liberty in the ancient world. He over-estimated the importance of economic liberalism in comparison with political freedom. This is evident in his study of the Roman Empire with the result that he hardly grasped the meaning of the political opposition to the Emperors and the importance of the senatorial class as a political *élite*.

(2) Rostovtzeff oversimplified the economic structure both of the Hellenistic and of the Roman period and never defined the term *bourgeoisie*. He never examined the means by which the cities governed themselves, nor asked the question: who governed them? He was not much interested in taxation and inflation, which are the main indications of changes in the social structure. He was lucky in being born early enough to escape the present ridiculous adoration of so-called prosopography (which, as we all know, claims to have irrefutably established the previously unknown phenomenon of family ties). But it may be regretted that he did not pay more attention to the general problem of the formation of the ruling classes.

(3) Rostovtzeff, as we have said, gave peasants and slaves sometimes less than their due, not because he ignored them, but because he focused his attention on middle class urban activities.

(4) Rostovtzeff, although he studied ancient religion, can hardly be said to have been aware of the profound impact that the religious needs of man have had upon his development. He never examined the implications of the fact that Christianity ultimately made its appeal to people of all classes. He assumed the fatality of the clash between the educated city-dweller and the less educated peasant, but Christianity did embrace both peasants and citizens and made them work together.

Perhaps other objections can be made to Rostovtzeff. One, obvious enough, is that he was more intuitive than logical (as Russians often are) and therefore seldom thought his theories out clearly. But he must be measured by his achievements, not by his shortcomings. He was a liberal man who loved life in his creative moments and had the gift of calling things back to life. His learning was enormous, but he cannot be confused with those people who know all about a thing without knowing the thing. He fought for the ideas in which he believed and was never quite at peace with the surrounding world, though America gave him his best years. At last, the Second World War and old age coming together were too much for him: he sank into melancholia and was never himself again. Those who have known him have known greatness. They will always cherish the memory of a courageous and honest historian to whom civilization meant creative liberty.

ADDITIONAL NOTE. – When I wrote this paper I was not acquainted with the biographical sketch (with bibliography) published by G. V. Vernadskij in *Seminarium Kondakovianum*, IV (Prague 1931) 239–52. Vernadskij gives many details about Rostovtzeff's family (his father was a student of Virgil) and makes it clear that Kondakov was the main influence in his intellectual formation. Later (1895–6) R. studied in Vienna with Bormann and Benndorf.

[1] *Cf.* C. Bradford Welles, *Gnomon* (1953) 140–4.
[2] *Vseobščaja istorija i ee predstaviteli v Rossii v xix i načale xx veka*, čast' vtoraja (Leningrad 1931) 172–4; 184; 207–10.
[3] O. I. Švedova, *Istoriki SSSR* (Moscow 1941) 147.
[4] *Russkaja Istoriografija* (1941) 492–3.
[5] N. A. Maškin, *Principat Avgusta* (Moscow 1949) 375 (*cf.* 355–6).
[6] A. Ranovič, *Vostočnye Provincii Rimskoj Imperii v I–III vv.* (Moscow–Leningrad 1949) 33 (*cf.* 5–6).
[7] *Journ. Rom. Studies* 19 (1929) 229; *cf.* H. M. Last, *ibid.* 16 (1926) 126.
[8] *Journ. Hellen. Stud.* 63 (1943) 116.

CHAPTER SIX

A HUNDRED YEARS AFTER RANKE*

ABOUT a hundred years ago a student of the University of Berlin would have been able to hear Boeckh lecturing on *Enzyklopädie und Methodologie der philologischen Wissenschaften* and Droysen lecturing on *Enzyklopädie und Methodologie der Geschichte* (*Historik*). He could also hear Ranke, whose *Epochen der neueren Geschichte* were delivered, not however in Berlin, in 1854.

Boeckh's *Enzyklopädie*, Droysen's *Historik* and Ranke's *Epochen*, as we know, had two features in common:

(*a*) They rejected the Hegelian *a priori* method of philosophy of history.

(*b*) They took the main task of the historian to be the discovery of the leading ideas of history.

As for the first point, not much comment is needed here. Hegel's *a priori* method was discredited. Historical research was more than ever safely founded on the careful examination of old sources and the discovery of new ones. Niebuhr, whom Hegel had despised, was universally hailed as the great master of the new historical method. The new historical school had re-established contact with the great *érudits* of the eighteenth century, after the over-production of philosophies of history. Great attention was again devoted to the rules whereby we ascertain the authenticity of documents, date them, and edit them.

It is more difficult to say something both sound and brief on the second point. In 1821 Humboldt had proclaimed that the task of the historian is to discover the ideas behind the facts, and his words had inspired the younger generation. Boeckh, Droysen and Ranke were Humboldt's ideal pupils. They agreed on the notion that history makes sense because men ultimately act according to leading ideas. By leading ideas they seem to have meant the general principles according to which religions are founded and states are built. Their interests were, generally speaking, confined to religion and politics

* *Diogenes* 7, 1954, 52–8.

with some excursion into the realm of literary and artistic activities: they concerned themselves with ideas relevant to these fields of research. State, Church, freedom, individuality, humanity, marriage, honour, redemption, are some of the ideas which were supposed to determine and characterize historical events. There was a general inclination to admit that the leading ideas of successive periods would form some sort of continuity and could be described as phases of a progressive development, but there was no unanimity on this point. Ranke himself was notoriously uncertain: according to him each epoch is in direct contact with God, though he would not perhaps deny some progress from epoch to epoch.

Ranke, Droysen and Boeckh can be considered as typical representatives of that German historical method that spread throughout Europe about 100 years ago. This method ruled the universities but was also largely accepted outside the universities. Where the native traditions of historical research were particularly strong, German influence had to compromise with them. In England the emphasis remained on strictly political history, that is, the history of party struggles. In France there was a preference for the history of civilization. But though no German was capable of writing a Greek history like Grote's or an *Histoire de la Civilisation en Europe* like Guizot's, the differences were not such as to imply a conflict of methods and purposes. These too were histories of leading ideas: it would not be unfair to call Grote a historian of Greek democracy or Guizot a historian of the influence of liberty on civilization.

It is, however, important to remind ourselves that other points of view remained or became vital a hundred years ago. The philosophy of history now took the shape of comtisme and historical materialism. Vico continued to inspire some writers. Strictly partisan, dogmatic history was flourishing, both in the field of political and of religious historiography. But it is perhaps more important to register the fact that the very notion of leading ideas was already becoming ambiguous. Nations were, of course, often supposed each to have their own ideas – the Germans were the *Träger der Freiheit*, and the Prussians the *Träger des Staats* – but this close identification of ideas and nations was no longer fashionable in every circle. Nationality as such was the good thing, without further justification; and one talked of natural borders, national spheres of interest, natural enemies, as if these things existed. It would indeed be interesting to make an exact study of the spreading of these notions. The national history as such was endangering the history of leading ideas embodied in states and religions.

Nor was all smooth in the field of source criticism. Many people suspected that what was called the German method of source criticism was arbitrary and fanciful. Some people, like Bachofen, objected to *Quellenforschung* because they believed in traditional data: others, like Cornewall Lewis, thought the Germans, and Niebuhr most of all, far too credulous. Lewis asked for stricter standards of judgment; he was suspicious of Niebuhr's intuitions. But the Bachofens and Lewises remained a small minority.

The German method of source criticism seemed to the majority to be founded on the solid rock of the direct examination of evidence. And the German history of leading ideas was corroded by internal ambiguities rather than by external enemies. The elevation of nationality to be the supreme factor in history was indeed momentous: it led away from the study of ideas to the study of material forces; it replaced the study of something dynamic, like ideas, by the study of something which was supposed to have been present from the very beginning.

I must now ask you to jump over a hundred years without even that pause over 1890 which would make argument easier. If we compare the situation of about 1850 with that of about 1950, I would say that two features emerge:

(1) Academically speaking, not much has changed in the matter of source criticism. The principles obtaining in Boeckh and Droysen are still ruling now. There has been some change in the technique of critical editions: the evaluation of manuscripts has of course become much less mechanical after Traube than it used to be after Lachmann. There has also been a conspicuous refinement in the study of linguistic evidence. But on the whole the approved technique of academic research is today not essentially different from that of the days of Droysen and Boeckh. Yet much of the present historical research is done with little respect for, if not with actual contempt of, the approved rules. The Marxists have gone back to obsolete *a priori* interpretations of history. Racialism has been another notorious source of an *a priori* approach to history. Psychoanalysis, existentialism and theology have made their contribution to *a priori* constructions.

Apart from these more or less frank *a priori* interpretations, there are abundant examples of relaxations of rules. In my own field of ancient history the phenomenon has assumed alarming proportions. There are many distinguished scholars who do not deal with sources according to generally approved methods. An accurate analysis of their departures from what I may perhaps call valid methods would involve us in a discussion of individual historical problems. I shall simply refer to my recent experience in dealing with the problem of the date of composition of the *Historia Augusta*. This is a conventional problem, but the arguments recently put forward by many distinguished researchers to solve it are so unconventionally absurd that a restatement of principles appeared necessary.

(2) Even more important, perhaps, is another feature of the present situation of historical studies. As I have mentioned, a hundred years ago it was generally admitted that one could understand history if one could grasp the ideas behind the facts. As history was, generally speaking, either political or religious history, the ideas would be either political or religious, which was simple enough. Today this situation has changed in four ways: (*a*) History is no longer chiefly political or religious. National histories look old-fashioned. Under Marxist influence social-economic history is probably the most popular brand, and covers a bewildering variety of products from the history of tools to the history of amusements, from the history of town planning to the history of the parson's wife in the Anglican tradition. If you happen to admit or suspect that there are ideas behind all these developments, the problem of how to track down these ideas becomes increasingly complicated. Theological thought provided a key to religious history, and political doctrines were deemed to explain political facts, but the ideas, if any, lurking behind the development of card games or silk-production are not so easily found and formulated in plain words.

(*b*) The evident fact that ideas are no longer so easy to discover can only increase the doubts already suggested from many other quarters that ideas are no explanation of history. Psychoanalysis, racialism, Marxism, the study of primitive and animal behaviour all suggest different competitive explanations. Do these explanations exclude ideas or simply supplement the interpretation of history by ideas? And do these anti-idealistic explanations exclude each other? Take the notion of aggressiveness as a historical factor. Is aggressiveness an explanation in itself, or does it presuppose the existence of some ideas or some ideals to be aggressive about? Furthermore, if you exclude the intervention of ideas or ideals, is aggressiveness the most elementary factor, or is it to be analysed in terms of economic competition? Even if aggressiveness is to be analysed in terms of economic competition there is the further question whether economic competition explains aggressiveness or aggressiveness is the condition of economic competition and class warfare. And this, of course, is not the end of the question: one can ask, for instance, whether human aggressiveness is different from animal aggressiveness; and whether religion is a sublimation of aggressiveness or a source of aggressiveness, or an antidote to aggressiveness, provided either by natural or by supernatural forces.

(*c*) Since the explanation of historical facts is now usually given in terms of social forces, the question of the relation between explanation of historical events and explanation of individual actions has become more acute. You can explain the French Revolution as you like, but there is always a moment in which you have to take account of the fact that a certain individual was either angry or in love or ill or drunk or stupid or cowardly. How are these individual features to be combined with the general explanation?

(*d*) The fourth and most obvious aspect of this state of affairs is that it is has become extremely difficult to speak of progress or even of a meaningful development of events in a certain direction. Not even all those who hold an *a priori* view of history would find themselves able to believe in progress. Marxists and Catholics perhaps can, but psychoanalysts, I am told, do not believe in progress. The great majority of ordinary historians simply do not know what to think about progress, and ask the philosophers for guidance. The philosophers, of course, answer that it is not their business to tell you what to think, but only how to think.

This picture, however sketchy and incomplete, is one of exceptional complication. It makes the life of a historian a hard one. To begin with, the historian is now supposed to know more facts than are compatible with the short span of an ordinary human life. He must know about statistics, technical developments, the subconscious and unconscious, savages and apes, mystical experiences and middle town facts of life: besides that he must make up his mind about progress, liberty, moral conscience, because the philosophers are chary in these matters.

I have no idea how one can simplify the present tasks of a historian. But I venture to throw out two remarks on marginal points:

(1) It is more than ever essential to be strict in the examination of evidence. We must not allow people to get away with doubtful pieces of evidence. Any searching question about the value of the evidence presented by Marxists, psychoanalysts, racialists, Catholics, sociologists, contributes towards the clarification of the general question of the value of their doctrines.

(2) We must get used to the fact that the purpose of our research has an influence on the methods of the research itself. If you study corn production in order to assess its influence on the growth of population, you will use different methods of research from those you would use if you were interested in collecting facts relevant to a proposed reform of land-tenure. In the latter case the mental habits of the peasants would presumably be of greater importance than in the former case. A candid admission of the purpose of one's own study, a clear analysis of the implications of one's own bias helps to define the limits of one's own historical research and explanation. To take the example of a great book, if Ronald Syme had clearly asked the question which was at the back of his mind when he wrote his *Roman Revolution* – was Augustus' revolution a fascist revolution? – his research would have been more clearly directed to a definite aim.

This point may perhaps help us to understand the role of ideas in contemporary writing of history. Dilthey has already dispelled the illusion that one can write the history of one or two isolated ideas or principles. But men still inevitably turn to history in order to clarify their own mind about ideas such as freedom, honour, justice or even marriage, war, trade, for which contemporary experience might well seem to be enough. These ideas provide the starting point of important historical research. The question whether ideas are principles of historical development is one that cannot be answered *a priori*: only historical research can say whether and how, for example, the idea of honour operated in history. But if we cannot be sure that ideas lead to historical developments, before having tried hard to find other explanations, we are sure that ideas lead to historical research. Ideas are themes of historical research – though not of all historical research. The clearer we are about the theme of our own research, the clearer we become about our own bias. And the clearer we are about our own bias, the more honest and efficient we are likely to be in our own research. Many of the rules laid down about the correct methods of historical research are in fact disguised declarations of the purposes of the research itself. For instance, if you assert that the only method of studying the history of Roman law is to analyse the interests of the Roman property classes, you are already selecting one of the many tasks of historical research on Roman law. Self-examination is a necessary step not only to personal redemption, but also to objective historical research.

Too much historical research is being done by people who do not know why they are doing it and without regard to the limits imposed by the evidence. An improvement in this respect is both possible and desirable.

CHAPTER SEVEN

SOME OBSERVATIONS ON CAUSES OF WAR IN ANCIENT HISTORIOGRAPHY*

RICHARD of Bury, bishop of Durham in the fourteenth century, wrote in his *Philobiblon* a lament for the ancient books that have not come down to us because of war. How many more interesting books by Aristotle and Seneca we could have read, he suggested, if they had not been destroyed by war. Aristotle would have transmitted to us the quadrature of the circle and would not have left the problem of the eternity of the world an open question. Furthermore, the grammar of Cadmus, the geometry of Joshua, the riddles of Samson, the antidotes of Aesculapius, the stratagems of Palamedes and countless other secrets of science are believed to have perished when the library of the Ptolemies was burned in the Alexandrian war, as we know from Aulus Gellius. '*Quis tam infaustum holocaustum, ubi loco cruoris incaustum offertur, non exhorreat?*' 'A lesser crime than this is the sacrifice of Jephthah or Agamemnon where a pious daughter is slain by a father's sword.'

If Richard of Bury were living today he would of course have even better reasons to lament the books destroyed by war. But perhaps he would have learnt that there is an even great calamity than books destroyed by war: it is the calamity of books and papers inspired by war, books and papers on causes of war, war psychology, war guilt, future wars. To this sad category of papers inspired by war belongs, I am afraid, the paper I am going to inflict upon you now. My only consolation, if it is a consolation, is that there is a third, even worse, category of books and papers: the category of the books that inspired wars and were themselves causes of wars. No international enterprise as yet has taken the initiative in collecting the hundred most dangerous books ever written. No doubt some time

* *Acta Congressus Madvigiani*, Proceedings of the Second International Congress of Classical Studies 1954, vol. I (1958), 199–211: a lecture delivered in the Aula Magna of the University of Copenhagen.

this collection will be made. When it is done, I suggest that Homer's *Iliad* and Tacitus' *Germania* should be given high priority among these hundred dangerous books. This is no reflection on Homer and Tacitus. Tacitus was a gentleman and, for all that I know, Homer was a gentleman too. But who will deny that the *Iliad* and the *Germania* raise most unholy passions in the human mind? It is fortunately not my task to speak here about the influence of Tacitus' *Germania.* One horror is enough for one day. But if I am going to speak about causes of war in ancient historiography I cannot pass over all the nefarious consequences of that great epic model – the *Iliad.* Not only did the *Iliad* create the model of all those Achilleses and Agamemnons who have troubled the world ever since, but all the bad historians have learnt from Homer to attribute silly causes to earnest wars.

Yet Homer was so nice – if I may apply to him this homely English adjective – Homer was so nice about war. He knew why people go to war and he stated it so simply: they may go to war by sheer necessity for their children and their wives; or they may go to war to avenge an offence, after the enemy has carried away their oxen or their horses or has wasted their harvest. Or they may fight to get glory for themselves and their chieftains. Or they may just want booty and wealth for themselves, though it is characteristic of Homer that this is rather implied than said in so many words. But war remains a sad necessity, the lot that gods have spun for miserable men that they should live in pain. Thus, *ab Homero principium.* In the first part of my paper I am going to summarize as briefly as I can what Greek and Roman historians discovered about causes of war. In the second part, for which I venture to claim some originality, I am going to discuss the place of ancient historical writing about war in the history of ancient political thought and also its influence on modern historical writing.

It is hardly necessary to say that there is nothing in Homer of the many things that later generations found in Homer – the conflict between Greeks and Barbarians, the permanent enmity between Europe and Asia. The *Iliad* was not meant to be a chapter in the history of the wars between East and West. Yet, as we all know, the *Iliad* was treated as such a chapter, and Herodotus was already aware of this. I am not certain that I understand fully what Herodotus implies in his introductory chapters of Book I. Notwithstanding Professor K. Reinhardt's ingenious remarks, I still fail to understand why Herodotus attributed stories that looked so obviously Greek to

Phoenicians and Persians. But on one point there can be little doubt. Herodotus was dismissing a current interpretation in mythical terms of the Persian wars. He definitely decided that if you want to know something about the causes of the Persian wars, you must not look at Greek myths, you must not look at Homer. The stories of Io, Medea and Helen are not episodes of the Persian wars. Here is part of the process whereby Herodotus quietly rebelled against Homer – a rebellion, incidentally, that has made history possible as we understand it. He freed himself from the fascination of the mythical past and looked at events in the recent past. He asked himself what is the value of the evidence. At the same time he was sensible enough to transfer to the events of the recent past that sort of sympathetic understanding for the complications of human life that Homer had displayed in dealing with mythical events. One thing Herodotus undoubtedly learnt from Homer – to do justice to intricacies. He promised to explain δι' ἣν αἰτίαν ἐπολέμησαν ἀλλήλοισι and he set out to fulfil his promise with the open mind and the leisure of a historian who has never read a book on historical method.

The question whether αἰτία meant to Herodotus cause rather than grievance is, of course, irrelevant. Herodotus had no reason to distinguish between subjective and objective causes of war. All that he knew was that people do not become enemies without some inducement. He wanted to know what made Greeks and Persians fight one another, and diligently registered all that he thought to be relevant to the conflict. The enquiry spread to and involved all the world of his time, but Herodotus never pretended to have exhausted his subject or to tell a fact only if it was relevant to his subject. Croesus' interference with the Ionians, Democedes' advice to Atossa that she should persuade her husband Darius to conquer the Greeks, the Ionian rebellion with all its complications, the part played by the democratic assembly of Athens in provoking Darius, and finally Xerxes' lust for glory and empire – all these causes, if you choose to call them so, are loosely mentioned by Herodotus. He is quite unsystematic. We can say that Democedes' advice does not lead to anything; yet we feel that Herodotus would have been wrong not to mention it: it remains one of those imponderable factors of the future. We can also observe that Darius' wrath against Athens is disproportionate; that Xerxes' decision to extend the war to the whole of Greece is not made fully intelligible. Yet again we feel that Herodotus is not far from the truth. Nor is Herodotus trying to make his opinions on the origins of the war agree with his own political opinions. He admires Athenian democracy and knows that democracy made Athens more efficient in war than any other Greek state: indeed, he praises the Athenians as the saviours of Greece. But when the Athenians, unlike Cleomenes of Sparta, are persuaded by Aristagoras to help the Ionians, he blandly remarks that it is easier to deceive thirty thousand men than one. He has no doubt that to help the Ionians was the worst thing the Athenians could have done.

Herodotus' approach to the causes of the war is both concrete and subtle. He is aware that it all started with Croesus and with the expansion of the Lydian state, but he is also convinced that the actual war originated in consequence of the interplay of disjointed factors. The mental horizon of Herodotus is both geographically and chronologically very wide: but even more admirable is the dexterity with which he avoids being enmeshed in his own net, wide as it is.

It is tempting to compare Herodotus with Eastern historical texts. I am not sure that the comparison is really illuminating just because the difference is too great. The records of Egyptian and Assyrian wars are official chronicles, and Herodotus is the denial of official history[1]. The biblical *Books of Kings* can tell a story as well as Herodotus. The rebellion of Absalom or the arrival of the Queen of Sheba is as good as anything in Herodotus. But the *Books of Kings* show little interest in wars. If we extend our enquiry to the books of *Judges* and *Samuel* we shall soon find those Hebrew constant factors – obedience or disobedience to God's order – which are incommensurable with Greek historiography. There is, of course, in Herodotus a reference to the intervention of gods in war but the passions that explode in war and the results of the wars themselves are always capable of description and almost always capable of explanation independently of the reactions of the gods. If one day we discover more of the private writing of Egyptians, Assyrians and Jews, we may well find that they were able to look at wars with a more detached and subtle attitude than their official historians.

As far as comparison is permissible and makes sense, I should say that three differences between Herodotus and Oriental chronicles emerge:

(1) Oriental chronicles are rather monotonous in their motivation of wars. Such and such people have committed some standard offence – they have been treacherous, they made a conspiracy, they refused to pay tribute – and were punished.

(2) The war is seen almost invariably from the point of view of the conqueror. Defeats are concealed. I do not know of any parallel to the history of the Spartans at Thermopylae.

(3) The victorious king automatically identifies his own cause with the cause of his own gods and presents victory as a straightforward divine judgment in his own favour.

At least, we can safely say that, as far as we know, Herodotus was the first to organize a vast enquiry about a war and its causes. This is indeed the legacy of Herodotus to European historiography, and I am not going to say that it is an enviable legacy from every point of view. It has made war the central theme or one of the very central themes of European historiography ever since. If I had to answer the famous question an Oxford undergraduate once put to Sir John Myres – 'Sir, if Herodotus was such a fool as they say, why do we read him for Greats?' – my answer would be that Herodotus was not only the founder of European historiography in a generic way: he provided European historiography with one of its leading and recurring themes, the study of a war, in its origins, main events, results.

It was, of course, Thucydides who, coming immediately after Herodotus and accepting this theme, contributed more than anybody else to making it an essential ingredient of European thought. It is not my purpose here to discuss some of the well-worn problems connected with Thucydides' approach to the causes of the Peloponnesian war. I have nothing to offer about the Megarian decree, nor have I a new theory to propose about the meaning of an αἰτία or πρόφασις. Naturally, I wish I were certain about what Thucydides really meant when he said in Chapter 23 τὴν μὲν γὰρ ἀληθεστάτην πρόφασιν, ἀφανεστάτην δὲ λόγῳ, where the major difficulty is rather in ἀφανεστάτην δὲ λόγῳ than in ἀληθεστάτην. When I was young I had of course an answer to all these questions, and I even printed it. I have now lost faith in my own theories, but I have not yet acquired faith in the theories of my colleagues. No doubt this will come with the years, too. Fortunately any theory is unnecessary for what I think is the really important point. If Herodotus' world is an open society, Thucydides' is a closed shop. He does not allow intruders to get in as Herodotus does at the slightest provocation. His world is that of the two Greek leagues involved in a mortal war against each other. What he wants to describe is that war and nothing else. As Professor Gomme has rightly observed, we should not ask of Thucydides what he is not prepared to give us. This isolation is necessary for Thucydides' great and on the whole successful experiment of studying how leaders behave in a war emergency and what results from their decisions. Thucydides' history is a study in political and military leadership which after 2400 years still defies comparison. But any isolation has its own disadvantages. Thucydides can no longer imitate Homer, as Herodotus could, in the picture of the intricacies of human life. We would hardly suspect from Thucydides that there was in Athens a powerful Strategos in love with Aspasia and that another Strategos, better known for his theatrical achievements, tried to steal a kiss from a boy of Chios and admitted that this was the strategy for which he was better suited. Thucydides indeed has become so Hellenocentric as to forget the peace of Callias: he turns his attention to the Persians only when he cannot help it. He tries to isolate rigorously the events which lead to the outbreak of the Peloponnesian war. He knows exactly what is relevant. He certainly puts his finger on some of the most important knots. The story of what happened at Corcyra and Potidaea is there for ever. But he himself realizes that this is not enough. As he has precluded himself from any excursion into the wider world, he tries to work in depth. He makes a distinction between the superficial and the profound causes of the war. The profound cause would be the distrust of Sparta and her allies for the increasing imperial power of Athens. This distinction – whatever its exact terminology may be – has been acclaimed by the moderns. Nothing else has contributed so much to Thucydides' reputation as the most scientific of the ancient historians – as the man whom any university would be proud to have as a Privatdozent. But surely there is a misunderstanding here. If there is something that Thucydides does not succeed in doing, it is to explain the remote origins of the conflict between Sparta and Athens. The whole of the diplomatic and social history of the thirty years before the Peloponnesian war is perhaps irretrievably lost for us just because Thucydides was not interested in it. There are so many things we do not know because Thucydides did not care to study them.

The remote causes of a war are as much plain facts as the immediate causes. If the facts are not produced, if we are left with a vague feeling of mystery, then we can be certain that we have been misled. Thucydides is vague about the ἀληθεστάτη πρόφασις. He is far superior to Herodotus in explaining the actual conduct of the war with which he is concerned, but he is much less convincing than Herodotus in discovering the remote origins of the war. His austere self-imposed limitations make him particularly unsuited to follow up the origins of a conflict: he does not allow himself the use of those factors which his predecessor manipulated so well. About fifty years ago, Professor Cornford created a sensation by stating that Thucydides was not a scientific historian because he was not interested in causes. We are now less certain than Cornford was in his youth that that is only one type of scientific history, but his main thesis still contains a great deal of truth. Thucydides tried to understand the mind of the people who decided to fight rather than the traditions and interests which were involved in the fight.

By distinguishing between αἰτία and ἀληθεστάτη πρόφασις Thucydides only gave a more precise formulation to a distinction that Herodotus already instinctively knew and used to better effect. The distinction proved to be useful in the subsequent development of Greek historiography in so far as the prevailing tendency was to be frivolous and anecdotal about causes of war. Thucydides' grave words reminded the historians that they had a duty to look beyond the immediate appearances. Two of the continuators of Thucydides – Xenophon and the author of the *Hellenica Oxyrhynchia* – applied the distinction to some of the wars which they described. Xenophon, for instance, used it to explain the hostility of Sparta towards Thebes, and the author of the *Hellenica Oxyrhynchia* has a peculiarly self-conscious passage in which he explains that Persian gold cannot be the only explanation for the coalition against Sparta. That the reminder of Thucydides was needed is shown by Ephorus. As far as we can judge from Diodorus' reports of what he said about the Messenian wars and the Peloponnesian war, he was unashamedly frivolous about causes of war. According to him, Pericles would have listened to young Alcibiades' advice and made war in order to distract attention from his own mismanagement of public funds. The importance of Thucydides' distinction as a warning against bad historiography cannot be exaggerated. But the fruit that he himself and his followers reaped from the approach to the causes of war is not very impressive. Neither Xenophon nor the author of the *Hellenica Oxyrhynchia* are at their best on the subject[2].

Polybius must have felt some uneasiness on this matter because in accepting Thucydides' distinction he corrected and improved it. He distinguished not simply between αἰτία and πρόφασις, but between αἰτία, πρόφασις and ἀρχή and attributed a different, or at least a better defined, meaning to the terms already used by Thucydides. One of his examples is the expedition of Alexander. The αἰτίαι are represented by the expeditions of Xenophon and Agesilaus which made the Greeks aware of the weakness of the Persian empire; the πρόφασις was Philip's declared intention to take revenge for the wrongs done by the Persians against the Greeks; and finally the ἀρχή is the very organization of the expedition. Here the remote causes are not vaguely expressed; they are plain historical facts, such as Xenophon's and Agesilaus' expeditions which help us to understand why the Macedonian kings felt safe in preparing war against Persia. Yet even Polybius' revised version of Thucydides' distinction is not particularly satisfactory. Even Polybius seems to us more successful in dealing with the military and diplomatic conduct of the wars than with their origins. He found the αἰτία of the Second Punic War in the personal hatred of Hamilcar Barca against the Romans, in the resentment of the Carthaginians at having been robbed of Sardinia and finally in the fears of the Romans about the Punic empire in Spain.

Some of us would say that Polybius is not paying enough attention to economic causes and to the structure of Roman society; others would say that he does not take into account the imponderable elements of a deep-rooted mistrust far earlier than the formation of a Punic empire in Spain; others would probably be inclined to widen the exploration and see what the Greek cities of the West – Massalia included – had to do with the war. But we would all agree, I believe, that Polybius simplifies and rationalizes the causes of war. While Thucydides is too vague, Polybius is too simple.

Now, Thucydides was not vague nor was Polybius simple when they talked about constitutional matters. Thucydides knows how to appreciate the differences between the Spartan and the Athenian way of life; he writes some of his most famous chapters about the internal strife of a polis; he devotes a considerable part of Book VIII to explaining how the oligarchs got hold of the machinery of the Athenian State. In the same way our dissatisfaction with Polybius' Book III on the causes of war gives place to admiration when we pass to Book VI on constitutional problems. In both cases sweeping and somewhat superficial statements on causes of war are replaced by careful observations. We feel that Thucydides and Polybius used a more advanced technique of study when they dealt with constitutional history than when they dealt with causes of war.

It seems to me that we have come up against a very important, and perhaps little noticed, feature of Greek historical writing and, more in general, of Greek political thought. Political thought in Greece tended to concentrate on the internal changes of the States, on constitutional problems. Causes of war, external conflicts remained marginal issues rather than central problems. Herodotus is still outside this development, the origins of which I would connect with the Sophistic movement. Of course he is affected by it, as the debate in Book III on the best constitution and the remarks of Book V on Athenian democracy show. He was certainly well acquainted with the contemporary discussion of philosophers, but his history as a whole still belongs to a world where not constitutional theories but individual actions and national customs predominate. Thucydides, on the contrary, reflects very much the new situation which is, when you come to think of it, a paradoxical one. War was an ever present reality in Greek life; it was a focus for emotions, ethical values, social rules. It was not by chance that Herodotus made war the centre of historical writing, and that his successors accepted his decision. War was the centre of Greek life. Yet the amount of attention that Greek political thinkers gave to causes of war is negligible in comparison to the attention they paid to constitutional changes. Professor Nestle collected in a useful little book what the Greeks thought about peace, and more recently Professor Loenen published a similar book about war in Greek thought. The very fact that the two collections hardly overlap each other is enough to show how unsystematic and superficial Greek reflection was on these topics. Plato and Aristotle can always be relied upon to produce something interesting, if not something sensible, on any subject, but their contributions on war and peace do not bear comparison with what they wrote on constitutional changes.

The reason, I suspect, is that the Greeks came to accept war as a natural fact like birth and death about which nothing could be done. They were interested in causes of *wars*, not in causes of *war* as such. Yes, the golden age had been free from wars, but then that was the golden age. In ordinary life you could postpone *a* war, but you could not avoid *war*. On the other hand constitutions were man-made and could be modified by men; the study of constitutional changes was considered to be profitable and was developed in consequence. Wars remained the centre of historiography, because you could not escape wars; but constitutions became the centre of political philosophy because, in a sense, you could escape a bad constitution by exchanging it for one better and more stable. Thucydides and Polybius were caught in this contradiction, one as the contemporary of sophistic thought, the other as the contemporary of Panaetius and the heir of Hellenistic political philosophy. They were provided with the surgical instruments necessary to dissect constitutions, but they found themselves lacking in comparable tools when wars came up for a post-mortem. All they could do was to improvise without the support of the technicians.

Thucydides' pupils, Xenophon and the author of the *Hellenica Oxyrhynchia*, confirm this point. Xenophon competently analysed the constitution of Sparta, and the author of the *Hellenica Oxyrhynchia* wrote his best chapter on the constitution of Boeotia. Their descriptive technique in the matter of constitutions is far superior to their technique in the matter of war causation.

Polybius certainly played a great part in transferring this feature of Greek historiography to Roman historians. There are many aspects of the attitude of Roman historians towards war that I cannot take into account on the present occasion. It is obvious that Roman historians identified themselves much more closely than did Greek historians with the victories and defeats of their own country. It is also obvious that Roman formalism about *bellum iustum* has left its trace on Roman historical writing. This and other features of Roman historiography about war deserve further study. The point I want to make about Roman historians is that their description of constitutional changes and of civil wars is usually more competent than their analysis of the origin of external wars. The only really impressive account of the origins of a war given by a Roman historian – in Sallust's *Bellum Iugurthinum* – is an account of the conflicts within the Roman aristocracy; whether reliable or not is another matter. Livy's account of the origins of the Second Punic War is very dramatic – we shall never forget Saguntum's fall – but glides over the surface of things. The same Livy knows what popular troubles are when he tells the story of the conflicts between Patricians and Plebeians. It may be true that his account of these conflicts is strongly coloured by the prejudices of Sullan annalists. But this would only confirm that a more direct experience of life accompanied the study of civil wars than that of external wars. The case of Appian is very relevant to this argument because, though Greek, he depends on Roman sources. The competently dull student of Roman wars during the Republic suddenly becomes a clear-minded historian when he touches upon the origins of the Gracchan movement. Without Appian we should understand even less about the *ager publicus.* He indirectly confirms that the Roman historians were better craftsmen when they talked about internal conflicts than when they discussed wars abroad.

Most telling is the case of Tacitus. When he has to talk about a rebellion or a civil war, he is splendid. Cartimandua and Caratacus and Boudicca and Julius Civilis live in our minds because Tacitus knew what could be offensive in Roman provincial government. But if you look for a dull patch in Tacitus, you have only to open the pages of Book XII of the Annals on the origins of one of the wars between Parthia and Rome.

One contributory factor of the situation which we are trying to describe becomes even more evident with the Romans than with the Greeks. To give a good account of the origins of a war one must know something about geography and about ethnography; more than that, one must have lived with the people of the other side. The man who understood causes of war so humanly – Herodotus – was an excellent traveller. His successors seldom compare well with him as fair-minded travellers, if they were travellers at all. Tacitus made a remarkable effort in ethnography as far as the Germans are concerned, but did not repeat his effort with the Parthians who, from his point of view, had the deplorable quality of not being barbarous enough. Another historian of Roman wars with barbarians, Ammianus Marcellinus, exhausted his curiosity in describing the Huns. At least in the surviving parts of his work he never studies the Germans closely; perhaps he thought that his model Tacitus had already done enough three centuries before.

I would therefore venture to offer the general conclusion that the Greek and Roman historians were much more competent on constitutional developments than on causes of war. I would also emphasize the point that this has something to do with the fact that they accepted war as inevitable though disagreeable, but considered bad constitutional developments as controllable, at least to a certain extent: after all they soon invented a mixed constitution as an artificial remedy for the dangers of corruption. The Christian historians of antiquity are no exception: the Christian idea of peace did not affect the historical study of the causes of war, at least until the end of the fifth century AD. St Augustine's thoughts about peace, remarkable as they are, did not inspire any new type of historical research about causes of war, as his faithful Orosius shows. If anything, the idea of original sin made war appear even more inevitable and natural.

I would further venture to make an even more irresponsible statement, though I am well aware that I am not competent to substantiate it fully. I think that there would be some truth in saying that historical writing from the Renaissance to the beginning of this century has been much more successful in dealing with causes of political revolutions than with causes of external wars, just because it has been so largely under the influence of Greek and Roman historiography.

Modern books on the history of war have the reputation of being tedious, while studies on constitutional changes and revolutions often make fascinating reading. There must be some reason why not all of us would read books on the wars of the Spanish succession or on the Napoleonic wars except for professional purposes, while we read for pleasure books on the Puritan or on the French revolution. The reason, I suggest, is that histories of wars seldom go beyond military technicalities, while histories of revolutions explain how revolutions came about. Illuminating pages like those in which Guicciardini explained how the balance of power was upset in Italy at the end of the fifteenth century and Charles VIII invaded the country are extremely rare in historiography; but there are dozens of good histories of the French Revolution. The fact is that until recently modern historians were better equipped to explain revolutions than to explain wars because they, like the ancient historians, took war as natural, but believed in controlling constitutional changes. The phenomenon of war as such – its place in human life – its relation to political and economic forms – the possibility of avoiding it, not just of postponing it to a better moment – were studied seriously for the first time in the nineteenth century, which is also the century in which histories of wars began to become less technical and more deeply concerned with political and social implications. The century that produced Constant's *De l'esprit de conquête* and Clausewitz's *Vom Kriege* is also the century in which Thierry's *Histoire de la Conquête de l'Angleterre par les Normands* and Sybel's *Geschichte des ersten Kreuzzuges* appeared. The very idea of studying ancient warfare in its moral, economic and social aspects is recent. E. Ciccotti's book on *La guerra e la pace nel mondo antico*, which appeared as late as 1901, was a pioneer work on the subject. The idea of controlling wars, like the idea of the emancipation of women and the idea of birth control, is part of the intellectual revolution of the nineteenth century and meant a break with the classical tradition of historiography about wars. The classical interpretation of war lasted until the nineteenth century. Its perfect formulation was provided by Polybius. He taught modern historians to distinguish between remote and immediate causes of war, between causes and pretexts. By remote causes he meant isolated episodes of past history rather than all-pervading economic, social, religious and psychological factors. His teaching came to an end when classically inspired constitutional theory came to an end. Today the students of war rely on a technique of research which embraces both external wars and civil wars, both social and personal conflicts – with the ultimate purpose of transforming both social and personal life. War is no longer regarded as a phenomenon to be examined in isolation: we are trying to understand how war came to take roots in the history of mankind and how we can eliminate the urge for it from human nature. With the classical tradition on causes of war goes the classical tradition on constitutional theory. This is the fact we must face. Nobody ever again will write histories of wars in the manner of Thucydides and Polybius, though it is perhaps too much to hope that nobody ever again will write a new version of Plato's *Republic*.

This means that we are now for the first time in a position to look at the wars of the ancient world with new eyes. We can now study the causes that the Greek and Roman historians attributed to ancient wars as characteristic features of a more primitive way of thinking. A whole new field of research is open to us. We have to classify and to interpret what ancient people thought about their own wars and we must also try to establish a connection between the wars they fought and the way they thought about war. The first task is that of collecting what the ancients thought about causes of war both in their guarded and in their unguarded moments. Here I can only list by way of conclusion some of the features that seem to me most interesting for future detailed study:

(1) First of all a declaration of war is often conceived as a religious act. This is strictly connected with the idea of a just war on which there is no exhaustive study, as far as I know.

(2) Another feature I have already mentioned is the propensity to attribute strictly personal reasons – sometimes silly ones – to declarations of war. This, too, is worth enquiry. Even if the origins of some legends are to be found in comic poets, it is remarkable that comic poets could influence serious historians.

(3) Traditional enmities, inherited rivalries are at any time features of military aggressiveness about which ancient sources are particularly informative.

(4) The mechanism of alliances in its relation to the outbreak of wars can be studied both on literary and epigraphical evidence. The same can be said about the various forms of armistice and provisional peace.

(5) The notion of war for religious causes – for instance to punish the profanation of a sanctuary – is another theme. The frequency and importance of this type of war in different centuries is also significant. More generally, a study is desirable on the direct intervention of gods through oracles, dreams, apparitions, in provoking, advising, encouraging or discouraging wars.

(6) Ancient sources, both Greek and Latin, tell us something about the part played by popular assemblies in deciding war. This could be a starting point for a study on the part played by public opinion in deciding, encouraging or discouraging war.

(7) It is obvious that war and colonization are very closely connected notions that help to explain each other. In a study of this kind special attention should be given to the various forms of *ver sacrum* which as we know from Herodotus (I, 94) existed also in the East.

(8) Ideal motives for war are the most difficult to estimate when one finds them in ancient sources. It is difficult to decide whether the historian attributes alien motives to the actors and to determine the exact meaning and degree of sincerity of the slogan used in a certain circumstance. But if Herodotus speaks of *eleutheria*, and Thucydides talks of *ananke*, if the fourth-century writers insist on the opposition between Greeks and barbarians, we may well believe that they are true to contemporary ways of thinking. When certain facts of war, like the destruction of Melos or the occupation of the Cadmea of Thebes by the Spartans, appear to be repugnant to public opinion, there are implications to be worked out about the ethics of war.

(9) The idea of war-guilt in the classical world is a well-worn subject. Yet as far as I know there is no comprehensive study of it.

(10) Again, it is obvious that the study of arbitration – another

subject on which good work has been done – can still throw further light on causes of war in antiquity. Arbitration was, of course, meant to remove ordinary causes of complaint, for instance about disputed territories.

I do not presume to have exhausted the various categories of facts which one can collect from the ancient sources. In surveying them it gave me some pleasure to notice that apparently no Greek writer ever thought that spring is the season in which kings go to war. Hesiod thought rather that spring is the season to prune the vines. And that wise king of Euboea gave the gold tripos to him in preference to Homer εἰπὼν δίκαιον εἶναι τὸν ἐπὶ γεωργίαν καὶ εἰρήνην προκαλούμενον νικᾶν.

[1] On Hittite historiography *cf.* now A. Kammenhuber, *Saeculum*, 9 (1958) 136–55.

[2] *Cf.* now R. Sealey, *Thucydides, Herodotus and the Causes of War, Class. Quart.*, N.S. V (1957) 1–11.

CHAPTER EIGHT

THE PLACE OF HERODOTUS IN THE HISTORY OF HISTORIOGRAPHY*

I HAVE often felt rather sorry for Dionysius of Halicarnassus. How embarrassing it must have been for a budding historian to have the father of history as his own fellow-citizen. No wonder that Dionysius left Halicarnassus and emigrated to Rome where the name of Herodotus, if adroitly used, could even become an asset. In Rome Dionysius was wholeheartedly devoted to the memory of his formidable predecessor. Dionysius is in fact the only ancient writer who never said anything unpleasant about Herodotus. Yet even he never dared to defend Herodotus from the most serious accusation of his enemies, the accusation of being a liar. To us it may perhaps seem odd that the ancients saw nothing incongruous in being at one and the same time the father of history and a liar. But, as far as I know, Francesco Petrarca was the first to notice the implicit contradiction between these two terms and to object to it.

Petrarch had never seen a manuscript of Herodotus, nor would it have made a great difference to him if he had: he never got beyond the most rudimentary knowledge of Greek. But he read most carefully what his Romans told him about the Greeks and was struck by what Cicero said about Herodotus. In the same sentence of *De Legibus* I, 1, 5, Cicero refers to Herodotus as 'the father of history' and brackets him with Theopompus as another notorious liar: '*quamquam et apud Herodotum patrem historiae et apud Theopompum sunt innumerabiles fabulae.*' This indeed, as Petrarch noticed, was not the only occasion on which Cicero treated Herodotus as a liar, '*fabulosus*'. In a passage of *De Divinatione* (II, 116) Cicero expressed the suspicion that Herodotus himself had fabricated and attributed to Delphi the ambiguous oracle about the results of the war between Croesus and Cyrus. In the same way, Cicero added, Ennius must have fabricated the story

* *History* 43 (1958), 1–13. A paper read at the Anglo-American Conference of Historians, July 1957.

of the ambiguous Delphic oracle that encouraged Pyrrhus to march against the Romans. Petrarch was shocked by the suggestion that the father of history could be the author of a forgery. There was no harm in attributing an oracle to the imagination of Ennius. A poet, Petrarch knew, had a right to invent – not so the father of history. '*Itaque satis credi potest hoc ab Ennio suo quodam iure fictum esse. De Herodoto autem, quem Cicero ipse patrem historiae vocat, quod superioris oraculi fictor extiterit, non tam facile crediderim.*'

This passage of the *Rerum Memorandarum* (IV, 25–6) is typical of Petrarch's shrewd, yet naïve, understanding of the classical world. If he had been able to read Greek, he would have seen that Cicero was simply conforming to a traditional opinion about Herodotus. Herodotus was not denied the place of '*primus inventor*' of history, but at the same time was distrusted to the point of being considered a liar.

Admittedly, the Greeks and Romans were not apt to kneel in silent adoration before their own classical writers. Historians were especially open to accusations of dishonesty. But no other writer was so severely criticized as Herodotus. His bad reputation in the ancient world is something exceptional that requires explanation. It does so the more because the ancient opinion had a considerable influence on Herodotus' reputation among the students of ancient history from the fifteenth century to our own times. The story of Herodotus' posthumous struggle against his detractors is an important chapter in the history of historical thought: it is also, in my opinion, an important clue to the understanding of Herodotus himself.

Herodotus combined two types of historical research. He enquired about the Persian war – an event of one generation earlier – and he travelled in the East to collect information about present conditions and past events in those countries. The combination of two such tasks would be difficult for any man at any time. It was particularly difficult for a historian who had to work in Greece during the fifth century BC. When Herodotus worked on Greek history, he had very few written documents to rely upon: Greek history was as yet mainly transmitted by oral tradition. When he travelled to the East, he found any amount of written evidence, but he had not been trained to read it.

Let us say immediately that Herodotus was successful in his enterprise. We have now collected enough evidence to be able to say that he can be trusted. Curiously enough we are in a better position to judge him as a historian of the East than as historian of the Persian Wars. In the last century Orientalists have scrutinized Herodotus with the help of archaeology and with the knowledge of languages that he could not understand. They have ascertained that he described truthfully what he saw and reported honestly what he heard. Where he went wrong, either his informants misled him or he had misunderstood in good faith what he was told. We are not so well placed for the history of the Persian Wars because Herodotus himself remains our main source. Wherever we happen to be able to check him with the help of inscriptions or of simple topography, we have no reason to be dissatisfied with him. This, however, does not mean that we are in a position to say how Herodotus wrote his history. We do not yet know exactly how he proceeded in his enquiry, compared different versions, wrote down his notes, gave them their present literary form. Above all we cannot say how much he owed to earlier writers. But we know enough about Herodotus' alleged predecessors – Cadmus of Miletus, Hecataeus, Dionysius of Miletus, Charon of Lampsacus, Xanthus of Sardes – to state confidently that they did not do the work for him. There was no Herodotus before Herodotus.

The almost total loss of the geographical and ethnographical literature that preceded and accompanied Herodotus' work makes it impossible for us to assess exactly how much he owed to earlier and contemporary writers. But any careful reader of his work will agree that his main research must have been done not on written, but on oral tradition. After all, Herodotus himself tells us that he used ὄψις, γνώμη and ἱστορία: his eyes, his judgment and his talent for enquiry. This can be confirmed by an analysis of the main episodes of the Persian wars. It is easy to see that what he knows about Thermopylae chiefly comes from Sparta, whereas Athenian traditions are behind his accounts of Marathon, Salamis and Plataea.

In other words Herodotus managed to produce a very respectable history mainly on the basis of sightseeing and oral tradition. He succeeded in putting together a trustworthy account of events he was too young to have witnessed and of countries whose languages he did not understand. We know that his history is respectable because we are now able to check it against independent evidence. But we must admit that if we had to give an *a priori* estimate of the chances of success in writing history by Herodotus' method, we should probably shake our heads in sheer despondency. Herodotus' success in touring the world and handling oral traditions is something exceptional by any standard – something that we are not yet in a position to explain fully. The secrets of his workshop are not yet all out. Therefore we cannot be surprised if the ancients found it difficult to trust an author who had worked on such a basis as Herodotus.

It is only too obvious that Thucydides ultimately determined the verdict of antiquity on his predecessor. He carefully read (or listened to) his Herodotus and decided that the Herodotean approach to history was unsafe. To write serious history, one had to be a contemporary of the events under discussion and one had to be able to understand what people were saying. Serious history – according to Thucydides – was not concerned with the past, but with the present; it could not be concerned with distant countries, but only with those places in which you lived and with those people whose thoughts you could put into your own words without difficulty. Thucydides did not believe that there was a future in Herodotus' attempt to describe events he had not witnessed and to tell the story of men whose language he could not understand. We now know that Thucydides was insensitive to Herodotus' bold attempt to open up the gates of the past and of foreign countries to historical research. But we must recognize that he knew what he was doing in criticizing Herodotus. He was setting up stricter standards of historical reliability, even at the risk of confining history to a narrow patch of contemporary events. Thucydides claimed that a historian must personally vouch for what he tells. He allowed only a limited amount of inferences from present facts to events of the past. He also implied that it is easier to understand political actions than any other type of action. With Thucydides history became primarily political history and was confined to contemporary events.

Now Thucydides certainly did not succeed in imposing his strict standard of historical reliability on other historians, but he succeeded in discouraging the idea that one could do real research about the past. Greek and Roman historians in fact, after Herodotus, did very little research into the past and relatively seldom undertook to collect first-hand evidence about foreign countries. They concentrated on contemporary history or summarized and reinterpreted the work of former historians. Search for unknown facts about the past was left to antiquarians, and the work of the antiquarians hardly influenced the historians. It can be doubted whether Polybius studied Aristotle's constitutions or whether Livy ever read his Varro thoroughly. Indeed, the very existence of the antiquarians was conditioned by the fact that historians interested themselves only in a small sector of what nowadays we should call history. Every generalization of this kind is bound to do violence to a certain number of facts. But on the whole it is apparent that the great historians of antiquity left their mark either on first-hand accounts of contemporary events or on the reinterpretation of facts already collected by previous historians. Xenophon, Theopompus, Hieronymus of Cardia, Polybius, Sallust were pre-eminently historians of their own time. Ephorus, Livy and Tacitus are at different levels to be considered original historians only in so far as they reinterpreted facts which previous historians had collected. The surviving books of Tacitus' *Annals* are the most conspicuous example of a great work of history written with a minimum amount of independent research. And Tacitus himself is an example of what can happen to a historian who relies on interpretation rather than on research: if he is not wrong in his facts, he is liable to be arbitrary in his explanations[1].

Ancient historiography never overcame the limitations imposed by what we can call the paramouncy of contemporary history. The more remote the past, the less likely historians were to contribute anything new to the knowledge of it. Ephorus and Livy were honest men. They were by no means deprived of critical sense. Ephorus decided that it was no use trying to tell the story of the Greeks before the Dorian invasion. Livy was acutely aware of the legendary character of the traditions he was bound to follow about the early history of Rome. But neither of them knew how to go beyond the literary sources for an independent enquiry about the past.

Thus Thucydides imposed the idea that contemporary political history was the only serious history; and Herodotus was cut off from the stream of ancient historiography. He was neither a contemporary nor a political historian. His tales, however attractive, looked oddly unprofessional. Even those who liked him as a patriotic and pleasant writer could hardly defend him as a reliable historian. Herodotus invited awkward questions: how could he tell so much about events he had never seen and about people whose language he did not know and whose countries he had only visited for a short time, if at all? *Either* he had concealed his sources, and was a plagiarist, *or* he had invented his facts and was a liar. The dilemma dominated ancient criticism of Herodotus. There was not a very great choice of predecessors, as we know, from whom he could have stolen his facts, but some could be found. A few were authentic enough: the geographer Hecataeus, the mythographer Acusilaus, the genealogist Pherekydes of Athens, perhaps also Xanthus the historian of Lydia, and Dionysius of Miletus the historian of Persia. Others were late forgers, but were accepted as authentic archaic writers by the majority of ancient critics: for instance the alleged first historian Cadmus of Miletus. Furthermore there were genuine historians whom Hellenistic scholarship placed before Herodotus, whereas some at least of the most authoritative modern scholars incline to take them for his younger contemporaries. To mention only the best instance, F. Jacoby has given very cogent reasons for dating Charon of Lampsacus not in the middle but at the end of the fifth century[2]. All these historians counted in the eyes of ancient scholars as potential sources of Herodotus and were made to contribute to the case for Herodotus' plagiarism. But even with the help of writers who were later than Herodotus and therefore may have used him, rather than having been used by him, the case for plagiarism can never have been a very impressive one. Many of Herodotus' enemies seem to have preferred the alternative line of attack which was to present him as a liar. It was obviously easier to dismiss his evidence than to trace his sources. After all, he could not have been considered the father of history if it had been so evident that he had copied from his predecessors. Though we shall see that there were books on Herodotus as a plagiarist, the final impression left by the ancient criticisms of Herodotus is that he was a story-teller – a liar. Here again we can measure the impact of Thucydides' verdict on his predecessor.

Herodotus had hardly ceased writing his history when Thucydides began to reflect on the mistakes and shortcomings of his predecessor. A few decades after Thucydides, Ctesias launched another attack against Herodotus by questioning his competence both as a student of Greek history and as an historian of the East. Ctesias had all the external qualifications for checking Herodotus' results. He had lived several years at the Persian court and must have understood Persian. He had opportunities of access to Persian records certainly denied to Herodotus. The impact of Ctesias' attack was somewhat reduced by its very violence and extravagance. A historian who puts the battle of Plataea before Salamis in order to impress on his readers his independence from the despised predecessor is likely to get himself into trouble. People were not slow to realize that Ctesias was no less open to suspicion than Herodotus. But, as we know, conflicting suspicions do not cancel each other out. Herodotus' reputation remained tarnished. Paradoxically, he was often associated with

Ctesias as an unreliable historian. Even Aristotle went out of his way to denounce Herodotus' mistakes over small details of natural history; and he formulated his criticism in such terms as to involve the reliability of the whole of Herodotus' history. He calls Herodotus a 'story-teller'.

The expedition of Alexander the Great, by opening up the East, certainly revealed lacunae in Herodotus' information. Strabo in his *Geography* repeatedly echoes and makes his own the criticisms of Alexandrian scholarship. Meanwhile, the Orientals themselves were being Hellenized. They learnt to read what the Greeks had written about them in former centuries and, not unnaturally, found it unsatisfactory. Manetho, the Egyptian priest who tried to present the history of his people to the Greeks, also wrote a pamphlet against Herodotus. The Greeks themselves became increasingly impatient with Herodotus for patriotic reasons. What may seem to us the wonderful serenity and sense of humour of Herodotus in judging the issues between Greeks and Barbarians was for them evidence that the historian had been 'a friend of the barbarians'. Even the local patriotism of Hellenistic Greeks operated against his reputation. Local historians and antiquarians were glad to show him up: he had not said enough about the glories of their own cities. All the anti-Herodotean literature of the Hellenistic age is unfortunately lost, but Plutarch's *De Herodoti Malignitate* can give us some idea of the complaints that were lodged against the father of history. Plutarch puts together a series of criticisms against Herodotus: excessive sympathy for the barbarians, partiality for Athens, gross unfairness towards the other Greek cities, lack of truthfulness where facts are concerned and lack of balance where judgments are involved. History was a form of encomium to Plutarch, and evidently Herodotus did not fit into the pattern. It is a pity that nobody has yet produced a competent commentary on Plutarch's pamphlet against Herodotus, both because it is typical of the way in which late Greeks looked at their past and because it influenced the judgment about Herodotus of many classical scholars from the fifteenth to the nineteenth century. Plutarch does not seem to have said the worst about Herodotus. To guess from the titles of lost works, even worse was in store for the father of history. Titles such as *On Herodotus' thefts* by Valerius Pollio or *On Herodotus' lies* by Aelius Harpocration – not to speak of the book by Libanius *Against Herodotus* – seem to imply that there was no dishonesty of which he was not capable[3].

With all that, Herodotus remained a classic. The immaculate grace of his style defied criticism. His information about Oriental countries was more easily criticized than replaced. Notwithstanding Manetho and Berossus, he remained the standard authority on Egypt and Babylonia. His epic tale of the Persian wars was a unique document of the Greek past. The accusation of lack of patriotism could hardly pass unchallenged. We can easily draw up a list of admirers of Herodotus. Theopompus summarized him in two books. No less a critic than Aristarchus wrote a commentary on him. The discovery of a fragment of this commentary has been enough to dispose of the legend that Herodotus was almost forgotten in the Hellenistic age. From the first century BC to the late second century AD Herodotus was in special favour as a model of style. Archaism operated in his favour. Dionysius of Halicarnassus, Arrian and Lucian were his champions. Dionysius says, 'If we take up his book, we are filled with admiration till the last syllable and always seek for more.' What more splendid compliment could Herodotus desire? Lucian is no less enthusiastic: 'If only we could imitate Herodotus – not all his good qualities because this is beyond hope – but at least one of them.'[4]

Yet there are very disturbing features in these apologies for Herodotus. Dionysius does not argue that Herodotus is a reliable historian: he compares him with Thucydides and gives reasons for the superiority of Herodotus that can persuade only those who do not care for reliability in a history. According to Dionysius, Herodotus chose a better subject than Thucydides, because he told the glories and not the misfortunes of the Greeks. He gave his history a better beginning and a better end. He wrote up his subject in a more interesting way and he arranged his materials better. In points of style he can at least compete with Thucydides. If Thucydides is more concise, Herodotus is more vivid; if Thucydides is more robust, Herodotus is more graceful. Herodotus' beauty is 'radiant', where Thucydides' is awe-inspiring. All is in favour of Herodotus – except truth.

In the same way Lucian admires him without ever implying that he is a reliable historian. Indeed Lucian positively denies that Herodotus is trustworthy. At least twice he couples him with Ctesias as one of the historians who are notorious liars. In the pamphlet of 'How to write history' (*Quomodo sit historia conscribenda*) Lucian definitely presents Thucydides as the model of the fearless, incorruptible, free, sincere and truthful historian. He emphasizes the fact that Thucydides developed his rules for the historian after having observed what Herodotus had done (41–2). Those who speak about Dionysius and Lucian as the great champions of Herodotus in antiquity too often forget to add that Dionysius implicitly and Lucian explicitly deny his truthfulness.

It is my submission that all this resulted from the fact that Herodotus had dared to write a kind of history of which Thucydides disapproved and which later historians found remote and uncongenial. The legend of Herodotus the liar is the result of the authentic achievements of Herodotus the historian. But it will have been observed that if Thucydides disapproved of writing on the past, he did not challenge Herodotus' assumption that history can be written from oral tradition. In the circumstances of the fifth century it was hardly possible to think otherwise. At least in Greece there were not enough written documents to make a sufficiently broad basis for history. Thucydides was far from being blind to the possibilities offered by the exploitation of written documents. Indeed he was one of the very few ancient historians to use written diplomatic records. But it could never occur to him that written records were the primary source for history: if he had thought so, he would never have written the history of the Peloponnesian War. More remarkable is the fact that later historians never tried to modify an approach that had originally been dictated by the conditions of fifth-century Greece. In Hellenistic Egypt there would have been an embarrassing wealth of written records to exploit; and written records were certainly not scarce in Rome during the late Republic and the Empire. But the study of written records remained to the end an exceptional occupation for the Greek and Roman historians. If Thucydides dictated the paramouncy of contemporary history, Herodotus determined the paramouncy of oral evidence. This explains why, though discredited, he remained the father of history.

The pre-eminence of personal observation and oral evidence lasted until historians decided to go to the record office. Familiarity with the record office, as we all know, is a recently acquired habit for the historian, hardly older than a century. It is true that the Roman and Greek antiquarians knew something about the use of documents and that the antiquarians of the Renaissance perfected this approach to the past. But this method became really effective and universally accepted only a hundred years ago. The antiquarians began to study systematically the records of the past in the fifteenth century, but only in the eighteenth century did the barriers between antiquarianism and history break down, and only in the nineteenth did it become established practice for the historian to look for new evidence before writing new books of history. The historians continued to compile ancient literary sources and medieval chronicles long after Spanheim, Maffei and Mabillon had worked out the proper method of studying coins, inscriptions and medieval charters. Gibbon was perhaps the first historian concerned with the classical world to pay attention to the results of antiquarian studies: he used the results of antiquarian labour. But even Gibbon made very little independent research in the fields of numismatics, epigraphy and archaeology. The documentary or antiquarian approach to the past is now so integral a part of historical studies that we sometimes forget that Mommsen was the first Roman historian systematically to use inscriptions and coins. Not until Rostovtzeff did archaeology come into its own for the history of the Roman empire. I am old enough to have witnessed the surprise caused by Rostovtzeff's mastery of archaeological data for historical purposes.

The antiquarian or documentary approach to history has been the most effective way of dealing with Thucydides' objection against a history of the past. We may indulge in the illusion that if Thucydides were to come back to life he would not reject our methods with the contempt with which he rejected the method of Herodotus. The labours of the antiquarians between the fifteenth and the nineteenth centuries prepared the way for an approach to the past that effectively undermined the paramouncy of contemporary history. By excavating sites, searching the files of the record office, comparing coins, reading inscriptions and papyri, we have gone into the past with the same confidence with which Thucydides and his informants went about the assembly places of contemporary Sparta and Athens. We can collect reliable facts without being eye-witnesses in the Thucydidean sense. In unguarded moments of pride we may even be tempted to tell Thucydides that we know more about Athenian tribute lists than he ever did.

It would however be a great mistake of historical perspective to belleve that the documentary approach to history has been the only way in which modern historiography has overcome the limitations imposed by Thucydides on ancient historiography. Before the study of documentary and archaeological evidence became a generalized practice, there was a revival of the Herodotean attempt to get into the past by way of enquiries founded on travels and the study of oral tradition. Defeated in antiquity, Herodotus triumphed in the sixteenth century. The revival of the Herodotean approach to the past, which happened then, is the first contribution of modern historiography to an independent study of the past[5].

In the sixteenth century historians travelled once more in foreign countries, questioned local people, went back from the present to the past by collecting oral traditions. In some cases they acted as ambassadors, in others they were missionaries and explorers: they were seldom professional historians. But they wrote history – a history extraordinarily reminiscent of Herodotus both in style and in method. The new diplomacy required careful examination of the traditions of foreign countries; religious propaganda made urgent the production of objective accounts of the peoples to be converted. Above all, there was the discovery of America with all that it implied. There is no need to assume that the Italian diplomats and Spanish missionaries who worked on their '*relazioni*' or '*relaciones*' were under the influence of Herodotus. Some of these writers – like Pietro Martire and Francisco López de Gómara – had had a good classical education; others, like Gonzalo Fernández de Oviedo, had the reputation of hardly knowing what Latin was. As the historical approach is approximately the same in all of them, it is evident that classical models counted far less than direct experience and contemporary needs. The influence of Herodotus and other classical scholars may colour some details, but the '*relazioni*' as a whole are certainly independent of classical models. What matters to us is that they vindicated Herodotus, because they showed that one could travel abroad, tell strange stories, enquire into past events, without necessarily being a liar. One of the standard objections against Herodotus had been that his tales were incredible. But now the study of foreign countries and the discovery of America revealed customs even more extraordinary than those described by Herodotus.

Classical scholars soon became aware of the implications of these discoveries. They were delighted to find the New World a witness in favour of the classical authors. As I recently wrote in another context, one of the consequences of the discovery of the New World was to confirm classical scholars in their belief that the perfect ancient world had been perfectly described by perfect ancient authors. If Herodotus did not inspire the students of America, students of

America and other foreign countries inspired the defenders of Herodotus. He regained his reputation during the sixteenth century.

My theory that Herodotus recovered from Thucydides' attack only after two thousand years in the sixteenth century can be proved both positively and negatively. I shall show that in the fifteenth century the old suspicions about him revived, but that in the sixteenth century his reputation improved considerably as a result of the new interest in ethnography.

I must admit that in order to dramatize the role of America I have so far underrated the part of Turkey in this development. The emergence of the Turks is another factor that must be taken into account in the story of the fortunes and misfortunes of Herodotus. What happened to Herodotus in Byzantine civilization is beyond my competence. But in the last century of the Byzantine empire the story of the old struggle between the Greeks and the Persians acquired a new poignancy. The Turks had replaced the Persians. Herodotus contained a tale of glory that could be a consolation in the present mortal predicament; but he seems to have been appreciated especially because in his quiet way he had understood the Persians, and through him the Turks could be seen more objectively. An understanding of the approaching rulers was perhaps more needed in that situation than celebration of past victories. The last great historian of Byzantium, Laonicus Chalcocondyles, was a student and imitator of Herodotus. It is impressive to see how he described the contemporary world from London to Baghdad in Herodotean terms. He was either the brother or the cousin of one of the Byzantine masters of the Italian humanists, Demetrius Chalcocondyles, and there can be no doubt that he was one of those who directly or indirectly transmitted interest and admiration for Herodotus to the Italian scholars of the first half of the fifteenth century.

The first reaction of the West to the rediscovery of Herodotus was indeed one of sheer delight, as it well ought to have been. Guarino, who translated the first seventy-one chapters of Herodotus about 1416, repeatedly expressed his joy in reading him. About 1452 Lorenzo Valla translated him entirely; though his translation was not printed until 1474, it made an impression even when it was only in manuscript. Not much later, about 1460, Mattia Palmieri Pisano produced another complete translation into Latin which was never printed. It can be read in an elegant manuscript of the university library of Turin and contains a most significant eulogy of Herodotus.

The father of history is appreciated not only for his style, but also for his method of working, for his journeys, for his free and independent mind.

But the Italian humanists, while learning to read Herodotus, were also learning to know his ancient critics. They realized that Thucydides had attacked him, knew of course Cicero's dubious compliments by heart, got to know what Aristotle, Strabo and Diodorus had said: above all they were impressed by Plutarch's systematic and ruthless attack. On top of all that, religious and scholarly controversies troubled the relations between the Italian humanists and their unfortunate Byzantine colleagues. The Greek name became disreputable again in many humanistic minds; and the psychological resistance to the belief that Herodotus had been a liar decreased correspondingly. The change in the situation is already clear about 1460. Giovanni Pontano was asked to write a preface for an edition of Valla's translation of Herodotus that did not materialize. We have this preface. We can see how prudent and reserved Pontano has become. He defends Herodotus, but he knows only too well that there is an old and impressive case against him. Ultimately he admits that in judging Herodotus one must keep in mind that when he wrote the standards of truth were not so strict as in modern times. A generation later, Ludovicus Vives had no difficulty in saying plainly that Herodotus deserved the title of father of lies rather than that of father of history. '*Herodotus quem verius mendaciorum patrem dixeris quam quomodo illum vocant nonnulli, parentem historiae*'[6]. The very fact that each translator and editor of Herodotus felt it necessary to defend him against Thucydides and Plutarch shows that at the beginning of the sixteenth century his reputation was, generally speaking, bad.

We can begin to notice a change of attitude in the preface of I. Camerarius to his edition of Herodotus of 1541. The change becomes complete, the defence of Herodotus against traditional accusations becomes confident and aggressive in the *Apologia pro Herodoto* by Henricus Stephanus, first published in 1566. It is an interesting coincidence that the Apologia by Stephanus appeared in the year in which Bodin published his *Methodus ad facilem historiarum cognitionem*. Both Stephanus and Bodin were fighting for a wider historical outlook and had perhaps more points in common than they would have liked to admit. But Bodin could not yet get over the fact that Thucydides, Diodorus and Plutarch had criticized Herodotus so severely. Stephanus, for once the more independent of the two, definitely rejected the judgment of the ancients. Stephanus' main argument is that a comparative study of national customs shows Herodotus to be trustworthy. Here the impact of the modern *relazioni* from distant countries is obvious. What we might call the comparative method of ethnography vindicates Herodotus. This is not the only argument produced by Stephanus. He remarked, for instance, that Herodotus could not be a liar, because he had a religious soul. But the strength of the *Apologia pro Herodoto* – a work of decisive importance in the history of European historiography – lies in its comparison between Herodotus' description and modern customs. As is well known, a few years later Henricus Stephanus used this comparison for satirical purposes in the *Apologie pour Hérodote*, which is no longer a study of Herodotus, but a satire on modern life. We can see the immediate effects of Stephanus' *Apologia pro Herodoto* in a book by Loys Le Roy, *De la vicissitude ou variété des choses en l'Univers*, which appeared in 1576. Loys Le Roy, also know as Ludovicus Regius, had long established his reputation as a pupil and a biographer of Budé and as a translator of Aristotle, when he published his meditation on universal history. He deals at length with Mesopotamia, Egypt, Persia, and Greece, and has an almost unlimited faith in Herodotus. Indeed he puts Herodotus and Thucydides together as the best two historians.

If the new ethnographic research was the main factor in the revaluation of Herodotus, the Reformation added a second motive. Interest in biblical history was revived, independent enquiries were encouraged up to a point. Herodotus proved to be a useful complement to the Bible. As David Chytræus put it in 1564, it was providential that Herodotus should begin '*ubi prophetica historia desinit*'. In the second part of the sixteenth century a new interest in Greek and Oriental history developed; it encouraged the study of Herodotus and was in its turn encouraged by a greater trust in his honesty. By the end of the century he had been recognized as the indispensable complement to the Bible in the study of Oriental history. This is not to say that the discussion of Herodotus' credibility did not go on well beyond the sixteenth century. There were still fierce controversies on this subject in the eighteenth century. Indeed the discussion is still going on as far as particular sections of his work are concerned. But after Henricus Stephanus there was no longer any question of relegating Herodotus among the story-tellers. He was the master of and the guide to archaic Greek history and Oriental history. As the greatest of the sixteenth-century scholars, Joseph Scaliger, said, Herodotus is '*scrinium originum græcarum et barbararum, auctor a doctis numquam deponendus, a semidoctis et pædagogis et simiolis numquam tractandus*'[7]. Scaliger himself made Herodotus one of the corner-stones of ancient chronology. One century later Sir Isaac Newton drew up chronological tables to 'make chronology suit with the course of nature, with astronomy, with sacred history and with Herodotus the father of history'. The course of nature, astronomy, sacred history – Herodotus was now moving in very respectable circles. About the same time, in 1724, the French Jesuit Lafitau discovered with the help of Herodotus a matriarchal society in America. His *Mœurs des sauvages Amériquains* revealed to the world the simple truth that also the Greeks had once been savages.

The stupendous developments of the study of Greek and Oriental history in the last three centuries would never have happened without Herodotus. Trust in Herodotus has been the first condition for the fruitful exploration of our remote past. The people who went to excavate Egypt and Mesopotamia had primarily Herodotus as their guide. But there is something more to Herodotus than this. It is true that professional historians now mainly work on written evidence. But anthropologists, sociologists and students of folklore are doing on oral evidence what to all intents and purposes is historical work. The modern accounts of explorers, anthropologists and sociologists about primitive populations are ultimately an independent development of Herodotus' *historia*. Thus Herodotus is still with us with the full force of his method of studying not only the present, but also the past, on oral evidence. It is a strange truth that Herodotus has really become the father of history only in modern times[8].

[1] For a different point of view, R. Syme, *Tacitus* (Oxford 1958).

[2] *Abhandlungen zur Griechischen Geschichtschreibung* (1956) p. 178.

[3] Details in W. Schmid, *Geschichte der griech. Literatur* II (1934) pp. 665–70.

[4] Dionysius, *Letter to Pompeius*, 3, ed. W. Rhys Roberts; Lucian, *Herodotus* (21), 1.

[5] *Cf.* my paper *Erodoto e la Storiografia Moderna, Aevum* 31 (1957) pp. 74–84 for other details.

[6] *Libri XII De Disciplinis* (ed. 1612) p. 87.

[7] *Thesaurus temporum Eusebii Pamphili* (1606), *Animadversiones*, p. 97 (*anno* 1572).

[8] Compare the excellent paper by H. Strasburger, *Herodots Zeitrechnung, Historia* 5 (1956) pp. 129–61. [W. von Leyden, *Spatium Historicum, Durham*

University Journal (1950) 89–104; T. S. Brown, *Herodotus and his Profession*, *Amer. Hist. Rev.* 69 (1954) 829–43; H. R. Immerwahr, *Aspects of Historical Causation in Herodotus*, *Trans. Am. Phil. Ass.* 87 (1956) 241–80; F. Mitchel, *Herodotus' Use of Genealogical Chronology*, *The Phoenix*, 10 (1956) 48–69; R. Lattimore, *The Composition of the History of Herodotus*, *Classical Philology*, 53 (1958) 9–21; K. Latte, *Histoire et historiens dans l'antiquité* (1958) 3–37.]

CHAPTER NINE

AN UNSOLVED PROBLEM OF HISTORICAL FORGERY: THE *SCRIPTORES HISTORIAE AUGUSTAE**

Quid fuerit consilii collectionis huius auctori quando in istam formam hoc corpus digessit vatibus relinquimus divinandum.
CASAUBON

WE can claim to have learnt reasonably well how to detect forgeries of ancient texts made either in the Middle Ages or in the Renaissance or later. It is true that there will always be somebody ready to believe that Tacitus' Annals and Histories were forged by Poggio Bracciolini; or vice versa that the *Consolatio* was written by Cicero and not in 1583. But generally speaking we know enough about transmission of texts, language and history to make it reasonably sure that a Greek or Latin prose composition of the fourteenth or sixteenth or nineteenth century will not be received as a historical document written any time between the fifth century BC and the fifth century AD.

On the other hand, it would be fatuous to maintain that we can readily expose a forgery when the forgery was made in antiquity. Indeed, in this case the name of forgery becomes a problem. What we are tempted to label as a forgery may, on closer examination, be a perfectly honest work attributed to the wrong author by mistake. To mention the most trivial example, the *Constitution of Athens*, which is transmitted among the works of Xenophon, is not a forgery but a genuine fifth-century work attributed by mistake to Xenophon. In

* *Journ. of the Warburg and Courtauld Institutes*, 17 (1954), 22–46. This paper was read at the Warburg Institute in May 1953 as one of a series on Forgeries. I am grateful to N. H. Baynes, H. Bloch, M. I. Henderson, A. H. M. Jones and H. M. Last for having read and discussed the text and to A. A. Barb and O. J. L. Szemerényi for useful information. I am of course alone responsible for the opinions here expressed, but I should like to dedicate the paper to the memory of my old friend G. M. Bersanetti whose article 'Storia Augusta' in *Enciclopedia Italiana*, Suppl. I (1938), pp. 1034–6, shows how well he knew the problems connected with the *Historia Augusta*.

other cases the name forgery may cover a playful imitation. It is uncertain whether the life of Homer going under the name of Herodotus is a straight forgery or a playful imitation of Herodotus' style and manner: it may even be an authentic fifth-century work which first circulated anonymously and then was attributed to Herodotus. It is only proper to admit that our knowledge of style, language, transmission and historical circumstances is not yet equal to solving all the problems concerning the ancient forgeries of ancient texts. This explains the persistent variety of opinions about certain works attributed to Plato and Demosthenes and Sallust, not to speak of such poets as Theognis and Tibullus.

If this is true of any period of Classical Antiquity, it is particularly true of Late Antiquity. We are here faced with a conspicuous mass of writings of doubtful authenticity. It is not enough to say that the language and the manuscript tradition of the Greek and Latin writers of the fourth and fifth and sixth centuries AD have been less studied than the language and the manuscript tradition of earlier writers. An additional reason why there are so many problems of authenticity regarding late Greek and Roman writers is perhaps to be found in the complications introduced by religious controversy into literary composition. Anyone who has read Harnack's introduction to his *Geschichte der altchristlichen Literatur* needs no further illustration. In his clear, unpretentious way, Harnack indicated the main factors of that process of deception and forgery – *Täuschung und Fälschung* – which polluted Roman and Greek literature after the third century under the impact of religious controversy. Orthodoxy with its faithful follower, persecution, encouraged literary dishonesty. No wonder that modern scholars are inclined to suspect forgery in fourth- and fifth-century documents, even in cases in which the reasons for a forgery are not immediately evident. Athanasius was accused of systematic forgery of documents by that great but erratic scholar Seeck. Eusebius' *Life of Constantine* is still the object of a lively controversy concerning both its authenticity as a whole and the authenticity of the documents included in it. The Donatist documents came under heavy fire until Duchesne rescued them, but the discussion about the authenticity of many Acts of Martyrs is still going on.

Even when we are certain of the forgery, it is sometimes difficult for us to understand the mind of the forger. Few forgeries are more glaring than the correspondence between Seneca and St Paul – though, in deference to human credulity, it must be said that I know at least one distinguished contemporary student of Christian literature who is prepared to take the correspondence as authentic. We are even reasonably certain that this correspondence was concocted in the fourth century AD, because Lactantius did not yet know of it, and St Jerome spoke of it as something made known in recent times. Yet it is almost impossible for us to enter the mind of the forger. He made Seneca and St Paul correspond about trivialities and obviously assumed that they would write to each other in Latin – and in an atrocious Latin at that. On the other hand the forger has taken some trouble about the chronology of the letters and has also utilized good sources about the fire of Rome under Nero. A mixture of naïvety, vulgarity, pedantry and roguishness distinguishes the concoction, but the ultimate motives for it are hard to perceive[1].

The so-called *Historia Augusta* is not a Christian product – indeed it is a remarkable document of the dying Paganism. But it cannot be examined in isolation – it must be related to what I should like to call the unstable standards of honesty of the late Greek and Roman writers. Theirs was an age of forgeries, interpolations, false attributions, tendentious interpretations. It would be surprising if the *Historia Augusta* should turn out to be more honest than the literary standards of the time required. The student of the *Historia Augusta* is bound to keep in mind that he is dealing with the product of an unhealthy age, but on the other hand he should be aware that in philology, as much as in a law court, the worst mistakes are made when vague suspicions take the place of precise evidence. The *Historia Augusta* was written in an age which was disposed to forgeries, but the *Ecclesiastical History* of Eusebius, if nothing else, shows that in the fourth century there were still people capable of collecting authentic evidence. Furthermore the critical problem of the *Historia Augusta* was first formulated by Hermann Dessau in 1889, when scholars were ready to suspect dishonesty behind any writer of late Antiquity. It is one of the difficulties in dealing with the *Historia Augusta* that we must constantly refer to the conflicting standards of two ages which were so different in matters of scientific integrity: the fourth century AD and the nineteenth century[2].

It is well known that *Historia Augusta* is a title given in modern times – I believe by Casaubon – to a collection of biographies of Roman emperors, caesars, usurpers for the period from Hadrian inclusive to Diocletian exclusive (117–284 AD). The present text is not complete. There is a certain lacuna for the years 244–59. Another lacuna may be suspected at the beginning, which is very abrupt. The authors profess to be admirers of Suetonius. If the collection originally included the biographies of Nerva and Trajan (besides a proemium) it would have continued Suetonius' work. But so far no certain trace of these allegedly lost biographies of Nerva and Trajan has been discovered. About twenty years ago Jan W. Crous, whom many of us affectionately remember as the kind and learned librarian of the German Institute of Archaeology in Rome, thought he had found fragments of lost biographies in a sixteenth-century antiquarian, Bartolomeo Marliani, author of an *Urbis Romae Topographia*[3]. A young Italian scholar, Guido Barbieri, soon proved that Marliani's quotations were not reliable[4].

According to the manuscript tradition the biographies were written by six different authors who lived in the time of Diocletian and Constantine. Some of the biographies are dedicated to Diocletian, some to Constantine, and some to private persons. Four of the authors – Aelius Spartianus, Julius Capitolinus, Vulcacius Gallicanus, Aelius Lampridius – say that they have written more biographies than those appearing in our present compilations. Indeed, Spartianus and Gallicanus announce in three complex statements their intention to write the biographies of all the emperors after Julius Caesar (*Hel.* 1, 1; 7, 5; *Avid.* 3, 3). Only two authors, Trebellius Pollio and Flavius Vopiscus, apparently never wrote more than the extant biographies which form the last portion of the *corpus* from Philip the Arab to Carus, Carinus and Numerianus. If we take this evidence *prima facie*, it follows that somebody must have chosen from among the biographies of the first four authors those which seemed worthy to be included in the present *Historia Augusta*: it does not follow of course that the editor should be identical either with Trebellius Pollio or with Flavius Vopiscus, the two writers who completed the series. It is important to keep in mind that the *prima facie* evidence about our present collection points to the existence of an editor, but does not make it clear whether the editor has to be conceived as a contemporary of the authors, and possibly one of them, or as some other person who lived later. The distribution of the biographies among the first four authors does not follow any clear order: Aelius Spartianus, for instance, appears to have written the lives of Hadrian, Didius Julianus and Septimius Severus, but Julius Capitolinus wrote the lives of Antoninus Pius, Marcus Aurelius and Pertinax. Vulcacius Gallicanus composed (his only contribution) the life of Avidius Cassius, and Aelius Lampridius wrote the biographies of Commodus, Elagabalus and Severus Alexander. One can of course dispute the attribution of individual lives with the help of various arguments, but the general picture of disorder will not be modified. Nor is any clear order to be found in the dedications to the emperors. Aelius Spartianus dedicates the life of Septimius Severus to Diocletian (20, 4), and the life of Geta to Constantine. Vulcacius Gallicanus dedicates his only biography to Diocletian, and Aelius Lampridius expressly states that one of his biographies, that of Elagabalus, was written by command of the emperor Constantine. The same Lampridius, we may remind ourselves, is given as the author of the idealized life of Severus Alexander, which would therefore be dated in the time of Constantine and written under the benevolent eye of the imperial convert.

Now modern critics claim to have discovered two different, though related, types of forgery in the *Historia Augusta*. The first type of forgery is plain enough and will not detain us long. The *Historia Augusta* follows Suetonius' model also in this, that it quotes documents extensively. There are about 130 documents, the majority of which are letters by emperors and other grandees. *Senatus consulta* and senatorial acclamations amount to twenty, and there are ten inscriptions. These documents are unevenly distributed[5]. The lives attributed to Spartianus have only three documents, and all of them are in the life of Pescennius Niger. The lives of important emperors, such as Hadrian and Septimius Severus, do not contain any document. Lampridius produces nine documents. Vulcacius manages to accumulate eleven in the life of Avidius Cassius. Even more remarkable is the case of Capitolinus. He has no document in his lives of Antoninus Pius, Marcus Aurelius, Lucius Verus and Pertinax, but more than forty documents in the lives of the second group beginning with Clodius Albinus and including the two Maximini and the three Gordiani. Trebellius has seventeen documents, but Vopiscus reaches the number of forty-four. It is enough to visualize this situation as a whole to become suspicious. The lives of the emperors about whom there was much to say contain no documents. The lives of little known emperors and even less known usurpers and members of the imperial household are filled with documents. This is a sign either of great diligence or of great dishonesty. It turns out to be a sign of great dishonesty. A closer analysis of the documents themselves proves that the majority of them cannot be authentic. It may be debated whether the majority of the documents have been forged by the authors of the *Historia Augusta* or by their sources, but forged they are. These pseudo-documents serve to fill up too meagre biographies. Their purpose is not to give facts, but to make up for the absence of facts. The *Scriptores Historiae Augustae* have no great taste for honest research[6].

Thus the *Historia Augusta* stands convicted of an extensive use of forged documents. Our question, however, is another. Must we also believe that the *Historia Augusta* as a whole is a forgery of a later age, the product of one or more writers who lived later than Diocletian and Constantine and yet wanted to pass themselves off as contemporaries of these emperors? What is called the problem of the *Historia Augusta* is not concerned with the forgery of documents in the *Historia Augusta*, but with the alleged forgery of the whole *Historia Augusta*. We have been asked to decide whether the six individuals whose names I have mentioned wrote the *Historia Augusta* under Diocletian or Constantine, as they claim to have done, or whether the *Historia Augusta* was written later, under Constantius II or Julian or Theodosius or even in the sixth century, by one or more individuals whose real names we do not know and who pretended to be contemporaries of Diocletian and Constantine.

At this point I should perhaps make two remarks. The first is about the word forgery in connection with the *Historia Augusta*. The majority of studies on the *Historia Augusta* have been written in German. German scholars often use the word *Fälschung* to describe the *Historia Augusta*. Italian being my own language, I do not feel competent to decide whether what they mean by *Fälschung* is in every case what English scholars would mean by forgery. All that I can do is to explain that for the purpose of this lecture I shall assume that you believe the *Historia Augusta* to be a forgery or *Fälschung*, if you believe that the *Historia Augusta* was written after Constantine by one (or more) people who intended to deceive the readers about the authorship and the time of composition of the *Historia Augusta* – and therefore probably attributed his (or their) own work to six imaginary writers of the time of Diocletian and Constantine. But I shall assume that you do not believe the *Historia Augusta* to be a forgery if you believe that it was written under Constantine by one or more people who concealed their identity and the true date of composition of their work. The reason for this distinction is, of course, that if you admit a date of composition under Constantine it becomes too difficult (at least for me) to draw a line between details introduced into the text with intent to deceive and features (such as anachronisms) unintentionally resulting from changes introduced into the text at a later stage by the authors themselves or by an editor.

Secondly, I may say that I felt some hesitation about choosing the *Historia Augusta* as a subject for a lecture in this series on forgeries. I am not unaware that the University of London, indeed my College, is proud to number among its Emeriti Professors the greatest living authority on the *Historia Augusta*, Norman Baynes. It is only too obvious that I cannot claim any comparable competence in this question. On the other hand the subject of the *Historia Augusta* is particularly suitable for discussion in a course on forgeries because, at least to my mind, it is still an open question whether the *Historia Augusta* is a forgery or not. In cases of indisputable forgeries we can look clever and talk as if nothing were more obvious. In the case of the *Historia Augusta* one has to make up one's mind for oneself. We are not talking about a *res iudicata*, but about a *res iudicanda*. The process of detecting the forgery, if any, is not yet concluded. Just because much depends on the choice we are going to make, we shall be wise not to commit ourselves until we are satisfied that our choice is a sound one. The *Historia Augusta* is not only our most important source for Roman history from Hadrian to Diocletian, but also a significant document of late Roman religious and political thought. It makes a great difference whether the authors, however unreliable they may be in the matter of documents, wrote under Diocletian and Constantine or half a century or a century later. Nowadays forgeries have become respectable. They are supposed to express the '*Weltanschauung*' of the forger. No doubt they do. But there remains some difference between the '*Weltanschauung*' of the man who wants to conceal his own identity, and the '*Weltanschauung*' of the man who does not. It is therefore necessary to suspend judgment until conclusive evidence is adduced in one sense or in another. The discussion of the *Historia Augusta* provides a classic example of a discussion in progress about forgeries. In this discussion I can perhaps claim the distinction, which must be almost unique among the students of the *Historia Augusta*, of not having any theory to propound about it. I have not found it either necessary or possible to formulate any new theory. What I think I can do is to apply to the study of the *Historia Augusta* the method of Simple Simon – who, when he had no penny, told the pieman that he had not any. Too many of the arguments which have been offered, especially in very recent years, about the *Historia Augusta* are imaginary pennies.

In 1889, Dessau contended, as is well known, that the *Historia Augusta* was not written in the time of Diocletian and Constantine, but in the time of Theodosius[7]. He also thought that the uniformity in phraseology and stylistic devices pointed to the conclusion that there was only one author behind the six names of the alleged biographers. Dessau's article is a recognized masterpiece. Its critical acumen still remains unsurpassed. As might be expected, Dessau immediately found an ally in that great man Otto Seeck, who never believed anything to be authentic if he could help it. Seeck produced arguments which would lead to an even later date, about 407[8]. But it is significant that another even greater man was only half convinced. Theodor Mommsen, whose pupil Dessau was, refused to believe that the *Historia Augusta* was anything else than a compilation written under Diocletian and Constantine. He only conceded later additions and a general revision at the end of the fourth century[9]. Still more sceptical was Hermann Peter who, as an editor of the text and a general student of historiography, was among the people best qualified to judge. He simply dismissed both Dessau and Seeck and argued that the collection was closed about 330[10]. In his conservative attitude he was helped by the analysis of language and style produced by E. Wölfflin and E. Klebs. One point seems to have been made probable by Wölfflin and Klebs – that the biographies were written by more than one author[11].

This was enough to open the gates to the flood of philological industry. The theories either extreme or compromising which have been formulated in the last sixty years make a library, not necessarily one of special attraction to book-lovers.

Four groups of researchers seem to emerge from this flood. The first group is that of Domaszewski and his school. Domaszewski tried to demonstrate that the *Historia Augusta* was written in the late sixth century, and that the author was born in Gaul and more precisely at Nîmes. His theory belongs to the merry curiosities of classical scholarship[12]. But Domaszewski, if often strange, was never foolish. His analysis of what the *Historia Augusta* has to say about the topography of Rome, personal names, political institutions and so on, is useful. Two other groups are more conventional in their respect for common sense. One is the group of the frank conservatives which is headed by De Sanctis in Italy and Lécrivain in France[13]. It can be said that De Sanctis' article of 1896 succeeded in exploding the majority of Dessau's and Seeck's original arguments[14]. The other group has rallied round N. H. Baynes' famous little book, *The Historia Augusta, its Date and Purpose* (1926). Baynes argued that the *Historia Augusta* was composed under the emperor Julian about the years 362–3, and was designed as propaganda to help the constitutional and religious programme of the Apostate. Baynes persuaded two such eminent students as Hohl and Ensslin[15]. Indeed the conversion of Hohl, a man of unique knowledge of the *Historia Augusta*, from Dessau's theory to Baynes' almost implied the establishment of Baynes' theory as the norm of orthodoxy. The fourth group is one that I mention with mixed feelings. It collects the most recent students of the *Historia Augusta* and follows the distant leadership of Seeck. One of this group, W. Hartke, tried to prove in 1940 that the five hundred pages or so of the *Historia Augusta*'s admittedly bad Latin were written in about three months towards the end of 394 AD. The *Historia Augusta*, in his view, was composed by a member of Symmachus' pagan circle, more precisely by Nicomachus Flavianus junior, to prepare a reconciliation between Theodosius and the pagan followers of the defeated usurper Eugenius[16]. The *terminus post quem* but not the *terminus ante quem* of Hartke was accepted by J. Straub in a book which appeared in 1952[17], while that acute scholar S. Mazzarino had shown himself in general sympathy with this date[18]. My mixed feelings are explained by the fact that Hartke has published another far bigger book to support his earlier date. The new book, *Römische Kinderkaiser*, though it appeared as late as 1951, has already become a classic example of how real learning can be frustrated by obscurity of thought and inclination to mystical formulas. Hartke now examines the *Historia Augusta* as a document of '*querschnittlich-akausale Denkform*'. He thinks that the *Historia Augusta* has no sense of time and so on. It may remain uncertain whether Hartke's formulas have any meaning[19]. But I am quite certain that they have no bearing on the question whether the *Historia Augusta* is a forgery or not. A fifth line of approach has just been announced by H. Stern in the latest issue of the *Revue des Études Latines*. He writes an article to suggest that the *Historia Augusta* is a forgery meant to please one of Constantine's sons, Constantius II, and promises a book to prove his suggestion[20].

In examining the evidence one is compelled to make a selection among the innumerable arguments for a post-Constantinian date which have been introduced into the question since Dessau's article. The choice is inevitably subjective and can do great injustice to some important argument. All that I can say is that I have gone through the literature on the *Historia Augusta* twice in my life – the first time sixteen years ago, when I gave a course of lectures on this subject in the University of Turin, and then again in recent months. The arguments that impressed me in 1937 are still (with one addition) the arguments that impress me now. They are seven altogether, and I propose to examine them briefly in order of cogency. It will by now be apparent that on one point my disagreement with Baynes is radical. In 1926 he thought that Dessau had definitely proved that the biographies cannot have been written at the time when they purported to have been composed. He did not believe that all the biographies had been written by one author, but accepted Dessau's main contention that the writers (whatever their number and names) had written after Constantine and assumed false personalities. Baynes' only concern was with that part of Dessau's thesis which would attribute the compilation to a date later than 363 AD. He admitted the forgery and tried to date it about 363. It seems to me that the basic question is still whether the *Historia Augusta* was written before or after the death of Constantine. In comparison with this vital point it becomes secondary (though by no means insignificant) whether the forgery, once admitted, should be dated in 354 or in 363 or thirty years later. Arguments tending to prove that the *Historia Augusta* was written in the age of Constantius II and Julian will therefore be discussed here together with the arguments for the Theodosian or post-Theodosian date. As has been explained before, it is not the aim of this paper to discuss whether the *Historia Augusta* was written under Constantine with intent to deceive. We shall discuss the question of the date, not the questions of the number and truthfulness of the authors.

I shall begin with what seems to me the strongest single argument for a post-Constantinian date and, by implication, for a forgery. It is a well-known fact that there is a close correspondence between the life of the Emperor Septimius Severus (17–19) and Aurelius Victor, *de Caesaribus* (Ch. 20). This similarity can be interpreted either as direct dependence of the *Historia Augusta* upon Aurelius Victor, or as due to a common source: the derivation of Aurelius Victor from the *Historia Augusta* is made extremely unlikely by the general method of composition of Aurelius Victor. If the direct dependence of the *Historia Augusta* on Aurelius Victor is proved it means that at least some sections of the *Historia Augusta* were written after 360, which is the date of Aurelius Victor. I have repeatedly examined the two texts, and it seems to me clear that *prima facie* the *Historia Augusta* appears to depend on Aurelius Victor though on this hypothesis certain additions in the *Historia Augusta* remain unexplained. This might seem to settle the matter. If the *Historia Augusta* utilized Aurelius Victor, it must have been written after 360 and therefore was not compiled under Diocletian and Constantine as it purported to be. Unfortunately, things are not so simple. Not that I seriously believe that the passage in question of the life of Septimius Severus was interpolated from Aurelius Victor much after the final composition of the *Historia Augusta*: the passage cannot be easily extracted from its context. But there are three other facts to consider: (1) In other cases the *Historia Augusta* and Aurelius Victor undoubtedly depend on a common source. (2) We are simply not in a position to compare the *Historia Augusta* and Aurelius Victor with this common source because the common source has not survived. We can therefore see all that is in favour of the thesis that the *Historia Augusta* used Aurelius Victor, but we are materially prevented from seeing all that is in favour of the thesis that the *Historia Augusta* and Aurelius Victor copied the same source. The present state of the evidence does not allow us to form an opinion with full knowledge of the facts. (3) It is now commonly admitted (for instance by Leo and Baynes) that in the case of an analogous but not quite so close correspondence between the *Historia Augusta* and Eutropius, a common source is the better explanation. There is a difference only of degree between the case concerning Eutropius who wrote after 364, and therefore would exclude the Julianic date, and the case concerning Aurelius Victor, who allows the theory of a Julianic date to stand. Baynes himself admits with exemplary fairness that his case is weakened by the fact that he attributed probatory value to the correspondence between the *Historia Augusta* and Aurelius Victor, but not to the correspondence between the *Historia Augusta* (Marc. 16, 3–

18, 2) and Eutropius (VIII, 11–14). I gladly admit that *prima facie* the *Historia Augusta* is shown to be later than Aurelius Victor, but before we proceed to build theories on this assumption, a word of caution is not superfluous[21].

I put next in importance a very good argument recently produced by Mazzarino. The life of Severus Alexander (chapter 39) speaks of coins called *tremisses* which were one-third of the aureus. Coins called *tremisses* worth exactly one-third of the solidus were struck by Theodosius. Thence the conclusion that the life of Severus Alexander contains a clear anachronism referable to the age of Theodosius. Here again things are not so simple. As I am no numismatist, I must apply to numismatic authorities. Mr R. A. G. Carson of the British Museum, who is preparing a catalogue of Severus Alexander coins, was kind enough to tell me that he is 'not altogether convinced that the mention of this denomination is completely the anachronism which most people take it to be. For Trebonianus Gallus there is certainly a two-third aureus, and under Valerian and Gallienus there is what may well be a third. These pieces are by weight close to a third of the aureus, and they are mentioned in *S.H.A.*, XXV, 17, 7.' So, according to Mr Carson, there is after all the possibility that the *tremisses* mentioned by the *Historia Augusta* were in fact third-century coins. Furthermore, I understand from Dr G. Elmer's article in *Deutsche Münzblätter*, 1935, that on the one hand we do not know when the name *tremissis* came into circulation, and on the other hand we do not know the name of the 1½ scripula coin of Constantine which, though not exactly one-third of the solidus, was not very far from it. If so, I do not see how one can exclude the possibility that the smallest gold denomination of Constantine was called *tremissis*. Finally, recent scholars seem to have forgotten that there is a mention of the *tremissis* in the so-called *Liber de asse* 15 (II, 74 Hultsch) – the numismatic tract made known in 1525. I have no opinion about the date of the *Liber de asse*. But I am bound to note that I have never seen it dated later than Constantine. In view of these uncertainties, I propose to consider the argument of Mazzarino as important but not decisive. It does not seem to me to be proven that the word *tremissis* was coined in the time of Theodosius, which is the necessary presupposition for the absolute validity of this argument.

I put third the argument about the genealogy of the emperor Claudius Gothicus which seemed decisive to Dessau. In certain biographies by Trebellius Pollio which are supposed to have been written before 305 the emperor Claudius Gothicus is celebrated as an ancestor of Constantine. But in 310 the official panegyrist of Constantine mentioned the descent from Claudius Gothicus as something which only few people knew and which he was going to reveal for the first time to the public[22]. Here there is certainly something odd. The descent from Claudius Gothicus was first divulged in 310, but the *Historia Augusta* gives it as well known before 305. After careful reflection I must agree with Mommsen and De Sanctis that this argument is not so serious as it looks at first[23]. The Panegyric establishes the fact that the descent from Claudius was officially accepted and broadcast in 310, but does not exclude the possibility that a few years before the same tradition was circulated by Trebellius Pollio. There is furthermore the possibility of a later editing of the *Historia Augusta* during the time of Constantine[24]. It will be admitted that the interest in Claudius Gothicus as the alleged ancestor of Constantine must have been greater under Constantine than later. Though, as Hirschfeld has shown, one can make a case for a dynastic interest in this tradition until the death of Gratian in 383[25], it seems to me that the use of Claudius Gothicus in the *Historia Augusta* smacks of the age of Constantine. I am therefore reluctant to take as conclusive evidence of a later date, and by implication of forgery, the conflict of evidence between the *Historia Augusta* and the Panegyrics. This is the third argument that I take to be in favour of the forgery, but not decisive.

I pass now to three arguments which I rate at less value than the former. I take first what Baynes considered to be the strongest individual argument in favour of his Julianic date. This is the so-called Ctesiphon oracle. It is to be found in chapter 9 of the life of Carus and says:

> This letter I have inserted for the reason that many declare that there is a certain decree of Fate that no Roman emperor may advance beyond Ctesiphon, and that Carus was struck by lightning because he desired to pass beyond the bounds which Fate has set up. But let cowardice, on which courage should set its heel, keep its devices for itself. For clearly it is granted to us and will always be granted, as our most venerated Caesar Maximian has shown, to conquer the Persians and advance beyond them, and methinks this will surely come to pass if only our men fail not to live up to the promised favour of Heaven'[26].

Here there is a sort of prophecy of a future victorious war of the

Romans against Persia. It is taken by Baynes to be an allusion to Julian's expedition against Persia. On the other hand Straub considers it to be a clear allusion to the times of Honorius and Arcadius. To my mind, it may allude to anything – or to nothing. I cannot derive any argument from this oracle. Any patriotic Roman could say at any moment: 'If we are brave, we shall go beyond Ctesiphon.'

Another argument, to which Mommsen lent his authority and which I consider very difficult to assess fairly, is found in another oracle contained in the life of Probus. The prophecy is that future generations of the family of Probus will rise to such distinction in the Senate that they will hold all the highest posts. The writer of the biography comments on this oracle in the following way (24, 1–3): 'We have not yet seen any (of these consuls). But after all, it would seem that the future generations are unlimited in time and not a definite number.' '*Sed adhuc neminem vidimus, posteri autem aeternitatem videntur habere, non modum.*' This is obviously said in a satirical vein, and I cannot see the point of the joke on '*aeternitas*' unless it was true, when the author wrote, that the prophecy had not yet been fulfilled.

Now the *Historia Augusta* connects the family of the descendants of the emperor Probus with Verona (24, 1). The family of the great Sextus Petronius Probus, consul in 371, was connected with Verona (*CIL* V, 3344 = *ILS* 1266). It is therefore fairly certain that the *Historia Augusta* assumed (rightly or wrongly) that the family of Probus, consul 371, descended from the emperor Probus. But the family of the consul in 371 was eminent throughout the fourth century. Petronius Probianus and Petronius Probinus were consuls respectively in 322 and 341: and it is assumed by modern scholars with a considerable degree of probability that Pompeius Probus, consul in 310, belonged to the same family. Any of these people may have claimed (or been credited with) descent from the emperor Probus. If there is anything to be deduced from the comment on the prophecy it is that it was written before 322, or possibly before 310, when no member of this family had yet become a consul, though the family itself was already much in the public eye.

As this conclusion may seem outrageous, some further remarks are not superfluous:

(*a*) If the writer wanted to flatter the Probi after they had already filled several consulships, his witticism would have been in doubtful taste.

(*b*) The *Historia Augusta* plays with oracles. There is at least one oracle that nobody has ever dared to take as a chronological argument. It is the oracle contained in the life of the emperor Tacitus. A descendant of this emperor will live 120 years, will extend Roman rule to most mysterious places – perhaps Ireland and Ceylon – and, finally, will hand over the government of the State to the Roman Senate. Here, too, the *Historia Augusta* has an ironical remark similar to that in the life of Probus: 'It showed no great skill, indeed, on the soothsayers' part to declare that such a prince would come after an interval of one thousand years . . . ' (15). It is clear from this passage that the *Historia Augusta* was not invariably concerned with prophecies *post eventum*.

(*c*) Of course, nobody likes *real* prophets. But in the age of Constantine a new aristocracy began to consolidate. A contemporary (*ex hypothesi* not the author of the life of Probus who did not believe in the prophecy) could venture guesses about the future fortunes of certain prominent families without undue risks. It cannot have been very difficult to single out a few families with a future. This applies also to the passage about the family of the Ceionii in the life of Albinus. A Ceionius Albinus was a city prefect in 335 AD; and Julian, who was born in 331, belonged, on his mother's side, to the Ceionian family, if we accept Seeck's conjecture. Thus anyone could say of this family '*per te aucta et augenda*' with reference to Constantine's favour (4, 2).

(*d*) Suppose, however, that we have to do with a prophecy *post eventum*. I do not see why we should necessarily date it after 360 or 370. Even a prophet *post eventum* may have believed (rightly or wrongly) that the consuls of 310 and 322 belonged to the same family. The prophecy on the Probi, even as a prophecy *post eventum*, need not be later than *c.* 322[27]. Admittedly, an allusion to the great consul Probus and to his sons would be the best interpretation of the prophecy as a prophecy *post eventum*. But we are bound in fairness to consider the other possibilities: that the oracle is not a prophecy *post eventum* or that it is a prophecy *post eventum* not alluding to the consul of 371.

The third argument of this second series is the *nomen Antoninorum*. Since G. Tropea noticed that the *Historia Augusta* attributes great importance to the Antonines it has become necessary to explain why these emperors of the second century fill a conspicuous place in the mind of the author or authors of the *Historia Augusta*[28]. Baynes' explanation is perfectly adequate in itself. The emperor Julian was a great admirer of Marcus Aurelius, and the *Historia Augusta* would try to please him by celebrating the Antonine dynasty. But I am not sure that any special explanation is needed. Antoninus Pius and Marcus Aurelius were certainly model emperors for any one of their successors. Diocletian apparently gave himself the cognomen Aurelius to honour Marcus Aurelius and referred to him as '*Divus Marcus, pater noster, religiosissimus imperator*' (*Cod. Iust.* V, 17, 5). Under Constantine himself one of his panegyrists referred to Antoninus imperator '*in toga praestans et non iners nec futtilis bello*' (IV [X], 24, 6). This Antoninus must be Marcus Aurelius rather than Lucius Verus. Antoninus Pius and Marcus Aurelius were still the ideal emperors at the end of the fourth century well after Julian: Symmachus speaks of '*bonus Nerva, Traianus strenuus, Pius innocens, Marcus plenus officii*' (*Ep.* I, 13). If the *Historia Augusta* in the life of Elagabalus states that Constantine had great respect for Pius and Marcus, this may be simply true (2, 4). I cannot recognize any argument for a post-Constantinian date in the insistence on the *nomen Antoninorum*.

I have left to the last an argument which I consider very important but difficult to evaluate exactly. Contrary to the other arguments, it is a cumulative one. I allude to Baynes' theory that the biography of Severus Alexander is written to a considerable extent with Julian the Apostate in mind: in fact many details would be true only if referred to Julian. The biography of Severus Alexander in his view is an idealized biography of Julian. I have tried to examine all the points of resemblance, first taking each of them in isolation and then assessing their cumulative effect. I must admit that I have been impressed to some extent by the cumulative force of the details assembled by Baynes. Yet I am not prepared to consider the resemblance between the real Julian and the ideal Severus Alexander as sufficient proof that the *Historia Augusta* was written under Julian or later. In some cases what is common is a mere commonplace of the fourth-century description of good kings. As Baynes saw, '*condemnationes perraras esse iussit, at quae factae fuerant non indulsit*' (*Alex. Sev.* 21, 1) applies to Julian as well as to Severus Alexander. But also mild Marcus Aurelius knew, according to the *Historia Augusta* (24, 1), how to remain '*contra manifestos et gravium criminum reos inexorabilis*'. Claudian reminds us (xvii, *Paneg. d. Manlio Theodoro Consuli* 227–9) that

dis proximus ille
quem ratio, non ira movet, qui facta rependens
consilio punire potest.

In other cases what is common is not the specific point, but a general tendency common to both individuals. For instance both Severus Alexander and Julian are described as favourable to the Jews, but we do not know that Julian was ever insulted as '*Syrus archisynagogus*' which is what the *Historia Augusta* says of Severus Alexander. In other cases the analysis must perhaps take into account more factors than Baynes seems ready to allow. Baynes is justifiably struck by the fact that both Julian and Severus Alexander are said to have had a strong and virile body, sparkling eyes showing power of mind and an exceptional memory. As Baynes says, 'the three characteristic features noted in Alexander by Lampridius are all noticed as characteristic of Julian by Ammian'. But a strong and handsome body, bright eyes and the gift of an uncommon memory were qualities often mentioned in Late Antiquity to denote what L. Bieler rather loosely, though effectively, has described as the θεῖος ἀνήρ, the superman of the age[29]. So the distinguished sophist Chrysanthius is described by Eunapius as possessing an untiring and even adamantine body, great memory, 'eyes testifying that the soul within him was leaping and dancing around the opinions he expressed' (502). The *Historia Augusta* gives great attention to the description of physical and mental qualities according to contemporary handbooks of physiognomy. Just because it gives all these details, it makes a pretence of contempt for them. 'It would be too long to include every trivial thing and tiresome to tell of his stature, his person, his comeliness, or how much he could eat and drink. Let others describe these things.' (*Quadr. Tyr.* 11, 4). The unusual length and idealization of the biography of Severus Alexander is certainly something to be accounted for. But the question concerning us here is only whether the interpretation of the biography of Severus Alexander as a disguised panegyric of Julian is either necessary or satisfactory or both. All things considered, my answer is that it is neither necessary nor satisfactory[30].

The net result of my cursory analysis of the seven arguments is that three or possibly four of them are signs of a post-Constantinian date and, by implication, of forgery. The question, however, is whether these signs are evident and numerous enough to put the forgery beyond doubt, and, if so, to date it. There is obviously a disproportion between the claim that about five hundred pages have been forged and the existence of a few very suspicious passages. Of course, nobody in his senses will deny that the circumstances of the composition of the *Historia Augusta* are obscure. Some of the statements the alleged authors make about themselves are certainly mischievous (the *locus classicus* is *Aurel.* 1) and perhaps purposely misleading. On the other hand certain matters that now look mysterious may have been explained in the proemium, if the *Historia Augusta* ever had one[31]. Furthermore, *ex hypothesi* the alleged writers composed their biographies in uncertain places and circumstances at various moments between, say, 285 and 337 AD and had plenty of time to revise what they wrote, if they cared, before the present collection of biographies was put together. The very fact that we must almost inevitably assume an editor (either inside the group of the original writers or outside it) represents by itself a complication. The editor *may*, for instance, have added the sentence of *Gallien.* 6, 9, '*nulla vetus familia apud Byzantios invenitur*', if this is a jibe at the Constantinian senate, which is by no means certain[32]. When one considers how many unknown factors there are in the so-called question of the *Historia Augusta* one wonders even more whether one is entitled to make capital out of a few passages and to elaborate theories presupposing (rather than demonstrating) that the *Historia Augusta* was composed under Julian or under Theodosius or later.

The answer to this question is made more difficult by other considerations. Though a new aristocracy came into being, the fourth century remains a typical period of grave political and economic changes. Money changed value rapidly, dynasties replaced each other, barbarians and Christians were on the ascendant, the administration of the State was by no means stabilized by Constantine's reforms. When Dessau and Seeck started the new epoch in the study of the *Historia Augusta* they were confident that they could show traces of post-Constantinian families and institutions in the *Historia Augusta.* Later writers showed the same confidence in matters of topography, coinage and religious ideas. Yet I think everyone would now admit that the supporters of the theory of forgery are at their weakest when they produce arguments from political institutions[33], religious ideas, the topography of Rome, or economic changes[34].

The attempt to find post-Constantinian anachronisms in the title

Francicus falsely attributed to Probus (*Prob.* 11, 9) and in the invention of a *praefectus Illyrici et Galliarum* for the third century (*Tyr. trig.* 18, 5) becomes less impressive when one remembers that the institution of *Ludi Francici* probably belongs to the Constantinian age (*CIL.* 1^2, p. 268) and that the regional *praefecti* were created by Constantine[35]. These are anachronisms, but not necessarily post-Constantinian anachronisms.

In one emphatic passage the *Historia Augusta* calls the prefect of the city of Rome *praefectus urbis Romae* instead of saying simply *praefectus urbi(s)* (*Valer.* 6, 6). It has been suggested that the writer thus betrays his knowledge of the existence of another *praefectus urbi*: the prefect of the city of Constantinople, who was created in 359. This is an attractive argument. But the proposer did not notice that an inscription of Rome (*CIL.* VI, 1696) calls *praefectus urbis Romae* the prefect of Rome of 307 AD – about fifty years before the creation of the prefect of Constantinople. This disposes of the argument and incidentally shows that *praefectus urbis Romae* is excellent Constantinian terminology.

In two letters which are certainly forged, the emperor Valerian addresses as 'father', *parens*, two of his close collaborators – more precisely a regional *praefectus* and a *praefectus urbi* (*Tyr. trig.* 18, 5; *Aurel.* 9, 6). It has been observed that there is no other extant example of an emperor addressing a *praefectus urbi* as *parens* before *c.* 370. Consequently it has been inferred: (*a*) that the emperor Valentinian was the first to use this formula about 370; (*b*) that the *Historia Augusta* imitated the terminology introduced by the emperor Valentinian. It is evident that both inferences are arbitrary. Three centuries before Valentinian, Nero greeted his general Corbulo as 'father', and then killed him (Cassius Dio 63, 17). If one prefers a fourth-century example, the son of Constantine, Constantius, embraced the ex-rebel Vetranio and called him 'father' (Zonar. 13, 7). Nobody can seriously believe that it was only in about 370 that *parens* was first used by an emperor addressing his close collaborators.

A regulation attributed to Severus Alexander allows the senators to lend money, but at a rate of interest not higher than six per cent (*Alex. Sev.* 26, 3). It has been suggested that Severus Alexander never enacted this regulation and that one must see the model of it in a law of 405 AD (*Cod. Theod.* ii, 33, 4). I am not concerned with the point whether the regulation can be attributed to Severus Alexander. But who will believe that the question of allowing senators to lend money at a stated rate of interest was never raised before 405 AD? Generally speaking, even if it were proved that a law mentioned by the *Historia Augusta* and similar to authentic legislation of the fourth and fifth centuries was fictitious, one could not yet take it for certain that the fictitious law was modelled on the authentic legislation of the fourth or fifth centuries. The *Historia Augusta* (or its sources) may have anticipated authentic legislation. Such projects may be in the air for a long time before being embodied in actual legislation.

As great an authority as J. Geffcken tried to show that the religious atmosphere of the *Historia Augusta* is that of the second half of the fourth century rather than that of the first half[36]. He was later supported by H. Mattingly[37]. I confess that their arguments seem to me so inconclusive that I would find it difficult to discuss them in detail. It is significant that a cautious critic like Baynes has almost entirely avoided using political and religious institutions, coins, topography to prove his case in favour of the Julianic date. Now this is obviously serious. Anyone can avoid the name of Constantinople, even writing fifty years after the foundation of Constantinople, if he chooses to deceive. But the *Historia Augusta* apparently manages to avoid hundreds of pitfalls. None of the prominent features of the period between 330 and 380 AD – such as the struggles inside the Christian Church, Julian's apostasy, the Germanic menace, the abandonment of Rome – seems to have left a clear mark on the *Historia Augusta*. But the religious, dynastic and economic problems of the Constantinian period are somehow present. Is this a sign of extreme competence in forgery or the simple result of the fact that the authors were not writing after Constantine? Why did they commit what we would call Constantinian anachronisms but apparently avoid post-Constantinian ones? Is it likely that the author(s) were unsubtle forgers of documents, but clever composer(s) of the context? I wonder. The fact that the author(s) are not well informed about the details of the history of the late third century can hardly prove that they wrote in the late fourth century. It is at least arguable that lazy and irresponsible people find it more difficult to inform themselves about almost contemporary events than about those of which authoritative accounts already exist.

Whether one ultimately decides for a post-Constantinian forgery or not, the difficulty of deciding can perhaps throw some light on the nature of the *Historia Augusta*. If the *Historia Augusta* had a definite axe to grind, as Baynes or Hartke believe, the forgery would probably be easier to discover. Anyone who wanted to make propaganda for Julian, in 362, as Baynes suggests, or to plead clemency after Eugenius' revolt in 394, as Hartke prefers, would come more plainly into the open. Mommsen's simple question '*cui bono?*' has never been answered in a really satisfactory way. This may suggest that, whether the *Historia Augusta* is a forgery or not, it has no definite cause to support. No doubt, the *Historia Augusta* is in favour of the authority of the Senate, it has some ideas about imperial succession and more generally about good emperors; it has also a cautious preference for paganism. But I cannot see that this amounts to propaganda for anything[38]. There are eight passages about Christianity which deserve special mention. Five are in the life of Severus Alexander. One is the famous and much discussed statement that Severus Alexander had a little sanctuary of his own with the images of Apollonius of Tyana, Christ, Abraham, Orpheus and others (29, 2). The second passage says that Severus Alexander, like Hadrian, meant to build a temple to Christ and receive Him among the gods; either Severus Alexander or Hadrian (the text is not very clear) was discouraged by the haruspices (43, 6–7). The third (49, 6) refers to Alexander's answer, favourable to the Christians, in a quarrel between them and the cook-shop-keepers ('*popinarii*')[39]. Two other texts (45, 7 and 51, 7) show Alexander's sympathetic interest in Jewish and Christian rules of life. Another passage is a rather objective allusion to the Christians in an answer by Aurelian about Sibylline books (20, 4). In the biography of Pertinax (13, 5) the manuscript tradition seems to say that his enemies called him either Christologum or Chrestologum '*qui bene loqueretur et male faceret*'. If the right reading is '*Christologum*' – which seems to me most unlikely – we have here a joke founded upon the phonetic identity of χρηστός, good, and Christos. Finally, in another of the minor lives – that of Firmus and Saturninus – a strange epistle is attributed to Hadrian in which he describes Egypt as a land of frivolity and money-making. There the worshippers of Serapis are Christians, and the Christians are worshippers of Serapis. There Christians, Jews and *tutti quanti* worship money: '*Unus illis deus nummus est. Hunc Christiani, hunc Iudaei, hunc omnes venerantur et gentes*' (*Firm. Sat.* 8). The paragraph introducing this letter – an invective against the Egyptians – contains the only explicitly hostile mention of the Christians: '*Nam in eis* (the Egyptians) *Christiani, Samaritae et quibus praesentia semper tempora cum enormi libertate displiceant*' (7, 5). The Jews are left out for some reason. All that one can deduce from these passages is that the *Historia Augusta* was compiled by one or more people who would perhaps have liked Christianity to be absorbed peacefully into a pagan Roman empire and who had a mild sympathy for or at least no bitter grudge against Judaism and Christianity. They could utter an offensive remark against Christians in a moment of bad temper, but the writer of *Firmus* 7, 5 hardly took himself seriously.

True, the author of the life of Aurelian is enthusiastic about Sibylline books (19–21) and Apollonius of Tyana (24) and is consequently delighted to have Aurelian on his side in these matters. But Aurelian is not an ideal emperor in every respect: '*severus, truculentus, sanguinarius fuit princeps*' (36); '*populus eum Romanus amavit, senatus et timuit*' (50). The most idealized emperors – Claudius, Tacitus, Probus – are not conspicuous for religious activities. A few short passages are all that the *Historia Augusta* has to offer on Christianity out of five hundred pages. This is very little indeed. Clearly Christianity was not the main concern of the author or authors of the *Historia Augusta* taken as a whole[40].

Nor was imperial succession. Here two passages are especially relevant. One is in the life of Septimius Severus (20–21). Aelius Spartianus, speaking directly to Diocletian, says: 'When I reflect on the matter, Diocletian Augustus, it is quite clear to me that practically no great man has left the world a son of real excellence or value.' The second passage is in the life of Tacitus (6) – a life allegedly written by Vopiscus before the death of Diocletian. A senator, Maecius Faltonius Nicomachus, is said to have entreated the emperor Tacitus not to name his young sons 'as heirs to the Roman Empire, or bequeath to them the commonwealth, the conscript Fathers and the Roman people as you would your farm, your tenants and your slaves. . . . It is a great glory to a dying prince to love the commonwealth more than his own sons.' These passages – and many others in the same sense (for instance *Marcus* 5, 1; 18, 4; *Avid. Cass.* 2, 8; *Carac.* 11, 3; *Carus* 3, 8) – imply that adoption was better than natural succession especially when the emperor had very young sons: proven merit, not birth, was what was required in any aspirant to imperial power.

It is however remarkable that the same group of lives attributed to Vopiscus, which in some points stresses the dangers of natural succession, elsewhere celebrates the natural successors of Claudius

Gothicus (*Aurel.* 44, 5). I know of more than one acute and elaborate explanation of the contradiction between the attack on bad sons and the celebration of the descendants of Claudius Gothicus[41]. But I distrust these explanations as being too good. The author, or authors, of the *Historia* may, after all, have been people who, on the one hand, wanted to flatter the alleged descendants of Claudius Gothicus, but on the other hand disliked certain consequences of hereditary monarchy and, rightly or wrongly, thought that Diocletian shared, or had shared, their own dislike. We have seen in our own time people more muddle-headed than the *Scriptores Historiae Augustae*. Admittedly, if we were certain about the date of the *Historia Augusta*, we should also be in a better position to appreciate the point of view of the *Historia Augusta* about imperial succession. But I doubt whether we could ever say that the *Historia Augusta* was written in order to put across an opinion about imperial succession – even less in order to make propaganda for adoption against hereditary monarchy.

Prima facie, there is no religious or political motive sufficient to explain why the writer(s) of the *Historia Augusta* should conceal their names and dates. As I see it, it would be more reasonable to suggest that the author knew that he had forged many documents and quoted many non-existent authorities, and wanted to safeguard himself against awkward questions. But this too would not be, *prima facie*, a sufficient explanation. To the best of my knowledge, forgers and plagiarists normally took the risk of publishing their 'discoveries' under their own authentic names if they worked for vanity or money. Annius of Viterbo, Resende, de la Higuera, Meyranesio took this risk: de la Higuera did not expect people to go to Fulda to enquire about his own findings there. This remains true now. It must have been even more so in the fourth century AD when neither the possibility nor the habit of checking references in libraries and archives was widespread. At least two of the writers of the *Historia Augusta* (if they were more than one) give the impression of speaking with their tongues in their cheeks when they mention research and documents (*Tyr. trig.*, 33, 8; *Aur.* 1–2; *Tac.* 8; *Firmus* 2). I can hardly believe that they would take such elaborate precautions in the mere expectation that somebody might turn up in the Bibliotheca Ulpia and ask for the '*liber elephantinus*' of the '*armarium sextum*'.

I suspect that I should understand the *Historia Augusta* better if I were used to reading popular papers rather than the *Observer* and the *Spectator*. The *Historia Augusta* deals with royalty on ordinary journalistic lines: plenty of inside information, intimate details. The authors, of course, are on familiar terms with Augusti, Caesars and other grandees. They show a great concern for ancestors and descendants of emperors. But all this gossip is not to be found in a pure state. It is mixed up with relics and pretence of scholarship – a degeneration of the Suetonian biography. Furthermore, as the times were hard anyway, and one cannot always be frivolous, there is nostalgia for the good old days of the Senatorial power, there is the usual escape into oracles, ideal kings, and a golden age whether of the past or of the future variety. One would like to say a good word for the spirit of tolerance of the writer(s). But it is only too obvious that they refused to face the moral and political issues raised by Christianity. This complex attitude deserves much further study. It throws light on the decline of paganism and is not necessarily incompatible with forgery, but may perhaps explain why I am so dull as not to perceive the forgery clearly.

My conclusions are, I am afraid, disappointing:

(1) The problem of the *date* of the *Historia Augusta* has not yet been solved.

(2) A date, if independently ascertained, would probably be a pointer to the purpose or *Tendenz* of the *Historia Augusta.* But I consider it very unwise to try to proceed from an alleged purpose or *Tendenz* to the date of the *Historia Augusta,* because I cannot perceive an unmistakable purpose or *Tendenz* in the *Historia Augusta.*

(3) The claims of the *Historia Augusta* to be taken as a product of the early fourth century cannot yet be dismissed, though a passage in the life of Septimius Severus points to a date later than 360, and there are other objections to an early date[42].

(4) Personally, I feel inclined to admit that the author(s) of the *Historia Augusta* tried to conceal their identity but I cannot produce enough evidence to prove this opinion.

A negative conclusion is bound to leave the writer dissatisfied and the readers enraged. I hope, however, that my remarks may stimulate someone either to reformulate the theory of the post-Constantinian forgery in a more persuasive way or to explore more closely the implication of dating the *Historia Augusta* under Constantine.

APPENDIX 1

Note A

Cf. for instance these two passages: *H. A. Alex. Severus* 47, 1: '*milites expeditionis tempore sic disposuit ut in mansionibus annonas acciperent nec portarent cibaria decem et septem, ut solent, dierum nisi in barbarico*'. Amm. Marc. 17, 9, 2 (Julian): '*ex annona decem dierum et septem, quam in expeditionem pergens vehebat cervicibus miles, portionem subtractam in isdem condidit castris sperans ex Chamavorum segetibus id suppleri posse quod ablatum est*'. What matters is the difference (*nisi in barbarico*) not the similarity between the two passages. Another delusive passage is *Alex. Sev.* 15, 2: '*nec quemquam passus est esse in Palatinis nisi necessarium hominem*'. This can certainly be compared with Amm. Marcell. 22, 4, 10 about Julian, but *cf.* also *Anton. Pius* 7, 7: '*salaria multis subtraxit quos otiosos videbat accipere*' and *Pacati Paneg. Theodosio Augusto d.* (*Pan. Lat.* II (xii)) 13–14. As for the dislike of eunuchs (*Alex. Sev.* 66, 3; *Gord.* 25; *Aurel.* 43, 1), we have no way of knowing when they began to be powerful in the imperial household; *cf.* Hug in Pauly-Wissowa Suppl. 3, s.v. '*Eunuchen*', and E. Stein, *Geschichte des spätrömischen Reiches* I, 169, n. 1. It is perhaps worth noticing that there is a law by Constantine against castration (*Cod. Iust.* IV, 42, 1). It has also been assumed that *Cod. Theod.* VI, 4, 9 of 356 AD, fixing a *quorum* of fifty senators for the designation of praetors, was the source of *Alex. Sev.* 16 (K. Hönn, *Quellenunters. zu den Viten des Heliogabalus und des Severus Alexander* (1911) 91, followed by Baynes and Stern). But the passage of the *H.A.* implies that the quorum was of seventy, not of fifty senators; the two texts have very little in common. Two further remarks can be added on this subject. W. Seston in *Rev. Étud. Anc.* 44 (1942) pp. 224–33 (*cf.* 45, 1943, pp. 49–60) argued that *P. Fay.* 20 = Hunt-Edgar, *Select Papyri* (Loeb) II, 216 is an edict attributed to Severus Alexander by Julian ('*un faux attribuant à A.S. des mesures prises en fait par J.*') because (according to Baynes) Julian admired Severus Alexander. I confess that the idea of an emperor forging (or tampering with) a document in order to express his admiration for one of his predecessors seems to me odd. The interpretation of *P. Fay.* 20 is already difficult enough without these complications. Incidentally, my colleague E. G. Turner tells me that its writing can hardly be as late as 360. On the other hand, Stern presses his texts when he states that '*Julien a manifesté un vif mépris pour Alexandre Sévère qu'il appelle, dans le* Banquet, *Hertlein* 402, 11 *sq. un fou et un enfant*' (*Rev. Étud. Lat.* (1952) 268, n. 4). *Cf.* on all this Baynes, *Class. Quart.*, 22 (1928) pp. 166–71 and H. G. Ramsay, *L'Ant. Class.*, 4 (1935) pp. 419–48; 5 (1936) pp. 147–76. It remains, however, true that if you follow Baynes it is not easy to account for Julian's lack of sympathy for Severus Alexander, as shown in the *Caesares*.

Note B

Straub, *Studien*, p. 86, suggests that the inscription of Timesitheus in *Gordian.* 27, 10, '*parenti principum . . . tutori rei p.*', would be an imitation of the inscription of 420 AD to Fl. Constantius, '*reparatori reipublicae et parenti invictissimorum principum*' (Dessau *I.L.S.* 801). *Cf.* also Straub, '*Parens Principum*', *Nouvelle Clio* 4 (1952) 94–115. The story of Timesitheus would, however, be an imitation of the story of Stilicho. And the *H.A.* could have learnt the words '*rei publicae necessarius*' (*Aurel.* 37, 1; *Av. Cass.* 2, 7) only from Eutropius 9, 14 (*cf.* pp. 120–2). I confess to a definite feeling of irritation with Straub's way of arguing. On p. 37 he suggests that as the *H.A.* (for instance *Gallien.* 13, 9) does not explain the word *carrago* which is explained (or at least mentioned as a foreign word) by Ammian. Marcell. 31, 7, 7, the *H.A.* must be later than Ammianus. Straub himself knows of course (p. 25) that different writers have different habits of explaining unusual or foreign words. (*Cf.* Stern, *Date et destinataire*, p. 12, n. 4). As even recent studies of the *H.A.* seem to make capital out of *Heliog.* 7, 7 about Hadrianopolis, '*quam saepe cruentari hominum sanguine necesse est*', I may add that the sentence is explained well enough by the battles of 313 and 324. As for the alleged attempt to make Valerian a censor (*Valer.* 5), it is arbitrary to say that nobody could have thought of it before Symmachus. See what Cassius Dio attributed to Maecenas (52, 21, 3–5), and Mommsen, *Staatsrecht*, III, 491, n. 1, not to mention Dalmatius' censorship under Constantine (M. Besnier, *Mélanges Glotz*, I (1932) pp. 85–91). *Cf.* also E. Hohl, *Gnomon*, 26 (1954) pp. 45–50, and F. Dornseiff, *Deutsche Literaturz.*, 75 (1954) pp. 138–52 in their reviews of Straub.

NOTE C

Arguments from numismatics, to judge from K. Menadier, *Zeitschr. f. Numism.* 31 (1914) pp. 1–146, do not seem, so far, to be very successful. A good example is this. Menadier, p. 56, discussed *Gallien.*, 12: '*Odaenathum participato imperio Augustum vocavit eiusque monetam qua Persas captos traheret cudi iussit*'. He argued that this type became fashionable only with Julian and provided a '*terminus post quem*' for E. Hohl, *Bursians Jahresb.*, 171 (1915) p. 120 (*cf.* O. Th. Schulz, *Gnomon*, 6 (1930) p. 607). But Menadier himself knew that the type is already to be found earlier, and more precisely in Constantine's time (*cf.* G. Rodenwaldt, *Jahrb. Deutsch. Archaeol. Instit.* 37 (1922) p. 29, n. 4; J. M. C. Toynbee, *Roman Medallions* (1944) p. 181). Some other extraordinary numismatic arguments can be found in J. Maurice, *C. R. Acad. Inscr.* (1913) p. 208, to explain '*Illi qui Serapem colunt Christiani sunt*' of *Firm. Sat.* 8. Seeck, Pauly-Wissowa, s.v. '*follis*', col. 2832, argued that '*follis*' is used in *Heliog.* 22, 3 in the sense of a bronze coin for which there would be no evidence before *Cod. Theod.* IX, 23, 1 of 352 AD. But he assumed (and was approved by G. Mickwitz, *Geld und Wirtschaft im röm. Reiche* (1932) p. 85, and Hartke, *Kinderkaiser*, p. 48) that the mention of *follis* as a bronze coin was to be deleted from the difficult passage of *Cod. Theod.* VII, 20, 3 of 326 AD (?). An examination of *Cod. Theod.* VII, 20, 3, will easily persuade the reader that this is a most dangerous way of arguing: the history of the word *follis* is not yet clear. *Cf. Thesaurus L.L. ad l.* Mazzarino, *Aspetti Sociali*, p. 349, again calls attention to the passage of *Aurel.* 45, 5: '*libra enim auri tunc libra serici fuit*'. He observes that this agrees with Diocletian's edict, if we take it with Mattingly that in the edict the pound of gold is worth 10,000 (not 50,000) denarii. He would therefore infer from *tunc* that the writer is later than Diocletian. But Mattingly's hypothesis (*Numism. Chron.*, 6, 6 (1946) p. 113) is almost certainly wrong (L. C. West, 'The Coinage of Diocletian and the Edict on Prices', *Studies A. C. Johnson* (1951) p. 294, n. 5, and A. H. M. Jones, *Class. Rev.*, N.S. 3 (1953) p. 114), and we do not know what interval *tunc* implies. In general I am impressed by Mazzarino's remark founded on *Heliog.* 24, 3; *Alex. Sev.* 22, 8, and contrary to his conclusions, that the *H.A.* prices '*si fondano su prezzi identici o non contrastanti con quelli segnati nell'editto dioclezianeo*'. Another important point made by Mazzarino is that the *H.A.* seems to be hostile to *adaeratio*, the compulsory conversion of payments in kind into payments in money. There is a passage in this sense in the almost certainly forged document of *Claud.* 14 ('*ut nihil adaeret*'). I have not to discuss here the far-reaching conclusions of Mazzarino. It is enough to say that on his own evidence hostility to '*adaeratio*' is to be found in the texts of the early fourth century. (*Cod. Theod.* VII, 4, 1 of 325 and probably *Pap. Reinach*, 56 = Wilcken, *Chrest.* I, 419.)

Note D

I collect here, for the convenience of the reader, the most important chronological references of the *H.A.* In my opinion, none of them necessarily implies a later date than Constantine's death. Spartianus dedicates to Diocletian the biographies of Aelius, Septimius Severus, Pescennius Niger. He calls Galerius and Constantius Caesares – as they were before May 305 (*Helius* 2, 2). He dedicates the life of Geta to Constantine as Augustus. Capitolinus dedicates to Diocletian the lives of Marcus, Verus, Macrinus, but to Constantine the lives of Albinus, Maximini duo, Gordiani tres. The *Gordiani* presuppose the defeat of Licinius in 324 (34, 5): also the allusion to the family of the Ceionii (*Clodius Albinus* 4, 2) takes the reader to Constantine's later period. Capitolinus is mentioned by Vopiscus in *Probus* 2, 7, allegedly written about 305 (see below).

Lampridius dedicates the lives of Elagabalus and Severus Alexander to Constantine. *Heliog*. 35, 2–7 implies a date later than 324: *ibid.* 7, 7, there may be an allusion to the battle of Hadrianopolis of 324. Lampridius is mentioned by Vopiscus in *Probus* 2, 7.

Trebellius Pollio allegedly wrote when the '*Thermae Diocletianae*' could be said to be '*exaedificatae*' (*Tyr. trig*. 21, 7): hardly long before 305 (*CIL* VI, 1130 = Dessau 646). He is referred to by Vopiscus in the conversation of *Aurelianus* 2, 1, the dramatic date of which seems to be 304 (see below). He mentions Constantius as Caesar (*Gallien.* 7, 1; *Claud.* 1, 1; 3, 1; 9, 9) – which he would not have done after 305. His grandfather is supposed to have known Tetricus iunior (*Tyr. trig*. 25, 3). Vopiscus allegedly had his conversation with the praefectus urbi Iunius Tiberianus either in 291–2 or, rather, in 303–4. For the latter date and its difficulties compare for instance Mommsen, *Hermes*, 25 (1890) 257, n. 2 = *Ges. Schriften* 7, 329, n. 2. He mentions Diocletian as already a privatus in

Aurel. 43[43] and calls Constantius '*imperator*' – that is, presumably, Augustus – in *Aurel.* 44: the life of Aurelianus would be dated May 305–July 306. This agrees with the allusion to the Thermae of Diocletian as already in full use (*Probus* 2, 1). But though Vopiscus says that he wrote his lives in chronological order (*Probus* 1, 5; *Firmus* 15, 10), he seems clearly to presuppose in the life of Carus that Constantius was a Caesar (before May 305: *cf.* 9; 17; 18). This, on the traditional theory, can be explained only by the admission of some revision[44]. In the life of Probus 23, 5 there is a difficult allusion to a civil war: '*eant nunc qui ad civilia bella milites parant*'. The supporters of the traditional date interpret it as an allusion to an expected conflict between Constantius and Galerius (Mommsen) or to the earliest phase of the conflict between Galerius and Maxentius. The mention of a consul Furius Placidus (*Aurel.* 15, 4) is sometimes interpreted as alluding to the consul of 343: this is not convincing. It is uncertain whether *Aurel.* 42, 1 contains an allusion to a grandson of Aurelian or to a grandson of Aurelian's daughter. Vopiscus' grandfather is alleged to have known Saturninus (*Firmus* 9, 4; *cf.* 15, 4) and Diocletian (*Carus* 13–15). Vopiscus' father is quoted in connection with Diocletian *iam privatus* (*Aurel.* 43). Vopiscus says of himself (*Probus* 1, 5): '*si vita suppetet omnes qui supersunt usque ad Maximianum Diocletianumque dicturus*' (*cf.* 24, 8); this does not make him an old man. Finally, the unkind allusions to Maximianus in *Heliog.* 35, 4 and *Aurel.* 44, 2 were allegedly written after Maximianus' abdication.

[ADDENDUM. In an important article C. E. Van Sickle (*L'Antiquité Classique*, 23 (1954) pp. 47–62) argues that *Claudius* 14, 2–15 is based on an authentic salary-warrant belonging to the period between 296 and 312 AD. But he assumes that the text in its present form is later than 370 because the formula *fortissima ac devotissima* appears first in *Cod. Theod.* (VII, 4, 17) in 377 AD and *privatum aerarium* is first mentioned in *Cod. Theod.* (XI, 36, 32) in 396 AD. I am not here concerned with the question whether the biographer utilized an authentic document of the early fourth century. But before I can accept the second part of Van Sickle's thesis I must satisfy myself (a) that a formula cannot appear in a literary text (*S.H.A.*) many years before it finds its way into official documents (*Cod. Theod.*); (b) that the earliest mention of a formula in the *Cod. Theod.* marks the date of its introduction into official language.]

APPENDIX II

AN ADDITIONAL NOTE (1958)

As I have made abundantly clear, I have no theory on the *Historia Augusta*. What I am trying to do is to test the arguments against the traditional date. A post-Constantinian date of the *Historia Augusta* must not simply be made plausible or attractive: it must be proved. When I wrote my paper in *Journal of the Warburg Institute* it had not yet been proved. Has it been proved after the appearance of my paper?

Professor Hohl – the great student of the *H.A.* whose death we all regret – thought he had established beyond doubt the priority of Aurelius Victor in his paper in *Historia* 4 (1955) 220[45]. I still believe the priority to be probable (at least in relation to the corresponding passage of the life of Septimius Severus), but I am not satisfied that Professor Hohl has added anything to what we knew before. If we assume that both the *H.A.* and Aurelius Victor copied the same source (which is unlikely, but not impossible), Aurelius Victor can no longer be taken as a '*terminus post quem*' for the *H.A.*

I attribute much more importance to A. Chastagnol's paper '*Notes chronologiques sur l'Histoire Auguste et le Laterculus de Polemius Silvius*', *Historia* 4 (1955) 172–88. This is an outstanding contribution. Chastagnol argues that the *H.A.* is later than 357 and earlier than 398. I am not concerned with his '*terminus ante quem*', but only with his '*terminus post quem*'. Chastagnol brilliantly analyses '*Vita Trig. Tyr.*' 24, 5: '*Pudore tamen victus (Aurelianus) vir nimium severus eum quem triumphaverat correctorem totius Italiae fecit, id est Campaniae, Samnii, Lucaniae, Bruttiorum, Apuliae, Calabriae, Etruriae atque Umbriae, Piceni et Flaminiae, omnisque annonariae regionis*'[46]. According to Chastagnol, Campania and Samnium are here to be taken as two separate provinces of the '*regiones suburbicariae*'. As the separation happened between 352 and 361 (according to Chastagnol, most probably in 357), 352 or 357 would be the '*terminus post quem*' for the *H.A.*[47]. The trouble is that we simply do not know whether the writer intended to use the official terminology of the '*regiones suburbicariae*'[48]. The last four names are explicitly arranged in couples, the first six are not. If we take the first six to be implicitly arranged in couples, then Campania and Samnium go together, and we are compelled to conclude that the passage was written before, not after, the separation of the two regions. As Mommsen thought, the passage becomes an argument in favour of the traditional date, not an argument against it. If we deny that the first six names are implicitly arranged in couples, the six names cannot be taken as administrative units, and the passage becomes irrelevant to the question of the date. In either case Chastagnol's argument fails.

Chastagnol also avails himself of the passage in '*Vita Sev. Alex.*' 33 which attributes the institution of 14 '*curatores urbis*' to Severus Alexander. Chastagnol argues that these '*curatores*' were probably created after 384 and before 418. But I am not yet satisfied that the author of the life of Severus Alexander was perverse in attributing this reform to Severus Alexander[49]. If he was not, Chastagnol's argument is valueless. But even if he was, the history of the '*Curatores regionum*' in the fourth century, both in Rome and Constantinople, is too obscure to provide a '*terminus post quem*' for the *S.H.A. Inter alia*, we have always to reckon with the possibility that the biographer attributed to Severus Alexander a reform which was discussed, but not yet realized, when the *H.A.* was written. After all, the life of Severus Alexander is a programmatic picture of a good emperor: it may include implicit suggestions of reform[50].

APPENDIX III*

H. Stern, *Date et Destinataire de l' 'Histoire Auguste'* (*Collection d'études latines sous la direction de J. Marouzeau. Série scientifique XXVII*). Paris: Les Belles Lettres (1953) pp. 108.

Dr Stern, though he writes on the *Scriptores Historiae Augustae*, is a reasonable man. One may – indeed in my opinion one must – disagree with his conclusions; but one is bound to admire his command of the subject, his lucidity, and his brevity. Since N. H. Baynes wrote on this topic (1926), nobody has combined so well these three qualities in discussing the *Historia Augusta*.

In 1905 U. Giri (*In qual tempo abbia scritto Vopisco le biografie degli imperatori*) suggested that Vopiscus wrote his section of the *H.A.* under Constantius II not much later than 343 AD. He mainly relied on the identification of the consul of *Aurel.* 15, 4 ('*vidimus proxime consulatum Furii Placidi*') with the consul of 343, M. Maecius Memmius Furius Baburius Caecilianus Placidus. His theory was discussed and rejected by E. Hohl in *Jahresb. d. klass. Altertumsw.* 171 (1915) 111–13, with the argument – already put forward in another context by Mommsen (*Ges. Schriften* VII, 346) – that Vopiscus presented himself as a man who had talked to the *praefectus urbi* of 303 AD (*Aurel.* 1) and therefore was not likely to give himself away by such childish anachronisms: there are many lacunae in our knowledge of the consular list for the Diocletianic-Constantinian period. Notwithstanding Hohl's criticism, part of Giri's theory was accepted by another Italian scholar, G. Costa, in a paper in which he suggested that chapters 1–37, 4 of the biography of Aurelian were written between 343 and 360 (*Bilychnis* 22 (1923) 127–33), but curiously enough Costa did not mention Giri. On the other hand, outside Italy Giri's little book was soon forgotten. Even Baynes had failed to obtain a copy when he wrote his monograph. His attention was later called to Giri by De Sanctis (*Riv. Filolog.* 55 (1927) 405), and he briefly expressed his opinion on him in *CQ* 22 (1928) 168–9[51]. Now Giri's theory is revived by Dr Stern and extended to the whole of the *Historia Augusta*. According to Stern, a team of writers hastily composed the *H.A.* for Constantius II after his victory over Magnentius. They intervened in favour of the Roman aristocrats who had helped Magnentius and presented to the emperor the point of view of the senatorial aristocracy of Rome. Constantius' policy after Mursa may have been determined to a certain extent by his acquaintance with the *H.A.* Stern does not rely only on the chronological arguments already put forward by Giri. He thinks that the double eulogy of the first tetrarchs and of the ancestors of Constantine was possible only under Constantius II, who was Maximianus' grandson.

As I have said, I am not persuaded by Stern. Whoever claims that the *H.A.* was written about 353 must prove first that it cannot have been written when it claims to have been (under Diocletian and Constantine)

* *Journ. Rom. Studies* 44 (1954) 129–31.

and secondly that the arguments for dating its composition to *c.* 353 are stronger than those that can be adduced for any other date. It seems to me that Stern, though a careful reasoner, fails on both accounts. He attributes much importance to his impression that the compliments to the first tetrarchs and the celebration of Claudius could have been combined only under Constantius II, but Baynes made an even better use of the same argument in favour of the Julianic date. I am not going into the details of the contrasting claims of Baynes and Stern because I have never been satisfied that *this* feature of the *H.A.* provides an argument against the traditional Diocletianic-Constantinian date. Conflicts and compromise between the hereditary and the adoptive principles were typical of the period of Diocletian and Constantine. There is nothing in the allusions of the *H.A.* either to the tetrarchy or to Claudius' descendants that compels me to go beyond the death of Constantine, though some of the passages (especially those about Claudius purporting to be written before May, 305) may easily rouse the suspicion that they were written or redrafted when Constantine was in power. Stern finds it difficult to explain why in *Heliog.* 35, 4, Diocletian is called '*aurei parens saeculi*', and Maximianus (Constantius II's grandfather!) '*ferrei parens saeculi*'. This is very different from, say, the eulogy of both in *Carus* 18, 3–4. But the difference between the two passages presents no difficulty to the traditionalist. The life of Carus is supposed to have been written under the first tetrarchy (see chapters 9, 17, 19), while the life of Elagabalus was apparently written after 324 AD, as the very chapter in question, 35, shows. Stern himself proves in a useful appendix that the reputation of Maximianus fluctuated under Constantine: even without the evidence of Lactantius, *De mortibus persecutorum* (written about 316?), and Eusebius (*HE* VIII, 13) we ought to take for granted that anyone writing about Maximianus after 312 was allowed considerable freedom of speech. Stern also devotes a whole chapter to proving that the biography of L. Aelius Caesar was written in 354 to support the senatorial point of view: '*l'intérêt suscité par ce personnage . . . surgi probablement dans les milieux sénatoriaux peut-être peu avant 354, il n'a pu survivre longtemps à cette année*' (p. 59). He does not seem to me to offer any valid proof for this contention, and the *H.A.* itself contains an explanation that *prima facie* is very plausible: '*nihil habet in sua vita memorabile nisi quod primus tantum Caesar est appellatus, etc.*' (*Aelius* 2, 2). This is alleged to have been written under Diocletian, and it must be admitted that it was a good moment for writing it.

If the opinions of the *H.A.* about the tetrarchs do not necessarily point to the years about 353, it cannot be said that Stern's position is reinforced by the passages he takes to be direct allusions to these years. One is the passage about the consul Furius Placidus, and we have already seen that there are difficulties in identifying this man with the consul of 343. A second passage is the allusion in *Probus* 23, 5, to a civil war. Stern (following G. Costa, *Raccolta di scritti in onore di G. Lumbroso* (1925) 296) refers it to Magnentius, but it is notorious that this passage can be made to agree with all the possible theories about the *H.A.* – including the traditionalistic, as Mommsen showed. A third passage is contained in the pseudo-letter of Hadrian (*Saturn.* 8, 4): '*ipse ille patriarcha cum Aegyptum venerit, ab aliis Serapidem adorare, ab aliis cogitur Christum*'. Stern, like Baynes, identifies the patriarch with Athanasius. I fail to see why this passage (which I hardly understand) should refer to Athanasius and why, if it refers to Athanasius, it should be explained by '*la situation religieuse à Alexandrie en 353*' (p. 67)[52]. Finally, according to Mr Stern, Vopiscus must have been an old man when he promised that he would go on with his biographical work '*si vita suppetet*' (*Probus* 1, 5; 24, 8): furthermore, as his father talked to him about Diocletian '*iam privatus*' (*Aurel.* 43, 2) and therefore was alive after 305, he must have lived until the middle of the century and have seen the rebellion of Magnentius. I do not want to express any opinion about the dubious fathers and grandfathers of the *S.H.A.*, but I maintain that any man, whether young or old, whether his father is alive or has been dead for forty years, may (indeed should) write '*si vita suppetet*'.

Thus Mr Stern fails to persuade me that his date for the *H.A.* explains passages that the traditionalistic date cannot explain. On the other hand he seems to me to have failed to dispose effectively of the main arguments that have been adduced since Dessau for a date later than 360. He fights valiantly to refute the most powerful argument produced by Dessau: the relation between *S.H.A. Sept. Severus* 17, 5–19, 4, and Aurelius Victor, *De Caes.* 20, 1–3. Indeed he fights his battle twice, in an article in *RÉL* 30 (1952) 251–84, and in the first chapter of this book. He attempts to prove that both authors copied the same source and that *Sept. Severus* 18, 7, preserves the succession of ideas of the common source, while Aurelius Victor 20, 6, breaks it on purpose. His argument is entirely subjective; other people with a sense of style, like Leo, have taken the opposite view. He is also weak in his discussion of the many similarities between the *portrait* of Severus Alexander contained in the *H.A.* and the *real* Julian which Baynes collected in order to prove that the biography of Severus Alexander is nothing but an idealized portrait of Julian himself. It is of course another matter whether Dessau and his followers have proved that Aurelius Victor (360–1) is a source of the *H.A.* and whether Baynes has proved that the Severus Alexander of the *H.A.* is Julian. I have discussed these questions in a paper on the *H.A.* in *Journ. of the Warburg and Courtauld Institutes* 1954, and do not propose to restate my point of view. But I should like to show by three examples that Stern's attack on Baynes' theory is both insufficient and misleading. Stern accepts (p. 39) Baynes' opinion that there is no evidence for Diocletian's admiration for Marcus Aurelius (Baynes made the point to prove that the celebration of the *nomen Antoninorum* in the *H.A.* is best explained by Julian's admiration for Marcus Aurelius). Here it is enough to say that both Baynes and Stern forget the very telling passage of *Cod. Iust.* v, 17, 5 – a law of Diocletian. In another point Baynes followed K. Hönn, *Quellenunters. zu den Viten des Heliogabalus und des Severus Alexander* (1911) 91, in assuming that *Cod. Theod.* vi, 4, 9, of 356 AD, fixing a *quorum* of fifty senators for the designation of praetors, was the source of *Alex. Sever.* 16. Stern (pp. 87–8) accepts the connection between the two passages, but, dating the *H.A.* in

353, reverses their order. The *H.A.* would have provided '*une suggestion qui aurait été retenue par la loi de 356*'. Here all one need say is that the passage of the *H.A.* has been misread. As Mommsen saw (*Staatsrecht* III, 990) the *H.A.* passage implies that the *quorum* was of 70, not of 50, senators: the two passages have nothing in common, except the existence of a variable *quorum* in the Senate. On the other hand Stern argues against Baynes (*RÉL* 30 (1952) 268, n. 4: this volume p. 34, n. 7) that Julian '*a manifesté un vif mépris pour Alexandre-Sévère*'. The evidence would be provided by the *Symposium* (= *Caesars*) 313 A, but it is very rash to identify Silenus' jests with Julian's considered opinions: see the passage in its context. It is however true (so far I would agree with Stern) that Severus Alexander must have meant little to Julian. I cannot follow W. Seston in taking *P. Fay.* 20 (= Hunt-Edgar, *Select Papyri* II, 216) as evidence to the contrary.

Stern's failure to solve the problem of the *Historia Augusta* by another simple formula is perhaps not surprising. We have not the prooemium of the *H.A.* which might explain much; we do not yet know the number of the authors (though there is now general agreement that there was more than one); above all, we do not yet know whether and when an editor put together the biographies if the authors were more than one. These circumstances are not favourable to the production of an account of the origins of the *H.A.* based on fact rather than on speculation[53].

[1] See my paper in *Rivista Storica Italiana*, 62 (1950) pp. 325–44 [*Contributo* (1955) 13–32]. In general G. Bardy, *Rev. Hist. Éccl.* 32 (1936) 5–23; 275–302.

[2] The modern studies on the *H.A.* are discussed by H. Peter in *Bursians Jahresb.*, 76 (1893) pp. 119–61; 130 (1906) pp. 1–40, and by E. Hohl, *ibid.*, 171 (1915) pp. 94–146; 200 (1924) pp. 168–210; 256 (1937) pp. 129–56. See also Hohl (whose invaluable work on the *H.A.* it would be impertinent to praise), *Neue Jahrb.*, 33 (1914) pp. 698–712; *Hermes*, 55 (1920) pp. 296–310; *Klio*, 27 (1934) pp. 149–64. *Cf.* the surveys by P. Lambrechts, *Ant. Class.*, 3 (1934) pp. 503–16, and E. Manni, *La Parola del Passato*, 8 (1953) pp. 71–80. The article 'Historia Augusta' by Diehl in Pauly-Wissowa I found very useful. In the absence of a modern commentary the notes by D. Magie to his Loeb text (1922–32) are helpful. Only the most relevant studies are quoted in this paper.

[3] *Röm. Mitteil.*, 48 (1933) pp. 50–6.

[4] *Annali Scuola Normale Pisa*, II, 2 (1933) pp. 376–83. *Cf.* Chr. Hülsen, *Rh. Mus.*, 83 (1934) pp. 176–80; E. Hohl, *Bursians Jahresb.*, 256, 131.

[5] I follow H. Peter, *Die Scriptores Historiae Augustae* (1892) p. 154. *Cf.* E. Diehl, Pauly-Wissowa, s.v. 'Historia Augusta', 2085; C. Lécrivain, *Études sur l'Histoire Auguste* (1904) pp. 45–101, and L. Homo, Les documents de l'histoire Auguste et leur valeur historique, *Rev. Histor.* 151 (1926) pp. 161–98; 152 (1926) pp. 1–31 (a useful summary).

[6] On the historical value of the *H.A.* the latest contribution is the excellent paper by E. Hohl, Ueber die Glaubwürdigkeit der Historia Augusta, *Sitz.-Ber. Berl. Akad.* (1953) n. 2; *cf.* also by him, Das Ende Caracallas, *Miscellanea Academica Berolinensia*, II, i (1950) pp. 276–93. I avoid on purpose the question whether the *H.A.* claimed to have utilized *literary* sources that never existed. [*Cf.* G. Barbieri, 'Mario Massimo', *Riv. Filol.* 32 (1954) pp. 36–66; 263–75.]

[7] *Hermes*, 24 (1889) pp. 337–92; 27 (1892) pp. 561–605. His paper in *Janus, Festschrift zu C. F. Lehmann-Haupts sechzigstem Geburtstage* (1921) pp. 124–8, suggesting that the Samaritans could not be known to the *H.A.* (*Heliog.* 3, 5; *Firmus* (*Quadr.*) 7, 5; 8, 3) before Theodosius adds little: the *H.A.* was interested in things Jewish (*cf. Claudius*, 2, 4). Hohl developed Dessau's ideas in *Klio*, 11 (1911) pp. 178–229 and pp. 284–324; 12 (1912) pp. 474–82; 14 (1914) pp. 380–4, and the papers earlier than 1927 quoted above. *Cf.* A. Rosenberg, *Einleitung und Quellenkunde zur römischen Geschichte* (1921) p. 238 and H. Dessau, *Woch. f. Klass. Philologie*, 35 (1918) pp. 389–93.

[8] *Jahrb. f. class. Philol.*, 141 (1890) 609–39; *Zeitschr. f. Numism.*, 17 (1890) 36; p. 113 ff. (especially p. 152); *Rh. Mus.*, 49 (1894) pp. 208–24 (the most important of Seeck's papers); *ibid.*, 67 (1912) pp. 591–608.

[9] *Hermes* 25 (1890) pp. 228–92 = *Ges. Schriften*, VII, pp. 302–62. F. Leo, *Die griechisch-römische Biographie* (1901) pp. 268–304, supported Mommsen by an illuminating analysis of the structure of certain lives, but he could not prove that each layer is the work of a different author. Later W. Soltau tried to write an 'Entwicklungsgeschichte' of the *H.A.* on Mommsen's premises: *Philologus*, 74 (1917) pp. 384–445; *Berl. Philol. Woch.* (1917) pp. 1541–4; (1918) pp. 1047–56. It was a clear failure. A return to Mommsen's position is announced by E. Manni, in his preface to *Le Vite di Valeriano e di Gallieno* (Palermo, Palumbo 1951). [*Cf.* also A. Piganiol, *Histoire de Rome*, 4 ed. (1954) 302.]

[10] H. Peter, *Die Scriptores Historiae Augustae* (1892). No less important the various papers by E. Klebs, *Hist. Zeitschr.*, 64 (1889) pp. 213–45; *Rh. Mus.*, 45 (1890) pp. 436–65; 47 (1892) pp. 1–52 and 515–49.

[11] E. Wölfflin. *Sitz.-Ber. Bayer. Akad.* (1891) pp. 465–538; *cf.* also E. Klebs, *Rh. Mus.*, 47 (1892) pp. 1–52 on Vopiscus and the remarks by S. Frankfurter, *Eranos Vindobonensis* (Vienna 1893) pp. 218–32. Hohl's speculations on Vopiscus, *Klio*, 12 (1912) p. 481, have inspired those about one of the alleged sources of the *H.A.*, Iunius Cordus, by W. Hartke in E. Hohl, *Julius Capitolinus, Maximini duo*, 'Kleine Texte', 172 (1949) p. 8. I agree with O. Gigon, *Mus. Helvet.*, 6 (1949) p. 236, on this matter.

[12] See his various papers in *S.-B. Heidelb. Akad.* (1916–20) of which *Die Personennamen bei den S.H.A.* in 13 Abh., 1918, is the most typical; and the bad-tempered criticisms by E. Hohl, *Bursians Jahresb.*, 200, 168, and *Philol. Wochenschrift* (1919) pp. 745–51. Many of the topographical arguments produced by D. were exploded by D. M. Robathan, *Trans. Amer. Phil. Assoc.*, 70 (1939) pp. 515–34. D. had of course to dismiss the 'terminus ante quem' of Q. Aurelius Symmachus, cos. 485, using the *H.A.* (ap. Jordan., *Getica*, 15, 83). On this *cf.* W. Hartke, *Kinderkaiser*, p. 427.

[13] G. De Sanctis, *Rivista di Storia Antica*, 1 (1896) pp. 90–119; C. Lécrivain, *Études sur l'Histoire Auguste* (1904). A careful study of De Sanctis' paper would save students of the *H.A.* from repeating obviously weak arguments.

[14] Agreement with this position has been emphatically expressed by F. Dornseiff, *Deutsche Literaturzeitung*, 66–8 (1945–7) pp. 72–5. *Cf.* O. Gigon's wise remarks in *Mus. Helvet.*, 6 (1949) pp. 236–7. L. Homo's paper (*Rev. Histor.*, 131 (1919) pp. 209–64; 132 (1919) pp. 1–38) is somewhat capricious.

[15] See Hohl's review of Baynes in *Philol. Woch.* (1927) 711 and Ensslin, *Klio*, 32 (1939) 103, and elsewhere.

[16] *Geschichte und Politik im spätantiken Rom, Klio*, Beih. 45 (1940). Hartke had already written *De saeculi quarti exeuntis historiarum scriptoribus quaestiones*, diss. (Berlin 1932) (see especially p. 56) and inspired E. Norden's page in *Altgermanien* (1934) p. 31 (*cf.* E. Hohl, *Bursians Jahresb.*, 256 (1937) p. 153). His theory did not survive the criticisms by Hohl in *Phil. Woch.*, 62 (1942) p. 236 and by Ensslin,

Gnomon, 18 (1942) pp. 248–67. [E. Demougeot, *L'Antiquité Classique*, 22 (1953) pp. 361–82, rashly identifies Vopiscus with Nicomachus Flavianus the Elder.]

[17] J. Straub, *Studien zur Historia Augusta*, Diss. Bernenses, 4 (1952). Straub is in general agreement with A. Alföldi who has however never published his announced study on the *S.H.A.* I am unfortunately unable to read Alföldi's Hungarian paper in *Egyetemes Philologiai Közlöny* (1929–30) (on which see Hohl, *Klio* (1934) p. 160), but gather his ideas from *Zeitschr. f. Numismatik*, 38 (1928) p. 166, n. 2 and 172, n. 3; *A Festival of Isis in Rome under the Christian Emperors of the IV century*, Diss. Pannonicae (1937) pp. 45–6; *Die Kontorniaten* (1943) pp. 59, 64, 75; *A Conflict of Ideas in the Late Roman Empire* (1952) p. 125, and minor papers quoted below. A criticism of Alföldi's approach to late Roman problems by J. M. C. Toynbee, *Journ. Rom. Stud.*, 35 (1945) pp. 115–21. It will be seen that, greatly as I value Alföldi's work, I find it difficult to accept his views on the *H.A.*

[18] *Aspetti sociali del quarto secolo* (1951) pp. 345–70 and *passim*. *Cf.* also *Doxa*, 4 (1951) p. 123, n. 1. (I think that Mazzarino would not care to press the argument given here.)

[19] See the excellent reviews by N. H. Baynes and H. M. Last in *Journ. Rom. Studies*, 43 (1953) p. 153 and by F. W. Walbank in *Class. Rev.*, N.S. 3 (1953) pp. 47–9.

[20] *Rev. Études Lat.*, 30 (1952) pp. 251–84. Stern's main contention is that 'les analogies entre certaines parties du premier panégyrique de Julien et les éloges conjugués des tétrarques et de la famille constantinienne dans l'*H.A.* nous suggèrent Constance II comme destinataire de cette dernière' (p. 284). This seems to me a *non sequitur*. [Stern's book has now appeared, *Date et destinataire de l'Histoire Auguste*, Paris, 1953, and contains very many acute remarks with which I agree, but its thesis seems to me unconvincing. See my review in *Journ. Rom. Stud.*, 44 (1954). In some of his arguments Stern was anticipated by U. Giri, *In qual tempo abbia scritto Vopisco le biografie degli imperatori* (Turin 1905); though Giri dates only Vopiscus' section under Constantius II. *Cf.* above, p. 172.]

[21] The case made by Stern, *Rev. Ét. Lat.* (1952) pp. 251–62 = *Date et destinataire* 17–27, for the non-dependence of the *H.A.* on Aurelius Victor is too subtle to carry conviction. *Cf.* F. Leo, *Die griech.-römische Biographie* (1901) p. 286, n.1. But too much subtlety is also to be found on the other side. E. Hohl, *Rh. Mus.*, 68 (1913) pp. 316–19, tried to prove that *Sev.*, 17, 6, 'non tam ex sua voluntate quam ex morum parsimonia', is a misunderstanding of Aur. Vict. *Caes.* 20, 10, 'ob vitae parsimoniam similem ipsum magis ascivisse'. *If* there is a misunderstanding by the *H.A.*, it could of course be not of Aurelius Victor, but of the source which the *H.A.* has in common with Aurelius Victor. On this question of sources G. Barbieri's contributions seem to me sensible: *Ann. Scuola Normale Pisa*, II, 3 (1934) pp. 525–38; *Studi Ital. Filol. Class.*, N.S. 13 (1936) pp. 183–206; *Riv. Fil. Class.*, 32 (1954) 36–66; 262–75. A. Maddalena, Sulle fonti per la storia di Diocleziano e Costantino, *Atti Istit. Veneto*, 95 (1935–6) pp. 247–75, is also useful.

[22] *Paneg. Lat.* 6 (7), 2: 'A primo igitur incipiam originis tuae numine, quod plerique adhuc fortasse nesciunt, sed qui te amant plurimum sciunt'.

[23] Mommsen's remarks, *Hermes*, 25, p. 254, n. 1 = *Ges. Schriften*, VII, p. 326, n. 2, remain decisive. F. Altheim thinks that Constantine's descent from Claudius was already stated by Dexippus who, according to *Literatur und Gesellschaft im ausgehenden Altertum*, I (1948) pp. 191–2, would have written 'nach 293' and, according to *Aus Spätantike und Christentum* (1951) p. 54 'vor 293'. His main argument is that Dexippus concluded his history with Claudius' death because he wanted 'Claudius als Neubegründer des Imperium Romanum betrachtet wissen'

Cf. E. Klebs, Das dynastische Element in der Geschichtsschreibung der römischen Kaiserzeit, *Hist. Zeitschrift*, 64 (1889) pp. 213–34. [Stern, *Date et destinataire de l'H.A.*, pp. 45–51, would date about 350 *Claud.* 11–13 on the Dardanian origin of Claudius and Constantius Chlorus. But Themistius, *Or.* 3, 43b, p. 52, Dindorf proves nothing about the date of this legend.]

[24] On this see below.

[25] *Kleine Schriften* (1913) pp. 887–91. The only way out (a poor way) is to think with Straub, p. 137, that the *H.A.* writes all that about Claudius in order to mislead the reader about its own date of composition.

[26] The translation quoted in the text of this and other passages is by D. Magie (Loeb).

[27] An alternative, less convincing, explanation is offered by E. Klebs, *Rh. Museum*, 45 (1890) p. 448, according to whom the oracle failed as far as the real descendants of Probus were concerned, but succeeded with another family of Probi. *Cf.* G. Vitucci's good remarks in *L'Imperatore Probo* (1952) 148. It is hardly necessary to add that the appearance in the *H.A.* of names like Toxotius, Ragonius Celsus and Faltonius Probus, which are known to us from the history of the second part of the fourth century, cannot be exploited as a chronological argument. Baynes (p. 46) approves of Seeck's argument *ex silentio* (*Jahrb. f. class. Phil.*, 141 (1890) 632–3) that, contrary to *Albin.*, 4, 1, the family alliance of the Ceionii and Postumii is later than 350 AD. But apart from the intrinsic weakness of such arguments, all that the *H.A.* says is that Albinus was 'nobilis apud suos et originem a Romanis familiis trahens, Postumiorum scilicet et Albinorum et Ceioniorum'. Postumii Albini did exist during the Republic.

[28] *Riv. Storia Antica*, 4 (1899) 233–41. *Cf.* C. E. Van Sickle, *Class. Philol.*, 27 (1932) pp. 51–2. For the evidence of the Philocalus calendar (*CIL*, I², p. 310) see H. Stern, *Le Calendrier de 354* (Paris 1953) p. 82, n. 14. [Notice that Lactantius in *De mortibus persecutorum*, written about 316, does not mention Marcus Aurelius' persecution. For one explanation, *cf.* the commentary by J. Moreau, II (1954) 210.]

[29] ΘΕΙΟΣ ΑΝΗΡ, *Das Bild des göttlichen Menschen in Spätantike und Frühchristentum*, I (1935). *Cf.* E. C. Evans, *Harvard Studies in Class. Philol.*, 46 (1935) pp. 43–84.

[30] See *Note A* in Appendix I.

[31] I cannot agree with Hartke, *Kinderkaiser*, pp. 326–8, that there are arguments to show that the *H.A.* originally started with Hadrian. His statistical argument to prove that if there had been a life of Trajan the name of this emperor would have been quoted more frequently in the biographies of the successors of Hadrian is misleading. Nor would I say that *Avid. Cass.*, 3, 1–3, and *Pescennius Niger*, 9, 2, presuppose the life of Hadrian to be the first of the series. *Helius* 1, 1, is, in any theory, difficult to reconcile with 7, 5, and therefore helps no theory. My impression, however, is that the contradiction between the two passages of *Helius* is more easily explained as a change of mind of one person than as the result of the intervention of a second person. [According to Stern, *Date et destinataire*, pp. 52–61, the interest in Aelius has 'surgi probablement dans les milieux sénatoriaux peut-être peu avant 354'. This would seem to me an arbitrary statement.]

[32] Domaszewski, *Rh. Mus.*, 57 (1902) p. 514, assumed that *Get.* 6, 4, speaking of only *one* Tribunus of the *cohortes urbanae*, must be later than 316. But both Domaszewski's interpretation of the passage and his date for the unified command of the *cohortes urbanae*, based on *CIL* VI, 1156 (D. writes 1186 by oversight), are questionable: *cf.* Mommsen, *Hermes*, 25, p. 236 = *Ges. Schriften*, VII, p. 309. Domaszewski's other argument that *Gall.*, 8, 6 'signa templorum omnium-

que legionum' shows an author no longer acquainted with points of pagan religion is even less cogent. The reference of *Clod. Albin.* 1, 4 (allegedly by Capitolinus) to *Pescenn. Nig.*, 8, 1 (by Spartianus) *may* have been added by an editor. But *Pescenn. Nig.*, 9, 3, *may* indicate that both lives were written by one author.

[33] See *Note B* in Appendix I.

[34] See *Note C* in Appendix I.

[35] J. R. Palanque, *Rev. Étud. Anc.*, *Mélanges Radet* (1940) pp. 494–7, suggested that the *praefectus Illyrici et Galliarum* was inspired by the fact that in 360 a *praefectus Galliarum* changed his position for that of a *praefectus Illyrici.* But what we want to explain is the double title. The surprising contention by Alföldi *ap.* Straub, *Studien*, p. 30, that *Claud.* 6, 2 depends on the *Notitia Dignitatum* about Grutungi-Austrogoti is, in my opinion, refuted by Altheim, Das Auftreten der Hunnen in Europa, *Acta Archaeol.*, Budapest, II (1952) pp. 273–6. The *proconsul Ciliciae* of *Aurel.* 42, 2 (*cf. Car.* 4, 6) is still unexplained: *cf.* P. Meloni, *Il regno di Caro* (Cagliari 1948) p. 39. As far as I know, J. B. Mispoulet never published his research on 'consulares' in the *H.A.* summarized in *C. R. Acad. Inscr.* (1906) p. 332. Even if he had proved his case, it would not date the *H.A.* after Constantine.

[36] *Hermes*, 55 (1920) pp. 279–96.

[37] *Harv. Theol. Rev.*, 39 (1946) pp. 213–15. Alföldi in *Festival of Isis* (1937) p. 44 argues that the passages on Commodus and Isis were written in the late fourth century and thinks that *Pescenn.* 6, 8 echoes Ps. Cyprian, *Ad Senatorem* (III, 302 Hartel). I cannot see any cogency in his arguments. *Cf.* Suet. *Otho* 12, 1, also quoted by Alföldi. In general his view that the *H.A.* is a 'pamphlet against Christianity' (*Cambridge Ancient History*, XII, p. 223; *ibid.* he speaks of 'its hatred for the Christians') does not seem to me supported by sufficient evidence.

[38] This was felt by a man who knew his fourth century, G. Costa, 'Un libello anticristiano del sec. IV?' in *Bilychnis*, 22 (1923) 127–33. He tried to date the main part of the life of Aurelianus between 343 and 360, 'quando non si poteva alzar la voce se non discretamente per tema di rappresaglie e punizioni'. But his *terminus post quem*, shared now by Stern – that Furius Placidus mentioned in *Aurel.*, 15, 4, must be M. Maecius Memmius Furius Baburius Caecilianus Placidus cos. 343 – is questionable (*cf.* Mommsen, *Hermes* 25, p. 275 = *Ges. Schriften*, VII, p. 346). Equally questionable is the argument used by W. H. Fisher, The Augustan Vita Aureliani, *Journ. Rom. Stud.*, 19 (1929) p. 129, to prove that this biography is later than 358.

[39] The arguments produced by Alföldi, *Klio*, 31 (1938) pp. 249–53, on the *popinarii* affair are not cogent. Those on the *iudiciale carpentum* (*Aurel.* 1, 1) have been shown to be erroneous by W. Ensslin, *Klio*, 32 (1939) pp. 89–105.

[40] If one separates the lives attributed to Vopiscus from the others, one may say that Vopiscus is more anti-Christian than his colleagues. But I am unable to understand what *Firmus*, 8, 4, means by 'ipse ille patriarcha cum Aegyptum venerit'. E. Hohl, *Ueber die Glaubwürdigkeit*, p. 53, n. 64, explains 'Aegyptum' but not 'patriarcha'. Baynes saw in it an allusion to Athanasius which would not rule out a date under Constantine. In *Kinderkaiser*, p. 300, Hartke takes up *Heliog.*, 6, 7: 'penum Vestae, quod solae virgines solique pontifices adeunt, inrupit'. He argues that the *H.A.* does not realize that Elagabalus, being the emperor, was also 'pontifex': the passage could have been written only after 379 when the emperor was no longer 'pontifex maximus', but before 395 when the 'pontifices' were abolished. It seems to me that texts cannot be pressed in this way. The *H.A.* was thinking of Elagabalus as an emperor, not as pontifex. If the *H.A.* had been written soon after the emperor gave up the title of 'pontifex maximus', it would probably be more acutely aware of the fact that previous emperors were

pontifices. The other argument used by Hartke, p. 298, connecting what *Heliog.*, 6, 5 says on the 'Floralia sacra' with a discovery allegedly made in 394 that the temple of Flora was an 'Unterpfand der Herrschaft Roms', is too much for me.

[41] *Cf.*, for instance, the discussion between De Sanctis, *Riv. Fil. Class.*, 55 (1927) pp. 404–5, and Baynes, *Class. Quart.*, 22 (1928) pp. 166–7. Baynes, in *Journ. Rom. Stud.* (1953) p. 138, gives a list of passages referring to imperial succession. The fact that in certain cases the *H.A.* justifies usurpers is clearly no chronological argument: after all Diocletian had been a usurper. Hartke, *Kinderkaiser*, has of course plenty to say on this subject. [See now Stern, *Date et destinataire*, pp. 69–72.]

[42] It would, of course, be a different matter if we could prove that Aurelius Victor, or Eutropius, or any other writer of the late fourth century, did follow for post-Constantinian events one of the sources which the *H.A.* followed for pre-Diocletianic events. But, as far as I know, such a demonstration has not yet been provided (the latest attempt was made by Hartke in 1940); and there is a simple reason for this. As A. Enmann saw in his research 'Eine verlorene Geschichte der römischen Kaiser', *Philologus*, Suppl. IV (1884) pp. 443–4 (*cf.* E. Hohl, *Klio*, 11 (1911) p. 187), even if we admit that a source *K* was used throughout both by the *H.A.* and (say) Eutropius, it does not follow that the *H.A.* and Eutropius used the same redaction of *K*. Eutropius may have used *K* 'auctus' (*K* increased by the addition of an account of the post-Constantinian period).

[43] 'Sed ego a patre meo audivi Diocletianum principem iam privatum dixisse.' This does not mean 'Diocletian, when still a commoner' (Magie) but 'post depositam purpuram' (Casaubon). *Cf.* Lessing, *S.H.A. Lexicon* s.v. 'iam', but notice Baynes, pp. 97–8, and Hohl, *Klio*, 11 (1911) p. 182 n. 1.

[44] For a different opinion H. Vermaat, *Disputatio de aetate qua conscripta est Historia Augusta* (Lugd. Batav. 1893) 111.

[45] *Cf. Gnomon* 28 (1956) 235 and *Wiener Studien* 71 (1958) 32–52.

[46] Hohl's punctuation – Campaniae, Samni, Lucaniae Bruttiorum, Apuliae Calabriae – is misleading.

[47] *Cf.* R. Thomsen, *The Italic Regions* (1947) 215.

[48] *Cf.* H. Stern, *Rev. Ét. Anc.* 58 (1956) 415 n. 5. I may perhaps be allowed to say that Stern's main argument against me (on the contradiction between *Aur.* 43 and *Carus* 9) had already been answered above p. 170.

[49] A Jardé, *Études critiques sur . . . Sévère Alexandre* (1925) 52 n. 2; G. Vitucci, *Ricerche sulla praefectura urbi* (1956) 105 n. 1.

[50] E. M. Štaerman, *Krizis Rabovladel'českogo Stroja . . .* (Moscow 1957) 21–3, seems to support the Constantinian date, but the article she announces (p. 21, n. 26) has not yet appeared. *Cf.* also *Cahiers d'hist. mond.* 4 (1958) 324–7.

[51] N. H. Baynes, *Byzantine Studies* (London 1955) 214–15.

[52] The authenticity of the letter is defended by F. Dornseiff, *Aus der Byzantinischen Arbeit der Deutschen Demokratischen Republik* I (1957) 39–45.

[53] *Cf.* P. Courcelle, *Rev. Ét. Anc.* 56 (1954) 502–4.

CHAPTER TEN

CASSIODORUS AND ITALIAN CULTURE OF HIS TIME*

WHEN I want to understand Italian history I catch a train and go to Ravenna. There, between the tomb of Theodoric and that of Dante, in the reassuring neighbourhood of the best manuscript of Aristophanes and in the less reassuring one of the best portrait of the Empress Theodora, I can begin to feel what Italian history has really been[1]. The presence of a foreign rule, the memory of an imperial and pagan past, and the overwhelming force of the Catholic tradition have been three determining features of Italian history for many centuries. These three features first joined together when Ravenna became the capital of the Ostrogothic kingdom. The beginnings of Italian history such as we have known it are contemporary with the building of Sant' Apollinare Nuovo, with the martyrdom of Boethius, and with that moving note left by a scion of a great house at the bottom of a manuscript of Macrobius: 'I, the Right Honourable Aurelius Memmius Symmachus, have emended and revised this manuscript in Ravenna with the help of the Right Honourable Macrobius Plotinus Eudoxius.[2]' Notwithstanding the crime, the cruelty, and the enormous destruction, one receives the impression that Italian society in the sixth century was humane and easy-going[3]. I always like to remind myself of that miracle so precisely told by Gregory the Great. Two Goths on their way to Ravenna paid a visit to Bonifatius, Bishop of Ferentium in Etruria. The bishop provided them with a bottle of wine. The more the Goths drank, the more

* *Proceedings of the British Academy* 41 (1955), 207–45: Italian Lecture delivered on 25 May 1955. *Cf.* the reviews by P. Courcelle, *Latomus* 16 (1957) 741–3 and H. Fuchs, *Museum Helveticum* 14 (1957) 250–1. I have returned to the argument in 'Gli Anicii e la storiografia latina del VI sec. d.C.', *Rendiconti Acc. Lincei* 8, 11 (1956) 279–97, republished in the volume of the *Fondation Hardt, Histoire et Historiens dans l'Antiquité* (1958) 249–76.

wine there was in the bottle. So the two Goths passed their days in Ravenna drinking, as the Goths are wont to do: '*biberunt ut Gothi*'[4]. Bonifatius was a very understanding Italian bishop.

Two members of the Italian aristocracy of that time – Boethius and St Benedict – have been chosen by universal consent to represent and symbolize what is highest in the Italian contribution to medieval civilization. Nobody will dispute this choice. Another member of the same aristocracy, Cassiodorus Senator, has been slower in receiving due appreciation. Though his *Institutiones* rank among the formative books of the Middle Ages, he was never an awe-inspiring figure[5]. Dante, who declared the greatness of Boethius and St Benedict in lines as good as any that he ever wrote, did not mention Cassiodorus. The many references in medieval literature do less than justice to his achievements and are sometimes curiously misinformed. One is surprised to see that John of Salisbury in his *Historia Pontificalis* took him to be a recent convert to Christianity: '*Cassiodorus ex gentili Christianus, monachus ex senatore*'[6].

I am quoting John of Salisbury because his statement that Cassiodorus was a convert to Christianity may have some remote connection with a strange tradition studied thoroughly, but not exhaustively, by Père Delehaye[7]. This tradition seems to go back to the eighth or ninth century and is presented both in a Greek and in a Latin version, but the Latin version depends on the Greek. We are told of three men, Senator, Viator, and Cassiodorus, who lived under the Emperor Antoninus. They were the sons of an officer of Delchemus, King of Sardinia, were baptized by Eusebius, Bishop of Caesarea, took part in a war between Caesarea and Carthage, and finally died the martyr's death in Calabria. Père Delehaye saw that Senator and Cassiodorus derive their names from Cassiodorus Senator, who was born and died in Calabria, while Viator is probably his contemporary, Flavius Viator, consul in 495; the whole legend must have been inspired by an inscription in honour of Viator and Cassiodorus Senator found in Calabria. I would only add that the war between Caesarea and Carthage, in which Cassiodorus and Senator are said to have taken part, may well be a recollection of the war between Justinian Caesar and the Vandals of Carthage. The tradition is worth further examination and shows that a vague memory of Cassiodorus lingered on in the land he loved so well. But this legend shows that little more than his name was popularly remembered. His reputation as a learned man was always confined to narrow circles and even in these it was never comparable with that of Boethius. Modern scholars also have been slow in taking a real interest in Cassiodorus. We had to wait until 1937 for a critical edition of his *Institutiones*, though when it came it provided our Academy with one of its most distinguished members. The *Historia Tripartita*, inspired, if not actually written, by Cassiodorus, was first critically edited in 1952. The *De anima* is still no man's land, though we have the promise of an edition from America and of a critical commentary from Switzerland. For Cassiodorus' *Commentary on the Psalms* there is not even the promise of a modern edition, as far as I know[7a].

A man of no heroic character and of no towering intelligence, Cassiodorus hardly appealed to generations for whom nothing less than unconditional heroism and indisputable intellectual greatness counted. We, the members of the race of iron, have learnt to appreciate the lesser men – the men who tried to save what could be saved and who did not disdain the task of elementary teaching when elementary teaching was needed. Cassiodorus's recent rise to universal fame is not due to doubtful theories about the survival of the books of Vivarium[8] nor to the equally doubtful theories about the connection between the *Regula Magistri* and Vivarium[9]: even the alleged discovery of his tomb at Squillace has failed to fire our imagination[10]. The change is simply due to our own recent experience in matters of scholarship and political life. We have learnt again what it means not to be able to consult a book because it was destroyed by war. Our gratitude for the monks who saved our classics in their monasteries has become something more than conventional homage. Indeed monastic life itself has become less alien to the modern scholar's taste: it may become a desirable alternative to the horrors of university committees.

But if the Vivarium period of the life of Cassiodorus is now properly appreciated, not much attention has recently been paid to Cassiodorus as the historian of the Goths. This is no easy subject, for of course we have not his *Gothic History* but only a summary made by Jordanes, and any attempt to define Jordanes' treatment of his source is likely to lead the unwary into trouble[11]. Yet there can be no doubt that Cassiodorus' *Gothic History* is a landmark in the history of Latin historiography and of Late Roman politics. It is about Cassiodorus's *Gothic History* that I feel I can offer a few suggestions this evening. The '*Getica*', however, cannot be appreciated in isolation. They emerge as an exceptional, yet timely, work only if they are examined against the background of the literary production of the first part of the sixth century.

In the ninth century the chronicler Agnellus could still see in Ravenna a mosaic in which Theodoric was represented between the images of Ravenna and Rome[12]. Rome was a woman with a helmet and a spear, but Ravenna was shown as jumping out of the sea – with a leg still in it – in her desire to meet the king. The whole representation has its iconographical interest into which I need not go, but it also has a plain historical meaning. Ravenna was at the end of both land and sea routes, and these routes pointed to the East. Under Theodoric and his Gothic successors Italy had no control of her seas. Cassiodorus himself says plainly that his king had no fleet of his own: '*Cum nostrum igitur animum frequens cura pulsaret naves Italiam non habere*'[13]. Theodoric's last-minute attempt to build up a fleet in Ravenna came to an end with his death[14]. But the Vandals too were no longer so powerful at sea[15]. Organized naval power existed only in the Eastern Empire. This is one of the main facts that explains why Italy again fell under the influence of the Hellenic East. The other fact is, of course, that Africa, Gaul, and Spain in their increasing barbarization had less to give.

We can hardly measure what the loss of Africa to the Vandals meant to the Church in Italy and, more generally, to Italian intellectual life[16]. Since the end of the second century the superabundant spiritual energies of African Christianity had inspired the Church in the West. These energies were still abundant enough to account for the stubborn resistance to the Arian Vandals and for the amount of apologetic literature thrown into the controversy. But the death of Augustine while besieged by the Vandals had signed the end of the intellectual supremacy of Christian Africa. Nor were Spain and Gaul ready to supply intellectual food of equivalent value. Spain seems to have been as good as lost to creative culture in the first part of the sixth century. Martinus of Bracara, who in the name of Seneca started something of a Renaissance about 550 AD, was an import from the East[17]. Things were of course not so bad in Gaul. But the circle of Sidonius Apollinaris did not survive *in situ*. If he had a follower it was Ennodius, who, though born in France, lived in Milan and Pavia: Milan, indeed, became a centre of learning that attracted not only Italians, but Gauls[18]. Sidonius' friend, Claudianus

Mamertus, also found his follower in Italy rather than in France: his *De statu animae* was one of the sources of Cassiodorus' *De anima.* About 500 AD there were only two writers of uncommon stature in France – Avitus, Bishop of Vienne, and Caesarius, Bishop of Arles. Their pastoral activities were absorbed in specifically local problems – which incidentally compelled Caesarius to come to an agreement with King Theodoric. Their strictly theological writing had not sufficient distinction to make a strong impression on Italy. Caesarius' biographer tells us that his hero distributed his sermons in Spain and in Italy[19]. If this is true, they served the pastoral rather than the theological interests of the Italian clergy.

St Augustine had of course not exhausted his influence. In dedicating his *De trinitate* to Symmachus, Boethius expressed the hope of being a good pupil of St Augustine. Eugippius prepared an anthology of St Augustine for the benefit of those who could not provide themselves with the Saint's *Opera Omnia* and dedicated it to that remarkable woman relative of Boethius, Proba[20]. Proba herself and Galla, Symmachus' daughter, maintained close relations with St Augustine's follower, Fulgentius of Ruspe[21]. But the theological controversies just then raging with the East in consequence of the *Henotikon* increased the need for recent, up-to-date, theological information. Besides, there was an aspect of St Augustine's philosophy that the aristocratic circle of Symmachus and Boethius could never make its own: this was his view of Roman history.

Symmachus and Boethius were not prepared to admit that pagan Rome had had little to show but disasters and robberies. They had succeeded in combining a genuine Christian faith with a devotion to all that was pagan in Roman tradition. Quintus Aurelius Memmius Symmachus, the senior leader of this intellectual revival, had chosen Cato as his model, *antiqui Catonis novellus imitator*[22]. He was a descendant of the last defenders of pagan Rome in the fourth century and was only too conscious of his ancestry. His care for the text of Macrobius was not uninfluenced by the circumstance that another Symmachus had been a speaker in Macrobius' *Saturnalia.* He wrote a Roman history in imitation of one of his ancestors, *parentes suos imitatus*: here, too, the model was pagan, if the allusion is to Nicomachus Flavianus' history[23]. Our sixth-century Symmachus is the only writer in antiquity who, to our knowledge, used and quoted the *Scriptores Historiae Augustae* – that mysterious compilation of the fourth century with a marked bias towards paganism and senatorial authority[24]. Another man of the same senatorial group and another descendant from one of the great pagan champions of the fourth century, Vettius Agorius Basilius Mavortius, emended the texts of both Horace and Prudentius – of the most pagan and of the most Christian of Latin poets[25].

These antiquarians were not frivolous. They were aware that their attempt to combine Christian devotion with pagan tradition could succeed only if it was supported by the strength of Greek thought and by the continuity of imperial tradition. They looked to the East where exciting things seemed to be happening. In Constantinople Priscian was opening new vistas to Latin grammatical studies[26]. In Alexandria the school of Ammonius was making a new effort to harmonize Plato, Aristotle, and Porphyrius and to reconcile all with Christianity[27]. These were intellectual events giving hope to men whose hearts never turned away from the classical past of Greece and Rome. Symmachus was already well known in Constantinople when he went there on a visit[28]. He befriended Priscian and brought back three of his rhetorical works with resounding dedications to himself[29]. Boethius may even have been educated in the East, if, as Courcelle has suggested, he was the son of Boethius, the prefect of Alexandria about 475[30]. Symmachus and Boethius certainly had a large number of Oriental connections which helped to bring about the reconciliation between the Church of Rome and that of Constantinople in 519[31]. In 515 and 517 Ennodius, who was a relative of Boethius, was sent to Constantinople to discuss the union of the Churches[32]. Indeed, a woman of their family group, Anicia Juliana, the daughter of the Emperor Olybrius, was in Constantinople to work for the union[33].

Symmachus encouraged Boethius to make Aristotle and Plato and their commentators known to the West in a Latin translation. But theology no less than philosophy was involved in this effort to capture the latest results of Eastern speculation and to harmonize them with Western tradition. Boethius complained bitterly in some of the prologues of his works about the hostility of those who did not know the meaning of their own words and more particularly of the theologians who disapproved of him[34]. Yet he was not alone in spreading knowledge of the Greek doctrines. At least three other Roman senators are known to have taken an interest in theological controversies. One was the patrician Senarius, a relative of Ennodius, who, as we said, was himself a relative of Boethius; another was

Faustus, probably the consul of 490, and the third was Albinus, who later was accused of treason by Theodoric and became the immediate cause of Boethius' fall[35]. At the service of this Italian group Dionysius Exiguus – a Scythian by birth, but a Roman in manner, as Cassiodorus said – passed his life in translating theological, philosophic, and ecclesiological treatises from Greek into Latin[36].

The mere fact that we find in Constantinople a man of Priscian's distinction shows that the efforts of the Romans to re-establish their cultural contacts with the Greeks were reciprocated by the Greeks themselves. Priscian was no isolated figure in Constantinople as a student of Latin grammar and rhetoric. We know the names and the works of some of his pupils. One of them, Flavius Theodorus, was in the office of the *quaestor sacri palatii* in Constantinople[37]. Priscian's protector, the consul and patrician Julian, is described as equally learned in things Greek and Latin[38]. The compliment is perhaps not undeserved if he was the Julian who is connected with the text of Statius[39]. The Latin interests of the court society of Justin and Justinian were not confined to Roman law. About 512 John the Lydian started his career of the perfect bureaucrat. The services of this comic figure towards Roman antiquities are well known: among his many boasts there is that of an exceptionally fine knowledge of Latin[40]. A few years later, a man of quite different calibre and importance, Peter the Patrician, who specialized in the knowledge of the West, wrote his history of the Roman empire from the death of Caesar to the death of Constantius II[41]. Men of his kind could of course sympathize with the Roman aristocrats of Symmachus' circle and established friendships that were to bear fruit during Justinian's determined struggle to destroy the Ostrogothic kingdom.

In judging this movement both from the Western and from the Eastern side, we must take it for granted that Boethius' *De Consolatione Philosophiae* does not belong to it. However prepared by long meditation in earlier life, *De Consolatione* went beyond anything Boethius had done before: it must have taken the author himself by surprise. Many people have turned to Christianity for consolation. Boethius turned to paganism. His Christianity collapsed – it collapsed so thoroughly that perhaps he did not even notice its disappearance. The God of the Greek philosophers gave peace to his mind. The arrogance with which he had dealt with Christian theology was replaced by a new humility. This may show that his earlier attempt to harmonize philosophy and Christianity was on an unstable basis, but it cannot be a guide to the conscious aims of the Roman group of which he was a member, nor of its Byzantine counterpart[42].

Nobody of course can say – perhaps even the men involved did not know – when the efforts to bring about a reconciliation between Rome and Constantinople began to imply a covert rebellion against the government of Ravenna. Symmachus, like some of his friends, was wise enough to avoid taking employment under Theodoric in Ravenna. He was content with his Roman honours. Boethius, after having long imitated his father-in-law, was persuaded to accept the *magisterium officiorum* in 522. It would have been a mistake in any case. The circumstances made it a tragedy[43].

Cassiodorus was so little involved in this tragedy that he succeeded Boethius in the *magisterium officiorum*. He had never been a full member of Symmachus' circle. He did not belong to the Roman aristocracy in a full sense. His family had come from the East and had been established in Calabria for four generations. Squillace, *prima urbium Bruttiorum*, was the city he felt his own. One of the *Variae* has a lyrical, almost incongruous, description of the countryside round Squillace that anticipates the famous description of Vivarium in the *Institutiones*[44]. Though Cassiodorus' estate must have been substantial, he went naturally into the civil service as his father and his grandfather had done. He did not take pride in independence as did Symmachus or, to some extent, Boethius. His education was correspondingly different. It is true that at a certain moment of his life he studied dialectics with Dionysius Exiguus, but his training was rhetorical rather than philosophical[45]. Some Greek he certainly knew, but how much is uncertain. In his later years he patronized translations from Greek works such as Josephus' *Jewish Antiquities*[46] and a conflation of the Church histories of Theodoretus, Sozomenus, and Socrates – the so-called *Historia Tripartita*. But as far as we know he did not translate any work himself. Among his contemporaries he has more points in common with the poet Arator than with Symmachus. Arator, too, was a powerful public speaker, who served Theodoric for many years, and later in life entered holy orders[47]. Cassiodorus' name does not appear in the works of Boethius or in those of Ennodius: this is particularly remarkable in the latter case, as Ennodius, though a priest and a relative of Boethius, was in close contact with Ravenna.

On the other hand it is of fundamental importance for the argument I shall soon develop about the history of the Goths to notice that Cassiodorus emphasized his family connections with Symmachus and Boethius. He never lost an opportunity to celebrate Boethius' family, the Anicii[48]. The most important evidence for Cassiodorus' family pride is his *Ordo generis Cassiodororum*, a sort of family history addressed to Flavius Rufius Petronius Nichomachus Cethegus, consul in 504 and probably a member himself of the group of the Anicii. Only an excerpt from the *Ordo generis Cassiodororum* is preserved, but it is enough to show that the original text contained a biography of all the members of the family who had contributed to literature together with a list of their publications[49]. The extract that has come to us preserves the sections or parts of the sections dealing with Cassiodorus himself, with Symmachus and with Boethius. Unfortunately the text is corrupt just at the point that would decide whether Cassiodorus explicitly claimed Boethius and Symmachus as his relatives[50]. But no other reason can easily explain why he included Symmachus and Boethius in the account of his own family. This interpretation is confirmed by a passage of the *Institutiones* in which Cassiodorus mentions Proba as *parens nostra*[51]. We have already had occasion to say that Proba was a close relative of Boethius and Symmachus: she was either Symmachus' daughter or his niece. Her very name Proba shows that she was connected with the Anicii[52]. Admiration for the nobility of the Anicii – and perhaps pride in it – is apparent from what Cassiodorus wrote at length in his *Variae* to celebrate them: he praised them as an almost regal family. It is hardly necessary to point out that the aristocrats of late antiquity gave a very wide interpretation to the term of family when they could claim illustrious relatives. Thus the poet Avitus talks of *nostra familia* with the son of Sidonius Apollinaris, simply because Sidonius had been son-in-law to the Emperor Avitus, who was in some way related to the poet Avitus[53]. One has the impression that there was a far greater desire on Cassiodorus' side to associate himself with the Anicii than on the side of the Anicii to admit Cassiodorus to their kin. Nor was Cassiodorus interested in emphasizing his relationship with the Anicii only before the fall of Boethius. All the evidence we have quoted seems to be later than Boethius' death about 524. Hermann Usener, who was the first editor of the *Ordo generis Cassiodororum* in 1877 – and what an admirable editor he was – tried to prove that the *Ordo* had been written before Boethius' death. But Mommsen was in my opinion quite right in refusing to accept this date. The mention of the *Variae* in the *Ordo* and other details point to a date at least as late as 538[54]. The addressee, Cethegus, was still alive and near Cassiodorus in Constantinople in 550[55].

The points that separated Cassiodorus from the circle of Symmachus and Boethius were of great importance, but one can understand that they alienated Boethius from Cassiodorus rather than vice versa. The intellectual horizon of Boethius included Greeks and Romans, whether pagan or Christian, but excluded the Germans. The Germans were ignored. It is difficult to imagine that Symmachus could be so thorough as his son-in-law in this omission, because he wrote history – and imperial history at that. It is at least arguable that he presented the Emperor Maximinus Thrax as the first Goth on the Roman throne[56]. But we have no further reason to believe that he tried to give a place to the Barbarians in his intellectual world. No doubt Boethius and Symmachus followed with anxious attention the daily movements of their Gothic masters, but they studied and wrote to forget them.

Cassiodorus faced the Goths not only in his daily work of a secretary and administrator but in his own studies. In Rome one could ignore them. In Ravenna he found it necessary to educate them and to give them a past and a future in the history of the Roman world. There were other Latin writers who did not ignore – could not ignore – the Goths. They were the writers of biographies of bishops and abbots and saints. The leaders of the Church were then playing an essential part in trying to reduce the horrors and the hardships of the Barbarian invasions, and their biographers could not forget this aspect of their activities. Thus Ennodius' life of Bishop Epiphanius and Eugippius' life of St Severinus provide invaluable evidence for this aspect of ecclesiastical history[57]. But this was of course a different point of view from that of Cassiodorus. He was not facing the Goths as the Christian representative of the native population; he was working in an exalted position for the Goths in Ravenna.

Day after day Cassiodorus tried to give Roman *dignitas* to the orders of his Barbarian masters. His eloquence, his historical and philosophic knowledge, and even his personal sympathies were transferred into the *Variae* and put into the mouths of the Gothic kings. He was pompous, but there are moments in which even pomposity can serve a serious purpose if it is an endeavour to dignify what is in itself undignified. There can be few other works in the literature of any country comparable with such a sustained effort to present a Barbarian as the embodiment of civilized justice and wisdom. Cassiodorus' zeal was such that the *Variae* became a sort of encyclopaedia: not unfairly German dissertations have been treating them as a document of *Kulturgeschichte*[58]. In his private conversations with Theodoric Cassiodorus was expected to convey the answers of Greek science to the naïve questions of the Barbarian king about natural phenomena[59]. In the *Variae* he tried to give the answers of Roman 'civilitas' to the political and administrative problems opened up by the Ostrogothic settlement in Italy: '*Gothorum laus est civilitas custodita.*' To preserve the ancient things – '*vetusta servare*' – that was the intention Cassiodorus liked to attribute to his masters[60].

In 519 a symbolic event seemed to confirm that the best hopes of peace between Constantinople and Ravenna were going to be realized. Euthariсus, the husband of Amalasuntha, was recognized by Justin as the heir presumptive of Theodoric. He was made a consul and had Justin himself as a colleague: he was the first German to be made a consul during the Ostrogothic rule in Italy. Cassiodorus celebrated the date in a typical Romano-Christian way. He produced a new version of the chronicle of Eusebius-Jerome and brought it up to date, giving the Goths pride of place. Thus the admission of the Gothic prince to the Roman consulship was presented as the beginning of a new period of world history[61].

Not long afterwards Cassiodorus must have started working on his history of the Goths. He says in the *Ordo generis Cassiodororum* that he started it to please Theodoric, that is before 526. In 533 his work was already finished or rather had progressed far enough to become the object of praise in a letter which King Athalaricus sent to the Roman Senate to announce that Cassiodorus had been made the prefect of the praetorium. Needless to say, the eulogy of Cassiodorus the historian had been written with conspicuous care by Cassiodorus the secretary. Thanks to this indiscretion we know what he wanted to do in his work: '*originem Gothicam historiam fecit esse Romanam*'[62].

This history in twelve books is lost. Jordanes, a man of at least partial Gothic origin, tells us that about 551 he was preparing a survey of Roman history – later to be known as *Romana* – when he was urged by his friend Castalius to interrupt it and to give priority to a compendium of Cassiodorus' *Gothic History*. Jordanes obeyed, but added apologetically that his task was difficult because he had only been able to borrow Cassiodorus' *History* for three days from Cassiodorus' steward: he admitted, however, that he had already read the book before. '*Ad triduanam lectionem dispensatoris eius beneficio libros ipsos antehac relegi*'[63].

There is certainly something mysterious about this statement. Three days are an impossibly short time to prepare a summary of twelve books. Besides, this passage is stylistically an imitation of Rufinus' Prologue to his translation of Origen's commentary on the letter to the Romans by St Paul; and Jordanes feels the need for introducing his excuse by *ut non mentiar* – 'let me lie not', which makes it doubly suspicious[64]. But if one may well doubt the story of the three days, there is no reason to doubt the main facts. Jordanes was urged to prepare in haste a summary of the history of the Goths, he did his work about 551 and used a copy borrowed from Cassiodorus' own library[65]. Now the year 551 falls within a period of some importance in the relations between Justinian and the Goths. In 550 Matasuntha, Theodoric's granddaughter, now an exile in Constantinople, had married Germanus, a cousin of Justinian[66]. The marriage had been arranged to attract Gothic loyalism. After a few months Germanus died, but a posthumous son of the same name was born to Matasuntha. This is the event with which Jordanes emphatically concludes his work. His line of thought is that Theodoric himself before dying had recommended to his people to 'love the senate and the Roman people, and to make sure of the peace and good will of the Emperor of the East as next after God'[67]. Theodahatus had called upon himself Justinian's wrath by killing Amalasuntha. After Belisarius' expedition and Vitiges' defeat there was only one hope left for the Goths: it was this marriage between Matasuntha and Germanus. Their son was a promise of reconciliation and peace between the two races.

Jordanes does not make any allusion to Narses' expedition which started in 552 with the definite aim of destroying the Ostrogoths for ever. The conclusion of his work is enough to show that he was evidently not a naïve Gothic monk living somewhere in Thrace, as Mommsen conjectured[68]. He did not summarize the Gothic history simply because it flattered his patriotic sentiments. His work had a clear political message. It invited the Goths to cease resistance, but also gave encouragement to those who worked in Constantinople for a *modus vivendi* between Goths and Romans.

The real question which I want to put before you is whether this political message was introduced by Jordanes into Cassiodorus' work or whether it was part of Cassiodorus' original work. In the former hypothesis Jordanes would have summarized Cassiodorus in order to make him serve a new political cause. In the latter hypothesis Jordanes would have summarized Cassiodorus in order to make more easily available for propaganda purposes a work that already contained a political message for the time.

So far as I can see, the almost unanimous opinion of modern scholars is that Cassiodorus concluded his work on the Goths in or before 533 and therefore could not describe the later developments to 551. As a matter of fact, a very substantial section of modern critics believes that he did not even write the history of the reign of Theodoric. Now let me first remind you that although we know that Cassiodorus had already a reputation as a historian of the Goths about 533, we have no reason to think that he stopped working on his *magnum opus* about 533. On this point I find myself in solitary agreement with the Belgian scholar Dom Cappuyns[69]. Between 535 and 550 many things happened to Cassiodorus, but none of them made it impossible for him to give further attention to his *Gothic History*. About 535 he made his unsuccessful attempt to build up a Christian university in Rome[70]. About 538 he relinquished his position as a *praefectus praetorio*, but remained on good terms with Vitiges[71]. He turned increasingly to religion and wrote *De anima*[72]. In 540 Ravenna was occupied by the Byzantines, and Vitiges was taken prisoner and transferred to Constantinople where he was treated very kindly[73]. We do not know whether Cassiodorus was one of those who followed Vitiges in 540, but in 550 (the date is significant) we learn from a letter of Pope Vigilius that he was an authoritative man in Constantinople[74]. Like Pope Vigilius and Cethegus, to whom he dedicated his *Ordo generis Cassiodororum*, he must have returned to Italy after the promulgation of the pragmatic sanction of 554 that fixed the organization of the reconquered territory[75]. Cassiodorus then was obviously a follower of Justinian even if, like his friends Pope Vigilius and Cethegus, he did not often see eye to eye with the emperor. Already in collecting his *Variae* about 538 he had carefully eliminated any piece of writing that might give offence to Justinian; and I do not see why we should rule out that he submitted his work on Gothic history to a similar revision in order to make it compatible with the new situation.

Questions of this sort, however, cannot be argued with *a priori* arguments. What I wish to do is to offer a very simple argument which in my opinion establishes that Cassiodorus really continued his work after 535 until 551 and supported the efforts for a final reconciliation between Goths and Romans under Justinian. My only hesitation in presenting my argument is that it is so simple; one would expect it to have been presented before. It is my considered opinion that Mommsen has already said all the right things about Roman history. I always feel uneasy when I discover that he has not yet said what I am going to say. My argument is this. As I have mentioned, Jordanes concludes his history with the baby Germanus as the new hope for the two nations. But he formulates this hope in a very remarkable way: 'And of them was born a son (also called Germanus) after the death of his father Germanus. This union of the race of the Anicii with the stock of the Amali gives hopeful promise, under the Lord's favour, to both peoples.' '*In quo coniuncta Aniciorum genus cum Amala stirpe spem adhuc utriusque generi domino praestante promittit*'[76].

The marriage of Matasuntha with Justinian's cousin Germanus is presented as a union of the family of the Amali with the family of the Anicii. It is only natural that Matasuntha should represent the Amali – the royal family of the Ostrogoths. But we are not told why Germanus should represent the family of the Anicii rather than the imperial family of Justinian. No doubt, some fact is behind this statement. Perhaps Germanus' mother belonged to the family of the Anicii[77]. But even if there must be some factual basis for this statement, the statement itself remains most extraordinary. The union of a member of the imperial family of Constantinople with a member of the royal family of the Amali is described as a union of the Roman family of the Anicii with the Amali – and no explanation is given. It seems to me clear that this passage is a shortened version of something more circumstantial about the same subject. If this is true, Jordanes summarized his source here as elsewhere – and his source was Cassiodorus.

But the clearest proof of the Cassiodorean origin of the passage is its very content. Nobody except Cassiodorus could represent the union between Matasuntha and Justinian's cousin as a union not of the royal family of Ravenna with the imperial family of Constantinople, but between the Amali and the Anicii. Here, it seems to me, Cassiodorus has put his seal. In all probability he considered himself connected with the family of the Anicii; and his friend Cethegus, next to the Pope the most eminent Italian exile in Constantinople, was very probably a member of the Anician family[78].

If there is some truth in what I am saying, important consequences follow. When Cassiodorus went to Constantinople he must have carried with him a copy of his *Gothic History*. He kept it up to date and modified it to serve the new situation. When the marriage between Germanus and Matasuntha took place and the preparation for a new expedition against the Goths of Italy was progressing, there were good reasons for bringing the work to a conclusion. His last chapters evidently expressed the hopes of the Italian aristocratic exiles who wanted to go back to Italy with a part to play in the reorganization of the country. They did not contemplate the utter destruction of the Goths – and of so much else – that Narses was soon to perpetrate. They may well have thought that the most advantageous situation for themselves would be one in which enough Goths were left to counterbalance Byzantine influence. Certainly they liked the marriage between Germanus and Matasuntha. By emphasizing the connection between Germanus and the family of the Anicii Cassiodorus was discreetly calling attention to his friend Cethegus and to himself. After all he had been in the service of the Amalian family for so many years. Thus the new edition of his own *Getica* expressed the opinions and the hopes of the Italian aristocrats who were exiles in Constantinople in 551.

But a work in twelve books was not the most suitable for propaganda. Anyone who felt that Cassiodorus' work could make an impression either on the Goths of Italy or on the Byzantine leaders would have been well advised to take steps for a shortened edition. The next question is whether Cassiodorus himself saw to it that his work should be summarized. This, of course, is not a question that can be answered with certainty. But there are two arguments that point to Cassiodorus' intervention. First, Jordanes admits to having borrowed Cassiodorus' work from Cassiodorus' steward. Cassiodorus must have known how to choose a steward who would not lend the manuscripts of his master's works without his permission. Secondly, there may be something in Jordanes' personality to corroborate this hypothesis. There is no evidence that Jordanes was a monk, as Mommsen suggested, but there is some reason to believe that he was a Gothic Catholic bishop of Italy. Jordanes dedicated his *Romana* to a Vigilius about 551. Now we know that a Bishop Jordanes of Crotone was in Constantinople together with Vigilius, Bishop of Rome, in 550, and we also know that Pope Vigilius was on friendly terms with Cassiodorus[79]. Furthermore part of the manuscript tradition calls Jordanes *episcopus*[80]. The conclusion seems inescapable that the Jordanes who summarized Cassiodorus' *Gothic History* is the Bishop Jordanes who was the friend of Bishop Vigilius who was the friend of Cassiodorus. Jordanes would have borrowed Cassiodorus' work in Constantinople.

This conclusion was already drawn by Jacob Grimm more than a hundred years ago, but after a period of general acceptance it has now been universally abandoned[81]. There is in fact a serious difficulty against the identification of Jordanes' friend Vigilius with the Bishop of Rome. Jordanes calls his friend Vigilius *nobilissimus et magnificus frater*, while we would expect *venerabilis* or *reverendissimus* or *sanctissimus frater*, if he addressed the Bishop of Rome. More generally one can say that Jordanes talks to Vigilius in a way that would be very clumsy if Vigilius were the Pope. However, I am inclined to suspect that Jordanes was a clumsy man: he could hardly keep his Latin together. Either we are prepared to admit that near Cassiodorus there were two Jordanes and two Vigilii, or we must admit that Jordanes was a boorish provincial bishop of Gothic extraction who did not know how to talk to his fellow exile, the Bishop of Rome. If Jordanes was the exiled Gothic Bishop of Crotone one can understand even better why he was selected in a hurry to compile a summary of Cassiodorus' views about the Goths. A last detail may be added. Jordanes addresses his work to his friend Castalius who is living 'near the Goths', *vicinus genti*. This would seem to designate a man living in Italy – precisely the place where the summary could be most useful.

Ranke already suspected in general terms that Jordanes wrote his summary in agreement with Cassiodorus and for political purposes. I rejoice at the idea that if I cannot agree with Mommsen, I have at least Ranke's support[82].

After von Sybel's dissertation of 1838 and even more after Carl Schirren's distinguished work of 1858, modern scholars have tried various methods to establish what Jordanes owed to Cassiodorus.

Two Italian contributions to this discussion, by C. Cipolla in 1893 and by R. Cessi in 1912, should not be forgotten[83]. These researches, however acute, never produced conclusive results, and we can now see that they were vitiated by three wrong assumptions in the matter of style, chronology, and geography. It is true that some of Jordanes' chapters are written in better Latin than others, but it does not follow that what is good comes from Cassiodorus and what is bad was added by Jordanes. No doubt in some cases Jordanes copied literally whole sentences from Cassiodorus, while in other cases he summarized long passages of his source in his own inferior Latin. On the other hand one used to assume that Cassiodorus wrote in the West under Arian kings and therefore one attributed to Jordanes all that in the present text of the *Getica* is definitely anti-Arian and shows an intimate acquaintance with the East[84]. But now we have to reckon with the strong probability that Cassiodorus revised his work in the East when he had become the subject of a Catholic emperor.

Jordanes' own declaration – 'I have put in an introduction and a conclusion of my own and have also inserted many things of my own authorship' – is not necessarily false[85]. He probably added the initial quotation from Orosius, the final paragraph, and a few details in the middle. But it is simply impossible to determine exactly the quantity and the quality of his own contributions. What we can say is that in all probability Jordanes' *Getica* reflects Cassiodorus' political ideas as reformulated by him about 550 when the Goths were on the wane.

Books about Gothic history probably existed before Cassiodorus: he himself mentions a source, Ablabius[86]; and if we accept an attractive emendation by W. Meyer of a passage of the *Variae*, Ablabius was a Greek[87]. Furthermore, there was a tradition already well established in the fourth century that *Getae* and *Gothi* were the same people[88]. This made it possible for Cassiodorus to incorporate in his history what Dio Chrysostom and other writers had written on the Getae. There seems to have been also another tradition identifying the Goths with the Scythians[89]. This, too, was exploited by Cassiodorus. He extended the range and respectability of Gothic history by adding what one knew about the Getae and the Scythians. Thus the Goths were shown to have been educated by the divine Zalmoxis and became the wisest of the Barbarians: '*pene omnibus barbaris Gothi sapientiores semper extiterunt*'[90]. Goths and Romans were born to help each other. Good emperors like Theodosius were lovers of peace and of the Goths: *amator pacis generisque Gothorum.*

It was a tragedy that the Emperor Valens chose to offend the Goths or that more than once the Goths went their own way without respecting the Romans[91]. Attila's story according to Cassiodorus demonstrated both the advantages of the collaboration between Romans and Goths and the disadvantages of mutual distrust[92]. Applied to contemporary events this lesson of history meant that the only hope for the Goths was the peaceful acceptance of Justinian's rule. But Justinian would be well advised to persevere in a policy of collaboration both with those members of the Gothic aristocracy who were prepared to help and with those Italian aristocrats who knew their Goths from long experience.

What unfortunately we can no longer assess is the scholarly effort of Cassiodorus. Unlike the referendarius Cyprianus and his sons, he was not able to read the Gothic language[93], but there must have been many people in Ravenna ready to help him if he ever wanted to go beyond his classical sources. It was indeed the first time, as far as we know, that a Roman historian had found himself in the position of writing the history of an alien group ruling Rome. Cassiodorus' work is as epoch-making in one way as Polybius' work had been in another. He tried to understand the Goths as Polybius tried to understand the Romans. He had an idea of Gothic psychology – of the pride, violence, gratitude to benefactors of these people – which must have been the result of long observation[94]. The first attempt to place the history of the Goths within the framework of Roman history and civilization was also the last great work of Roman historiography. Not long afterwards the Barbarians of the West began to speak for themselves. There are less than forty years in the chronology I have adopted between Cassiodorus' *Gothic History* and the *History of the Franks* by Gregory of Tours[95].

Cassiodorus' *History*, even if it was not the product of a very critical and independent mind, showed love of knowledge, realism about the present, and a considerable amount of kind and humane feeling[96]. It was meant to help the cause of a peaceful coexistence of Goths and Romans. If my hypothesis is right, we can also say that Cassiodorus remained faithful to his policy of collaboration – for what it was still worth – even on the eve of Narses' expedition. The old universal spirit of Roman tradition was still at work in the last representative of Roman historiography.

Justinian's policy of extermination of the Goths must have come as a deep disappointment to Cassiodorus. Now there was really nothing left for him to do in the world of politics. We shall probably never know whether he had already turned his beloved estate of Squillace into a monastery before going to Constantinople. He certainly concentrated his attention on Vivarium after his return and perhaps became a monk[97]. Though old, he was vigorous enough to start a new life for himself and to open new ways to Latin culture. The task he set himself was to make pagan learning the servant of Christian knowledge. If political life was disintegrating, St Benedict was there to teach that it was possible to build up new unities of economic and spiritual life in the form of monasteries[98]. Classical scholarship would contribute to monastic life. The cloister would replace the court as a centre of culture[99]. The last chapter in the biography of Cassiodorus is undoubtedly more important than that which I have tried to reconstruct on the basis of Jordanes' *Getica* – but it is one on which other members of this Academy can speak more competently than myself.

A SELECT BIBLIOGRAPHY

The best recent works on Cassiodorus are:

J. J. van den Besselaar, *Cassiodorus Senator en zijn Variae* (Academisch Proefschrift, Nijmegen-Utrecht 1945).

Idem, Cassiodorus Senator, Leven en Werken (Haarlem-Antwerpen, n.d., but about 1950).

M. Cappuyns, *Cassiodore* in A. Baudrillart, *Dictionnaire d'histoire et de géographie ecclésiastiques*, xi (1949) 1349–1408.

These have excellent bibliographies. Other references can be found in:

M. Manitius, *Geschichte der lateinischen Literatur des Mittelalters*, i, (München 1911), 36–52 (Cassiodorus); 210–15 (Jordanes).

M. Schanz, *Geschichte der römischen Litteratur*, iv, 2 (München 1920), 92–108 (Cassiodorus); 115–20 (Jordanes).

O. Bardenhewer, *Geschichte der altkirchlichen Literatur*, v (1932), 264–77.

B. Altaner, *Patrologie*, 5 ed. (Freiburg 1958), 442–52.

W. Wattenbach and W. Levison, *Deutschlands Geschichtsquellen im Mittelalter*, i (Weimar 1952), 67–81.

[1] It will be enough to refer to E. Dyggve, *Ravennatum Palatium Sacrum* (Copenhagen 1941) (Arkaeol.-Kunsthist. Meddelelser Danske Vidensk. Selskab, iii. 2); S. Fuchs, Bildnisse und Denkmäler aus der Ostgotenzeit, *Die Antike*, xix (1943) 109–53; A. M. Schneider, Die Symbolik des Theoderichgrabes, *Byz. Zeitschrift*, xli (1941) 404–5; C. O. Nordström, *Ravennastudien. Ideengesch. und*

ikonographische Untersuch. über die Mosaiken von Ravenna (Stockholm 1953) which has an excellent bibliography; M. Mazzotti, *La Basilica di Sant'Apollinare in Classe*, Studi di Antichità Cristiane, Pontificio Istituto Archeol. Cristiana (Rome 1954). [E. Dyggve, *Studi A. Calderini–R. Paribeni* III (1956) 765–73.]

[2] O. Jahn, Ueber die Subscriptionen in den Handschriften römischer Classiker, *Berichte Sächs. Ak. Wiss.* iii (1851) 347.

[3] There is no satisfactory modern account of Italian life in the sixth century. O. Bertolini, *Roma di fronte a Bisanzio e ai Longobardi* (Rome 1941) provides, however, an excellent introduction to the evidence.

[4] *Dialogi*, i, 9 pp. 55–6, ed. Moricca (Fonti per la Storia d'Italia).

[5] *Cf.* A. Franz, *M. Aurelius Cassiodorius Senator* (Breslau 1872) 122–7; Manitius i–iii, index s.v.; P. Lehmann, Cassiodorstudien, *Philologus*, lxxi (1912) 278–99; lxxii (1913) 503–17; lxxiii (1914) 253–73; lxxiv (1917) 351–83; H. Thiele, Cassiodor. Seine Klostergründung Vivarium und sein Nachwirken im Mittelalter, *Studien und Mitteil. z. Geschichte d. Benediktinerordens*, L (1932) 378–419; L. W. Jones, The Influence of Cassiodorus on Medieval Culture, *Speculum*, xx (1945) 433–42 (*cf. ibid.*, xxii (1947) 254–6); M. L. W. Laistner, The Value and Influence of Cassiodorus' Ecclesiastical History, *Harv. Theol. Rev.* xli (1948) 51–68; J. J. van den Besselaar, *Cassiodorus Senator* (Haarlem, n. d. [1950]) 253–263. L. W. Jones's papers are utilized in his introduction to the translation of the *Institutiones* (New York 1946) 47–58.

[6] *Historia Pontificalis*, ed. R. L. Poole (Oxford 1927) p. 2: 'Cassiodorus quoque ex gentili Christianus, monachus ex senatore, ex oratore doctor ecclesie, palmas Christiane militie visas et acceptas a patribus preconatur et sicut previos in cronicis descriptionibus habuit, sic illustres viros huius studii reliquit successores' [*cf.* ed. M. Chibnall (London 1956) p. 2].

[7] P. Delehaye, Saint Cassiodore, *Mélanges Fabre* (Paris 1902) 40–50. *Cf. Acta Sanctorum*, Sept., IV, 349–50.

[7a] An edition has now been provided by M. Adriaen in the *Corpus Christian* (1958). Also *De anima* has been edited by J. W. Halporn in *Traditio* xvi (1960).

[8] It will be enough to mention: R. Beer, Bemerkungen über den ältesten Handschriftenbestand des Klosters Bobbio, *Anz. Phil.-Hist. Klasse Wiener Akad.* xlviii (1911) 78–104; *idem, Monumenta Palaeogr. Vindobonensia*, ii (1913), 14–50; W. Weinberger, Handschriften von Vivarium, *Miscellanea F. Ehrle*, iv (1924) 75–88. *Contra:* E. A. Lowe, Some Facts about our oldest Latin Manuscripts, *Classical Quarterly*, xix (1925) 205, and *Codices Latini Antiquiores*, iv (1947) pp. xx–xxvii, and above all G. Mercati, in *Prolegomena* to *M. Tulli Ciceronis De re publica libri . . . phototypice expressi* (*Codices e Vaticanis selecti*, xxiii) (Città del Vaticano 1934) 1–174. *Cf.* R. Devreesse, La Bibliothèque de Bobbio et le palimpseste du De Republica, *Bull. Ass. Budé* (1935) 27–33; F. Blatt, Remarques sur l'histoire des traductions latines, *Classica et Mediaevalia*, i (1938) 226–42; A. Souter, Cassiodorus' Library at Vivarium, *Journ. Theol. Studies*, xli (1940) 46–7; Card. I. Schuster, Come finì la biblioteca di Cassiodoro, *La Scuola Cattolica*, lxx (1942) 409–14; P. Courcelle, *Les Lettres grecques en Occident. De Macrobe à Cassiodore*, 2nd ed. (Paris 1948) 357–88; H. Bloch in his review of E. A. Lowe, *Codices*, iv, *Speculum*, xxv (1950) 283–7. About the *Amiatinus* I shall only refer to H. Quentin, *Mémoire sur l'établissement du texte de la Vulgate* (Rome 1922) 438–452; Lowe, *Codices*, iii (1938) no. 299 with bibl.; Courcelle quoted; M. Cappuyns, *Dict. Hist. Géogr. Eccl.* ii, 1384–8 ; H. Blum, Über den Codex Amiatinus und Cassiodors Bibliothek in Vivarium, *Zentralbl. f. Bibliothekswesen*, lxiv (1950) 52–7. For a curious detail of the Codex Amiatinus *cf.* C. Roth, The Priestly Laver as a Symbol on Ancient Jewish Coins, *Palest. Explor. Quart.* lxxxiv (1952) 91–3; other literature in Wattenbach-Levison, *Deutschlands Geschichtsquellen*, i

(1952) 47 n. 32; 75 n. 139, and (for archaeological criticism) in F. Saxl, *Journ. Warburg and Courtauld Inst.* vi (1943) 15 n. 1. [M. P. J. Van Den Hout, *Prolegomena* to *M. Cornelii Frontonis Epistulae* (Leiden 1954) XII–XIII.]

[9] It is impossible and would be superfluous to give here the whole literature on the question whether the *Regula Magistri* was written by Cassiodorus or can at least be associated with Vivarium. Cassiodorus's authorship has not been demonstrated, and the connection with Vivarium seems to be a vague probability at best. *Cf.* Dom H. Vanderhoven and F. Masai, *Aux sources du monachisme bénédictin*, i. *Regula Magistri* (Paris–Bruxelles 1953) with the reviews of H. I. Marrou, *Rev. Étud. Lat.* xxxii (1954) 414–20; P. Courcelle, *Rev. Étud. Anc.* lvi (1954) 424–8; and F. Vandenbroucke, *Rev. Bénéd.* lxiv (1954) 277–82. Among the earlier papers the following can be singled out *exempli gratia*: J. Pérez de Urbel, *Rev. Hist. Eccl.* xxxiv (1938) 707–39; A. Genestout, *Rev. d'Ascétique et de Mystique*, xxi (1940) 51–112; M. Cappuyns, *Recherches de théolog. ancienne et médiévale*, xv (1948) 209–68, who suggested the name of Cassiodorus; F. Vandenbroucke, *ibid.* xvi (1949) 186–226; F. Masai, *Scriptorium*, ii (1948) 292–6; F. Renner, *Stud. Mitt. Geschichte Benedikt.* lxii (1950) 87–195; E. Franceschini, *Aevum*, xxiii (1949) 52–72; *idem* in *Liber Floridus . . . P. Lehmann gewidmet* (St Ottilien 1950) 95–119; O. J. Zimmermann, *Amer. Bened. Review*, i (1950) 11–36; H. Vanderhoven, *Rev. Hist. Eccl.* xlv (1950) 707–70; P. Blanchard, *Rev. Bénéd.* lx (1950) 25–64; F. Vandenbroucke, *ibid.* lxii (1952) 216–73. Now see C. Mohrmann, *Vigiliae Christianae*, viii (1954) 239–51 (with an excellent bibliography) and J. Froger, *Rev. d'Ascétique*, xxx (1954) 275–88. [Later bibliography in G. Penco, *S. Benedicti Regula* (Florence 1958) XI–XVIII: I. Gomez, *Hispania Sacra* 9 (1956) 1–55 is especially concerned with C.]

[10] I know only G. Iacopi, *Brutium*, xxxii (1953) nos. 3–4, pp. 8–9, a provisional note substantially repeated in Πεπραγμενα του Θ' Διεθνους Βυζαντινολογικου Συνεδριου, i (Athens 1955) 201–5, that leaves me sceptical. But we must wait for further details. I have not yet seen P. Courcelle, Nouvelles recherches sur le monastère de Cassiodore, *Actes du Ve Congrès International d'archéol. chrétienne 1954*. We owe to Courcelle the most important research on Le Site du monastère de Cassiodore, *Mélanges École Rome*, lv (1938) 259–307. [*Cf. Actes* quoted (Città del Vaticano 1957) 511–28, where Courcelle takes a positive view of Iacopi's discoveries.]

[11] The most recent treatments known to me are Wattenbach and Levison, *Deutschlands Geschichtsquellen*, i, 75–81, and F. Giunta, *Jordanes e la cultura dell'alto medio evo* (Palermo 1952). I understand that a new edition of the text of the *Getica*, which will make use of the ninth-century manuscript noticed by E. Sthamer in the Archivio di Stato of Palermo, is being prepared in England. On the Palermo manuscript *cf. Forschungen und Fortschritte*, v (1929) 45, and Giunta, pp. 188–202. R. Cessi's suggestion that the second section of the *Anonymus Valesianus* (c. 36–78) goes back to Cassiodorus is not well founded (*cf.* the ed. of the Anonymus in *Rer. Ital. Script.* xxiv, pp. lxxvii–lxxxviii). F. Rühl's alleged discovery of another excerpt of Cassiodorus's *Gothic History* (*Neue Jahrb. f. Phil.* cxxi (1880) 549–76) was soon disproved by Th. Mommsen, *Chron. Minora*, ii, *Monum. Germ. Hist.* [*M.G.H.*], xi, 308–22 (*Exordia Scythica*): 'Cassiodori Geticis tantum abest ut auctor usus sit, ut ne Iordanianorum quidem certa indicia deprehendantur.'

[12] *Agnelli Liber Pontificalis*, ed. O. Holder-Egger (*M.G.H.*), 94: 'In pinnaculum ipsius loci fuit Theodorici effigies, mire tessellis ornata, dextera manu lanceam tenens, sinistra clipeum, lorica indutus. Contra clipeum Roma tessellis ornata astabat cum asta et galea: unde vero telum tenensque fuit, Ravenna tessellis figurata, pedem dextrum super mare, sinistrum super terram ad regem properans.'

E. Dyggve (quoted in n. 1), p. 50. *Cf.* also E. Bishop, *Liturgica Historica* (Oxford 1918) 370–83.

[13] *Variae*, 5. 16. 2.

[14] *Cf.* W. Ensslin, *Theoderich der Grosse* (1947) 321.

[15] The extent to which the Vandals interfered with communications in the western Mediterranean after 500 is still disputed. For an extreme view *cf.* N. H. Baynes, *Byzantine Studies and other Essays* (London 1955) pp. 309–20 (from *J.R.S.* xix (1929) 230). More cautious in the same sense: G. Mickwitz, Der Verkehr auf dem Westlichen Mittelmeer um 600 n. Chr., *Wirtschaft und Kultur. Festschrift A. Dopsch* (Leipzig 1938) 74–83. For the view minimizing Vandal interference: A. R. Lewis, *Naval Power and Trade in the Mediterranean, 500–1100* (Princeton 1951) 1–30; *idem*, Le Commerce maritime et les navires de la Gaule occidentale (550–570), *Études Mérovingiennes* (Paris 1953) 191–9, and to a certain extent C. Courtois, *Les Vandales et l'Afrique* (1955) 207–9. But Ennodius, *Paneg. Theol.* xiii, 70, and Cassiod. *Variae*, 5. 17, mention troubles, and the existing evidence on the relations between Africa and Gaul (*cf.* C. Courtois, *Cahiers de Tunisie*, ii (1954) 127–34) and between Africa and the other Western regions (Courtois, *Les Vandales*, 205, n. 3) is not too clear. *Cf.* also W. H. C. Frend, North Africa and Europe in the Early Middle Ages, *Trans. Royal Hist. Soc.* v, 5 (1955) 61–80. [*Cf.* F. Giunta, I Vandali e la Romania, *Kokalos* II (1956) 20–36.]

[16] *Cf. inter alia* G.-G. Lapeyre, *Saint-Fulgence de Ruspe* (Paris 1929); W. Pewesin, *Imperium, Ecclesia Universalis, Rom. Der Kampf der afrikanischen Kirche um die Mitte des 6. Jahrh.*, in *Geistige Grundlagen römischer Kirchenpolitik* (Stuttgart 1937); P. Courcelle, *Histoire littéraire des grandes invasions germaniques*, 151 ff.; C. Courtois, *Victor de Vita et son oeuvre* (Alger 1955); *idem*, *Les Vandales*, 284 ff. R. R. Bezzola, *Les origines et la formation de la littérature courtoise en Occident*, i (Paris 1944) 7, seems to me to overrate the Vandals.

[17] He came from Pannonia: 'Pannoniis genitus, transcendens aequora vasta Galliciae in gremium divinis nutibus actus' (*Martini Episcopi Bracarensis Opera Omnia*, ed. C. W. Barlow (1950) p. 283).

[18] The new great collective *Storia di Milano*, ii (Fondazione Treccani, Milano, 1954) (*Dalla invasione dei barbari all'apogeo del governo vescovile, 493–1002*), is disappointing about Milan as a centre of learning in Late Antiquity.

[19] *Vita Caesarii*, lv, p. 480 (with note), ed. B. Krusch (Passiones Vitaeque Sanctorum Aevi Merovingici, *M.G.H.*). *Cf.* M. Dorenkemper, *The Trinitarian Doctrine and Sources of St Caesarius of Arles* (Fribourg 1953); G. Bardy, L'Attitude politique de saint C. d'A., *Revue d'histoire de l'église de France*, xxxiii (1947) 241–257.

[20] See the *Epistula ad Probam Virginem* preceding the *Excerpta* (ed. P. Knoell in *Corp. Script. Eccl. Lat.* [*C.S.E.L.*]), where Eugippius says 'cum bibliothecae vestrae copia multiplex integra, de quibus pauca decerpsi, contineat opera, placuit tamen habere decerpta.' *Cf.* Cassiodorus, *Inst. I* (*div. litt.*) 23: 'Hic ad parentem nostram Probam, virginem sacram, ex operibus sancti Augustini valde altissimas quaestiones ac sententias diversasque res deflorans.' *Cf.* Max Büdinger, Eugippius, eine Untersuchung, *Sitz.-Ber. Wiener Akad.* xci (1878) 804. I may mention here G. Morin, Une Compilation antiarienne inédite sous le nom de S Augustin issue du milieu de Cassiodore, *Rev. Bénéd.* xxxi (1914–19) 237–43 (not very cogent). [On Ennodius and St Augustine *cf.* P. Courcelle, *Hist. Jahrbuch*, lxxvii (1957) 451–3.]

[21] Fulgentius, *Ep.* ii, 16 (*Patr. Lat.* [*P.L.*] lxv, 320); *Vita Fulgentii*, xxv (*P.L.* lxv, 144), edited by G.-G. Lapeyre (Paris 1929) p. 119. *Cf.* G.-G. Lapeyre, *Saint Fulgence de Ruspe*, 234–6.

[22] So Cassiodorus, *Ordo generis Cassiodororum* ('Anecdoton Holderi') in *Variae* rec. Mommsen, p. v.

[23] *Cf.* the genealogical tree of the Symmachi in Seeck's edition of Q. Aurelius Symmachus, *M.G.H.*, p. xl.

[24] *Cf.* Jordanes, *Getica*, xv, 83, and the discussion by W. Hartke, *Römische Kinderkaiser* (1951) 427–39. *Cf.* H. Löwe, Von Theoderich dem Grossen zu Karl dem Grossen, *Deutsches Archiv*, ix (1952) 354–6.

[25] O. Jahn, *Ber. Sächs. Akad.* iii (1851) 353; J. Sundwall, *Abh. z. Geschichte d. ausgeh. Römertums* (1919) 139 (about Horace), and M. Schanz, *Gesch. Röm. Lit.* iv, I, 2nd ed., 258. Sidonius associates Horace and Prudentius in *Ep.* 2. 9. 4.

[26] P. Courcelle, *Les Lettres grecques en Occident*, 2nd ed., 307. *Cf.* J. Martin, *Grillius. Ein Beitrag zur Geschichte der Rhetorik* (Paderborn 1927) (Studien zur Geschichte und Kultur des Altertums, xiv). *Cf.* also L. Hahn, Zum Sprachenkampf im Römischen Reich bis auf die Zeit Justinians. Eine Skizze, *Philologus*, Suppl. x (1907) 675–718.

[27] The two basic researches are by K. Praechter, Richtungen und Schulen im Neuplatonismus, *Genethliakon C. Robert* (Berlin 1910) 105–56, and Christlich-neuplatonische Beziehungen, *Byzant. Zeitschrift*, xxi (1912) 1–27. *Cf.* furthermore P. Courcelle, *Les Lettres grecques*, 257 ff.; R. Vancourt, *Les Derniers Commentateurs alexandrins d'Aristote. L'école d'Olympiodore, Étienne d'Alexandrie* (Lille 1941); H.-D. Saffrey, Le chrétien Jean Philopon et la survivance de l'école d'Alexandrie, *Rev. Étud. Grecques*, lxvii (1954) 396–410.

[28] *Gramm. Lat.* iii, 405 Keil: 'Fama quidem antea nobis absentem venerabilem faciebat; nunc autem praesentem veritas supergressum laudes praedicationis ostendit'.

[29] *Cf. Gramm. Lat.* iii, 405; notice in this passage a sentence remarkable from the political point of view: 'petimus igitur sapientem eloquentiam vestram ut . . . Romanorum diligentiam vestrorum ad artes suorum alacriorem reddatis auctorum, quibus solis ceteras cum Grais gentes superasse noscuntur'. *Cf.* in general R. Helm in Pauly-Wissowa, s.v. 'Priscianus', and V. Schurr, quoted below, n. 31.

[30] *Les Lettres grecques*, p. 299.

[31] *Cf.* the admirable book by V. Schurr, *Die Trinitätslehre des Boethius im Lichte der skythischen Kontroversen* (Paderborn 1935) 198. Part of the evidence is given in the following notes. But one fact deserves to be emphasized with Schurr. A corrector of manuscripts of Boethius called *Renatus v.s.* appears as the transmitter of a letter by Senarius to Iohannes Diaconus with questions about 'catechumeni', etc. (the reference in n. 35). The same Renatus of Ravenna was apparently in Constantinople about 510 to argue with the monophysite Severus (J. Lebon, *Le Monophysisme sévérien* (Louvain 1909) p. 46, n. 3, on the evidence of *Severi Antiocheni Liber contra Impium Grammaticum Orat. III Pars Posterior* (Paris 1933), ed. J. Lebon, ch. 29, p. 72 of the translation). On the background see E. Caspar, *Geschichte des Papsttums*, ii, 149 ff., and A. A. Vasiliev, *Justin the First* (1950) 160 ff.

[32] *Epistulae Romanorum Pontificum*, ed. Thiel (1868) 755; *Avellana quae dicitur collectio*, ed. O. Günther (*C.S.E.L.*), *Ep.* 115.

[33] Cyrilli Scythopolitani, *Vita Sabae*, c. 53, p. 145, ed. Schwartz (1939); Theophanis *Chronographia*, p. 157, ed. De Boor; *Avellana . . . collectio*, nos. 164, 179, 198 (*C.S.E.L.*). *Cf.* J. Aschbach, 'Die Anicier', *Sitz.-Ber. Wiener Akad.* lxiv (1870) 392; E. Schwartz, *Kyrillos von Skythopolis* (1939) 379–83; E. Stein, *Histoire du Bas-Empire* (1949) ii, p. 67, n. 1; 172. *Cf.* also E. Schwartz, Publizistische Sammlungen zum acacianischen Schisma, *Abh. Bayer. Akad.* (1934) p. 245, and A. von Premerstein, Anicia Juliana im Wiener Dioskorides-Codex, *Jahrb. d.*

Kunsthist. Sammlungen, xxiv (1903) 106–23 (*cf.* R. Delbrueck, *Die Consulardiptychen* (1929) 55).

[34] *Liber contra Eutychen et Nestorium*, Prooemium.

[35] Senarius: *P.L.* lix, 399; A. Wilmart, *Analecta Reginensia* (Studi e Testi, lix (1933) 170–9. *Cf.* Avitus, *Ep.* 36 (*P.L.* lix, 252; *M.G.H.* vi, 2, p. 68, ed. Peiper); Ennodius, *Ep.* i, 23, and J. Sundwall, *Abh. zur Geschichte des ausgeh. Römertums*, 153. Faustus: *P.L.* lxiii, 534; E. Schwartz, *Publizistische Sammlungen zum acacianischen Schisma*, 115–17; J. Sundwall, 117. Albinus: *Avellana . . . collectio* (*C.S.E.L.*), *Ep.* 173, p. 629; J. Sundwall, 87. On Senarius, O. Fiebiger, *Denkschr. Wiener Akad.* lxxii (1944) 2. Abh., 10, is misleading.

[36] *Cf.* Cassiod. *Instit.* i, 23, 2. His work collected in *P.L.* lxvii. *Cf.* Schanz, iv, 2 (1920) 589; E. Schwartz, *Zeitschr. Savigny-Stift.*, Kan. Abt. xxv (1936) 1–114; H. Wurm, *Studien u. Texte zur Dekretalen-Sammlung d. Dionysius Exiguus* (Bonn 1939) (Kanonistische Studien und Texte 16), pp. 10–30, and bibl. there quoted. *Cf.* also B. Altaner, Zum Schrifttum der skythischen (gotischen) Mönche, *Historisches Jahrbuch*, lxxii (1953) 568–81; H. Steinacker, Die römische Kirche und die griechischen Sprachkenntnisse des Frühmittelalters, *Mitt. Inst. Oesterr. Gesch.* lxii (1954) 28–66, especially 51 ff., and in general the article by J. Rambaud-Buhot, Denys le Petit, *Dict. Droit Canon.* iv (1949) 1131–51. P. Heck, *Übersetzungsprobleme im frühen Mittelalter* (Tübingen 1931) must be consulted on the nature of mediaeval translations [W. M. Peitz, *Studia Gratiana* 1 (1953) 53–79].

[37] The evidence in Schanz, iv, 2, 230.

[38] *Inst. Gramm.* ii, 2, Keil 'non minus Graecorum quam Latinorum in omni doctrinae genere praefulgentem'.

[39] *Codex Iuliani v.c.* in the subscriptio of Stat. *Theb.* iv, in the Cod. Puteanus. The identification was suggested by F. Vollmer, *Rh. Mus.* li (1896) 27, n. 1. But *cf.* R. Helm, Pauly-Wissowa, s.v. 'Priscianus', 2329.

[40] E. Stein, *Histoire du Bas-Empire*, ii, 729, 838; A. H. M. Jones, *Journ. Rom. Studies*, xxxix (1949) 52. For his love of Latin *De Magistr.* iii, 20, 27, and especially the pathetic passage, ii, 12.

[41] E. Stein, *Histoire du Bas-Empire*, ii, 723–9. *Cf.* the telling chapters by John Lydus, *De Magistr.* ii, 25–6. About him *cf.* also E. Schwartz, Zu Cassiodorus und Prokop, *Sitz. Bayer. Akad.* (1939) n. 2 – a study of his diplomatic activity; his conclusions are not accepted by Stein, ii, 337, n. 1; 342, n. 2, but the matter deserves further consideration. See O. Veh, *Zur Geschichtsschreibung und Weltauffassung des Prokop von Caesarea*, iii (Bayreuth 1953) 3–11.

[42] It will be enough to register here my disagreement with the admirable essay by F. Klingner on Boethius in *Römische Geisteswelt* (Leipzig 1943) p. 432.

[43] Here again I shall be content to refer to C. H. Coster, The Fall of Boethius, *Ann. Inst. Phil. Hist. Orient.* xii (1952) 45–87, for recent literature, but G. B. Picotti, Il senato romano e il processo di Boezio, *Arch. Storico Italiano*, vii. 15 (1931) 205–28, mentions previous Italian works and clears away wrong hypotheses. Coster's theory that Boethius was arrested in 525 and executed in 526 seems to me untenable: it goes against the Anonymus Valesianus and the date at which Cyprianus was still referendarius (*Variae*, 5, 40).

[44] *Variae*, 8, 32.

[45] *Instit.* i, 23, 2: 'qui [Dionysius] mecum dialecticam legit'. Note his autobiographical remark in *Anecdoton Holderi* 'iuvenis adeo dum . . . laudes Theodorichi regis Gothorum facundissime recitasset'.

[46] *Instit.* i, 17, 1: 'Hunc tamen ab amicis nostris, quoniam est subtilis nimis et multiplex, magno labore in libris viginti duobus converti fecimus in Latinum'. On Cassiodorus's knowledge of Greek see the remarks by H. Steinacker, *Mitt.*

Inst. Oesterr. Geschichtsforschung, lxii (1954) 46, n. 76a. [See now F. Blatt, *The Latin Josephus*, I (1958) 17.]

[47] Biographical details in Schanz, iv, 2, 392. For his clerical status *Epist. ad Parthenium*, 69; *Epist. ad Vigilium*, 11 (now in Aratoris Subdiaconi *De Actibus Apostolorum*, ed. A. P. McKinlay (C.S.E.L.) (1951) p. 152; 4).

[48] *Variae*, 10, 11, and 12, 'Anicios quidem paene principibus pares aetas prisca progenuit'. This was written in 535. Significantly enough, the family 'vere dicitur nobilis, quando ab ea actionis probitas non recedit'. After 533 the family of Boethius was mentionable again in Ravenna (Procopius, *B.G.* i (5), 2, 5) – a fact not without importance for the question of the date of the *Ordo generis Cassiodororum*; *cf.* n. 54.

[49] The most recent edition of the text – first published by H. Usener, *Anecdoton Holderi* (Bonn 1877) and then by Mommsen, *Cassiodori Variae*, p. v – is in J. J. van den Besselaar, *Cassiodorus Senator en zijn Variae* (1945) p. 206.

[50] 'Ordo generis Cassiodororum qui scriptores exstiterint ex eorum progenie vel ex quibus eruditis'. Usener's emendation 'ex civibus eruditis' will not do. Mommsen wavered between 'vel qui eruditi' in his edition of Jordanes, p. xli, and 'vel ex quibus eruditis profecerint' in *Variae*, p. v. The emendation 'vel qui eruditi' would make it certain that Boethius and Symmachus were included in the *Ordo generis Cassiodororum* as relatives, not as teachers. But even if one accepts 'ex quibus eruditis profecerint' it is hard to believe that Boethius was mentioned by Cassiodorus as a teacher. Professor Mynors, whom I consulted on this passage, wrote to me (13. x. 1955): 'Really we have not the needful resources to solve the problem. None of the suggestions so far made seems to me at all on the right lines; if I had to add to their numbers, it would be to supply a verb, which must be in the third person singular: e.g.

qui scriptores extiterint ex eorum progenie vel ex quibus eruditis <claruerit>

the subject being either *genus* or *progenies* understood, preferably *genus*. I cannot begin to explain why the verb should have fallen out; but when one is dealing with (*a*) a title, (*b*) an excerpt, one cannot be expected to explain omissions as one normally has to when dealing with continuous literary text'. Another conjecture in *Dict. Hist. Géogr. Eccl.* xi, 1367.

[51] *Instit.* i, 23, 1: 'ad parentem nostram Probam virginem sacram'.

[52] J. Sundwall, *Abhandlungen*, 161; J. J. van den Besselaar, *Cassiodorus Senator en zijn Variae*, pp. 13–14; Seeck, Pauly-Wissowa, s.v. 'Symmachus' ii, 4, 1161.

[53] Avitus, *Ep.* 51, p. 80, Peiper (*M.G.H.*).

[54] In his edition of the *Variae*, p. xi, Mommsen thought that in the corrupt sentence of the *Anecdoton Holderi*: 'Postmodum dehinc magister officiorum et praefuisset', there was an allusion to the dignity of a praefectus praetorio received by C. in 533; this seems to be confirmed by Dom Cappuyns, *Dict. Hist. Géogr. Eccl.* xi, 1368. Van den Besselaar, *Cassiodorus Senator en zijn Variae*, defends Usener's date not very convincingly (p. 5), though one must admit that the present state of the text of the Anecdoton does not allow any certainty about its date. For another suggestion, R. Cessi, *Studi critici preliminari* to his edition of the *Anonymus Valesianus*, pp. cxxxvi–cxxxvii. I was unable to consult R. Anastasi, La fortuna di Boezio, *Miscellanea Studi Letteratura Cristiana Antica*, iii (1951) 93–109, which deals with the *Anecdoton Holderi*.

[55] See the text quoted in n. 74. Furthermore Mansi, *Conciliorum Omnium Amplissima Collectio*, ix, 50 and 347. *Cf.* Sundwall, pp. 107–8.

[56] *Cf.* W. Ensslin, Des Symmachus Historia Romana als Quelle für Jordanes, *Sitz. Bayer. Akad.* (1948) no. 3, 5–12. Ensslin has made a powerful case for

Symmachus as the chief source of the *Romana*. I may add that, if the thesis on the *Getica* defended in the present lecture is correct, Jordanes's *Romana* also needs reconsideration.

[57] *Cf.* G. M. Cook, *The Life of St Epiphanius by Ennodius* (transl. and commentary) (Washington 1942). About Eugippius, *Vita S. Severini* (ed. Th. Mommsen *M.G.H.*: transl. and commentary by R. Noll, Linz 1947). I. Zibermayr, *Noricum, Baiern und Oesterreich, Lorch als Hauptstadt und die Einführung des Christentums* (Berlin 1944); F. Kaphan, *Zwischen Antike und Mittelalter*, 2nd ed. (München 1947); E. Schaffran, Frühchristentum und Völkerwanderung in den Ostalpen, *Arch. f. Kulturgesch.* xxxvii (1955) 16–43. *Cf.* also R. Noll, *Mitt. Inst. Oesterr. Geschichtsf.* lix (1951) 440–6.

[58] A. Th. Heerklotz, *Die Variae des Cassiodorus Senator als kulturgeschichtliche Quelle*, diss. (Heidelberg 1926). *Cf.* also G. A. Punzi, *L'Italia del secolo VI nelle Variae di Cassiodoro* (Aquila 1927). But I recommend the shrewd remarks by E. Sestan, *Stato e Nazione nell'alto Medioevo* (Napoli 1952) 221–31.

[59] *Variae*, 9, 24: 'Nam cum esset publica cura vacuatus, sententias prudentium a tuis fabulis exigebat, ut factis propriis se aequaret antiquis. Stellarum cursus, maris sinus, fontium miracula rimator acutissimus inquirebat, ut rerum naturis diligentius perscrutatis quidam purpuratus videretur esse philosophus.'

[60] 'Civilitas' in *Variae*, 9, 14, 8. In the same sense 1, 27, 1; 3, 24, 4; 4, 33, 1, etc. 'Vetusta servare', 3, 9, 1; *cf.* 2, 4.

[61] 'Eo anno multa vidit Roma miracula, editionibus singulis stupente etiam Symmacho Orientis legato divitias Gothis Romanisque donatas', etc., ed. Mommsen, *Chronica Minora*, ii, *M.G.H.* xi, 161. *Cf.* M. Büdinger, Die Universalhistorie im Mittelalter, *Denkschr. d. Kais. Akad. Wien*, xlvi (1900) 26. [A.-D. v. Den Brincken, *Studien zur lateinischen Weltchronistik* (Düsseldorf 1957) 86.]

[62] *Variae*, 9, 25. This passage is generally taken to imitate Justinus's prooemium to his Summary of the *Historiae Philippicae*. [For the meaning of Origo in this passage *cf.* my *Secondo Contributo*, 149. I cannot accept the far-reaching conclusion by O. Seel, *Die Praefatio des Pompeius Trogus* (Erlangen 1955): indeed I am no longer certain that Cassiodorus imitates Justinus, as F. Rühl suggested].

[63] *Getica*, i, 3. The meaning of 'relegi' is not clear to me: it seems to imply that Jordanes had already read Cassiodorus before. *Cf.* Wattenbach and Levison, i, 77, n. 149; on the interpretation of this passage *cf.* A. von Gutschmid, *Kleine Schriften*, v (1894) 331–3, *contra* C. Schirren, *De ratione quae inter Iordanem et Cassiodorum intercedat*, 92–3. [H. Fuchs, *Mus. Helv.* 14 (1957) 251 is probably right in postulating two lacunae and reading 'eius beneficio < admissus > libros antehac < iam diligenter lectos > relegi'.]

[64] This was shown by H. von Sybel, *Allgemeine Zeitschrift für Geschichte*, vii (1847) 288.

[65] The date is approximately fixed by *Romana*, 4: 'In vicensimo quarto anno Iustiniani imperatoris'; the year 24 started on April 550 (Stein, *Histoire du Bas-Empire*, ii, 821, but the reasons given by Stein for dating the *Getica* in the spring of 552 are not cogent). Another suggestion in A. van de Vyver, *Speculum*, VI (1931) 259, n. 1.

[66] Procopius, *B.G.* iii (7), 39, 14; Jordanes, *Getica*, 314.

[67] *Getica*, 304.

[68] Mommsen, preface to his edition, pp. x–xiv. W. Wattenbach, *Deutschlands Geschichtsquellen*, i, 6th ed. (1893) p. 77, remarked: 'Ich halte es für vollkommen undenkbar, dass ein Mönch in einem Kloster in Mösien ein solches Werk hätte zu Stande bringen, dass er das neueste Annalenwerk hätte erhalten und über die politischen Angelegenheiten der Gegenwart hätte schreiben können'. Other not

very convincing suggestions in L. Erhardt, *Gött. Gel. Anz.* (1886) 676, n. 1; B. von Simson, *Neues Archiv*, xxii (1896) 741–7; J. Friedrich, *Sitz. Bayer. Akad.* (1907) 379–442.

[69] In the excellent art. *Cassiodore* of Baudrillart, *Dictionn. d'histoire et de géogr. ecclés.* xi (1949) col. 1366: 'en complétant à Constantinople son ouvrage de 519–522, à l'occasion de la naissance de Germain (551), l'ancien ministre entrevoyait la possibilité d'une restauration romano-gothique . . . Trois années plus tard cette possibilité était irrémédiablement exclue.'

[70] *Inst.*, *Praefatio:* 'nisus sum cum beatissimo Agapito papa urbis Romae ut, sicut apud Alexandriam multo tempore fuisse traditur institutum, nunc etiam in Nisibi civitate Syrorum Hebreis sedulo fertur exponi, collatis expensis in urbe Romana professos doctores scholae potius acciperent Christianae'. H. Marrou, Autour de la bibliothèque du Pape Agapit, *Mél. d'archéol. et d'hist.* xlviii (1931) 124–69 (fundamental, but pp. 157–69 are somewhat speculative). About the model *cf.* J. B. Chabot, L'École de Nisibe, *Journ. Asiat.* ix, 8 (1896) 43–93. The preserved inscription of the library (Diehl, *Inscr. Lat. Christ. Vet.* I, 1898) is a monument to Cassiodorus's intentions:

Sanctorum veneranda cohors sedet ordine [longo]
divinae legis mystica dicta docens.
hos inter residens Agapetus iure sacerdos
codicibus pulchrum condidit arte locum.
gratia par cunctis, sanctus labor omnibus unus,
dissona verba quidem, sed tamen una fides.

On the school of Nisibis, *cf.* also Th. Hermann, *Zeitschr. f. Neutest. Wiss.* xxv (1926) 89–122. [On the historical situation W. Ensslin, *Hist. Jahrbuch* 77 (1957) 459–66.]

[71] This is shown by the conclusive page of *De anima*, 'Invidit [diabolus] (pro dolor!) tam magnis populis, cum duo essent' (*P.L.* lxx, 1307). The past *essent* does not necessarily imply the end of the Gothic régime: see A. van de Vyver, *Speculum*, vi (1931) 253.

[72] Cassiodorus himself considered *De anima* as the thirteenth book of the *Variae*, *Expos. in Psalterium* 145 (*P.L.* lxx, 1029). *Cf.* also *Variae*, 11, praef. 7, and above all the preface to *De anima* itself: 'Dixi propositiones has non praeceptis regum, quae nuper agebantur, sed profundis et remotis dialogis convenire' (*P.L.* lxx, 1281). This dates *De anima* about 538–40.

[73] Jordanes, *Getica*, 313; Procopius, *B.G.* iii (7), 1, 2.

[74] 'Nec non et per gloriosum virum patricium Cethegum et religiosum virum item filium nostrum Senatorem aliosque filios nostros commoniti noluistis audire' (Mansi, *Concilior. Omn. Ampliss. Collectio*, ix, 357). *Cf.* Jaffé, *Regesta Pontificum*, i, 2nd ed., p. 122; Procop. *B.G.* iii (7), 35, 10 (where Cethegus is called Γόθιγος) and Liber Pontific. *Vita Vigilii*, vii (ed. Duchesne, p. 298).

[75] Liber Pontific. *Vita Vigilii*, ix (ed. Duchesne, p. 299); Victor Tonnensis, *Chronica*, pp. 203–4, Mommsen, *M.G.H.* xi. *Cf.* Stein, ii, 669. In *Instit.* i, 17, 2, Cassiodorus may express some authentic admiration for Justinian, though the words are conventional: they are paralleled by *Variae*, 11, 13, 5, 'si Libya meruit per te recipere libertatem'.

[76] The manuscript tradition is divided between 'utriusque generi' and 'utriusque generis' and between 'genus' and 'gens'.

[77] As we have seen (n. 33), a branch of the family was in Constantinople. *Cf.* J. Aschbach, *Sitz. Wien. Ak.* lxiv (1870) 416–17.

[78] This cannot be stated confidently as J. Aschbach, *Sitz. Wien. Ak.* lxiv (1870) 415, and J. J. van den Besselaar, *Cassiodorus Senator en zijn Variae*, p. 14, do; but Flavius Rufius Petronius Nicomachus Cethegus was the son of Petronius

Probinus, consul 489 (Ennodius, *Opusc.* 6, p. 314, Vogel), and Petronius-Nicomachus-Probinus are names typical of the Anician groups. As Besselaar rightly says, 'Op deze wijze zou men zoowel de opdracht als den inhoud van den "Ordo generis Cassiodororum" beter kunnen verklaren.' About the importance of the Anicii in the Gothic war *cf.* also Procop. *B. G.* iii (7), 20, 26–31; on Cethegus, *ibid.* iii (7), 13, 12.

[79] Mansi, *Sacrorum Concil. . . . Collectio*, ix, 60 D (551 AD): 'Cum Dacio Mediolanensi . . . Paschasio Aletrino atque Iordane Crotonensi fratribus et coepiscopis nostris.' *Ibid.* ix, 716 (556 AD): 'directam a vobis relationem, defensore ecclesiae nostrae Iordane deferente, suscipientes satis mirati sumus' (a letter of Pope Pelagius I). The text of the former now in E. Schwartz, Vigiliusbriefe, *Sitz. Bayer. Ak.* (1940) 2, p. 14; of the latter in *Pelagii I Papae Epistulae*, ed. P. M. Gassò and C. M. Batlle (Montisserrati 1956) p. 31.

[80] Manuscripts PVS of *Romana*: 'Incipit liber Iordanis episcopi'. In XZY of the third class of the manuscripts of the *Getica*: 'episcopus ravenatis civitatis' (or similar expressions). About the 'versus Honorii scholastici ad Iordanem episcopum' (Riese, *Anth. Lat.* 666) I accept Mommsen's suggestion that Jordanes's name is a later addition (pref. to Jordanes, p. xlvi, but *cf.* Pauly-Wissowa, s.v. 'Iordanis', col. 1911). Jordanes is called episcopus also in old catalogues. See M. Manitius, *Neues Archiv*, xxxii (1906) 651.

[81] Grimm, *Abh. Berlin* (1846) p. 11; *Kleinere Schriften*, iii (1866) 182, identified Vigilius with the pope but did not yet know that a Jordanes was mentioned as a bishop of Crotone. The identification of Jordanes with this bishop was suggested by S. Cassel, *Magyarische Alterthümer* (Berlin 1848) 302, n. 1, from Mansi, *Sacrorum Concil . . . Collectio*, ix, 60, quoted above. Mommsen, *Jordanes*, p. xiii, n. 22 is clearly embarrassed: 'quod ut non inepte excogitatum est, ita vincitur indiciis plurimis et certissimis originis libellorum Thracicae.' The possibility of identifying Vigilius with the pope had already presented itself to J. E. Metzgerus, *De Jornande* (Altdorf 1690) p. 18.

[82] *Weltgeschichte*, iv, 2 (1883) 313–27, a magnificent analysis: 'Jordanes hätte nur den Namen gegeben, durch welchen der eigentliche Ursprung verborgen gehalten werden sollte; er wäre mehr Redaktor als Autor' (p. 327).

[83] C. Cipolla, *Memorie Accad. Torino*, ser. 2, xliii, 99–134; R. Cessi, Introd. to his ed. of the *Anonymus Valesianus* (Rer. Ital. Script, 24, 4), pp. lxxxix ff. A survey of opinions on the date of composition of Cassiodorus's Gothic History in Wattenbach and Levison, i, 71. F. Altheim, Waldleute und Feldleute, *Paideuma* (1953) p. 427, dates the *Hist. Gothorum* about 526–33. Waitz in *Nachr. Göttingen* (1865) p. 101, followed by A. Gaudenzi, *Atti e Memorie Deputazione . . . Romagna* (1884–5) 278, thought that Jordanes was responsible for mistakes about Clovis's family. This is possible, but nobody can tell what mistakes Cassiodorus could make and any inference about the terminal point of Cassiodorus's history would seem to me unjustified.

[84] It will be enough to mention one *locus classicus*: *Getica*, 133, 'sic quoque Vesegothae a Valente imperatore Arriani potius quam Christiani effecti.'

[85] i, 3: 'Ad quos et ex nonnullis historiis Grecis et Latinis addidi convenientia, initium finemque et plura in medio mea dictione permiscens.' I cannot go into the question of the relation between Jordanes's text and the continuation of the Chronicle of Marcellinus. In any case the answer to this question cannot be decisive for our problem whether Jordanes had Cassiodorus's work before him for the period after Theodoric. But remarks on the connections of this *auctarium* of Marcellinus preserved in Bodleianus Auct. T. ii, 26 with Cassiodorus are to be found in Courcelle, *Rev. Étud. Anc.* lvi (1954) 428.

[86] *Getica*, 28, 82, 117.

[87] *Variae*, 10, 22, 2: 'et abavi (*Ablavi* Meyer) vestri historica monimenta recolite'. L. Schmidt, *Geschichte d. deutschen Stämme*, i² (1934) 28, n. 2, does not accept the emendation and altogether minimizes the importance of Ablabius. Sidonius refused to become the historian of the Visigoths: *Ep*. 4, 22.

[88] For instance, Orosius, 1. 16, 'Getae illi qui et nunc Gothi'. *Cf. Scr. Hist. Aug.* (Spartianus) *Anton. Carac.* 10; *Geta*, 6. As is well known, the identity of Getae and Gothi was still defended by J. Grimm. The point was elaborated by C. Schirren, *De ratione quae inter Jordanem et Cassiodorium intercedat* (1858) 54 ff., and before him by S. Cassel, *Magyarische Alterthümer*, 302 ff. 'Getae' instead of 'Gothi' is also found in inscriptions: for instance Dessau, *I.L.S.*, 798.

[89] Sidonius Apollinaris, *Panegyr. Aviti*, 403: 'Obstupuere duces pariter Scythicusque senatus.' *Cf.* 498.

[90] *Getica*, 40.

[91] *Getica*, 146; *cf.* 131 ff. [But see 154 ff. with Mommsen's note.]

[92] *Getica*, 180 ff. The analysis of the sources in M. Schuster, Die Hunnenbeschreibungen bei Ammianus, Sidonius und Iordanis, *Wiener Studien*, lviii (1940) 119–30, is unsatisfactory. *Cf.* also D. Romano, Due storici di Attila: Il Greco Prisco e il Goto Jordanes, *Antiquitas*, ii (1947) 65–71.

[93] *Variae*, 8, 21, 7: 'Pueri stirpis romanae nostra lingua loquuntur.' Their father was, of course, 'instructus trifariis linguis', *Variae*, 5, 40, 5.

[94] A study of this aspect of Jordanes-Cassiodorus in its relation to the methods of ancient historiography would be rewarding. Sections 121–63, 180–229 are particularly interesting. Some good remarks in H. Helbling, *Goten und Wandalen. Wandlung der historischen Realität* (Zürich 1954) 29–32.

[95] Gregory died in 593 or 594, Wattenbach and Levison, i, 101. *Cf.* J. M. Wallace-Hadrill, *Trans. Royal Hist. Soc.* v, 1 (1951) 35–6. [*Histoire et Historiens dans l'Antiquité* (1958) 278.]

[96] 'Diese Widersprüche und Inkonsequenzen dem Jordanes beizumessen, geht nicht an', L. Schmidt, *Geschichte der deutschen Stämme*, i² (1934) 27.

[97] In the preface of *De orthogr.* (*Gramm. Lat.* vii, 144 K.) Cassiodorus speaks of 'conversio mea': 'post commenta psalterii, ubi praestante domino conversionis meae tempore primum studium laboris impendi'. About the meaning of 'conversio' see Kappelmacher in Pauly-Wissowa, s.v. Jordanis, col. 1911; J. J. van den Besselaar, *Cassiodorus Senator*, Haarlem, n.d. [1950] 146–51. I am not convinced by C. Mohlberg, *Ephemerides Liturgicae*, xlvii (1933) 3–12, that the 'Sacramentarium Leonianum' was C.'s prayer-book. Mohlberg is followed by G. de Jerphanion, *Rech. de science religieuse*, xxvi (1936) 364–6. [L. C. Mohlberg, *Sacramentarium Veronense* (Rome 1956).]

[98] I may perhaps refer to L. Salvatorelli, *San Benedetto e l'Italia del suo tempo* (Bari 1929); Dom J. Chapman, *St Benedict and the Sixth Century* (London 1929); S. Brechter, St. Benedikt und die Antike, *Benedictus der Vater des Abendlandes* (München 1947) 139–94; Ph. Schmitz, *Histoire de l'Ordre de Saint Benoît*, i, 2nd ed. (Maredsous 1948); G. Aulinger, *Das Humanum in der Regel Benedikts von Nursia* (St Ottilien 1950); J. J. van den Besselaar, *Cassiodorus Senator* (Haarlem, n.d. [1950]) 134 ff. For anti-ascetic tendencies in the fifth–sixth centuries notice G. A. Cary, A Note on the Mediaeval History of the Collatio Alexandri cum Dindimo, *Class. et Mediaevalia*, xv (1954) 124–30. [B. Steidle, ed., Commentationes in regulam S. Benedicti, *Studia Anselmiana* 42 (1957); *Il Monachesimo dell'alto Medioevo e la formazione della civiltà occidentale* (Spoleto 1957); *cf.* also *Studia Anselmiana* 44 (1959).]

[99] *Cf.* M. Roger, *L'Enseignement des lettres classiques d'Ausone à Alcuin* (Paris 1905); G. Manacorda, *Storia della scuola in Italia. I. Medioevo* (Milano 1913); G. Hoerle, *Frühmittelalterliche Mönchs- und Klerikerbildung in Italien* (Freiburg

1914); F. Ermini, La scuola a Roma nel VI secolo, *Archivum Romanicum*, xvii (1934), 143–54; B. Gladysz, Cassiodore et l'organisation de l'école médiévale, *Collectanea Theologica* (Lwów), xvii, 1 (1936) 51–69; P. Courcelle, Histoire d'un brouillon cassiodorien, *Rev. Étud. Anc.* xliv (1942) 65–86; E. R. Curtius, Das mittelalterliche Bildungswesen und die Grammatik, *Romanische Forschungen*, lx (1947) 1–26; H. I. Marrou, *Histoire de l'éducation dans l'antiquité* (Paris 1948) 435 ff. Other references in P. Renucci, *L'Aventure de l'humanisme européen au Moyen-Âge* (Paris 1953) 210–14; R. R. Bolgar, *The Classical Heritage and its Beneficiaries* (Cambridge 1954) p. 416 (*cf.* also p. 405). There is much, of course, to learn from A. Viscardi, *Le origini*, 2nd ed. (Milano 1950), and R. Bezzola, *Les origines et la formation de la littérature courtoise en Occident*, i (Paris 1944). *Cf.* E. Bickel's review of Mynors's edition of the *Institutiones*, in *Gnomon*, xiv (1938) 322–8, and E. K. Rand, *Speculum*, xiii (1938) 438–47. [Dom J. Leclercq, *L'amour des lettres et le désir de Dieu* (Paris 1957) 25–8.]

CHAPTER ELEVEN

HISTORIOGRAPHY ON WRITTEN TRADITION AND HISTORIOGRAPHY ON ORAL TRADITION*

THE origin of Greek historiography lies in Ionic thought. We recognize dimly that without Xenophanes there would be no Hecataeus; but the precise relationship between the two is unknown to us, and even the connection that, for us, links Herodotus with his predecessor Hecataeus is uncertain. Xenophanes showed the uncertainties and the relativism of human knowledge, without, however, allowing them to discourage him: he sought to investigate the past, by examining its traces in the present; he was interested in fossils and, as far as can be seen, wrote on the foundation of Colophon. The inevitable result of his casting doubt on current conceptions of the gods was research on the borderland between gods and men, which, for the Greeks, was myth. This research was undertaken by his contemporary Hecataeus. A geographer and a mythologist, Hecataeus compared Greek traditions with Oriental (or at least with Egyptian) traditions, and realized that Oriental history was considerably longer than Greek, with the result that the mythical period was, in Egypt, placed in a more remote past than in Greece. What precise deductions he drew from his discovery we do not know, but we do know that he set out, albeit intuitively and not systematically, to minimize the miraculous and supernatural in the Greek traditions. Although he was among the most important figures in the drama of the Ionian revolt, he does not appear to have written on the Greek history of his time. His scientific interests were the structure of the earth and the legends of the mythical past, and knowledge of foreign lands nourished his scepticism of Greek traditions – which he declared to be 'many and ridiculous'.

Herodotus derived from him his concern with geography, the

* *Atti della Accademia delle Scienze di Torino*, 96 (1961–2), 1–12.

passion for travel, and interest in non-Greek mythology; he was like Hecataeus a barbarophile but, as a friend of Sophocles, as one who had reached maturity in Periclean Athens, he was far from systematically despising the Greek traditions; he declared his respect for the gods and emphasized his intention of preserving the record of the great deeds of Greeks and Barbarians. The transfer of the Homeric note to historiography means that the first duty of the historian is to collect and preserve traditions: respect for traditions is placed higher than criticism; and since criticism could not refrain from the irreverent disclosure of what was hidden, Herodotus is scrupulous not to relate details of a religious kind. The positive value of this caution and respect lay in the new calling of Herodotus: he wished to open up for '*historia*' the territory of contemporary or almost contemporary events, which, without the help of the historian, would have been soon forgotten. By emphasizing preservation and respect as opposed to criticism, Herodotus put himself in a position to collect people's memories of the events which had been at the heart of his adolescence.

There is, without doubt, in Herodotus a mingling of different, and sometimes opposed, motifs and inspirations. In terms of pure rationalism he is weaker than Hecataeus. But he lays bare the fact that to write history is above all to remember and register a long and complex series of events in all its details; and for this discovery we are all in his debt. For this reason Herodotus moves from the zone of myth to that of the recent past. And he gives to the combination of geography and research ('*historia*') about inhabitants a new meaning, showing how the description of foreign lands can be accompanied by the narrative of an event which brings into contact foreigners (Barbarians) and Greeks. Having made this discovery, he can let many critical suggestions of Hecataeus operate in his narrative: the description of Egypt bears clear traces of this. Hecataeus' tendency to minimize the miraculous works in him too. But his problems as a historian are definitely different. For him it is more important to collect new facts than to criticize those that are already known, it is more essential to give a comprehensive and unified representation of events than to examine individual episodes and to judge of their verisimilitude. As a result Herodotus was obliged to construct his own method of collecting, ordering, and unifying events. He directed his powers as a collector towards the oral tradition of Greeks and Barbarians; he preferred the accounts of living people to written documents. Perhaps, in the circumstances, this was the more natural choice. In Greece written documents were rare, and seldom dealt with those political and military events in which Herodotus was interested. Oriental chronicles were at the time linguistically inaccessible to the historian who knew only one language. Nevertheless, what little written documentation, Greek and Barbarian, he did use in his history shows that, if he had wished, he could have proceeded in another direction. Just as he made use of interpreters for his oral communications with the Egyptians, so could he probably have drawn upon interpreters for the written sources; they cannot have been lacking in the Persian empire.

His preference – it was not exclusive, but dominant – for the oral tradition entailed a series of consequences. Above all Herodotus sought to guarantee the credibility of all that he had collected. Hence his well-known habit of distinguishing between what he has seen personally and what he has heard from others; and the less precise, but none the less constant, effort to report different versions and to establish their relative value. But the collection of oral traditions involved also the need to construct a chronology that would unite the isolated facts and give them order. Herodotus had to combine Oriental dynasties with Greek genealogies in a first attempt at international chronology. His equation of the sixth year after the death of Darius with the archonship of Kalliades at Athens (VII, 51, 1) is even today one of the fundamental dates of history.

Contemporaries recognized, and posterity confirmed, that the '*historia*' of Herodotus was more important than Hecataeus' criticism. For the Greeks and Romans he was the father of history. Sophocles was his friend, Aristophanes parodied him, Theopompus epitomized him, and Aristarchus wrote commentaries on him. The historians who recounted the events of individual foreign nations (for example Ctesias) or embraced several regions (Timaeus and perhaps Posidonius) referred to his example. Stylistically his influence can be traced from the beginning to the end of ancient historiography, and beyond, in Byzantine historiography. And yet the father of history was never, or almost never, recognized as a model historian, because he was never considered trustworthy, even by his admirers. Even his fellow-citizen, Dionysius of Halicarnassus, who admired him in all other respects, is silent about his veracity.

This paradoxical situation is easily explained. Herodotus was the father of history, because Thucydides implicitly recognized him as such; but he was believed to be untrustworthy, because such was the verdict of Thucydides. In other words the reputation of Herodotus in antiquity depends fundamentally on the direction that Thucydides imposed on historiography.

Thucydides accepted the presupposition of Herodotus that history is made of predominantly oral traditions. The importance of this basic agreement can never be emphasized enough. Written documents are marginal for Thucydides as they are for Herodotus: even if they are documents of a different sort (treaties instead of inscriptions and oracles). Moreover Thucydides followed Herodotus in his interest in the most recent events. But the criteria that he adopted for the study of the oral tradition were more rigorous than those of Herodotus. The historian had to have been present at the scene of action or to have used the reports of those who were present. Even the speeches had to be constructed with precise criteria of verisimilitude. The temptation to collect traditions that had not been thoroughly checked was strictly repressed. One could indeed, according to Thucydides, move from the present to make conjectures on the past, somewhat in the manner of Xenophanes; but it was again a controlled and brief conjecture, very different from the unlimited collection of traditions and legends of the world at large which Herodotus had put together precisely because he had not excluded what he could not guarantee. It will be noted that Thucydides records different versions considerably less often than Herodotus, and seldom indicates the source of his version or allows it to be discovered. He assumes the responsibility for what he says, and feels no need to leave a choice to the reader.

Indeed, as is well known, behind Thucydides' methodological objection on the criterion of certainty in history lies the different orientation of his interests in life. Thucydides concentrated on political life; it was here that he found the meaning of human effort. By understanding the political life of the present, and its military consequences, he believed that he had understood the nature of man in its perennial elements. He refrained almost completely from descriptions of foreign lands, unusual occurrences (with the exception of the plague), anecdotes about famous individuals, myths and cults, or information about monuments conspicuous for beauty or greatness. He was at pains to understand the Peloponnesian War as the sum of human nature – so much so that he entertained no doubt whatsoever about the premises of his method.

Undoubtedly, Thucydides persuaded the majority of his readers, at least in antiquity, that in comparison with his own criteria of truth Herodotus did not deserve belief. He then succeeded also in persuading his successors that the only true history is political, or politico-military. Xenophon, Theopompus, and the author of the *Hellenica Oxyrhynchia* headed the line of historians who differ from Thucydides in a multitude of ways and yet, like him, are political historians. The geography which Herodotus had interspersed with history is now separate; at the most it serves as a preface (Ephorus). With the notion of political history Thucydides also hands on a preference for contemporary or almost contemporary history constructed on direct experience or on the recollections of others which have been rigorously controlled. This goes to confirm how Thucydides consolidated Herodotus' preference for oral tradition. Rarely, and then only subordinately, do the political historians of Greece and Rome have recourse to documents. So when, in opposition to Thucydides and with, ultimately, a bad conscience, they decide to go beyond near-contemporary history to the remote past, they still apply as best they can the Thucydidean criterion of research. Even for the distant past it is only rarely and subordinately that they draw upon what we call primary material. The normal method is to make use of the accounts drawn up by historians living at the time of the events. The non-contemporary historian avails himself, as much as he can, of contemporary historians, not of documents. An oral tradition is definitely preferred, since contemporary historians who are the ultimate source to which one returns use for preference an oral tradition.

Thucydides, then, carries to triumphant fulfilment a demand for veracity that is more rigorous than Herodotus', and encourages his successors to limit their particular interests to the realm of politics, but he does not change the basis of historic documentation, which in antiquity remains principally oral in character, and only secondarily archivistic. Of those who consolidate the Thucydidean position, it will suffice here to name Polybius. Not only did he accept in substance the Thucydidean method (although, as far as I know, he quotes Thucydides only once in the extant parts); he also systematically demolished Timaeus, the only great historian of the third century to connect himself with Herodotus. And, since Timaeus had begun to have a following in Rome (Fabius Pictor), the success of Polybius meant in fact the triumph of Thucydides' school at Rome. It is noteworthy that for the ancients Polybius did not represent a new school. Even the Greek historians who are specifically concerned with Rome, like Dio Cassius, remain faithful to the model of Thucydides. And according to Lucian it is Thucydides who teaches that the historian says ὡς ἐπράχθη, a definition which was perhaps remembered by that great admirer of Thucydides, Ranke.

When Thucydides showed such rigour in limiting his history to contemporary history of Greece based on predominantly oral sources, he perhaps presupposed – certainly he encouraged – as a reaction the tendency shown in Sophist circles to deal with certain aspects of the past in erudite monographs based on a tradition that was in part written. The list of Olympic victors compiled by Hippias, the same writer's monograph on the names of nations, Critias' study of different constitutions, not to mention the list of the priestesses of Hera at Argos compiled by Hellanicus (who was not a Sophist) are among the earliest examples of what we call antiquarianism (and what Hippias seems to have called archaeology). There has never been an absolute divorce, a precise criterion of separation between antiquarianism and historiography. One could make a long list of subjects about which it has always been uncertain whether they belong to historiography or to antiquarianism. All local histories have this stamp of ambiguity between history and antiquarianism. The ambiguity dates from their origin, and goes back to the age of Thucydides. Anyway, in broad terms, the distinction exists, and can be recognized. Historiography from Thucydides onwards was above all political in subject-matter, it set out to explain and instruct, it followed a chronological order, and was concerned with great events, with important nations or cities. Erudite research on religion, art, customs, proper names, events of obscure cities or nations and so on was excluded; usually (though not, of course, in local history) it was hostile to chronological order. But just because it was often presented in systematic order, erudite research reflected philosophical interests or lent itself to offering material to philosophers. In the Hellenistic age, as had already happened during the Sophistic period, erudition and philosophy became allied in certain philosophical schools, principally in the Peripatetic. This alliance between erudition and philosophy was to appear again in later ages, often assuming the character of religious libertinism. And even at the beginning this antiquarian research was concerned with written sources, with collecting and reporting documents from archives, describing statues and buildings, interpreting foreign languages. The technique of erudite research spread to the field of biography; indeed it dominated the study of the lives of men of letters and philosophers, leaving on one side for the most part the lives of statesmen (but Suetonius applied the technique of antiquarian biography to the emperors). In political historiography the antiquarian technique is seldom to be found, and where it does appear (for example in Dionysius of Halicarnassus and Tacitus) it is confined to the age of origins or limited to digressions. It goes without saying that one cannot speak of antiquarian method when a senator like Tacitus, instead of consulting his own notes on a meeting of the Senate, went to read over the *Acta Senatus*. There is a sole exception: ecclesiastical history. It was the last to develop, in the fourth century AD, and it followed the model of erudite research. There is no doubt that in creating it Eusebius had in mind the technique used in the biography of philosophers as we find it in Diogenes Laertius. The unconventional spirit of the Hellenizing Christians, who culminate in Eusebius, is confirmed in their relinquishing the usual historiographical method that was based on oral sources and had a marked interest in contemporary history. A passage of Sozomen (I, i, 13) clearly indicates the written sources of ecclesiastical historiography.

Leaving this ecclesiastical historiography on one side for a moment, we must emphasize that the study of written sources of an archivistic nature, the use of primary documents, is in antiquity the custom not of historians but of 'archaeologists', 'philologists', 'grammarians', that is, of antiquarians.

The separation between political historiography and antiquarian erudition reappears with the resurgence of the authority of ancient historiography in the fifteenth century, and continues until very recent times. It cannot be chance that the only branch of historiography ready to display a huge documentary apparatus should again be ecclesiastical historiography, a field of great importance yet discredited in humanist circles and scarcely considered in treatises on the art of history. The persistence of this division explains why the ancient historians remained for so long the model for modern historiography. Modern historians as late as the nineteenth century are concerned less with collecting material than with telling a story and understanding it adequately. Although the use of written sources becomes ever more general even for near-contemporary history, research into archives, when there is any, is secondary. The ideal persists of the historian who sees, remembers what he has seen, and gives his own judgment. Anyone who wished to write the history of the respective fortunes of Herodotus, Thucydides, and Polybius (and one might add Livy and Tacitus) from the Renaissance to the nineteenth century could leave out of consideration – or almost – their reputation as students of sources. Their authority is determined by other factors. Until the nineteenth century Thucydides remains relatively in the shadow. Hobbes's admiration for the History of the Peloponnesian War is a taste not widely shared. Even the parallel between Thucydides and Livy drawn by Father Rapin (1681) is exceptional, and besides he leaves it in doubt which of the two is to be preferred. The wise Polybius takes supremacy over Thucydides, because – among other reasons – he deals with a Roman subject. As for Herodotus, he finds unexpected support in the Bible, to which he provides a complement and an explanation. At the same time incredulity about his stories decreases little by little. The new geographical explorations show that there are in the world things stranger than those related by Herodotus. The judgment of Dionysius of Halicarnassus, who is held in great consideration, whether as a Greek historian of Rome or as a literary critic, favours Herodotus, and is unfavourable to Thucydides. The revolution that places Thucydides at the head of all the ancient historians is the Romantic revolution. Thucydides is the artist, the patriot, the indefatigable seeker after truth. Polybius is neither patriot nor artist, and not being an artist he merely skims over the prosaic surface of human life. This objection is, naturally, not valid against Herodotus, and indeed there is plenty of sympathy for Herodotus among the Romantics. But it is not surprising that in the end Thucydides prevails in the opinion of the majority: for his political passion and for his scrupulousness about truth he is deemed superior.

Now in this story of Thucydides' fortunes one point should be noted, for it is essential to our argument. Even in the eighteenth century the barrier between antiquarian research and historiography had remained fairly strong. Certainly the great Benedictine erudition of the early eighteenth century had made an enormous impression;

but no one (to my knowledge) had dared to suggest that this should replace Livy or Guicciardini. In the second half of the century the prestige of Benedictine erudition was shaken. With Voltaire and the Encyclopaedists comes the affirmation of a philosophy that repudiates the old alliance between philosophy and erudition and substitutes the new alliance between historiography and philosophy. Racy and generalizing, historiography offers its services to the propaganda of the enlightened. Only in the third phase (which begins with Winckelmann and culminates in Gibbon) does there appear the possibility that erudition could re-enter the new history of civilization, and the philosopher and the antiquarian collaborate again on a new basis. But it would be a mistake to think that this ideal of a synthesis between antiquarianism and historiography progresses without hindrance throughout the nineteenth century. The truth is that the more forms are taken by erudite research the more there persists a nostalgia for those historians like Thucydides who kept firmly to the essential lines and did not allow themselves to be carried away by the mass of documents. It is just that combination of art, exactness, and absence of pedantry which makes Thucydides the ideal historian in a century where pedantry inevitably becomes a method in itself. It is enough to read the most significant nineteenth-century book on Thucydides, by W. Roscher (1842). Here Thucydides, the artist, is contrasted with the professional historian, pedantic and erudite, who, devoid of inspiration, copies out the sources. True enough, Niebuhr, the artist-historian, the new Thucydides, had at the end of his life edited Byzantine sources, but only because like a true leader he wished to pass on an impulse to others. The cult of Thucydides, which lasts until E. Meyer, has this ambiguous basis in the almost nostalgic admiration for a history with all the characteristics of the new austere and erudite research, yet not getting lost in it, nor losing the ancient simplicity of direct evaluation of the facts. The so-called 'Archaeology' – the opening chapters of the work of Thucydides – assumes a new importance as linear reconstruction of the past on the basis of clues.

An orientation of this kind was possible while the separation between historiography and antiquarianism, though ever weaker and weaker, was still defensible: it is to be noted that the distinction was still accepted by Eduard Meyer. But the elimination of the distinction came about not only through the work of those historians who were making ever more use of full documentary research; the change was also at work in those antiquarians who transformed their systematic works of erudition into fascinating historical reconstructions, and among this number were Mommsen and Burckhardt. More and more, sociology was now collaborating with antiquarianism and historiography, so closely as to make it in certain cases impossible to distinguish what was history, what was antiquarianism and what was sociology: the case of Max Weber is the most noted example. Once the dualism between antiquarianism and historiography, which goes back to the time of Thucydides, has disappeared or is about to disappear, it becomes even easier to realize that modern historiography, in leaning on Herodotus and Thucydides and their Greek and Roman pupils, has appropriated a method highly suitable for orally based historiography, but much less so for research drawing upon archives, linguistic data, archaeological excavations, and systematic inquiries. The breakaway from Thucydidean method is now an accomplished fact: and it allows us also to understand how much was lost (as well as gained) in the rigorous delimitation of Thucydides by comparison with Herodotus. But because of this it is all the more necessary to refer back to Herodotus and Thucydides if we wish to understand how different is our contemporary historiography, which for the first time since the Renaissance is a non-Greek historiography, although still animated by the Greek spirit of 'enquiry'.

CHAPTER TWELVE

HISTORICISM IN CONTEMPORARY THOUGHT*

FOUR years after the appearance of *Lo Storicismo tedesco contemporaneo* (Turin, Einaudi, 1956), Pietro Rossi has taken up his earlier theme again and completed his exposition, thus consolidating his reputation as one of the greatest experts on contemporary problems of historiography[1]. As can happen to those who resolutely follow their own course, Rossi is not perhaps sufficiently aware of his debt to Carlo Antoni (a debt that is not peculiar to him, but shared by us all). Antoni was the first to separate the fortunes of German historicism from Italian, Crocean historiography. Now Rossi accepts the premise in substance, but upsets the conclusion. He sees Dilthey and Max Weber as the masters of a historicism liberated from metaphysical presuppositions. This ought to take the place of Croce's historicism inasmuch as the latter carried with it a theological inheritance of Hegelian origin. What is admirable in Rossi is the clarity with which he masters a difficult and intricate subject. His analysis extends to all the most important theorists of history of our time except those in the Slavonic languages, and satisfies the widely felt need to ascertain the relationships between sociological research and historical research.

It would be inappropriate for me to enter into a discussion with Rossi in a field which he knows so much better than I do. But there is perhaps in his book an implicit presupposition which I can help to discuss here. Rossi's aim is above all, explicitly, to encourage a theory of history that is a methodical discussion of how the facts can be understood, instead of being an interpretation of the global significance of history. But, if I am not mistaken, he implicitly assumes that in contemporary historiography there are convergent movements towards a new historicism derived from, or akin to,

* *Rivista Storica Italiana*, LXXIII (1961), 104–19.

that of Dilthey and Weber. While I am not arguing here about what ought to be the case, I have the impression that the real state of affairs in contemporary historiography is different. And since every programme for the future, which is what Rossi's basically is, has to start from present circumstances, I believe that one should take account of a resistance to German historicism that is much stronger than he seems to assume. In short our task is to measure the influence of German historicism on the actual work of the historians of the post-war period. Let my impressions be worth what they may; they belong to a historian who, outside his own field, has read desultorily and little. But the question cannot be avoided.

In the following pages, I ask this question of fact: whether, and to what extent, contemporary historiography is inspired by German historicism. My answer is that, however much Nazi and Fascist persecutions have scattered all over the world historians and philosophers who were brought up on Dilthey and Weber, contemporary historiography does not seem to have received its greatest stimuli nor the solution of its difficulties from German historicism.

Before we can begin to discuss whether, and how, German historicism can in the future recover its position as the theory of history for our times, we should be quite clear what the historians of our day are doing and to whom they owe their inspiration. I open the discussion with this preliminary question.

With the advent of Nazism, Germany quickly lost her position as the principal forge of historical methods and problems, which she had held since the beginning of the nineteenth century. The methodology of racialist historiography, which was imposed by violence and accepted usually more through fear than conviction, did not succeed in producing historical research of real value, even if it did give rise to some interesting studies, for example the work of F. Schachermeyr in early Greek history.

The suppression of all free speech, and the forced exile (the alternative to legal assassination) of many historians (Jews, or related to Jews, or simply anti-Nazi) meant a suspension of all the work of revising historicism, which great historians and sociologists such as E. Troeltsch, M. Weber, G. Simmel, F. Meinecke had carried forward after Dilthey, and which a younger generation (including, for instance, K. Mannheim, K. Löwith, F. Saxl) was already following up. The discussion had to remain interrupted at a moment of vital importance. Relativistic thinkers were just beginning to face the need to preserve both the individual and the absolute (Troeltsch, Meinecke). Marxist determinism was confronted with the complex typology of the forms of social action elaborated by Max Weber (G. Lukács, K. Mannheim). The contention that man cannot escape the destiny imposed on him by the civilization to which he belongs (O. Spengler) was being opposed by the theory of a possible, though limited, choice between different experiences which lies at the root of the thought of W. Dilthey and Max Weber. The devaluation of ideologies as conditioned by the social situation was being replaced by the revaluation of the autonomy of culture through a sociology of knowledge (A. Weber, Max Scheler, K. Mannheim). Finally, with M. Heidegger, the theory of history was introduced into an existentialist philosophy. In the field of concrete historical research the interruption was no less dramatic. As a result of Nazism, the movement to establish a new humanism, which was led by W. Jaeger and centred round the journals *Die Antike* and *Gnomon*, disappeared within a few years. The revaluation of the heritage of the classical world, which had been undertaken by A. Warburg and embodied in his institute at Hamburg, could no longer be expressed in German. The movement to reinterpret the whole of European history in terms of great personalities, initiated by Stefan George with the co-operation of authentic historians such as E. Kantorowicz and F. Gundolf, was forced into silence. Even the conflict – essential to German historiography – between *Grossdeutschland* and *Kleindeutschland*, which was still finding expression in the grand manner in the works of K. Brandi and H. von Srbik, was concluded by order: as witness the dismissal of Meinecke from the *Historische Zeitschrift*.

In relation to this enforced adjournment of the debate, two questions arise: (a) whether, and in what way, the debate has begun again in Germany since the fall of Nazism; (b) whether it has proved possible to transplant the problems of German historicism and elaborate them further outside Germany. Among other things, the fact that the process is not yet finished, and must be defined here only in a transitory phase, makes both these questions difficult to answer.

In post-war Germany there has been an obvious effort to take up once again the problems that were left in suspense and to return to the historiographical traditions of the periods of Wilhelm II and the Weimar republic. Witness the remarkable reappearance of the

Monumenta Germaniae and the *Historische Zeitschrift*, and the number of reprints of classic books and articles: witness moreover the enthusiastic study of the lives and works of the great masters of the past, such as Theodor Mommsen and Max Weber. Hence the authority acquired by G. Ritter, the historian who has most thoroughly examined the problems posed by the conflict between political power and moral life on the lines already indicated by Meinecke (Meinecke himself, moreover, lived to see the fall of the régime he hated and to bear witness to its nature). But approximately half of Germany, with university centres such as Leipzig, has had imposed upon it a Marxist doctrine of historiography which, to judge from the results in the field of classical studies, does not seem to hold much inspiration for the Germans. In West Germany, where the greater part of serious historical work is going on, the most characteristic movement seems to be not the renewed study of problems intrinsic to pre-war historicism, but rather the theological interpretation of history. This was still superficial and combined with heterogeneous elements in the work of K. Jaspers, *Vom Ursprung und Ziel der Geschichte* (1949), but to give only one example, was already much more strongly marked in the almost contemporary work of K. Löwith, an exile who returned to Germany and to religion (*Meaning in History*, 1949, republished in German in 1953 as *Weltgeschichte und Heilgeschehen*). It is now at the centre of the discussions in the most lively and original journal of post-war German historiography, *Saeculum*. This explains the fact that the beginnings of Christianity (R. Bultmann, W. Kamlah), Constantine and the theological Middle Ages are more than ever subjects for enquiry. The research directed by P. Schramm on the political symbolism of the Middle Ages, and the History of the Council of Trent by H. Jedin are typical, but no less indicative are books like those of E. R. Curtius on the medieval rhetorical tradition, H. Planitz on the German city in the Middle Ages (1954), and A. Borst's *Der Turmbau von Babel* (1957 ff.), a study of ancient and medieval theories on the origins of peoples – not to mention other influential authors such as H. Grundmann, H. Mitteis, W. von den Steinen. On the other hand (and the two aspects are, of course, in no way contradictory), German historiography is today intensely concerned with themes of recent and contemporary history, both for obvious reasons and also for the less obvious reason – which A. Heuss brought dramatically into focus in *Der Verlust der Geschichte* (1959) – that the average German seems to have a tendency to avoid, by obliterating from his awareness the history of the post-Bismarckian period, the problems, the responsibilities and the feelings of guilt left as the legacy of Nazism. Another favourite theme of German research is the relationship between West and East, the East being represented now by the Mongols (B. Spuler), now by the Turks (F. Babinger), now by Byzantium (B. Rubin in his colossal work in progress on Justinian). It is probable that this motif has added a new interest to studies of ancient Oriental history (particularly important among these are the studies in Egyptology of H. Kees). Certainly, after the hate-propaganda of the Nazi period, the need was felt for a new view of the relationships between Jews and Christians, especially at the beginning of Christianity, and H. J. Schoeps has taken the lead in this. The programme of research formulated by O. F. Anderle to check and correct Toynbee's theories objectively is still too new to be able to give results.

It is difficult enough to say what has happened to historicism in Germany, but it is even more difficult to decide what the dissemination of German historical questions outside Germany following the Nazi persecutions has meant. The case of Lukács was exceptional: after years in Russia he returned to Hungary, the country of his birth, to find himself caught up in new difficulties created by the different and freer direction of his own Marxism compared with that of the local orthodoxy. For well-known reasons, the emigration largely centred – Israel apart – on the Anglo-Saxon countries, on Turkey and on Latin America. In these last two, where there is a tradition of interest in German thought but where original developments are rare, the situation does not seem to have been radically changed by the immigrants. Moreover it is obvious that those exiles who were scientifically most authoritative were more likely to find work in the Anglo-Saxon countries, and that it is therefore mainly to them that we should look for the transfer of German thought. It was to England that the Warburg Institute moved, under the guidance of F. Saxl. K. Mannheim worked there during and after the war, and republished in English translations his studies on the sociology of knowledge; and K. Popper extended his critique of scientific methods to include Marxism. Here in England, especially at Oxford, a group of outstanding classical philologists and art historians was reunited, amongst them F. Jacoby, the editor and commentator of the fragments of the Greek historians. The historians and sociologists of German or German-Jewish origin, however, settled for the most part in America, where, for instance, W. Jaeger completed his history of Greek thought (*Paideia*), P. O. Kristeller and H. Baron have become the leading spirits in the study of Humanism, S. Kuttner has reinvigorated research into canon law, E. Panofsky has disseminated a methodology of art history derived from the Warburg Institute, L. Strauss in his Chair at Chicago has carried out a penetrating critique of historicism with the object of reviving the idea of natural law (*Natural Right and History*, 1953), E. Kantorowicz has helped to establish new links between Byzantine thought and Western thought in the Middle Ages, and, finally, L. Spitzer, L. Olschki and E. Auerbach have continued the tradition of '*Geistesgeschichte*' in the history of literature and language.

In England the sphere of influence of these representatives of German thought has been limited: the conspicuous exception is the Warburg Institute, now an integral part of the University of London, but even here one must distinguish between the general interest it has aroused for the study of the figurative arts, and the more limited following for its specific research projects in the history of the classical tradition and its symbols. American historical studies being so vast and diversified, the present writer is of course unable to give a comprehensive impression. Where he has direct experience of American institutions and books, it would seem to him that the facility with which the representatives of German thought (especially those who were products of the school of Meinecke and the two Webers) brought themselves into contact with American historiography and sociology has some aspects that are deceptive. The kind of direction that A. O. Lovejoy and G. Boas, for example, were able to give to the history of ideas could indeed easily cohere with analogous German interests, and give rise to that typical German-American product, the *Journal of the History of Ideas*. A strong German influence can also be seen in the journal of medieval studies, *Speculum*, and in various sociological periodicals. But where the fusion has come about, it has come about with a clear prevalence of American sociological and historical methods, which tend to subordinate the more strictly epistemological problems of historical research to problems of the correlation between the technique of research and its objects. There has been no continuation in America of the more characteristic German historiographical movements (like the third humanism or the cult of the hero-leader in the circle of Stefan George): W. Jaeger and E. Kantorowicz, to cite two examples, have themselves entered into American culture rather more than they have shaped it to their original ideals.

At this point there arises the problem (which differs in details as between England and America, but is basically the same for both): what has enabled Anglo-Saxon historical culture to offer such resistance to the ideas imported with so much authority by the best representatives of German historico-sociological thought? To ask this question means analysing in brief the situation of historical research in Britain and America at present. A general explanation in terms of Anglo-Saxon traditionalism would merely be a mistake, for in adjacent fields of study Anglo-American culture has shown itself to be very open to ideas of Austro-Swiss-German origin – one has only to consider the pervasive influence of L. Wittgenstein in English philosophy, and of R. Carnap amongst American logicians, and the more general success of Freudian and Jungian psycho-analysis in both countries. What is more, between 1830 and 1870 historiography in English (whether English or American) absorbed what was then called the critical method of the German School; so it would not be wholly erroneous (though, as we shall see, it would be subtly deceptive) to conclude paradoxically that in England and America German historicism of the twentieth century has been meeting opposition from a German historicism of the nineteenth-century type.

In England the tradition of party-political historiography has survived until the present day, extending English political conflicts to Greece, Rome, the French Revolution, the Italian *Risorgimento*, and so on. H. A. L. Fisher's *History of Europe* belongs to this tradition, and not for nothing did it come under attack in a programmatical critique by the Marxist Christopher Hill. But this tradition has been subjected to penetrating internal criticism by H. Butterfield (*The Whig Interpretation of History*, 1931, *The Englishman and his history*, 1944), and it is discredited today amongst professional scholars, although it still has a following among the cultured public thanks to the prestige of writers like G. M. Trevelyan, and Winston Churchill himself. The dominant figure in contemporary English historiography is (I need hardly say it) the Polish Jew Lewis Bernstein Namier. He was educated at Balliol College, Oxford, but, as a militant Zionist, he remained outside British intellectual society until the publication of his book *The Structure of English Politics at the Acces-*

sion of George III (1929) gave him almost at once a unique position of authority, and transformed him, to his own surprise perhaps, into the model for the younger generation of English historians. In substance Namier applied to English history continental sociological methods of examining the ruling class, and he added to this a special knowledge of the situation in modern and contemporary Central Europe – which he was to show even more clearly in subsequent essays and research. Yet in his extraordinary ability as a minute and rigorous researcher and in the simplicity of his guiding principles he satisfied his English readers steeped in a historiographic tradition that had been formed under the influence of the first German historicism. Namier has instigated the most complex collective undertaking of contemporary English historians, the history of the English Parliament: and his example has influenced historians as different as J. A. Neale (who progressed from his early biography of Queen Elizabeth to the history of the Parliaments of her reign) and A. J. P. Taylor, the historian of Hapsburg Austria. It is impossible to separate from Namier's work R. Syme's studies in Roman history (*The Roman Revolution*, 1939), although it is to be noted that in Syme's more recent books (*Tacitus*, 1958; *Colonial Élites*, 1958) there is a different preoccupation, namely with studying the relationship between provinces (colonies) and motherland in a large empire. Namier has been criticized by H. Butterfield in an attempt to re-establish a religious perspective which is Methodist in origin (*Christianity and History*, 1949 etc.); but if the credit for the reawakening of interest in the history of historiography is due to Butterfield, his specific criticism of Namier's books has not found favour. In the Namier-Butterfield controversy one can clearly see the twofold tendency in British historiography today – towards analysis of politico-social forces, or towards a religious interpretation of history. The Catholics have made a strong contribution to this second tendency, both by emphasizing the Christian character of European culture (Christopher Dawson) and by producing a model history of the English medieval monastic orders (by the Benedictine David Knowles, Regius Professor of History at Cambridge). But, especially in the period 1935–50, the rigidly Marxist interpretation has not been negligible, and from another point of view this helped to weaken the 'Whig' interpretation of history, particularly in underdeveloped areas such as prehistory (Gordon Childe) and classical philology (B. Farrington on ancient science, G. Thomson on Greek literature, E. A. Thompson on the later Roman empire): today (1960) orthodox Marxism is in crisis because of the desertion of its most authoritative representatives, such as Christopher Hill. On the other hand English historical literature has affirmed, or continued to develop, a strong taste for narrative freed from doctrinal preoccupations and concerned with describing the characteristics of 'remarkable' people and events – which is embodied in an enormous number of biographies, and is elevated to research on the grand scale in the *History of the Crusades* by S. Runciman. Nor has interest in diplomatic history (C. Webster) declined. Compared with these movements, the two names that have given rise to most discussion in international circles, A. J. Toynbee and R. G. Collingwood, remain for the moment of marginal significance in English historiography. Toynbee, who has steered a middle course between a pragmatic interpretation and a religious view of the succession of civilizations, has met with almost unanimous hostility from the professional historians of his country. Collingwood, in his oscillation between idealistic neo-historicism of a Crocean type and a theory of metaphysical presuppositions derived from Dilthey, has earned more discussion amongst philosophers (W. H. Walsh, P. Gardiner, W. Dray) than amongst historians – with only one exception, though a significant one. Collingwood, who besides being a philosopher was also a brilliant archaeologist and epigraphist, has made his fellow-British archaeologists aware that the purpose of excavation is to resolve particular historical problems, and he has thus contributed to a characteristic tendency of archaeological research in his country (L. Woolley, M. Wheeler). The marginal position of Toynbee and Collingwood in the historical culture of their own country does not, however, detract from their relevance. In the present state of English historiography two difficulties emerge: first, how to find worthwhile subjects of research and, second, how to overcome the present lack of interest among the most influential philosophers for questions of fact or values. The first difficulty, while it is less conspicuous, is perhaps the more serious of the two. In the past century the English were in the habit of deriving the subjects of their research from themes of German historiography, producing those solutions based on 'judicial' examination of documents and on simple common sense that the Germans have always found difficult to reach. Even recently this derivation of themes was evident in studies of ancient and medieval history (for instance, in the books on Roman citizenship by A. N. Sherwin-White, on the Greek city from

Alexander to Justinian by A. H. M. Jones), not to mention classics such as R. H. Tawney's *Religion and the Rise of Capitalism*, which is clearly of Weberian origin. Now that the relationship between German historicism and English historiography has become less close, the latter will have to find, within itself or without, other sources of inspiration, both for single subjects of research and for the methods of research itself. The works of Collingwood and Toynbee represent clear attempts at autonomy of subject and method, and are recognized as such abroad, if not in England. The presence of Collingwood and Toynbee in the background, and of Namier and Butterfield in the forefront, explains why English historiography has derived no stimulus from methods which did not seem to offer the extensive documentary evidence supplied by Namier, the satisfaction of religious needs afforded by Toynbee and Butterfield, or Collingwood's familiarity with the language of English philosophy.

The situation in America is, again, one on which the present writer can speak with much less confidence. The striking feature of American contemporary historiography is its maturity, its self-confidence: and it seems that at least two reasons for this can be suggested. One is the essential function that historiography has assumed in clarifying for the inhabitants of the United States their own national problems, and in offering signposts for future progress to a nation that believes in progress, with all the disadvantages of easy deviation towards propaganda (especially in times of panic), but also with the advantages of a discussion in which anyone who distorts the facts ends up by disqualifying himself (the most recent in this series of historian-leaders is D. Boorstin, *The Genius of American Politics*, 1953; *The Americans*, 1959). The other reason is the co-operation of philosophers, especially of J. Dewey, in the creating of bonds between the social and the historical sciences, giving America a primacy, which she has not yet lost, in the use of sociological enquiry both for characterizing a historical situation and indicating a practical solution in modern terms. Analysis of historiographical methods in relation to the social and physical sciences has become quite rigorous. There is a tendency to recognize the specific character of historical knowledge, but within a framework of active mutual exchange with all other sciences (see, on this point, the two collective reports of the Social Science Research Council, *Theory and Practice in Historical Study*, 1946, and *The Social Sciences in Historical Study*, 1954; and works such as the recent *Nature and Historical Experience* by J. H. Randall Jr, 1958). Hence also the further characteristic of American historiography, that of having its own experimental field of methodological research in its own national history. 'America's coming of age', in Van Wyck Brooks' felicitous phrase, has been expressed not only in a literature which remains close to American life, but also in a historiography which, ever since the times when F. J. Turner posed the frontier problem (1893), C. Beard proposed an economic interpretation of the American Constitution (1913), and Carl Becker analysed the Declaration of Independence (1922), has exemplified new methods of research in terms of American historical problems (and naturally this is continued in more recent work from V. L. Parrington to R. Hofstadter). Master in its own home, American historiography has perhaps until now felt itself less at ease in treating the political history of other lands – except for certain periods of South American and English history which are directly connected with her own history. Here American historiography has drawn heavily on first-generation immigrants.

But in cultural and social history, particularly of the Middle Ages and the Renaissance, America is making independent progress, and has opened new avenues (L. Thorndike for the history of science, S. Baron for the social history of the Jews). And the trust with which the Americans welcome foreign historians who import new knowledge and ideas (M. Rostovtzeff and A. D. Nock in ancient history) must not conceal the fact that, in the end, the testing-ground for the validity of historical theories of any kind is, in America, American history. Even the historians of theological inspiration, who are at present a minority without much prestige, are successful where they reinterpret American history (R. Niebuhr, *The Kingdom of God in America*, 1937, and the more original part of the important *History of the Expansion of Christianity*, by the Baptist K. S. Latourette, 1937–45).

This brief analysis of the Anglo-Saxon position has perhaps indicated some of the reasons why German historicism is today a 'problem', above all in France and in Italy. France and Italy are, for the time being, the countries where Marxism occupies a central position in the political and cultural structure of the country, whereas in the Anglo-Saxon countries it is marginal. For both countries, this naturally poses in a more acute form the question (which exists for all countries) of the relationship between local

Marxism and Russian Marxism. A clear formulation of the position in this respect would demand a more exact knowledge of Russian historiography than the present writer possesses – the more so since the situation is complicated by the fact that the majority of Italian and French Marxists do not seem to have any real, first-hand knowledge of what is being written in Russia. A few names of historians who are basically pre-revolutionary in their background and interests, such as E. V. Tarlé and E. A. Kosminskij, are of little use in characterizing contemporary Russian historiography. In the field of ancient history, it is clear that the strength of Russian Marxists lies in certain types of archaeological research (Urartu, civilization of the Steppes), and more in the very broad horizon of their general interests which, as has been shown recently by the *Universal History*, embraces the whole East. The Russians can, however, teach us little about method because they have much to learn about elementary things such as the interpretation of texts, and about less elementary things like the analysis of a complex social structure. The recent easing of the curb on Soviet historiography has shown that the Russians themselves are not unaware of the retrograde and dogmatic state of their studies in ancient history; as witness the inconclusive end of the long debate on the dissolution of the slave society in the '*Vestnik Drevnej Istorii*', and the cautious tone, substantially expressed in bourgeois language, in certain works like that of A. I. Dovatur on Herodotus (1957) and E. M. Štaerman on the crisis of the slave society in the western provinces of the Roman empire (1957).

Leaving aside for the moment the relationship between Western historicism and Eastern Marxism, it is plain that the problems of dialectics are today inevitable in the debates on historical method in France and Italy, but more so in France than in Italy (M. Merleau-Ponty, L. Goldmann) because in Italy there was so much discussion on dialectics in the idealist period that people are less inclined to discuss it now in a period when historical materialism is clearly resurgent.

In France, at any rate, R. Aron can claim the credit for having disseminated a knowledge of the more recent German historicism, and for having attempted a synthesis of the thought of M. Weber and W. Dilthey in his *Introduction à la philosophie de l'histoire* (1938). Later a Catholic historian of great perception, H.-I. Marrou, also made use of Dilthey for an analysis of historical knowledge (1954). The development of existentialism naturally implied the taking over of the Heidegger problem of the relationship between existence and history, and there have been books on these lines (E. Dardel, 1946). But it is perhaps right to say that the only theoretical work to gain authority amongst historians, that of H.-I. Marrou, owes its success above all to the grafting of a specific historical experience (broadly speaking, that of the *Annales*) on to the stem of Dilthey. For in France too the theory of historical knowledge preoccupies historians less than does the elaboration of a method that will capture the living reality of events. However much Marxism may have left its imprint on historians like G. Lefebvre and E. Labrousse, the majority of French historians are today dominated by the methodological teaching and the moral example of Marc Bloch – the historian martyred for his France – and of his older friend and companion in arms, L. Febvre. It is impossible to read the pages of these historians and to observe their constant efforts, both intuitive and analytic, to do justice to the object of enquiry, without being reminded of H. Bergson. It is not easy, however, for me to say what is the nature of the general relationship that certainly exists between the most recent French historiography and Bergsonianism (even if we set aside specific theories on history by Bergsonians like H. Gouhier). It is sufficient to point out the importance of Bergson for a great researcher into medieval thought like E. Gilson. The *Annales* have given France a model of the interchange between sociology and historiography which, although infinitely more subtle and varied than the American example, has not yet perhaps to its credit the sureness of touch, the abundance of results, and above all the political importance, of American historico-sociological research. But, from the pioneer work of the *Annales*, thanks principally to F. Braudel, there has developed a systematic organization of historical research at the École des Hautes Études. It is this organization which is gradually taking the place in Europe of the German historical school as the central forge of future historians, and which shows the measure of the difference between French historiography and German historicism. One of its achievements is a very detailed reconstruction of the social history of France which takes into account demographic factors, religion and 'electoral sociology'. Within the flexible framework of present-day French historiography, the most varied personalities, from C. Morazé to G. Le Bras, can find room to move. Awareness of the variety of points of view and of problems, has given rise to series of handbooks of a new kind, designed to underline problems rather than solutions (*Clio*, *Mana*, *Que-sais-je?*). Other series, like those on everyday life and on the history of international relations, reflect typical lines of research. The relative agreement on method (not to mention the centralization of studies in Paris) favours works in series and collective enterprises; and the collective character of the research is heightened by the strong and competent participation of the religious orders (particularly the Dominicans and Jesuits). The method now prevalent demands research of the utmost minuteness, yet it must ultimately lead to broad generalizations. Finding the exact point where the particular conclusion can be generalized is a classic difficulty that recurs in every age. It is not surprising that in France today this dilemma is apparent even in the field of studies on the French Revolution, which has become the experimental field *par excellence* for new historiographical techniques. It will, therefore, be all the less surprising to note the obvious weakness and the excess of schematization in other fields, where documents are fewer in number and less groundwork has been done. This is clear, for instance, in the study of the history of religions, where M. Eliade, a Rumanian who has become French in culture (but who has recently been made a Professor at the University of Chicago), and G. Dumézil, among others, have produced brilliant generalizations on insufficient and sometimes refractory material. But, on the other hand, it is France, from the Abbé Brémond onwards, which has produced explorations of states of mind, of paradigmatic legends and collective religious phenomena for which it is difficult to find parallels elsewhere (for example, A. J. Festugière on the history of Graeco-Roman religion, R. Folz on the legend of Charlemagne).

What are striking are, in short, the distinctive features of contemporary French historiography in contrast to the German historiography of the inter-war period. It is enough to read side by side two works devoted to the same subject, for instance W. Jaeger's *Paideia* and the *Histoire de l'éducation dans l'Antiquité* by H.-I. Marrou.

The position in Italy is well known to us, and a detailed discussion of it is not appropriate here. But it is, nevertheless, evident that the separation between Italian and German historicism has become more marked, if anything, in the past twenty years. The basic fact is that in Italy, unlike Germany, the fall of the totalitarian government has not been followed by disorientation in historical studies. Thanks to

Benedetto Croce, to Gaetano De Sanctis, to Adolfo Omodeo, to the exile Gaetano Salvemini and to the historians who modelled themselves on them, Italian historiography in the Fascist period remained substantially in opposition, and emerged with problems and methods which could be passed on to the younger generation for disagreement and for agreement. Nor is it a coincidence that we owe to Benedetto Croce the foundation in his home at Naples of the most important centre of historical research in post-war Italy, entrusted to the directorship of F. Chabod. This research centre has influenced all branches, including that of ancient history, but, characteristically, it has been able to work in harmony with other schools. There are, of course, differences between historical studies before 1939 and after 1945. The younger generation has shown a marked preference for problems of social history: and erudite, exact research, with all its technical difficulties, has come into its own again – not without a polemical character – in those fields, such as the history of literature and culture, where it had been practised less. M. Bloch and G. Lefebvre are read quite as much in Italy as in France; and a master of erudition like Cardinal Giovanni Mercati rose in the last years of his life to become a revered example. Linguistic research is preferred to aesthetic criticism: and the first two histories of the Italian language (G. Devoto, B. Migliorini) have appeared. Travel abroad and cultural exchanges have facilitated research into non-Italian history, while the politico-social situation in Italy is a permanent subject for investigation – whence, among other things, a new flowering of municipal histories (Milan, Venice, etc.). And there is clear evidence of renewed interest in sociology, with the resulting need to clarify the relationships between sociological research and historical research. Nevertheless the implicit or explicit discussion of the Crocean conception of history is for the moment still at the centre of Italian historiographic experience. The authority of Croce in the last fifteen years of Fascism can be exemplified by the fact that even a historian as independent as Gaetano De Sanctis (who, moreover, was a Catholic) should have modelled his *Storia dei Greci* on the *Storia d'Europa* by B. Croce. On the eve of the war, Carlo Antoni, in his collected studies *Dallo storicismo alla sociologia* (1940), had already pointed out the profound gulf between Crocean historicism and the multifarious forms of German historicism – a gulf whose existence was confirmed in the amicable dispute between Croce and Meinecke. Traces of it can be seen in a different context in the published correspondence between Croce and K. Vossler. But at the very core of Crocean historicism the conflict between humanism and providentialism was growing ever more evident, and in all his teaching F. Chabod left no doubts as to his preference for the first of these tendencies. This preference, expressed in historiographical terms in what is perhaps the most considerable post-war Italian historical work – the first volume of the *Storia della politica estera italiana dal 1870 al 1896, I, Le premesse*, 1951 – was afterwards confirmed by the same author's study of Croce as a historian (*Riv. Storica It.*, 1952). Hence it was possible for Chabod and his school, both in variety of experiment and, more specifically, in new economic and social interests, to draw near to the French school of Bloch and Febvre. The interaction of the two schools has in recent years become closer, while the influence of the Neapolitan school has been spreading to foreign circles. With aims that were not dissimilar C. Antoni devoted his energies (which were cut short by his premature death in 1959) towards eliminating dialectic from Crocean philosophy and re-establishing the value of the individual personality. For reasons that would merit more precise analysis, there has been no real convergence of aims between Chabod and Antoni. At present, they seem rather to represent alternative solutions, one founded on the elimination of any precise philosophical theory from the humanistic interests of Croce's historiography, and the other bent on giving a new lease of life to the Crocean philosophy of 'distinctions' without much regard for actual historical research. The grafting of the *Annales* on to the *Critica* seems at the moment to be the dominant phenomenon of Italian historiography. If I read the situation aright, a Marxist historiography, fully distinguishable from the Crocean one, does not yet seem to have emerged. The Italian Marxist historians work in an atmosphere that is certainly unfavourable to any rigid theorization of class struggle and to any clear-cut distinction between structures and superstructures. This explains why the suggestions so abundantly provided in the posthumous publication of the writings of A. Gramsci have been taken up as much outside the Communist party as within: it is outside the party that one of the most penetrating Italian historians of culture, E. Garin, has acknowledged his debt to Gramsci. This also explains why the best contributions to the urgent task of studying the political and social movements of Russia and the Central European countries have come from left-wing historians who are hostile to Communism (F. Venturi).

On the other hand it is equally characteristic that it is much less easy to single out a Catholic historiography in Italy than it is in France. A few Catholic historians with distinct religious personalities can be found among the older historians – one thinks of A. Ferrabino and A. C. Jemolo. But with the majority of Catholic historians whom I have had occasion to read, Catholicism is disclosed in their choice of subject and in their final judgment on events rather than in a particular mode of interpretation. There are too, as is well known, especially in the field of history of religion, historians who refer readily to existentialist or Jungian interpretations. Sometimes I have the impression that Santo Mazzarino, a historian who is as rich in suggestions as he is difficult to grasp in his guiding thoughts, is coming close to these existentialist interpretations. Nevertheless, existentialism, Jung, Altheim, and also Toynbee and Teilhard de Chardin, do not seem for the present to have put down deep roots in Italy. If I were required to indicate the direction which Italian historicism seems to be taking in its gradual withdrawal from Crocean positions, I should want to name, at least for non-Catholic historians, the 'neo-illuministic' tendency, reflected in the special importance that the eighteenth century and the French Revolution have in research, which has many links with the anti-Fascist tradition from P. Gobetti to L. Salvatorelli and G. De Ruggiero.

The separation attempted by Antoni between Crocean historicism and the various forms of German historicism may well pave the way towards a greater influence of the latter. But though I see clear signs of this in philosophical works like those by Pietro Rossi, I could not say the same of concrete historical research. The fact that many young men take an interest in sociology is perhaps due more to their reading French and American books than to the study of Simmel and Weber. The only Italian historian known to me who has adopted Weberian concepts is a jurist of the old guard, P. De Francisci[2].

This discussion, growing ever more vague, could go on to other cultures that as a whole are even less familiar to me, and from which only individual names stand out. Thus Americo Castro has surprised us with a work that has been nourished on the thought of Dilthey. But is Dilthey the real guide of Castro? Like Delio Cantimori, I find it difficult to classify Castro's work. It seems to me that his books are essentially a revolt against the Spain of the Counter-Reformation in the name of the late medieval Spain with its three faiths. The theoretical justification he seeks in concepts derived from romantic nationalism (the idea of national genius), from Dilthey and the existentialists is perhaps a superfluous one. Finally, when I read the Dutch historians, P. Geyl, J. Romein, W. Den Boer (*Tussen Kade en Schip*, Daamen, 1957), all in the shadow of their great Huizinga, I find them all in search of absolute values (liberal Marxism for Romein, Calvinism for Den Boer, and a very personal mixture of rationalism and nationalism in Geyl). So I come back again to my initial question: 'In what way and to what end can Dilthey and Weber still be the guides of historical work that has been developing on such varied and different premises?'

[1] Pietro Rossi, *Storia e storicismo nella filosofia contemporanea* (Milan, Lerici, 1960) p. 518. It is useful to compare F. Wagner, *Moderne Geschichtsschreibung* (Berlin, Duncker and Humblot, 1960).

[2] *Cf.* N. Valeri, '*Su alcune tendenze della storiografia contemporanea in Italia*', in *La Filosofia Contemporanea in Italia* II (Rome 1958) pp. 305–23.

CHAPTER THIRTEEN

THE CONSEQUENCES OF NEW TRENDS IN THE HISTORY OF ANCIENT LAW[1]

To A. C. Jemolo

WE are here, I feel, to celebrate a historical event of some importance, the end of history of law as an autonomous branch of historical research. Few parts of history can boast the antiquity and the authority of the history of law: few can boast such results. But, I believe, it is now clear to almost everyone that we can no longer maintain a distinction between historians' history and jurists' history. For hundreds of years – at least since the days of the 'cultivated' jurists of the Renaissance – the distinction has been maintained because jurists were using political history to interpret the reasons for and the meaning of legislative measures, while historians were using legislative measures to throw light on political events[2]. The eighteenth-century notion of the history of civilization did not eliminate the distinction, precisely because the historians' attitude to legal texts remained different from that of historians of law. To the legal historians it was important to see how different civilizations expressed themselves in various forms of legislation; for the historians, what was important was to use legislative documents as expressions of different civilizations[3]. Differences of style, of literary tradition, and separate university faculties combined to maintain the distinction. The legal historians spoke a language – lawyers' terminology – which was not always accessible to the uninitiated; their points of departure were their own literary forms, such as the gloss and the systematic treatise; their teaching was designed not for historians, but for professional jurists.

Now the only remaining distinction between 'pure' historians and legal historians is the last one I mentioned: the separation between the teaching of the different faculties. This is a separation that seems ever more absurd. Intrinsically, at least in the field in which I can claim some knowledge – ancient law – the distinction no longer exists. I have here before me, in my imagination, a pile of books on ancient law. Need I name a few of them? Here they are: V. Arangio-Ruiz, *Lineamenti del sistema contrattuale nel diritto dei papiri*; U. Coli, *Il diritto pubblico degli Umbri*; P. De Francisci, *Primordia Civitatis*; F. De Martino, *Storia della Costituzione Romana*; P. Noailles, *Fas et Ius*; U. von Lübtow, *Das Römische Volk*; W. Kunkel, *Untersuchungen zur Entwicklung des römischen Kriminalverfahrens*; J. Gaudemet, *La formation du droit séculier et du droit de l'église aux IVe et Ve siècles* . . . These are jurists' books, but I find no intrinsic differences from ordinary history books. At the most, a certain peculiarity in phraseology, almost the tone of another age, draws my attention to distinctions that are now merely formal. If one wished to be paradoxical, one might say that today historians proper overdo their interest in juristic formalism, while legal historians are bent upon discovering the social realities that underlie their institutions. No one has a more exact knowledge of formal particulars than three great historians who come from philology, L. Gernet, K. Latte and E. Bickerman. But it was a jurist, W. Kunkel, who wrote the book on the *Herkunft und soziale Stellung der Juristen*, and it was another jurist who wrote the first (perhaps the last) biography of Gaius[4]. This paradox can be illustrated by a statement from one of our most eminent masters in the sociological school of law, Henri Lévy-Bruhl. In order to maintain the last semblance of a distinction between 'pure' historians and jurists, he asserts that historians want to know what happened, and are therefore tempted to reject apocryphal documents and successful forgeries as being valueless, whereas the jurist, on the other hand, knows that legend is truer than history[5]. But I am sure that Lévy-Bruhl would be the first to admit that interest in forgeries, as representing an epoch, is a typical historical interest that 'pure' historians have passed on to jurists[6].

Indeed the elimination of history of law as independent history now seems to me to be settled. It is implicit in the programme for a history of the law and the institutions of the Western Church formulated in the *Prolégomènes* by Gabriel Le Bras (1955). Nor is it important here to debate whether it was Max Weber or the French school of sociology or the teaching of Marx and Engels or, finally, the influence of Marc Bloch that precipitated this solution. It is inherent in the general recognition that law, as a systematization of social relations at a given level, cannot be understood without an analysis of the sexual orientations, the moral and religious beliefs, the economic production and the military forces that characterize a given society at a given moment, and are expressed in associations of individuals and in conflicts. It is conceivable today that history of literature, history of art, history of science and history of religion can retain some sort of autonomy, inasmuch as each is concerned with a specific activity of man. But what is no longer conceivable is that history of law should be autonomous; for by its very nature it is a formulation of social relations rooted in manifold human activities. And if, in some civilizations, there is a class of jurisconsults with special rules of conduct and of reasoning, then this too is a social phenomenon to be interpreted.

The changed nature of the history of law is clear, not so much from theoretical considerations, as from the sense of uneasiness that one feels on seeing an ordinary problem of legal history being approached in traditional terms. It is difficult to show the error of an argument that starts from the presupposition that the *gentes* are patrician formations, deduces from this that the *curiae* were confined to patricians, and hence that testation before the *comitia calata* was reserved for the patricians. But one feels immediately that this is not the question. The real question is whether in the Roman society of the fifth century BC, which created the Twelve Tables, such a distinction between patricians and plebeians on the subject of *gentes* and testation could subsist; and whether we have sufficient information on the period before the Twelve Tables to allow us to formulate any hypothesis on the nature of the *gentes* – not to mention testation[7].

It is not, therefore, the elimination of the antithesis between 'pure' history and legal history that is worth discussing. It is, rather, the consequences of the elimination that we must consider. Some of these are of a practical nature. Others – the most difficult ones – are theoretical.

To begin with the practical consequences, it is obvious that the present state of historical research demands that every historian should be able to understand law as well as economics, religion as well as politics. This requirement is formidable enough: but it is made even more so by the lack of adequate education for future historians. I can speak here only from my experience of Italian, English and American universities. I do not know what happens in

France and Germany: though many of us look with envy at the variety and depth of teaching at the École des Hautes Études. In Italy the student of ancient history educated in the Faculty of Arts never studies Roman law, and almost never Greek law. Vice versa the historian of Roman law educated in the Faculty of Law knows little of political history and has no direct experience of philological research: it is not surprising if the criticism of interpolations is sometimes conducted by methods that make us smile. It is plain that we must arrive at a radical reform of university history teaching. Once the distinction between 'pure' history and legal history has been eliminated from our teaching, then we shall also have eliminated, to all practical purposes, nine-tenths of the dualism between sociology and history. I do not want to enter into a theoretical discussion here on the question of the relationship between sociology and history, or, to use the modern terms, between nomothetic and idiographic sciences. A large part of what is called the sociology of the ancient world is in fact custom or law, seen in a synchronic rather than a diachronic arrangement. For the ancient world at least, as soon as the distinction between history and law is forgotten, then the distinction between history and sociology will be forgotten too.

On the theoretical side, the old questions whether the history of Roman law should be transformed into the history of ancient law, or whether the *Staatsrecht*, Roman public law, should give way to *Verfassungsgeschichte*, constitutional history, are becoming useless. These are ideas which served, in their time, to clarify the connection between Roman law and other ancient laws, or to reveal the weaknesses of a purely static description of the institutions of public law. But who today is interested in finding out whether the constitution of Servius Tullius is part of *Staatsrecht* or of *Verfassungsgeschichte*, whether it is history of Roman law or of ancient law?

Even in more complicated subjects than these, a clear identification of social history and legal history serves to eliminate old ambiguities and old problems. I shall deal with only two of these. In his *Untersuchungen über römische Verfassung und Geschichte* (1839), J. Rubino formulated one of the most fortunate criteria for combating the scepticism about early Roman history that was disseminated by G. B. Niebuhr. Individual kings may never have existed, the banquet-songs on which Niebuhr pinned his last hopes may be deceptive; but the Roman constitutional tradition leaves no doubt as to the existence of the monarchy and makes it permissible to classify and characterize it. Mommsen, and even Eduard Meyer, accepted this criterion as valid. And yet a cautious judge like Gaetano De Sanctis was able to repudiate it in one of his most characteristic formulas: 'Tradition is a great deal less trustworthy for the internal history than for the history of the foreign wars of Rome[8].' De Sanctis was clearly alluding to the constructions of jurists and the falsifications of politicians as causes of the distortion of the internal history of Rome. The opposition between Rubino and De Sanctis seems complete. Nevertheless, if one proceeds to analyse the dominant social groups in Rome in the last centuries before Christ, which had an interest in keeping alive archaic forms of public life and also in reinterpreting and distorting the civil conflicts of the fifth century, the opposition diminishes to vanishing point. The truth is that Rubino and De Sanctis were speaking of two different things – one of certain institutions, the other of the conflicts between patricians and plebeians.

The second problem to which I referred is the one that has been worked on recently by scholars such as E. Wolf in his *Griechisches Rechtsdenken* and E. A. Havelock in *The Liberal Temper in Greek Politics*: that is, the nature of Greek democratic thought. As long as one limits oneself to political theorists, the results of research are not only poor, but plainly contradictory. Democritus, who is, according to Havelock, the democrat *par excellence*, is relegated to non-political thought by Wolf. The fact is that Greek democrats did not write theories, or, if they did, they have not left them for us; whereas they did formulate constitutions, reforms that were radical and coherent, like that of Cleisthenes at Athens. Only by considering constitutional history, political thought and social conflicts together can one understand who were the democrats at Athens and elsewhere. Anyone in search of a democratic Plato is sure not to find one[9].

Yet we are obviously interested not so much in the difficulties that can be easily resolved as in those which are aggravated by the destruction of watertight compartments. If religion, economics, politics and law are considered together, the probability of multiplying errors is increased. A wrong interpretation of economic or religious facts can easily lie at the root of a wrong interpretation of legal facts, and vice versa. We have only to look around us. The notion of a primitive communism is a starting-point for interpretations of the legal structure of early Greece and Rome. I need scarcely point out that it is easier to cite a modern author on this primitive communism than an ancient document. It may have existed, but it is not easy to prove that it did, family property being something quite different. I have before me a very recent study by B. Borecky on *The primitive origin of the Greek conception of equality*[10], which deals with the changes in meaning of words like μοῖρα, λαγχάνω, δαίομαι as a result of the evolution from the collective property of the tribal community to private property. But at the decisive point the proof comes in the formula 'George Thomson has shown . . .', and George Thomson is not an ancient document.

In a recent and extremely interesting short study, Jean-Pierre Vernant has declared that the Greek myths of the wars between Gods and Titans represent the remains of the monarchical ideology of the Mycenaean *anax*, remains that were buried under the new rationalistic and democratic thought of the sixth and fifth centuries BC. But we can object that we do not know whether these wars between Gods and Titans, or these myths of sovereignty, were known to the Mycenaean kings, whereas we do know very well that they were popular with the Greeks of the democratic period in the sixth and fifth centuries BC, and are found in the poetry of the democrat Aeschylus, while the related story of the Gigantomachia has a place of honour in the Parthenon of Pericles[11]. In more general terms, the present vogue of divine monarchy is doing harm both to Greek history and to Roman history, because so far – with all respect to the most ardent Mycenists and Romists – we have no way of knowing how the inhabitants of the fortress of Mycenae and the huts of the Palatine thought of their kings. In the case of Rome, one of the consequences is reinterpreting the *lex curiata* in ways that are highly imaginative but do not correspond to what little we know of the *lex curiata* in the historical period, that is, in the last centuries of the republic. An ingenuous acceptance of theories on the primitive mentality of the Romans, on the precedence of magic over religion, on predeism, leads to explanations of Roman legal symbolism and of the distinction between *fas* and *ius* that are *a priori* because they are not based on the texts[12]. We know something of the cults at Rome in the sixth and fifth centuries BC, but almost nothing of the religious ideas current among the subjects of the Tarquins or amongst the contemporaries of M. Horatius Pulvillus. It is a bold man indeed who believes he knows what *ius* or *fas* meant even in the fourth century BC, not to mention in the sixth century BC. The more so as we continue to accept pictures of early Rome derived from the *De agricultura* of Cato – the famous countryman, simple, austere, and superstitious, the stern *pater familias* – which may be valid for the second century, when Cato was writing, but cannot be transferred, except arbitrarily, to the sixth century BC. After all, *we* are contemporaries of Claude Lévi-Strauss, and so we ought to learn something from his analysis of pseudo-archaic cultures[13]. One of our scholars who has contributed most towards liberating us from preconceived notions on early Rome, Massimo Pallottino, has moreover observed that for an understanding of early Rome Simonides and Ibycus are perhaps more useful than Cato and Livy[14]. When anyone contrasts the rationalistic mentality of the Roman jurists with the 'primitive' mystic or mythical mentality of which Numa would be representative, I like to remind him of a scholar who lived in the bright light of the sixteenth century AD: the Portuguese Jew, Joseph Karo, who was forced to emigrate to the East and, as is well-known, is the most famous modern interpreter and codifier of rabbinical law. Karo, the subtle casuist, was a cabbalist who maintained that he was in nocturnal communication with a spirit, a Maggid, with the significant name of Mishnah, who revealed to him the truth – just as the nymph Egeria inspired the worthy Numa[15].

Once the interpretation of any historical fact has become multilateral, even the use of the comparative method has to adapt itself to this multilaterality. Today comparisons can no longer be made on the one-dimensional principle that linguistics and the history of law still accepted as right some time ago. The comparison of isolated institutions – matrimony, let us say, or buying and selling – is as useless as the comparison of individual words. On the one hand, this change eliminates superficial resemblances. For a comparison of the *flamen* and the *brahman*, the fact that the terms probably have a common origin is not enough nowadays, just as an identical number of members (twelve) is not enough to establish a significant relationship between the Ionian league and the Etruscan league. On the other hand the very character of a multilateral comparison can lead to colossal errors: a few mistaken identifications are enough to upset the interpretation of whole civilizations. On the interpretation of a few terms concerning landed property depends the way we characterize the economy of the Mycenaean kingdom compared with that of, say, the Hittite kingdom[16]. On our interpretation of the nature of the Roman *curiae* depends the legitimacy of a comparison between the tribal structure of Rome and that of some Greek races.

The more the maker of comparisons is victim of the illusion that there are uniform laws of development for different peoples, the greater will be the danger of falsification. Collective property, totemism, tribal structure, magic mentality are *per se* already ambiguous notions, liable to be interpreted in very different ways[17]. If the illusion is then added that human society develops uniformly from collective property to private property, from animism to totemism, then fantasy has simply taken over from reality. It is obvious (but not superfluous to repeat it in the present situation) that comparison must assist in the understanding of existing documents, not in filling the gaps in the documentation in the name of a supposititious uniformity of development. But comparison can be even more dangerous, if it presupposes not so much uniformity of developments as an original, now disappeared, unity of structure, on which would supposedly depend divergent later developments. This is not the place for a detailed discussion of the various attempts to reconstruct an Indo-European, Semitic, or even only Mediterranean civilization earlier than the cultural units known to us from archaeological and literary documentation. But let us not forget the implications of the most famous and the most influential contemporary attempt to reconstruct a prehistoric mentality: that of Georges Dumézil. He holds that certain aspects of Roman civilization – among them the actual organization of Romulus' State – can be interpreted only as the remains of an Indo-European ideology, that so-called functional tripartition, which in its turn is reconstructed on the basis of the comparison of Roman survivals with the survivals of the same tripartite ideology in other Indo-European areas. Leaving aside other objections – such as J. Brough's contention[18] that with a little goodwill the same threefold division can be recognized outside the Indo-European field, e.g., in the Bible – it will be noticed that the explanatory fact (the Indo-European ideology) is deduced from the facts which it has to explain (early aspects of existing civilizations). The characteristics of a hypothetical civilization are formulated on the basis of a hypothetical interpretation of existing civilizations.

As I have already suggested, it is part of the situation created by these pluridimensional comparisons that the scholar should find himself faced with texts in languages that are now dead, and often they are languages that are not yet sufficiently known, or have even, like Indo-European, been reconstructed by indirect means. The first step in this direction was taken when Mommsen recognized the need for full mastery of Italic dialects in order to understand Roman history. Today a historian like Franz Altheim who is not afraid to make mistakes tackles texts in dozens of languages; and it would be ungenerous to reproach him if, in conformity to his own premises, he makes mistakes. But it is no good ignoring the fact that whole societies are being reconstructed on the basis of texts of doubtful interpretation. I do not wish here to allude to what are obvious, indeed frequent, errors of method: for example, interpreting the nature of an institution on the basis of an etymology, as if the nature of *ius* or the powers of the *rex* could become clearer on an etymological basis. And if *pontifices* were originally builders of bridges, the etymology is no help in explaining the functions of the *pontifices* of the historical period. But even in cases where the procedure is correct, there remains the intrinsic obscurity of languages that are insufficiently known in grammatical structure and vocabulary. The recent epidemic of Mycenaean and the endemic sore of Etruscan are a lesson to be learned. One thinks with nostalgia of Paul Maas, who, when offered a text in the classical Greek we learned at school, invariably began to examine it with the remark: '*Ich verstehe nichts.*'

In a certain sense, there is a simple remedy to all this: it is the *ars nesciendi*, the suspension of judgment wherever information is too uncertain. But if the *ars nesciendi* is good advice for a book-reviewer to give to over-audacious authors, it is not, of course, a general solution for a science which by definition tries to be an *ars sciendi*. The problem facing all scholars who have reached the conclusion that they cannot know is to discover the way to find out. No rule can be offered for escaping from ignorance, even from learned ignorance. But if on the one hand the situation I am describing accentuates the difficulties of knowing, and hence the necessity to confess one's own ignorance, it also shows certain ways out. We all know that there exists a traditional dualism between the annalistic attitude of historians and the systematic description of jurists. The separation goes back to antiquity and has good reasons of its own. In the history of a war or of a political conflict, what counts is the chronological succession of events; in the study of institutions, what counts is the structural connection between the various institutions, which gives each political organism its particular physiognomy[19]. Nevertheless, each of the two traditions of thought has its own characteristic defects and limitations. With the pure historian the much vaunted respect for chronology often turns into a lack of attention for semi-permanent forces, the long-term movements and, above all, for natural phenomena, which seem to be outside what is commonly understood by history. On the other hand, the jurist, with his inveterate predilection for systematic constructions, constructs even when documents are missing, trusting in the internal coherence of his hypothesis. If we are to be sincere, the true objection to the so-called gentilicial theory of the Roman state formulated by Pietro Bonfante is that it is founded on a historical void: he delineates institutions of a period which we have no reason to believe ever existed. Now it is precisely here, at the meeting-point of two mentalities as different as those of the annalist historian and the historian of institutions, that there are possibilities of new discoveries, beyond the first confession of ignorance. The thesis that I should like to propose in these brief observations of mine is that an appropriate exploitation of the situation created by the mingling of the historico-annalistic tradition and the juristic tradition will be successful enough in the end to surmount the difficulties of method inherent in the actual situation.

It is not a coincidence that the most convincing scholars of our time should be precisely those in whom – either instinctively or deliberately – the art of following a historical process step by step according to the annalistic method is blended with the art of fitting the facts within a well-defined framework of institutions. When I was a student it seemed almost inconceivable that Felix Jacoby should have organized his collection of the fragments of the Greek historians not in chronological order, but by literary *genres*. How could a historian of historiography ignore the principle of chronology in assembling his material? Today there is no dispute that Felix Jacoby was right and that his greatness as a philologist – a greatness that recalls Scaliger – lies precisely in his resolute decision never to judge of a fragment without fitting it into the *genre* to which it belonged. The same applies to Louis Robert, the epigraphist, whose strength lies in never considering an epigraphic text in isolation, but rather examining it in the geographic cadre in which it originated, in the formular tradition of which it is part: hence his principle that 'the epigraphist should be unaffected by horror of the void'[20], that is, the epigraphist should never arbitrarily fill in what is not there. Similarly with Elias Bickerman, the acute way in which he formulates a particular problem is always subordinated to the awareness that the value of a piece of evidence depends on the documentary or historiographic tradition in which the evidence is found: through the study of formulas he interprets the political and religious consciousness of Jews, Pagans and Christians in the Hellenistic and Roman world. Three historians of religion will continue to be exemplary, M. Nilsson, K. Latte and A. D. Nock. They are very different as historians, yet united not only by their friendship but also in their purposes, by the absence of superfluous conjectures and empty speculations, and by the presence of a constant frame of reference for particular religious manifestations. The anthropologist and student of religious associations prevail in Nilsson. With Latte there is a mingling of the juristic tradition of Mommsen, the comparativism of Usener and the linguistic analysis of W. Schulze*. Of A. D. Nock, whom we have lost all too soon, it could at first sight have seemed that his principal aim was to restrict the sphere of religiosity, in favour of custom: he himself once said to me with a smile that he hoped when he died to leave behind less religion than he had found when he was born. But a closer look reveals that Nock combined an exact appreciation of what was new in all religious experience with the conviction that religion is passed on in formulas, and that the formulas tend to become customs deprived of definite emotional and rational values. All these historians – and I could mention others closer to strictly juristic research, such as the historian of Greek federalism, J. A. O. Larsen – are indicative of our time because they combine feeling for institutions with a sense of the individual, and they avoid arbitrary conjectures. Quite the contrary of those historians, so well known that I need not give their names, who, being unable to control their own fertile – often ingenious – imaginations by the study of institutions, linguistic usage, historiographic conventions, lapse continually into the arbitrary. But if knowledge of structures (among which linguistic and juristic structures are the most important) serves to limit arbitrariness in the interpretation of individual documents, respect for the particular fact is equally necessary to prevent systematizations that stand condemned when they are defined as 'elegant'. The mentality of the institutionalist and the mentality of the annalist historian must exercise external vigilance over each other.

It will be objected – it certainly should be – that this interpretation of the present situation does not correspond to the facts in two ways:

* When this was written, K. Latte was still alive.

on the one hand, there have appeared in the past few years some important works on ancient law which are far removed from any interpretation in terms of social history; on the other hand, there are many recent works on the political and cultural history of antiquity that disregard and even disparage law. Both these points merit attention.

In the past decade there has undoubtedly been a revival of publications in which certain Oriental legal systems, Greek law and Roman law – or certain essential aspects of each of these – are presented in systematic and descriptive form. I am referring to works such as R. Yaron's *The Law of the Aramaic Papyri*; F. Pringsheim's *The Greek Law of Sale*; E. Seidl's *Ptolemäische Rechtsgeschichte*, and to the recent books which have allowed us a clearer vision both of classical Roman law, and of postclassical but pre-Justinian law by Fritz Schulz, *Classical Roman Law*, and Max Kaser, *Das Römische Privatrecht*. To my mind, these are works of compromise, and, like all compromises, they can be satisfying only until something better is done – which, by the way, will not be easy. The compromise, in some cases at least, is recognized or felt by the authors themselves. As early as in his preface, Kaser declares that he has set out to indicate the various forces, moral, religious, cultural, political, economic and social, that helped to make Roman juristic order in its different phases of development. But he does not go beyond generalities, and I am not sure that he is right even in these generalities. Others, such as Fritz Pringsheim, would probably not be willing to recognize the existence of a compromise. Nevertheless, in this very case, M. I. Finley has shown that Pringsheim arbitrarily combines legal systems of various states and regions in what is presumed to be Greek law[21]. I would add that the very wealth of details in Pringsheim's analysis reveals even more plainly what was also the defect of his great predecessor and teacher, Josef Partsch: scant attention to actual conditions of trade and to the social pressures that conditioned the Greek forms of buying and selling.

The case of F. Schulz calls for more detailed analysis because, to my knowledge, he represents the most coherent recent effort to reduce to a minimum the intervention of so-called extraneous factors in the development of juristic thought and juristic institutions. Fritz Schulz, with whom I was lucky enough to become friends in the years we shared at Oxford, would lose his habitual mildness if one quoted to him the *Summum ius summa iniuria* of J. Stroux. The idea that ancient rhetoric could have contaminated the purity of juristic thought made him physically ill. Classical Roman law, which he knew and admired more than anyone, was for him the product not of a society, but of an *élite* of jurists: and he sought to understand the guiding lines of thought of these jurists, whom he accurately distinguished from school masters like Gaius. For him, then, the mentality of the jurists was the starting-point. Hence the logical progression of the three works which he devoted to classical law, beginning significantly with the *Principles of Roman Law* (1934)[22] – lectures which he gave in Berlin in the face of the spreading flood of Nazism, before he took the road of exile – an exile which for him was particularly hard. There followed the volumes on the history of jurisprudence (1946) and on classical law (1951), which cannot be understood without reference to the first book. In reading the *Principles* one cannot avoid being struck by the strange mixture of notions that are placed at the foundations of Roman law: simplicity, abstraction, tradition, nation, humanity, liberty, *fides*. These principles themselves are not always found in the facts. The principle of nationality is not at the base of Roman law, unless one confuses nationality with citizenship. *Humanitas* perhaps existed as a principle, but paradoxically Schulz is one of those who consider that all the passages of classical jurists in which the word *humanitas* appears are interpolated[23]. Schulz himself, in *Classical Roman Law*, had to admit here and there a functionalism of law in respect to economics, for example concerning mortgages, but he did so against his will, and not without lapsing into naïvety. In short, Schulz's work confirms the impossibility of leaving Roman society out of the history of Roman law.

These extreme attempts at a self-contained legal history have their counterpart in contemporary tendencies to undervalue the institutional and juristic aspects of all political and cultural questions. To avoid ambiguity I should add straight away that it does not seem to me that the so-called prosopographic school of political and cultural history is guilty of a systematic neglect of law. It is true that one of the eminent leaders of this school, R. Syme, reacted against the atmosphere of Oxford, where he was educated and now teaches, by giving little scope to constitutional questions, and losing no opportunity to make known his distaste for his colleagues' discussions on the Augustan constitution. But Syme's attitude is by no means typical of prosopographers. It seems to me already significant that Syme's best pupil, E. Badian, should have sought to clarify the foreign policy of Rome in the last centuries of the Republic by introducing the concept of *clientela*. Another English historian, A. H. M. Jones, is able to combine the direction of the projected Prosopographia of the Later Roman Empire with an attentive study of the juristic sources. This combination is normal in France, as the works of H. G. Pflaum, P. Petit, A. Chastagnol bear witness; and it is clearly represented in Germany by the admirable works of W. Ensslin, as well as in Italy, for example by the now famous *Economia e Società nell'Italia annonaria* by L. Ruggini. Some conflict between prosopographic method and juristic sources is – or was – to be noticed, if anywhere, in Russia in the sense that prosopography was accused there of being excessively preoccupied with the ruling class as compared with the subordinate classes, but in this case it was of course interest in juristic sources and institutions that won the day. In any case, ancient juristic sources are being studied in Russia, even if the research is usually limited to a few themes, principally slavery.

Real neglect of institutional problems and juristic sources, with all that it entails, is more evident in the cultural and political histories that flourished in Germany after 1920. The antijuristic current, to which I would attribute long-term effects, is that which is represented in Greek history by W. Jaeger's *Paideia* and, at a lower level, by *Der hellenische Mensch* by Max Pohlenz (recently translated into Italian as *L'Uomo greco*), and which for Roman history begins perhaps with *Von den Ursachen der Grösse Roms* by Richard Heinze (1921) and is continued in a series of studies, some of which have recently been collected by Hans Oppermann with the title *Römertum* (1962). In all these works, concrete situations, economic and juristic relationships, institutions, are left on one side. Jaeger speaks of Paideia, but the history of education in antiquity has been written by a very different historian, the Frenchman H.-I. Marrou. Pohlenz has succeeded in writing what in the Italian translation amounts to 869 pages on Greek man without telling us what the so-called Greek man ate, how he bought and sold, how he was educated, what he did in a political assembly, in what particular ways (sacrifices, prayers, processions, oracles) he expressed himself in his relationship with the gods in whom he believed. If one takes Erich Burck's essay *Die altrömische Familie*, one will search in vain for any information whatsoever on the nature of *heredium* and of *consortium*, on the origin of testation, the relationship between *adrogatio* and *detestatio sacrorum*, the existence or not of a domestic tribunal. What one will find is a description of the happiness of the slaves under such a régime, and if Cato gives a few recommendations about them that are somewhat cruel, that is considered a sign of the dissolution of the '*alte römische Lebensordnung*'. The fate of the *addictus*, perhaps because he was not given time to belong to the *familia* ('*tertiis nundinis partis secanto; si plus minusve secuerunt, se fraude esto*'), is not, as far as I can see, recorded[24].

It would be erroneous to say that this historiography is a child of Nazism: this would go not only against chronology, but also against the fact that distinguished scholars like W. Jaeger were themselves victims of Nazism. Nor should we forget the conspicuous contribution of Jaeger, Heinze and certain of their disciples to the understanding of Greek and Roman ethics. But this historiography, with its scant grip on reality, bears the mark of an epoch of political dissolution: at any rate W. Jaeger himself, in the very productive years he spent in free America, returned to the most important of his early undertakings, publishing and expounding the works of Gregory of Nyssa. That this historiography could degenerate into Nazism was a danger, which was confirmed by some of Jaeger's pupils who had remained in Germany. Collective works like *Sparta, Der Lebenskampf einer nordischen Herrenschicht* (1940); *Das neue Bild der Antike* (1942); *Rom und Karthago* (1943), not to mention books by single authors, are clear proof of this connection. The time has, perhaps, not yet come to write the history of German historiography in the years between 1920 and 1945; and indeed one would want the Germans themselves to write it. But it is not too soon to admit that this ideological historiography was, and – given its vast ramifications – still is, an impediment to the understanding of ancient law and political institutions.

Before us is the ideal of a historiography in which the long-term phenomena – natural conditions, biological and psychological presuppositions, constants of language, economics and institutions – would be appreciated on a par with the creative act of the single individual, with his contribution to scientific progress and to the improvement of economic and political life. From the point of view of historiographic methodology, reference to the long-term phenomena offers the advantage of a control over hypotheses which are not sufficiently documented as regards linguistic usage, juristic tradition, or physical environment. In this way there comes into being a new situation of security in the interpretation of historical facts, even amongst the dangers of a research that is ever more extended and complex[25]. In this atmosphere of research, the study of ancient law is obviously destined to prosper, no longer in isolation, but as part of ordinary ancient history. In no case is this clearer than in recent historical writing on the ancient Orient. It is precisely because Oriental legal systems have never attained a stable position in university faculties, and, generally, in academic circles – in this they are even less fortunate than Greek law, which found refuge in Departments of Classics – that they are today capable of showing us most conspicuously the advantages of research that moves from formalities to social, religious and economic presuppositions. I shall of course leave specialists in Oriental history to speak on Oriental law. A second Koschaker is clearly not yet with us. But may I be allowed, in concluding, to indulge in a little *Lokalpatriotismus* and recall that some of the most penetrating among recent researches, for instance that on the symbols of property-sale in the law of ancient Mesopotamia, are due to a Piedmontese scholar – indeed she comes from my 'civitas' Cuneo – Elena Cassin, who works at Paris[26].

If this Congress of ours helps us to distinguish between the useful directions of research and the *culs-de-sac* and the paths that simply go round in a circle, that will be a true reward for the labour of the organizers, especially my friend B. Paradisi[27]: it is thanks to him that we are gathered here today.

[1] *Rivista Storica Italiana*, LXXVI (1964), 133–49. The complete and unrevised text of a paper read to the Accademia dei Lincei di Roma on 18 December 1963 on the occasion of the First International Congress of the Società Italiana di Storia del Diritto. Only a few indispensable references have been added. For further information on Greek and Roman law, see J. Ellul, *Histoire des institutions de l'Antiquité* (1961 ed.), and E. Meyer, *Römischer Staat und Staatsgedanke* (1961 ed.). The *Revue Internationale des Droits de l'Antiquité* is particularly useful for keeping abreast with studies of Oriental law. Of recent works on Roman law, the excellent study by B. Biondi, *Il diritto romano* (Bologna 1957), is addressed to the non-specialist reader.

[2] *Cf.* V. Piano Mortari, *Diritto romano e diritto nazionale in Francia nel secolo XVI* (Milan 1962); J. H. Franklin, *Jean Bodin and the Sixteenth-Century Revolution in the Methodology of Law and History* (New York 1963).

[3] This distinction must be taken *cum grano salis*. For the eighteenth century I know of no work comparable to G. Solari's book (never completed, unfortunately), *Storicismo e diritto privato* (written in about 1915, published Turin,

Giappichelli, 1940). *Cf.* E. Weis, *Geschichtsschreibung und Staatsauffassung in der Französischen Enzyklopädie* (Wiesbaden 1956) and, above all, not only for Italy, F. Venturi's introductory notes to the *Illuministi Italiani*, Vols. III and V (Milan-Naples 1958 and 1962). In general, *cf.* F. Wieacker, *Privatrechtsgeschichte der Neuzeit* (Göttingen 1952), in addition, of course, to the classic work of P. Koschaker (1947) and the studies in his honour, *L'Europa e il diritto romano* (Milan 1954).

[4] A. M. Honoré, *Gaius* (Oxford 1962).

[5] *Aspects sociologiques du droit* (Paris 1955) p. 42, but *cf.* the essay '*Le fait historique*' in the same volume. A bibliography of Lévy-Bruhl's work in *Droits de l'antiquité et sociologie juridique, Mélanges H. L.-B.* (Paris 1959).

[6] There is, however, to my knowledge, no history of the research on falsifications of which there is a sketch in J. G. Droysen, *Historik* (ed. R. Hübner, Munich and Berlin 1937) pp. 99 ff. *Cf.* the references in A. von Brandt, *Werkzeug des Historikers* (Stuttgart 1958), p. 125; and G. Tessier's chapter on charters in *L'histoire et ses méthodes* (Encyclopédie de la Pléiade 1961), pp. 633–76.

[7] For a different opinion see P. Voci, *Diritto ereditario romano* I (Milan 1960) and the same author's important critical contribution on Bonfante in the *Studi Arangio-Ruiz* I (1952) pp. 101–46 (*cf. Studia Doc. Hist. Iuris* 19 (1953) pp. 307–15).

[8] *Storia dei Romani* I (1907) p. 397.

[9] *Cf. Riv. Stor. Ital.* 72 (1960) pp. 534–41, and also M. I. Finley, *Athenian Demagogues*, Past and Present 21 (1962) pp. 3–24.

[10] In the collective volume *Geras. Studies presented to George Thomson* (Charles University, Prague 1963) pp. 41–60. For another recent Marxist viewpoint, *cf.* M. Móra, *Acta Antiqua* 11 (Budapest 1963) pp. 103–20.

[11] J.-P. Vernant, *Les origines de la pensée grecque* (Paris 1962).

[12] *Cf.* P. Voci, *Diritto sacro romano in età arcaica, Studia Doc. Hist. Iuris* 19 (1953) pp. 38–103; G. Gioffredi, *Religione e diritto nella più antica esperienza romana, ibid.* 20 (1954) pp. 259–302. For the charismatic theory of the Roman monarchy, references in E. Meyer, *Römischer Staat und Staatsgedanke*, pp. 470–1. As examples of recent Italian discussions on method, I should like to cite the writings of G. Grosso mentioned by the author himself in *Studi Arangio-Ruiz* (1952) pp. 33–46; the works of E. Betti, for example *Wesen des altrömischen Familienverbands, Zeitsch. Savigny-Stiftung, Rom. Abt.* 71 (1954) pp. 1–24; A. Guarino, *L'ordinamento giuridico romano* (3rd ed., Naples 1959). The most recent discussion of *fas* and *ius* is H. Fugier, *Recherches sur l'expression du sacré dans la langue latine* (Paris 1963) pp. 127–52 – which did not convince me.

[13] *Anthropologie structurale* (Paris 1958) pp. 113–32.

[14] *Studi Romani* 5 (1957) p. 261 (*La Prima Roma*).

[15] R. J. Z. Werblowsky, *Joseph Karo, Lawyer and Mystic* (Oxford 1962).

[16] *Cf.* F. R. Adrados, in *Emerita* 29 (1961) pp. 53–116; L. R. Palmer, *The Interpretation of Mycenaean Greek Texts* (Oxford 1963); P. E. Pecorella, in *Mem. Accad. Colombaria* 27 (1963) pp. 1–50, and bibliographies given by them.

[17] For totemism, *cf.* C. Lévi-Strauss, *Le totémisme aujourd'hui* (Paris 1962).

[18] *Bull. School Orient, and African Studies* 22 (1959) pp. 69–85. I hope to deal with this subject again at length. The most recent comprehensive work by Dumézil is *L'idéologie tripartie des Indo-Européens* (Brussels 1958).

[19] On this point, see e.g. my article *Storiografia su tradizione scritta e storiografia su tradizione orale, Atti Accad. Scienze Torino* 96 (1961–2) pp. 186–97 [here above, p. 211]. *Cf.* V. Frosini, *La struttura del diritto* (Milan 1962).

[20] *L'histoire et ses méthodes*, p. 487.

[21] *Seminar* 9 (1951) pp. 72–91.

[22] Oxford 1936. Translated into Italian by V. Arangio Ruiz (Florence 1946).

[23] On this question, *cf.* for example C. A. Maschi, in *Annali Triestini* 18 (1948) p. 263.

[24] *Cf.* the apposite observations of F. Hampl in *Historische Zeitschrift* 188 (1959) pp. 497–525 (*Römische Politik in republikanischer Zeit und das Problem des Sittenverfalls*).

[25] I myself can provide an example. In a recent note in *Maia N.S.* 15 (1963) pp. 47–8 (*Ambarvales Hostiae*), while examining the passage of Festus in the summary of Paulus Diaconus, p. 5 Lindsay '*ambarvales hostiae appellabantur, quae pro arvis a duobus fratribus sacrificabantur*', I implicitly assumed that '*sacrificabantur*' represented the text of Festus. This is not excluded. But E. Fraenkel has rightly pointed out to me that Paulus regularly substitutes the imperfect tense for Festus' present tense. Any deduction must therefore leave it uncertain whether Festus actually used the present or the imperfect tense. Fortunately I was basing little deduction upon this.

[26] *L'Année Sociologique*, 1952 (1955) pp. 107–61. Cassin's works begin with *L'Adoption à Nuzi* (Paris 1938). Of the many well-known works by E. Volterra on Oriental laws, it will suffice to mention here two of the most recent, so that his name should not be left out: *Rend. Acc. Lincei* 18 (1963) pp. 131–73; *Iura* 14 (1963) pp. 29–70.

[27] Of Paradisi's work, I would mention here especially the two studies *I nuovi orizzonti della storia giuridica, Riv. Ital. per le Scienze Giuridiche* 3, 6 (1952–3) pp. 134–207, and *Due aspetti fondamentali nella formazione del diritto internazionale antico, Annali di Storia del Diritto* 1 (1957) pp. 169–259.

I

INDEX OF SUBJECTS

II

INDEX OF NAMES